21st Century Coo

MW01048392

This edited volume explains the importance of regional public goods (RPGs) for sustainable development and shows why they are particularly important in the context of 21st-century international relations. By presenting a new and original data set and by presenting original essays by renowned scholars, this book lays the foundation for what will become an increasingly important focus for both economic development and international relations as well as for their intersection.

The volume contains four parts. The first introduces the core issues and concepts that are explored throughout the book as well as a new and original data set on RPGs. The second part further develops specific concepts important for understanding 21st-century RPGs: regional leadership, alliances, networks, and outcomes. The third examines how cooperation takes place worldwide for a range of important RPGs. Finally, the fourth part discusses how public goods are produced in specific regions, stressing that each region has a distinct context and that these contexts overlap in a decentered "multiplex" manner.

Global economic cooperation will be different in the 21st century, and this volume will be of interest to students and scholars of global governance, economic development, international political economy, sustainable development, and comparative regionalism.

Antoni Estevadeordal is Manager, Integration and Trade Sector, Inter-American Development Bank (IDB).

Louis W. Goodman is Professor and Emeritus Dean, School of International Service, American University.

21st Century Cooperation

Regional Public Goods, Global
Governance, and Sustainable
Development

**Edited by Antoni Estevadeordal and
Louis W. Goodman**

Routledge
Taylor & Francis Group
LONDON AND NEW YORK

First published 2017
by Routledge

2 Park Square, Milton Park, Abingdon, Oxfordshire OX14 4RN
52 Vanderbilt Avenue, New York, NY 10017

Routledge is an imprint of the Taylor & Francis Group, an informa business

First issued in paperback 2020

British Library Cataloguing in Publication Data
A catalogue record for this book is available from the British Library

Library of Congress Cataloging in Publication Data
A catalog record for this book has been requested

ISBN: 978-1-138-72259-0 (hbk)
ISBN: 978-0-367-59509-8 (pbk)

Typeset in Bembo
by Swales & Willis Ltd, Exeter, Devon, UK

Contents

Figures

Tables

Contributors

Amitav Acharya is Distinguished Professor of International Relations and The UNESCO Chair in Transnational Challenges and Governance at the School of International Service at American University, Washington, D.C.

Paulo Barbieri is Regional Public Goods Consultant at the Inter-American Development Bank, Washington, D.C.

Suh-Yong Chung is Professor of the Division of International Studies at Korea University.

Uri Dadush is Senior Fellow, OCP Policy Center, Rabat. He is also Non-Resident Scholar at Bruegel, Brussels.

Michelle Egan is Jean Monnet Professor *Ad Personam* at the School of International Service at American University, Washington, D.C. She is also Global Europe Fellow at the Woodrow Wilson Center for International Scholars.

Antoni Estevadeordal is Manager of the Integration and Trade Sector at the Inter-American Development Bank, Washington, D.C.

Louis W. Goodman is Professor and Emeritus Dean of the School of International Service at American University, Washington, D.C.

Jacint Jordana is Professor of Political Science and Public Administration at the Universitat Pompeu Fabra. He is also Director of the Institut Barcelona d'Estudis Internacionals.

Theodore Kahn is a doctoral candidate at the School of Advanced International Studies at Johns Hopkins University.

Masahiro Kawai is Professor of Economics at the Graduate School of Public Policy at the University of Tokyo.

Teng Liu is Research Associate in International Economics at the Council of Foreign Relations, Washington, D.C.

Tom Long is Lecturer at the Department of Politics and International Relations at the University of Reading, UK.

Johanna Mendelson-Forman is Scholar in Residence at the School of International Service at American University. She is also Senior Advisor of the Managing Across Boundaries Program at The Stimson Center.

Richard Newfarmer is Country Director, Rwanda, South Sudan, and Uganda, at the International Growth Centre at Oxford University and London School of Economics.

Carlos Portales is Research Professor at the Latin American Faculty of the Social Sciences, Santiago, Chile.

Jayant Prasad is Director-General of the Institute of Defence Studies and Analysis, New Delhi.

Miguel Rodríguez Mendoza is Senior Associate, International Centre on Trade and Sustainable Development, Geneva.

Manuel Suárez-Mier is a Consultant on Economic and Financial Issues and a Weekly Columnist for *Excelsior*, Mexico City.

Kati Suominen is chief executive officer of Nextrade Group and Visiting Adjunct Assistant Professor of the Anderson School of Management at the University of California, Los Angeles.

Joaquim Tres is Principal Specialist of the Integration and Trade Sector at the Inter-American Development Bank.

Craig VanGrasstek is Lecturer at the John F. Kennedy School of Government at Harvard University.

Preface

Antoni Estevadeordal and Louis W. Goodman

This book contains four parts. The first introduces the core issues and concepts that are explored throughout the book as well as a new and original data set on regional public goods (RPGs). The second part further develops specific concepts important for understanding 21st-century RPGs: regional leadership, alliances, networks, and outcomes. The third part examines how cooperation takes place worldwide for a range of important RPGs. The fourth part discusses how public goods are produced in specific regions, stressing that each region has a distinct context and that these contexts overlap in a decentered "multiplex" manner.

There are two chapters in Part I. The first, "21st-century cooperation, regional public goods, and sustainable development" by Antoni Estevadeordal and Louis W. Goodman, introduces the core concepts and research questions for the study of RPGs, global governance, and sustainable development. It points out the importance of public good production for sustainable development, the implications of the possibility of slowing worldwide growth, prospects for change in regional cooperation configurations, and the concern that there is a growing gap between needed public goods and great power capacity to produce them. Building upon Kindleberger's observation of the unlikelihood that the stability needed for sustainable development can be provided by a hegemon, the chapter suggests that increased public goods will need to be generated from other sources, including regional sources. The chapter links concerns of economists and international relations analysts to suggest that a wide range of possible public goods should be examined, and that the dynamics of sequencing, geography, institutional design and cooperation outcome be taken into account in understanding relationships among RPGs, global governance, and sustainable development.

The second chapter, "Regional public goods cooperation: an inductive approach to measuring regional public goods" by Teng Liu and Theodore Kahn, offers an inductive data-driven approach for measuring and analyzing RPGs. It presents an original data set based on the United Nations Treaty Collection series to systematically measure international cooperation for producing RPGs. This data set is a resource for clarifying, with empirically based evidence, the boundaries of regions and the geographical jurisdictions of public goods. The chapter provides a methodology for empirically measuring the intent to create RPGs by examining more than 50,000 international treaties on file in the UN Treaty Collection. Data on these treaties are coded based on functional areas important to international development, ranging from economic integration to peace and security. The resulting database provides an overview of RPG cooperation worldwide. While the results are preliminary, some points are clear: RPG cooperation is unevenly distributed, with developed countries like the United States dominating the landscape; RPG cooperation in economic matters outweighs other functions both in terms of amount and sequencing; finally, while the geographic sense of "region" still matters, nations may cooperate and constitute a "region" based on a particular function. This chapter and its accompanying database serve as a starting point for further research into the implementation and impact of RPGs.

Part II, "Regional leadership, alliances, networks, and outcomes," contains three chapters that further develop specific RPG-related concepts. Chapter 3, Amitav Acharya's "Regionalism in the evolving world order: power, leadership, and the provision of public goods," examines the roles, new and old, that RPGs have played and will play in the global order. It discusses global public goods, regional public goods, and national public goods in what the author calls "the multiplex world." The multiplex world order is decentered and involves states large and small as well as state and nonstate actors in multiple layers of governance with complex global links. The chapter contrasts hegemonic (EU) regionalism and more open, integrationalist (Asian) regionalism with multiplex regionalism, and argues that a communitarian leadership style is most effective in the multiplex world order. The "ASEAN Way" is cited as an important example of regional cooperation for the generation of public goods in this type of multiplex world. The chapter concludes by suggesting that there are "a variety of pathways and mechanisms" for creating RPGs and that traditional mechanisms are evolving toward wider, more complex functionality, some under the influence of emerging powers.

Chapter 4, Jacint Jordana's "Transnational policy networks and regional public goods in Latin America," begins with the observation that regionalism in Latin America has been characterized for decades by a constant failure to advance institutionalization and economic integration beyond globalization pressures. In discussing this challenging situation, Jordana argues that a particular and distinctive driver for regionalism is emerging in Latin America. The driver is rooted in a myriad of nonhierarchical policy networks operating across countries and sectors throughout the region. This network mode of regional integration is capable of providing RPGs and contributing to processes of policy diffusion. Using examples from the banking and telecommunication industries, Jordana suggests that networks of regulatory governance allow the emergence of informal mechanisms of regional cooperation, namely a rapid diffusion of regulatory innovations. However, Jordana observes that these networks have not necessarily been able to enlarge the provision of public goods in their policy areas, or to evolve toward stronger institutional forms. He argues that promoting regulatory governance networks could help provide public goods, but that it cannot be the sole solution to the integration problems of the region. More promising are hybrid modes of governance that incorporate formal institutionalization and the provision of tangible public goods.

Chapter 5, "Can regional standards be above the national norm? Impact evaluation issues for regional public goods" by Joaquim Tres and Paulo Barbieri, discusses the impacts of small-scale RPGs such as multilateral arrangements for promoting phenomena including regional educational infrastructure standards, pharmaceutical purchasing capacity, civics teaching guidelines, migrant workers' social security rights, and bicycle cooperative operations from the standpoint of how to create organizations to support the provision of these goods and their impacts. The chapter draws upon the experience of ten years of Inter-American Development Bank programs involving more than 700 entities in more than 100 projects, each of which has created public goods that are seen as "small scale." These small-scale public goods are of a different dimension to those most frequently discussed in the literature, such as goods that facilitate the operation of a regional trading and investment system or a regional defense umbrella. Nevertheless, these smaller-scale public goods can have significant sustainable development impacts as well as the capacity to generate externalities that expand development cooperation within Latin America, Asia, and other regions.

Part III, "New frontiers in functional cooperation," contains six chapters, each of which discusses the provision of RPGs in a separate and important functional area. Chapter 6, "Regional public goods: the case of migration" by Uri Dadush, discusses the set of institutions and policies that allow people to move freely across borders. Dadush argues that, in contrast to the proliferation of regional trade agreements, the international coordination of migration has fallen short of what might be expected. This chapter compares the provision of public goods at the global, regional, national and local levels and examines migration regimes as public goods, with particular focus on developing regions, especially the Middle East and North Africa and Latin America. The lack of political representation of migrants, along with the asymmetry of benefits between the origin and destination countries, constrains the creation of regional arrangements despite migration's development-promoting benefits such as remittances. The chapter argues that the provision of migration RPGs can be successful if certain conditions are present, such as political will, complementarity of economic structures, ability to learn from each other, and effective coordination among countries. Most importantly, the biggest needs are domestic reforms, bilateral negotiations among partners in the largest migration corridors, and increasing engagement with the diaspora.

Chapter 7 is "Connectivity and infrastructure as 21st-century regional public goods" by Jayant Prasad. Paying special attention to South Asia, Prasad discusses the importance of connectivity phenomena in five distinct clusters: trade, transportation, information and communication technologies, energy, and peoples. He argues that connectivity-related public goods are foundational for regional integration and sustainable development. The key is envisioning specific projects that can leverage geographic proximity for mutual benefit. Initially, such projects may or may not be linked to regional integration schemes—some might begin with fewer partners so as to overcome political obstacles and demonstrate early success—and institutional design should provide space for both public- and private-sector actors and should be clear about financing. Since connectivity public goods often accumulate in small discrete steps, care should be taken to anticipate sequencing, and to document and communicate benefits resulting from increased connectivity and from the cumulative impacts of the diverse connectivity clusters spread across a region.

In Chapter 8, "Open borders: a regional public good," Johanna Mendelson-Forman discusses the evolution of borders from "public bads" separating nations to public goods facilitating international peace and prosperity. Following a review of Latin American history in which borders have largely separated nations, the chapter discusses ways that borders can be used to bring nations together and promote multilateralism. Mendelson-Forman stresses the impacts of borderless threats such as organized crime and natural disasters that push nations to cooperate, as well as domestic economic and social forces that wish to form links with neighbors. Brazil's geopolitical situation and its 28 twin border city arrangements are discussed at length because Brazil shares borders with 13 other countries in South America. The chapter concludes by suggesting metrics that can be used to evaluate the extent to which open borders can generate public goods.

In Chapter 9, "Advancing digitization as a regional public good," Kati Suominen suggests that existing regional and global cooperation have yet to align with the digitization of international trade. The chapter reviews the impact of digitization on growth and trade and analyzes the state of digitization in different world regions and the extent of digital flows (including data flows and e-commerce) within different regions. Suominen finds that, despite the potentials of digital trade, governments around the world face challenges in broadening access to the Internet and digital technologies and translating access into usage by consumers and companies. Suominen proposes ways for countries to overcome these regulatory and technological obstacles so that they may translate digitization into trade, economic development, and inclusive growth through regional cooperation. These strategies include regulatory harmonization, trade facilitation, development aid to promote e-commerce, and regional innovation hubs. The author argues that regional actions can complement national and global policies and that creating digital scale economies and spurring on regional e-commerce would contribute to a more fluid and frictionless global economy.

Chapter 10, "Building regional environmental governance: Northeast Asia's unique path to sustainable development" by Suh-Yong Chung, discusses the importance of creating public goods relating to environmental issues, especially among countries that are relatively isolated from their neighbors. The author focuses on the countries of East Asia (China, Japan, the Republic of Korea, and the Democratic People's Republic of Korea), which have not concluded any multilateral treaties. This is a serious problem because environmental degradation in the region has been escalating: the Yellow Sea is one of the most heavily polluted oceanic bodies of water in the world, and air pollution in the region has reached record levels. The resulting damage includes negative impacts on human health, interstate commerce, and possibilities for conflict resolution. The chapter argues that enhanced cooperation on a range of fronts would benefit these nations. It discusses Northeast Asia's regional environmental governance approach, which is based on cooperation and "soft" environmental institutions and arrangements, in contrast with Europe's older and more formal "convention protocol" approach. The author suggests that this cooperation-based approach may lend itself to the creation of RPGs in East Asia beyond the environmental sphere and argues that the construction of RPGs must take the distinct challenges of each regional situation into account.

The final chapter in this part, Chapter 11, "The multilateral trading system and regional public goods" by Miguel Rodríguez Mendoza and Craig VanGrasstek, argues that the international trading system consists of two distinct layers: the multilateral trading system, embodied by the World Trade Organization (WTO), and a large and growing system of regional trade arrangements (RTAs). The chapter describes the current state of the trading system, especially the increasing emphasis on regionalism over multilateralism. It also discusses the implications of this shift using a global public goods perspective, considering how regionalism may contribute to discrimination while also strengthening the system. On the one hand, RTAs may transform the trading system, a true public good, into excludable club goods. From the perspective of global public goods, however, the same processes seem more like opportunities for countries to cooperate. The chapter provides recommendations on how to reinforce the positive aspects of regionalism and ameliorate its less desirable consequences to ensure that the net result is positive for the multilateral trading system. Rodríguez Mendoza and VanGrasstek assert that the net value of RTAs depends on whether countries have the wisdom and the will to incorporate them more fully into the multilateral trading system. While it is important to acknowledge the challenges that RTAs pose, insofar as they compete with the WTO and may undermine it, the authors argue that one must also recognize that RTAs have the capacity to help create a more solid and stable global trading system.

The final part of the book, "Old and new regions in a multiplex world," contains five chapters that discuss RPGs in Europe, North America, Latin America, Asia, and Africa. In Chapter 12, "European regional public goods: insiders and outsiders," Michelle Egan discusses how the production of regional goods in Europe has changed since the creation of the European Union. This is particularly salient given the streams of refugees entering Europe and putting pressure on the continent's open borders. The chapter provides an analytical discussion of the current situation and others in which attempts to provide public goods uniformly within a region have led to stratification and sociopolitical backlash due to the varied factor endowments and historical contexts of the countries/regions in question. It explains how the provision of RPGs evolved in the growing and maturing European Union and how this can produce conflict between market freedoms and "public service" objectives. It also discusses the difficulties in promoting economic development and addressing economic inequality, as well as the question of what types of RPGs it is feasible to generate in a context of budgetary constraints and austerity measures in member states. In this context, Europe has begun to move to "soft law" to provide flexibility of governance within its increasingly heterogeneous polity. Egan concludes by suggesting that these new modes of generating and evaluating RPGs in Europe may produce insiders and outsiders relative to Europe's boundaries. One of the established objectives of the European Union has been to use its influence to induce non-European states to adopt European standards in a number of policy areas, thus producing another dimension of non-European stratification. This capacity may also be diminished in a situation of austerity and uncertainty, thus causing the uniform provision of European public goods to diminish aspects of integration both within and outside of Europe—hardly a smooth path toward regional and extraregional integration.

Chapter 13, "Regional public goods in North America" by Tom Long and Manuel Suárez-Mier, discusses how Canada, Mexico, and the United States have created RPGs in North America. The impact of these goods on sustainable development was slowed by the reaction of the North American partners in these arrangements (especially the United States) to 9/11 and by other political considerations. Against a backdrop of nearly two centuries of hegemonic threat by the United States, Canada and Mexico signed the North American Free Trade Agreement in 1994. By 2001, the region's share of global GDP had grown from 30% to 36% but by 2015, due to the end of the dot-com boom and the 9/11 terrorist attacks, this percentage had fallen back to below 27%. The chapter examines these shifts and stresses that a resumption of the capacity for RPGs generation will depend on effective rule of law, especially regarding crime and disputes in Mexico and immigration in the United States. It also discusses how RPGs in the areas of economic cooperation, social development, environment and energy, conflict resolution, connectivity, and governance impact the region.

In Chapter 14, "Public goods and regional organizations in Latin America and the Caribbean: identity, goals, and implementation," Carlos Portales discusses the history of regional cooperation in the Americas and the evolution of regional and subregional public goods production as these arrangements have changed. While since the early 1800s Western Hemispheric regionalism was a goal of political figures as distinct as James Monroe and Simón Bolívar, attempts to include or exclude the United States from organizations embracing the rest of the hemisphere have resulted in a diverse variety of regional and subregional organizations (with corresponding public goods), especially since the creation of the Organization of American States (OAS) in 1948, and there has been increasing overlap in the 21st century. Changing and limited public goods generation in the region has been one outcome of the different groupings and organizations that have formed over the years, including ones in Latin America and the Caribbean (ALALC/ALADI), the Caribbean (CARIFTA/CARICOM), Central America (CACM/SICA), North America (NAFTA), South America (UNASUR), the Southern Cone (MERCOSUR), and ones based on an antihegemonic position (ALBA) and an Asia-oriented/open economy (Pacific Alliance). The chapter argues that a common definition of goals and the development of specific joint projects are indispensable for increasing public goods in Latin America and the Caribbean.

In Chapter 15, "Asia's financial stability as a regional and global public good," Masahiro Kawai argues that financial stability is an essential public good that provides the necessary conditions for economic growth and employment creation. This chapter examines regional arrangements that promote financial stability in Asia: the Chiang Mai Initiative (CMI), a network of bilateral currency swap arrangements now multilateralized as CMIM; the Economic Review and Policy Dialogue (ERPD), a regional surveillance process; and the ASEAN+3 Macroeconomic Research Office (AMRO). In particular, the chapter analyzes whether Asia has the capacity and expertise to manage possible future financial crises through various measures for prevention, response, and resolution. The chapter also compares Asian institutions with other regional arrangements, particularly the European Stability Mechanism and the International Monetary Fund. Kawai suggests that Asian financial RPGs face the following challenges: inadequacy of financial resources, limited effectiveness of surveillance, close links with the IMF, and lack of procedural clarity and certainty in activating the CMIM. The chapter argues that, with significant progress in institutional quality, Asia can contribute to global financial stability by improving regional liquidity facility and surveillance arrangements.

The final chapter in Part IV and the book, Chapter 16, is Richard Newfarmer's "From small markets to collective action: regional public goods in Africa." It is widely acknowledged that Africa emerged from colonialism with many nations having small national markets rife with tribal division. In this context, by providing common rules to widen markets, deepen infrastructure, and work collectively to provide security—in other words, RPGs—regional cooperation holds the promise of contributing to the region's peace and prosperity. However, integration efforts have fallen short of their ambitious objectives. This chapter examines why. Newfarmer looks at regional cooperation in Africa with the objective of deriving lessons about the sequencing of agreements, institutional design, and outcomes. He considers the political economy of efforts at regional cooperation, reviews recent literature on the effectiveness of Africa's regional trade agreements in promoting trade and changing the structure of trade, and concludes with observations about the next phases of Africa's integration.

Acronyms and abbreviations

ADB	Asian Development Bank
AEC	ASEAN Economic Community
AfDB	African Development Bank
AIIB	Asian Infrastructure Investment Bank
ALADI	Latin American Integration Association
ALBA	Bolivarian Alliance for the Peoples of Our America
ALBA-TCP	Bolivarian Alliance for the Peoples of Our America—Peoples' Trade Treaty
AMF	Asian Monetary Fund
AMRO	ASEAN+3 Macroeconomic Research Office
APEC	Asia-Pacific Economic Cooperation
APIBM	Afghanistan–Pakistan–India–Bangladesh–Myanmar
APSC	ASEAN Political-Security Community
APT	ASEAN Plus Three
ARC	Asia Research Centre
ARF	ASEAN Regional Forum
ASBA	Association of Supervisors of Banks of the Americas
ASBALC	Association of Banking Supervisory Organizations of Latin America and the Caribbean
ASCC	ASEAN Socio-Cultural Community
ASEAN	Association of Southeast Asian Nations
ASEM	Asia-Europe Meeting
AU	African Union
BBIN	Bangladesh, Bhutan, India, Nepal Initiative
BCIM	Bangladesh–China–India–Myanmar
BIMSTEC	Bengal Initiative for Multi-Sectoral Technical and Economic Cooperation
BRICS	Brazil, Russia, India, China, and South Africa
CAATEL	Andean Committee of Telecommunications Authorities
CACM	Central American Common Market

CAN	Andean Community
CAREC	Central Asia Regional Economic Cooperation
CARICOM	Caribbean Common Market
CARIFTA	Caribbean Free Trade Association
CASA-1000	Central Asia–South Asia Electricity Transmission and Trade Project
CASAREM	Central Asia–South Asia Regional Energy Market
CBP	US Customs and Border Protection
CCSBSO	Central American Council of Superintendents of Banks, Insurance, and other Financial Institutions
CEBS	Committee of European Banking Supervisors
CEC	Commission for Environmental Cooperation
CEE	Central and Eastern Europe
CELAC	Community of Latin America and Caribbean States
CEMAC	Central African Economic and Monetary Community
CEMLA	Center for Latin American Monetary Studies
CFA	*Communauté financière africaine*
CGE	computable general equilibrium
CITEL	Inter-American Telecommunication Commission
CJEU	Court of Justice of the European Union
CMI	Chiang Mai Initiative
CMIM	Chiang Mai Initiative Multilateralization
COMESA	Common Market for Eastern and Southern Africa
COMISCA	Council of Ministers of Health of Central America and the Dominican Republic
CRA	Contingency Reserve Arrangement
CUSFTA	US–Canadian Free Trade Agreement
DAC	Development Assistance Committee
DPRK	Democratic People's Republic of Korea
EAC	East African Community
EAS	East Asia Summit
EBA	European Banking Authority
EC	European Commission
ECB	European Central Bank
ECJ	European Court of Justice
ECLAC	Economic Commission for Latin America and the Caribbean
ECOWAS	Economic Community of West African States
ECSG	Electronic Commerce Steering Group
EEC	European Economic Community
EEU	Eurasian Economic Union

EFSF	European Financial Stability Facility
EIA	Energy Information Administration
EIB	European Investment Bank
ERPD	Economic Review and Policy Dialogue
ESF	European Social Fund
ESM	European Stability Mechanism
EU	European Union
EULAC	European Union, Latin America, and the Caribbean
FCL	flexible credit line
FDI	foreign direct investment
FEALAC	Forum for East Asia-Latin American Cooperation
FELABAN	Latin American Federation of Banks
FLAR	Latin American Reserve Fund
FTA	free trade agreements
FTAA	Free Trade Area of the Americas
FTAAP	Free Trade Area of the Asia-Pacific
GATS	General Agreement on Trade in Services
GATT	General Agreement on Tariffs and Trade
GDP	gross domestic product
GEF YSLME	Global Environment Facility Yellow Sea Large Marine Ecosystem Project
GHG	greenhouse gas
GMS	Greater Mekong Subregion
GNI	gross national income
GPG	global public good
GSP+	Generalized System of Preferences Plus
HST	hegemonic stability theory
IACHR	Inter-American Commission on Human Rights
IADC	Inter-American Democratic Charter
IATRA	Inter-American Treaty of Reciprocal Assistance
ICANN	Internet Corporation for Assigned Names and Numbers
ICGL	International Conference on the Great Lakes
ICTs	information and communication technologies
ICTSD	International Centre on Trade and Sustainable Development
IDB	Inter-American Development Bank
IEA	International Energy Agency
IGAD	Intergovernmental Authority on Development
IIAG	Ibrahim Index of African Governance
IIRSA	Regional Initiative for Infrastructure in South America
IMF	International Monetary Fund

INSTC	International North-South Transport Corridor
IRR	internal rate of return
IT	information technology
ITA	Information Technology Agreement
ITTO	International Tropical Timber Organization
ITU	International Telecommunications Union
IXP	Internet exchange point
LAC	Latin America and the Caribbean
LAFTA	Latin American Free Trade Association
LDCs	least developed countries
LLDC	landlocked developing countries
M&HLM	ministerial and high-level meetings
MENA	Middle East and North Africa
MERRAC	Marine Environmental Emergency Preparedness and Response Regional Activity Centre
MFN	most favored nation
MHT	Mahila Housing SEWA Trust
MOMEP	Military Observer Mission Ecuador–Peru
NAFA	North American Framework Agreement
NAFTA	North American Free Trade Agreement
NAO	network administrative organization
NEPAD	New Partnership for African Development
NGO	nongovernmental organization
NOWPAP	Northwest Pacific Action Plan
NPV	net present value
OAS	Organization of American States
OAU	Organisation of African Unity
ODA	official development assistance
OECD	Organisation of Economic Cooperation and Development
OOCUR	Organisation of Caribbean Utility Regulators
PA	Pacific Alliance
PDFF	Development Program for the Frontier Strip
PPP	purchasing power parity
PSC	Peace and Security Council
PTA	preferential trade agreements
QuARTA	Quantitative Analysis of Road Transport Agreements
RCEP	Regional Comprehensive Economic Partnership
RCT	randomized control trial
REC	regional economic community
RFI	rapid financing instrument

RFID	radio frequency identification
ROI	return on investment
ROK	Republic of Korea
RTA	regional trade agreement
SAARC	South Asian Association of Regional Cooperation
SABAH	SAARC Business Association of Home Based Workers
SACU	Southern African Customs Union
SADC	Southern African Development Community
SAFTA	South Asia Free Trade Area
SAGQ	South Asia Growth Quadrangle
SAPARD	Special Accession Programme for Agriculture and Rural Development
SARS	Severe Acute Respiratory Syndrome
SBA	Stand-By Arrangement
SCO	Shanghai Cooperation Organization
SEATO	Southeast Asian Treaty Organization
SEWA	Self Employed Women's Association
SICA	Central American Integration System
SIEPAC	Central American Electrical Interconnection System
SISFRON	Integrated Border Monitoring System
SMEs	small and medium-sized enterprises
SOLVIT	an informal EU trade barrier resolution mechanism
SSC	South–South cooperation
STC	Survey of Triangular Cooperation
STRI	Services Trade Restrictiveness Index
TAPI	Turkmenistan–Afghanistan–Pakistan–India
TDA	Transboundary Diagnostic Analysis
TFA	Trade Facilitation Agreement
TFTA	Tripartite Free Trade Area
THAAD	Terminal High Altitude Area Defense
TiSA	Trade in Services Agreement
TPP	Trans-Pacific Partnership
TTIP	Trans-Atlantic Trade and Investment Partnership
UEMOA	West African Economic and Monetary Union
UK	United Kingdom
UN	United Nations
UNASUR	Union of South American Nations
UNCTAD	United Nations Conference on Trade and Development
UNDP	United Nations Development Programme
UNEP	United Nations Environment Programme

UNTC	United Nations Treaty Collection
UNTS	United Nations Treaty Series
USA	United States of America
USAID	United States Agency for International Development
WFP	World Food Programme
WTO	World Trade Organization

Part I

Introduction

1 21st-century cooperation, regional public goods, and sustainable development

Antoni Estevadeordal and Louis W. Goodman

Introduction

Global economic cooperation will be different in the 21st century. There may be a "new normal" of slower economic growth worldwide with resultant adjustment difficulties for citizens and policy makers (El-Erian 2010). There may be changing international cooperation configurations as nations try to find new partners and/or undermine existing relationships.

Spurts and shocks have increasingly shaped worldwide economic growth with the expansion of global trade. By the 1870s, the triumph of liberalism opened the doors to five great growth-propelling innovations: electricity, urban sanitation, chemicals and pharmaceuticals, the internal combustion engine, and modern communication, which the economist Robert J. Gordon (2000) has described as the "Great Inventions." Over the past 150 years, the impact of these inventions and subsequent discoveries in other fields has been shaped by shocks that include the rise and fall of colonialism, two world wars, the Cold War, and its aftermath. A modern way of life has been created by the application of these innovations and their spread beyond the North Atlantic nations in which they were initially commercialized.

With the unfolding of the 21st century, there has been increasing concern that the growth in the impact of the Great Inventions is slowing and that new innovations in fields like information technology and biology, while important, will not match the depth of the impact of those of the late 19th century (Gordon 2016). It has been predicted that annual global economic growth may fall to long-term levels that could be half of that experienced since the 1870s. Further, in the 21st century demand has grown for the fruits of those inventions as the world's population has swelled. An increasing share of this population has adopted a modern lifestyle and more state and nonstate actors are able to impact the capacity to sustain those lifestyles, for good or for bad.

In North Atlantic and other nations that reaped the benefits of these innovations early on, there is concern that the foreseeable future may be a time of slow growth or stagnation (Gordon 2016). In nations whose citizens have only recently adopted modern lifestyles on a broad scale, the question of how to sustain this growth is referred to as "avoiding the middle-income trap." The desired outcome is sustaining economic growth so that standards of living can improve continuously. Best-case examples of this are the recent experiences of nations such as Singapore, Taiwan, and South Korea.[1]

Sustaining this economic growth in the 21st century will require new forms of innovation beyond the natural science-based changes initiated in the 1870s. Some of the most important innovations will occur in the fields of economics and global politics, which will facilitate new ways of organizing the benefits of the Great Inventions. The foremost of these will be the way in which "public goods"[2] are generated. With the end of the two world wars of the 20th century, continuing economic growth has been dependent on the global availability of goods such as a clean environment, widespread peace, global economic stability and predictable trade arrangements, stable financial and monetary systems, effective enforcement of the rule of law, and adequate numbers of healthy workers and consumers. A large but shrinking proportion of the capacity to produce these public goods has been provided by the world's great powers, including the United States. As these nations' capacities to produce all of the necessary public goods has contracted, new actors have stepped up to supplement them. These include nations other than the great powers, as well as states, cities, municipalities, nonstate actors and—the subject of this book—groups of often-contiguous nations, or regions.

Questions have been raised about precisely how these public goods can be provided in the future by these many entities. Rapid changes in the 21st-century world economy mean that answering them is a complex matter. Assumptions that were once unassailable can no longer be sustained. For example, the 21st-century world does not have a simple global North-South wealth hierarchy with the North constituting the "rich few" and the South the "poor many." The gross domestic product of the South, which represented about 20% of the global total in the late 20th century, had doubled to about 40% by 2012. Furthermore, as of 2010, 72% of the world's population lived in what are now known as "middle-income countries."[3] Therefore, avoiding the middle-income trap and sustaining economic progress is a core issue for policy makers and citizens in nations throughout the world, be they rich or poor, and located in the North or in the South.

Another question is precisely which configurations of nations will cooperate to produce public goods, be they global or regional. Through its "One Belt One Road" initiative, China is seeking to regain cooperative relations with states with which it once had mutually beneficial relations, some for nearly 2,000 years (Rowe 2009). Many nations that cooperated in the 20th century under the aegis of the Warsaw Pact and the Soviet Union have now joined the European Union or look to it for significant economic cooperation, much to the dismay of the Russian Confederation. Britain's vote to leave the European Union, increasing economic inequality among European countries, along with pressures brought to reinstate border controls in the Schengen Area by migration from some countries including Syria and Iraq, suggest that the nature of European cooperation is in flux. Political and economic change in

Mercosur and the evolution of the Pacific Alliance trade bloc, all suggest that new patterns of cooperation for the production of public goods may develop in Latin America.

In the United States, a cottage industry has developed that examines what we consider to be the flipside of this coin—the consequences of the relative decline of the power of the United States in an increasingly multipolar world. Underpinning this discussion is the observation that, while retaining its place as the world's most powerful nation, the United States likely will not be able to continue to provide its current share of the world's global public goods (GPGs). The provision of GPGs by the United States has been particularly important for maintaining world order and sustained economic development since the mid-20th century.[4]

Our advice to those who share this concern is the following:

- Take this matter very seriously. The GPGs produced by the United States and other powerful nations will continue to be critical for worldwide cooperation for the foreseeable future.
- Focus, too, on other sources of public goods—specifically city-based public goods, national public goods, and regional public goods (RPGs). It is our contention that, as the 21st century proceeds, global cooperation will depend increasingly on the coordinated production of public goods at all levels, including the global, regional, national, and municipal.

The shrinking salience of global public goods

Theorists from Kant (1795) to Kissinger (2014) have postulated that, beyond the power of hegemons, alliances are held together by common interests. In the contemporary world, an important source of common interest is creating and benefitting from public goods. While it would be ideal to promote international cooperation through public goods that are equally available to all nations and citizens—that is, GPGs—this has become increasingly infeasible. This is the case for a number of reasons:

- The number and types of public goods that are expected to be available have increased and are increasing year by year.
- Different types of public goods are required for specific regional, national, and municipal contexts. Thus it is unreasonable to expect that all public goods can come from a single source.
- It is beyond the capacity of even the world's wealthiest nations to produce all desired GPGs while responding to their own national needs.

One solution to the problem of instability caused by shortfalls in the production of public goods has been derived from the economist Charles P. Kindleberger (1973) in his book *The World in Depression: 1929–1939*. Kindleberger contended that the economic chaos that afflicted the world during the early mid–20th century could be blamed in part on the fact that no nation had a globally dominant economy. He argued that the condition of a single nation having a globally dominant economy could only occur under very special (and unlikely) circumstances, an option he thus presented merely as a heuristic rather than as a condition that one should expect in empirical reality. Applying this heuristic to the field of international relations has resulted in what has been called "hegemonic stability theory"—the idea that the stability of the global system, in terms of politics and international law, relies on a hegemon to develop and enforce the rules of the system.

The case for the literal form of this theory was the foundation for Michael Mandelbaum's *The Case for Goliath* (2006). Mandelbaum argued that there is no feasible alternative to the United States as the provider of public goods for the global system. He stated that no other nation has the political will, the military and economic capacity, and the ability to generate sufficient international acceptance. He worried that self-destructive US domestic politics might critically weaken the United States' capacity to provide GPGs.

The limitations of hegemonic stability based on a single hegemon have been widely noted. In a much-cited article, Duncan Snidal (1985) argued, as did Kindleberger (1973), that "the range of the theory (hegemonic stability theory) is limited to very special conditions . . . [the case of] . . . one large actor and many small ones." In fact, Snidal posited that hegemonic stability theory should be "viewed as a beginning rather than a reliable conclusion to international politics," and that the central question raised by hegemonic stability theory should be "how the distribution of interests and capability affects possibilities for collective action" (1985, p.613). The contemporary world is now far from being one in which there is a single dominant economy as imagined by Kindleberger in his heuristic, or the special case of one large actor and many small ones described by Snidal. Rather, with the rise of China, India, Germany and a host of lesser powers, the world is becoming increasingly multipolar, a process described by Peter J. Katzenstein in *A World of Regions* (2005).

The growth of regional, national, and municipal public goods

Thus it is logical that, if an increasing proportion of the means for responding to the needs of the ever wealthier and more multipolar world is to be found at the regional, national, and municipal levels, how this capacity might come into being should be a serious and detailed subject of study. A particularly important factor is understanding the circumstances under which public goods are provided by regional and local initiatives.

While it may require coordination so that gaps do not develop in the creation of critical public goods such as financial regulation, the management of fissile material, or crime control, producing public goods on a regional level will create more local buy-in as well as the potential for the creation of instruments that are more appropriate for specific circumstances. This importance of local buy-in is described by Amitav Acharya (2009) in his book *Whose Ideas Matter?* which pays special attention to cases as temporally diverse as the spread of Buddhism to China and the consolidation of the Association of Southeast Asian Nations (ASEAN). Acharya argues that the key factor in sustainable international relations is outside practices being adapted to local circumstances (a process he calls "constitutive localization"). His conclusion is that change is much more likely to be accepted and sustained by citizens if it is adopted through constitutive localization rather than through the imposition of hegemonic power.

In addition to RPGs, increased production of national and municipal public goods will be required to provide the practical foundations needed to engage in global and regional economics and politics. Physical infrastructure such as highways, ports, dams, higher education systems, and connectivity capacity beyond telephony to broadband, are becoming increasingly important for nations and cities to be poised to engage in the evolving global knowledge economy.

Public goods can be available at the global, regional, national, and community levels. If, as theorists such as Acharya (2014) and Ikenberry (2011) have argued, regional alliances are becoming more important in global affairs, then regional cooperation and RPGs will be important for (1) binding nations together to form regional alliances helpful for navigating the fast-changing international political order; and (2) enhancing capacities for economic, political, and social development.

Regional public goods and regional economic integration

The economics literature presents a market-driven vision of integration, including RPGs, where efficiency is maximized when economic activity—and the policies to regulate it—extend across national borders. The processes, institutions, and actors that bring about expanded markets are left in the background. How regional groupings form, take shape, and include or exclude members is addressed in comparative politics and international relations theories. An early reference in the politics of regional integration is Haas's (1958) functionalist framework in which interdependence through economic linkages creates demand for formal integration. According to Haas, the success of such projects depends on the constellation of urban-industrial interests that stand to gain from integration, the potential to forge cross-country coalitions among such groups, and the level of bureaucratization of decision making.

Public finance literature on federalism suggests that regional integration and cooperation are determined by the benefits of size—due to externalities and economies of scale and scope—and the costs associated with heterogeneity of preferences and asymmetry of information. The optimal level of regional cooperation occurs when there are significant economies of scale and externalities, together with a low heterogeneity of preferences and information asymmetries. This implies that there is potential endogeneity between the two factors. For example, increased commercial relations can reduce the degree of heterogeneity of preferences and information asymmetries. Similarly, a regional integration agreement can create a large "region" that can, in turn, create conditions that give potential regional policies greater opportunities to take advantage of economies of scale.

In addition to the underlying motivation for regional integration, it is important to understand *how* integration agreements come about. Often RPGs cannot be supplied by national governments acting unilaterally, and therefore cooperation among multiple countries is necessary. This requires the establishment of a formal agreement along with institutions to support it. The design and implementation of an effective cooperation agreement depend on the actions of the other countries. Generally speaking, RPGs are easier to supply than GPGs since countries in regional groupings tend to be more homogenous, face fewer constraints in the form of information asymmetries, and have more opportunities for identifying the advantages of scale economies.

Further issues relating to institutional design are explored in the so-called "subsidiarity principle." According to the subsidiarity principle, a GPG is optimally allocated by a global institution, while an RPG is better provided by a regional institution. This implies additional advantages for using regional integration agreements for the provision of RPGs. Using the most localized jurisdiction reduces transaction costs by limiting participants, drawing on shared culture, and fostering repeated interactions. Furthermore, common values and benefits facilitate the development of regional institutions, which allows them to adapt more quickly to new circumstances.

The payoffs from using regional integration agreements for the provision of RPGs come from the cost saving created by the institutional architecture that allows the demand for RPGs to be aggregated among members. Regional integration agreements can achieve economies of scope by offering "multiple" or "joint" regional goods and support complementary activities through mechanisms or redistribution to the least developed members of the group. Regional integration agreements can also improve the ability of the regional group to act jointly, for example, by acting as a "demandeur" of regional goods when dealing with the international donor community. In addition, the institutions involved in supporting the regional integration agreement can act as intermediaries in global networks that can contribute to a more optimal provision of GPGs.

Regional public goods and sustainable development

Attention to regional cooperation and RPGs is critical as efforts evolve to avoid the middle-income trap through strategies for national and local development. Regions are increasingly important for international relations as the role of the United States as the lone superpower diminishes. While the United States will remain the world's most important nation for some time, the importance of other nations is growing. This change means that, to prevent disruptive international relations, attention must be paid both to sustaining the strength of the United States and to supporting the strength of other nations. With 21st-century international relations moving with great speed and complexity, it is a challenge for a given nation or group to attempt to negotiate these relations without partners. One logical set of partners are regional neighbors: RPGs bind neighbors together and enhance their abilities to negotiate international relations both singly and as members of a group.

RPGs are similarly useful for development. Working together to create public goods—as large as a defense umbrella or a trading system or as small as capacities for creating bicycle cooperatives or teaching civics in primary schools—increases the possibilities for development through both economies of scale and transferring best practices. Such creation echoes the work of Joseph Schumpeter's (1942) "putting together the pieces" during the "creative destruction" of social and economic change or Albert O. Hirschman's (1958) "forward and backward linkages" and his notion of "voice" (Hirschman 1970), all discussions of how individuals can take the initiative and create value in development contexts. In fact, Hirschman's first book, *National Power and the Structure of Foreign Trade* (1945), is a discussion of the creation by post-World War I Germany of an RPG (an eastern and southeastern European trading system) to enhance its political influence and its capacity for economic development.

Regional public goods and sustainable development: key concepts

To more fully lay the groundwork for understanding the role of RPGs in the global order, we suggest that five sets of concepts need to be discussed in a context in which regional cooperation is understood as being important both for the global order and for national development. These are:

1   The definition of "public goods";
2   Sequencing in the process of public goods creation;
3   The geographic scope of "regions" as they relate to public goods;
4   An institutional design for RPG creation; and
5   Measuring the output of RPG cooperation agreements.

The following sections explore these concepts in more detail.

1. Public goods

The classic definition of public goods offered by Paul Samuelson (1954, pp.387–389) in his paper "The Pure Theory of Public Expenditure" is " [goods] which all enjoy in common in the sense that each individual's consumption of such a good leads to no subtractions from any other individual's consumption of that good." This is the property that has become known as *nonrivalry*. In addition, a *pure public good* exhibits a second property called *nonexcludability*: that is, it is impossible to exclude any individuals from consuming the good. The opposite of a public good is a *private good*, which does not possess these properties. A good which is rivalrous but *nonexcludable* is sometimes called a *common-pool*

Table 1.1 Types of Goods

	Excludable	*Non-excludable*
Rivalrous	**Private goods** food, clothing, cars, personal electronics	**Common goods (common-pool resources)** fish stocks, timber, coal
Non-rivalrous	**Club goods** cinemas, private parks, satellite television	**Public goods** free-to-air television, air, national defense

Source: Based on http://en.wikipedia.org/wiki/Common-pool_resource

resource. A good that is excludable and rivalrous is called a *club good*. Table 1.1 summarizes the qualities of these four types of goods.

The Inter-American Development Bank project that produced the publication *RPGs: From Theory to Practice* (Nguyen, Estevadeordal and Frantz 2004) used a relaxed concept of public goods that included some excludable and some rivalrous goods that were important for development and for international relations, but no private goods. This is important for understanding the roles of a wide range of regionally generated commodities for regional cooperation—beyond trade regimes, defense agreements, health measures, and environmental accords.

2. Sequencing

An important next question is to examine the extent to which trade cooperation is the first step toward regional integration or if, in specific circumstances, other functional areas such as transportation, logistics, border monitoring, connectivity, and labor agreements are foundational for cooperation.

Much of the literature supports the notion that cooperation tends to be dynamic. Economic integration that takes place via cross-border transactions (and is formalized in regional trade agreements) generates demand for cooperation in other policy domains where the externalities of economic activity are directly felt, such as regulation, infrastructure, and environmental management. Cooperation in these areas could, in turn, provide momentum for further policy integration.[5] At the same time, economic and political integration have been acknowledged as being distinct realms, and the degree of cooperation among a set of states can vary across functional areas. This is particularly salient when one considers the distinct contextual arrangements in which different nations and regions have found themselves at different points in history.

3. Geography

A fundamental phenomenon for research on RPGs is the notion of "region"— a basic concept for international relations. While national physical contiguity is a tempting measure of regionality, the fluid nature of national alliances and the

21st century's capacity to transcend such contiguity suggests that a function-based definition of "region" may be appropriate in some circumstances. Thus, finding ways to measure "region" or using nongeographic but functionally related terms to denote the basis for cooperation among nations is important for understanding the various ways public goods can be created.

In addition, the concept of "region" itself may be dynamic. Cooperation initiatives can expand or contract geographically to incorporate more partners, as has been the case in many formal regional organizations. However, in the absence of clear boundaries demarking one region from another, it is unclear how far this process might extend. At the same time, the subsidiarity principle suggests there may be an optimal regional scale for public goods provision, and that this scale will likely be different for different policy domains. This suggests that the traditional set of "regions"—corresponding more or less to broad geographic areas or well-established regional projects—may not be the natural locus for cooperation in all policy domains.

4. Institutional design

There is ambiguity surrounding the ideal institutional mechanism for achieving cooperation. While it is logical to question whether cooperation can succeed without empowered, formally incorporated, supranational bodies, the proliferation of small-scale agreements in narrowly defined policy realms suggests that a broad range of options is available to states in order to provide RPGs. By mapping a large sample of existing agreements according to their policy domains and institutional mechanisms, and applying metrics to assess outcomes, it may be possible to identify the most propitious institutional arrangements for RPG provision. In sociological studies, it is often the case that "informal" groupings are found to be as effective as or more effective than formally constituted organizations. Identifying the formal and informal patterns of association that generate public goods and produce desired outcomes could help map the evolving structure of international cooperation and create understandings of how it might best facilitate sustainable development.

5. Outcome of cooperation

Avoiding the middle-income trap, preventing stagnation and sustaining economic development is no simple feat. Many intermediate and parametric outcomes are required if this result is to be achieved. The effect of trade agreements, for example, has often been gauged simply by whether or not they stimulate trade flows between partners. Similarly, fora such as the Group of Twenty or the Summit of the Americas can be evaluated by the contents of the formal declarations resulting from such meetings. However, outcomes and externalities—be they of the hard or soft power variety—need to be investigated in terms of the actual economic and political cooperation they imply. Thus, at a minimum, in addition to impacts on economic phenomena such as trade, investment, and employment, scholars and policy makers should strive to understand the relationship between RPGs and a nation's ability to navigate the global order. Avoiding the middle-income trap may appear to be a pale substitute for Kantian perpetual peace, but it may very well be an important step in that direction.

Notes

1 For a discussion of the middle-income trap and sustainable development, see Kohli (2011).
2 Public goods are commodities that are available to all members of an alliance. When consumed by one member, the consumption potential for other alliance members is not actually or potentially reduced. Examples of public goods include lighthouses, defense umbrellas, trade and finance systems, public entertainment, clean air and water, healthcare, and open-source software.
3 See De La Torre et al. (2015:3).
4 See, for example, Acharya (2014), Brzezinski (2012), Ikenberry (2011), Kupchan (2012), and Lieber (2012).
5 See, for example, Estevadeordal and Suominen (2009).

References

Acharya, Amitav. 2009. *Whose Ideas Matter?* Ithaca, NY: Cornell University Press.
———. 2014. *The End of American World Order.* Cambridge: Polity Press.
Brzezinski, Zbigniew. 2012. *Strategic Vision: America and the Crisis of Global Power.* New York: Basic Books.
De La Torre, Augusto, Tatiana, Didier, Alain Ize, Daniel Lederman, and Sergio L. Schmukler. 2015. *Latin America and the Rising South: Changing World, Changing Priorities.* Washington, DC: World Bank Publications.
El-Erian, Mohamed A. 2010. "Navigating the New Normal in Industrial Countries." Per Jacobsson Foundation Lecture, International Monetary Fund. Washington, DC, December 15.
Estevadeordal, Antoni, and Kati Suominen. 2009. *The Sovereign Remedy? Trade Agreements in a Globalizing World.* Oxford: Oxford University Press.
Estevadeordal, Antoni, Frantz, Brian and Nguyen, Tam Robert (eds). 2004. *Regional Public Goods: From Theory to Practice.* Washington, DC: IDB/ADB.
Gordon, Robert J. 2000. "Does the 'New Economy' Measure Up to the Great Inventions of the Past?" *Journal of Economic Perspectives* 14, no. 4: 49–74.
Gordon, Robert J. 2016. *The Rise and Fall of American Growth.* Princeton, NJ: Princeton University Press.
Haas, Ernst B. 1958. *The Uniting of Europe: Political, Social, and Economic Forces, 1950–57.* Palo Alto, CA: Stanford University Press.
Hirschman, Albert O. 1945. *National Power and the Structure of Foreign Trade.* Berkeley, CA: University of California Press.
———. 1958. *The Strategy of Economic Development.* New Haven, CT: Yale University Press
———. 1970. *Exit, Voice and Loyalty: Responses to Decline in Firms, Organizations, and States.* Cambridge, MA: Harvard University Press.
Ikenberry, G. John. 2011. *Liberal Leviathan: The Origins and Transformation of the American World Order.* Princeton, NJ: Princeton University Press.

Kant, Immanuel. 1795. *Perpetual Peace: A Philosophical Sketch.* Königsberg, Germany: Friedrich Nicolovius.

Katzenstein, Peter J. 2005. *A World of Regions.* Ithaca, NY: Cornell University Press.

Kindleberger, Charles P. 1973. *The World in Depression: 1929–1939.* Berkeley: University of California Press.

Kissinger, Henry. 2014. *World Order.* New York: Penguin Press.

Kohli, Harinder S., ed. 2011. *Asia 2050: Realizing the Asian Century.* Thousand Oaks, CA: Sage Publications.

Kupchan, Charles A. 2012. *No One's World: The West, the Rising Rest, and the Coming Global Turn.* Oxford: Oxford University Press.

Lieber, Robert J. 2012. *Power and Willpower in the American Future: Why the United States Is Not Destined to Decline.* New York: Cambridge University Press.

Mandelbaum, Michael. 2006. *The Case for Goliath.* New York: Public Affairs Press.

Nguyen, Tam Robert, Antoni Estevadeordal, and Brian Frantz. 2004. *Regional Public Goods: From Theory to Practice.* Washington, DC: Inter-American Development Bank.

Rowe, William T. 2009. *China's Last Empire: The Great Qing.* Cambridge, MA: Harvard University Press.

Samuelson, Paul. 1954. "The Pure Theory of Public Expenditure." *The Review of Economics and Statistics* 36, no. 4: 387–389

Schumpeter, Joseph A. 1942. *Capitalism, Socialism and Democracy.* New York: Harper & Brothers.

Snidal, Duncan. 1985. "The Limits of Hegemonic Stability Theory." *International Organization* 39, no. 4: 579–614.

2 Regional public goods cooperation

An inductive approach to measuring regional public goods

Teng Liu and Theodore Kahn

Introduction

Regional public goods (RPGs) are a complex concept. The core features of "publicness"—nonrivalry in consumption and nonexclusiveness of benefits—are well known to any economics student and continue to be the basis for analysis in the literature. At first blush then, an RPG is simply a public good that provides nonexclusive and nonrival benefits to individuals in a well-defined region.[1] RPGs thus occupy a middle ground between strictly national and global public goods (GPGs). So far, so straightforward. However, a close examination quickly uncovers problems with both the "regional" and the "public goods" concepts as they are commonly applied in both policy and academic discussions of RPGs.

First, there is a lack of conceptual and empirical clarity on the boundaries of a region (De Lombaerde et al. 2010). A fundamental problem in studying RPGs, therefore, is that we do not precisely know the boundaries and location of the regions themselves. Are they groups of neighboring countries, areas with similar geographic characteristics, or formal political organizations above the level of the nation-state? Each of these conceptions of region has been implicitly or explicitly used in work on RPGs.

A second, related problem is the challenge of knowing a priori the geographical extent of a given public good. Many "classic" national public goods such as highway systems or defense can have regional spillovers, and, at the other end of the spectrum, it is particularly difficult to distinguish RPGs from GPGs. Thus, not only do we not know where the regions are, we also cannot be sure precisely which public goods they should be producing.

This ambiguity clearly poses problems for the measurement of RPGs, which is the main concern of this chapter. In light of the conceptual challenges previously outlined, much of the (small) literature aiming to measure RPGs focuses on development financing from aid agencies to support regional public provision in developing countries.[2] While this approach can uncover useful information, it has several drawbacks. First, the tendency to view RPGs through the lens of official development assistance (ODA) risks conflating the two concepts, with potentially negative consequences for the provision of both regional (or global) public goods and development assistance to poor countries (Kaul and Le Goulven 2003). More fundamentally, this approach completely excludes developed countries, and it captures only one of many mechanisms through which RPGs can be produced.

Far from being a secondary concern, the mode of provision is absolutely central to the RPG concept. We explain how two core concepts in the theoretical analysis of RPGs—subsidiarity and aggregation technology—suggest that when it comes to RPGs, the "how" matters. The mechanisms, actors, and jurisdictions that provide the RPG are critical for efficient provision. But we know very little about how and where RPGs are actually produced.

This chapter aims to address this gap through an inductive, data-driven approach to analyzing RPGs. We present an original data set, based on the UN Treaty Collection series, which allows us to systematically measure a *particular mode of RPG provision*: cooperation among national governments to produce RPGs. In defining such cooperation, we exclude ODA;[3] while ODA can also promote RPGs, we are interested here (for reasons later explained) in the efforts of states to provide RPGs through cooperative arrangements rather than the provision of bilateral or multilateral aid.

This approach enables us to map the existing ecosystem of RPG cooperation and observe patterns across space, time, and types of public goods. Through this exercise, we can gain empirical traction on the core conceptual questions that befuddle discussions of RPGs: what are the relevant boundaries of "regions"? How do these differ for different public goods? Which public goods should be properly thought of as "regional"?

These questions are not merely of academic interest. RPGs are increasingly important to the prospects of developing economies, but the conceptual and empirical challenges previously discussed prevent us from drawing systematic conclusions about their effectiveness. While this data set *does not* measure the coverage, quality, or impact of actual public goods provision, knowing which groups of countries are cooperating to produce which public goods is an important step toward doing so.

The chapter proceeds as follows. Section 2 lays out the motives behind our approach to measuring RPG cooperation by reviewing the existing definitions and concepts surrounding RPGs and their provision. Section 3 describes the data set and methods employed in our empirical analysis. Section 4 presents the framework and an overview of our results, and section 5 provides our conclusions.

Defining, producing, and measuring regional public goods

Definitions

As discussed above, RPGs can be defined in a straightforward way as public goods whose nonrivalrous and nonexcludable benefits extend to individuals in a well-defined region.[4] Of course, this formulation is problematic precisely because regions are rarely well defined. In policy and academic discourse, the label is applied to formal supranational political institutions and geographic neighborhoods whose precise boundaries are unspecified. Efforts by scholars of RPGs to better specify the boundaries of regions underscore this point (Reisen, Soto and Weithöner 2004), for example, define the spillovers from RPGs as extending to "countries in the neighborhood of the producing country, in a region which is smaller than the rest of the world." Other authors explicitly acknowledge the complex and multifaceted nature of regions. Sandler (2004) writes that a region is "a territorial subsystem that may be geological; geoclimatic; geographical in terms of continental placement; cultural; or political." Nor is the ambiguous nature of regions confined to discussions of RPGs. Genna and De Lombaerde (2010) argue that studies of regional integration are plagued by "a lack of conceptual clarity concerning the population of 'regions.'"

Given this inherent ambiguity, some analysts have sidestepped the issue of the boundaries of regions and deductively defined the group of public goods that are likely to be regional in their extent (see Raffer 1999; Te Velde, Morrissey and Hewitt 2002). These authors review project portfolios and classify them as "global" or "regional" based on their estimation of the likely spillovers. The issue here is that it is very difficult to distinguish a priori between RPGs and GPGs. In policy domains such as environmental protection or public health measures, efforts to produce public goods may generate positive spillovers across many parts of the world without being truly global. Thus there exists considerable ambiguity in both the "regional" and the "public goods" components of existing definitions of RPGs, which poses formidable challenges to measurement.

Of course, there is also a rich debate surrounding the public nature of goods, which has led to efforts to measure the "publicness" of various shared goods.[5] In the context of GPGs, Kaul and Mendoza (2003), for example, argue that "publicness" is not an inherent quality of goods but instead depends on a triangular interaction among policy making, distribution of benefits, and consumption. While it is important to acknowledge this additional ambiguity surrounding the concept of "publicness," we sidestep this debate and use an expanded definition of public goods that include those commonly classified as club or common goods.[6] This approach allows us to focus on the specific conceptual issues that arise when public goods are regional in scope, which, as this chapter argues, have important theoretical and practical implications.

Producing RPGs: aggregation technology and subsidiarity

There are two additional concepts of fundamental importance for the analysis of RPGs that suggest an alternative approach to measurement. The first is *aggregation technology*, which refers to how the contribution of different countries determines the overall level of provision. Aggregation technology differs for different RPGs. The possibilities, in principle, include summation (each country's efforts are substitutable, and the total level equals the sum of each country's contributions); best shot (the largest country contribution determines the aggregate level); and weakest link (the lowest country contribution determines the aggregate level), with several intermediate or hybrid possibilities.[7] The nature of the aggregation technology affects the optimal vehicle for provision. For example, if the overall level is determined by the contribution of the least capable country (as is the case with regional air traffic control systems), the best scenario may involve financial or technical assistance to weaker partners.

The introduction of diverse aggregation technologies does not, at first glance, help make headway on the issue of measurement. In fact, it would appear to present yet another concept that does not easily lend itself to empirical analysis.

However, the notion of aggregation technology as a core characteristic of RPGs does provide traction on the measurement issue by highlighting the importance of *how* RPG production occurs. The presence of diverse aggregation technologies means that a group of countries seeking to provide a common RPG will have to coordinate their individual contributions in order to ensure an efficient use of available resources. If the RPG is characterized by summation technology, then the group can increase overall provision by exhorting individual governments to contribute more. On the other hand, if the good features best-shot or better-shot technology, then additional efforts by less capable partners will be wasted.

RPG production, therefore, requires an institutional arrangement that allows for coordination, monitoring, and adjustment. In the absence (for the most part) of regional governance institutions with binding authority, such an approach generally requires voluntary cooperation and collective action (Anand 2002). The importance of this coordination mechanism for the production of RPG is so fundamental that Sandler (2001) argues the key obstacle to RPGs provision is not financial but institutional.

The principle of subsidiarity provides additional support for the proposition that the institutional arrangements supporting RPG provision are a paramount concern. A pillar of public finance theory, subsidiarity holds that the political jurisdiction responsible for administering a public good should correspond to the economic jurisdiction—that is, the extent of the good's beneficiaries (Oates 1972). Adherence to subsidiarity makes an efficient level of provision more likely ceteris paribus, as policy makers will take into account the full population of beneficiaries. At the regional level, therefore, some form of regional institution or forum would be ideally situated to provide RPGs.[8]

The goal of this brief discussion is to underscore that the "how" matters in thinking about RPGs provision. The nature of RPGs is such that efficient provision likely requires institutional mechanisms that allow for coordination and cooperation among two or more countries. At the same time, the discussion thus far has shown that from an empirical standpoint it is difficult to know ex ante which groups of countries form the relevant "regions" and which particular public goods they should be jointly providing. The next section explores the implications of these statements for measuring RPGs.

Implications for measurement

As is the case with private goods, one can in principle measure several aspects of public goods: production, supply, demand, consumption, and impact. In practice, however, measuring these aspects is inherently difficult, requiring the use of proxies and indirect measures (for example, measuring schooling and test scores instead of directly measuring education).[9]

On the supply side, researchers are often interested in measuring the efficiency of governments in providing public goods. A common approach here is to measure coverage. For example, one might take the kilometers of paved highways per overall surface area as an indicator of transportation infrastructure or the percentage of households connected to a formal electricity grid in a municipality as a measure of energy provision.

Implicit in the logic of measuring public goods coverage is that the relevant jurisdiction is known. In other words, we understand the boundaries over which the public good should extend as well as the level of government responsible for its provision (i.e. the political jurisdiction). If we are interested in the provision of local sanitation services in a particular country, we have well-defined states, provinces, and municipalities across which to measure coverage. Naturally, researchers choose to analyze the jurisdiction responsible for provision if the aim is to assess the public sector's effectiveness in providing a particular public good. If states are responsible for basic education, we should look at schooling indicators at the state level to evaluate their efforts.

The same cannot be said, however, about RPGs. In light of the ambiguity surrounding the boundaries and population of regions, the relevant jurisdictions over which we would expect an RPG to extend, as well as the actors responsible for its provision, are in many cases uncertain. This state of affairs clearly presents challenges for measuring coverage of RPGs. As we do not know ex ante what the boundaries of the region are, we lack a clear benchmark.

Other approaches to measuring public goods confront similar problems at the regional level. Contingent evaluation, initially developed in environmental economics, uses surveys "to elicit the willingness of respondents to pay for (generally) hypothetical projects or programs" (Portney 1994). As many public goods are not exchanged in markets, this method provides important insights into the demand for them. However, applying this method to RPGs may prove challenging due to cultural differences and the inherent uncertainty over the distribution of benefits from transnational projects (Laffont and Martimort 2005).

There are also ways to measure the benefits and impact of public goods ex post. Adhikari and Weiss (2004) have devised a framework to assess the economic outcomes of multi-country development projects using net present value (NPV) and internal rate of return (IRR). This method is most useful when financial parameters of both inputs and outcomes are well defined and therefore is not appropriate for RPGs such as environmental protection, disease prevention, and institutional building.

Impact evaluation has come to be regarded in some circles as the gold standard for measuring project outcomes. However, this approach has stringent requirements in terms of sampling, counterfactual selection, and limiting spillover effects of the program intervention (i.e. the counterfactual becomes affected by the project) that impose increasingly complex logistical challenges as the scale of the project increases. While impact evaluations of RPG projects exist—see, for example, the Inter-American Development Bank (IDB) project to reduce medical supply prices (2007–2012)—most impact evaluations examine local or municipal-level projects.

This brief survey suggests that the complex characteristics of "region" and regionalization pose considerable challenges in applying existing techniques for measuring public goods to RPGs. In light of these circumstances, a logical and necessary first step would be to measure the various efforts to produce RPGs. In other words, we should start by measuring inputs rather than outputs. These inputs may be financial or institutional. The former would measure the quantity of public resources invested in RPG provision; the latter the creation of organizations, forums, agreements, or treaties among groups of countries that aim to produce RPGs or that provide the institutional basis to support RPG provision. In turn, a refined technique for measuring RPG inputs will provide a basis for measuring other aspects of RPGs such as their coverage, quality, and impact.

Unlike in the case of national public goods, data sets on public spending by governments on RPGs are not widely available.[10] There have, instead, been some attempts to measure financial inputs via studies of ODA for GPGs and RPGs. Several papers at the turn of the 21st century pioneered this approach, using OECD Creditor Reporting System data on ODA allocations, which are classified at five-digit level categories according to their objective (Raffer 1999; Te Velde et al. 2002; World Bank 2001). These studies then identify the outlays oriented toward GPG provision according to their own criteria. The results suggest that ODA for GPGs is considerable (estimates range from US$3 billion to US$14 billion a year) and has increased considerably since the 1970s. Reisen et al. (2004) use a similar approach to estimate that 15 percent of grant allocations were aimed toward provision of RPGs (GPGs accounted for another 15 percent) between 1997 and 2002, totaling around US$5 billion a year. The variation among these estimates attests to the inherent ambiguity in determining ex ante what constitutes a GPG as well as distinguishing between GPGs and RPGs.

Studies of the amount of ODA spent on RPGs, while useful and informative, capture only one aspect of the universe of RPG production. By definition, they exclude RPGs involving developing countries as well as cooperative efforts to produce RPGs among developing countries themselves that are independent of aid.

More fundamentally, they primarily identify financial rather than institutional inputs into RPG production. Multilateral institutions, and regional development banks in particular, can play a key institutional role by coordinating the production and distribution of RPGs and acting as an honest broker (Estevadeordal 2004). However, given the importance of collective action at the regional level for efficient RPG provision for the reasons previously discussed, it is necessary to develop tools to measure this mode of RPG production as well.

The rest of this chapter presents a new data set that provides just such a tool. The data set consists of cooperation agreements among countries to produce RPGs.[11] In contrast to existing approaches that focus on ODA, the scope of RPG cooperation spans the entire globe and captures the efforts of sovereign states to form voluntary, cooperative arrangements with the *explicit* and *primary* objective of producing RPGs. In this way, the key variable of interest—RPG cooperation—can be seen as an institutional input to RPG provision, rather than a financial one. To our knowledge, the only similar approach to measuring RPG creation is Estevadeordal and Suominen (2008), which uses data on trade and cooperation agreements to study the relationship between economic integration and cooperation in public goods areas.[12]

The data set offers an inductive, data-driven approach to the core conceptual problems surrounding RPGs. Rather than relying on preconceived regional boundaries[13] or specifying ex ante which public goods have regional spillovers, we can observe which groups of countries are actually making efforts to create RPGs and which public goods are actually being produced at the regional level. This approaches also embraces the possibility that the geographic locus of RPG production will likely vary from one public good to the next. Importantly, a better understanding of the geographic and functional breakdown of RPG production—that is, knowing which groups of countries are cooperating to produce which public goods—is a critical first step toward measuring the output and effectiveness of such efforts. Understanding the relevant regional jurisdictions of different RPGs allows us to apply commonly used approaches to measuring public goods provision at the local and national levels.

Of course, cooperation agreements are only one among many technologies for producing RPGs, and the purpose of the data set is to complement rather than replace existing measures based on ODA. Such agreements are, however, an important mode of RPG production, considering the potential efficiency of *regional* provision of RPGs (an application of the subsidiarity principle) and the importance of collective action in light of various aggregation technologies and the need for flexibility and potential cost sharing. The next section describes the construction of the data set and presents initial descriptive statistics.

Data set and methods

Measuring RPGs: the variable

As discussed above, we use formal international agreements (i.e. institutional arrangements) to depict the universe of RPGs. In essence, we are empirically measuring the input into RPGs by constructing a methodological framework and an original indicator through the quantification of international agreements. This variable is "RPG cooperation," which illustrates the frequency/number of RPGs that national governments intend to create within a given period. More specifically, international treaties serve as indicators of RPG cooperation.

It is worth stressing once again that this variable measures the existence of an *instrument* of RPG creation rather than the *outcome* of RPGs. An RPG is not always created after the signing of a pertinent international agreement. Therefore, we only measure efforts to attempt to create RPGs as approximated by numbers of international treaties.

Signing formal treaties is only one of the many instruments for creating RPGs; informal international agreements may also facilitate cooperation and RPG creation. For instance, members of the Association of Southeast Asian Nations (ASEAN) use a consensus principle for their decision making which does not necessarily result in treaties. Additionally, the "RPG cooperation" variable does not account for RPG projects directly funded by regional organizations such as the Asia-Pacific Economic Cooperation (APEC) or multilateral institutions such as the IDB or ADB.

While the absence of formality facilitates flexible arrangements, it also creates challenges in sustaining cooperation. Because a treaty is legally binding, the incentive for participants to defect is considerably reduced. This is an important rationale for using treaties as proxies of international cooperation. Admittedly, the focus on formal cooperation in this study may leave out RPGs created through informal mechanisms.

To construct the "RPG cooperation" variable, we employed an empirical approach based on quantitative analysis of legal texts. The World Trade Organization (WTO) and the World Bank have previously developed this approach. The World Bank's "Quantitative Analysis of Road Transport Agreements (QuARTA)" report examines the openness and restrictiveness of 77 bilateral agreements, and their relationship to international trade smoothening. It evaluates an agreement based on criteria pertaining to openness, using a scoring template. Through this approach, each international agreement will have a numerical score, reflecting the strength of its openness.

Inspired by this study, our research uses an even simpler approach: we counted the number of agreements that nation-states have signed, while partially examining the legal texts themselves. Due to the large sample size (initially over 100,000 observations), it was impractical to evaluate all the treaties' contents in great detail. This means that the variable only measures the quantity but not the quality or depth of RPG cooperation.

Data sources and sampling

The research sourced data from the United Nations Treaty Collection (UNTC)[14], more specifically the United Nations Treaty Series (UNTS). UNTS contains both bilateral and multilateral treaties.[15] Pursuant to Article 102 of the United Nations Charter, member states must register all international agreements that they sign with the UN Secretariat, which then publishes these legal texts (UNTS 2012, p.29).

Due to this requirement, the UNTC is probably the most comprehensive database of international agreements and provides a representative sample. However, it is important to note what the database does not include. First, there is no clear deadline for registration, which means that some active agreements have not been recorded. In some cases, there is a lag of years between an agreement entering into force and being registered with the UN. On the other hand, all the treaties deposited with the secretariat have been ratified.

Despite clear registration guidelines, the types of documents that should be registered remain ambiguous. In the United States, for instance, "treaty" and an "executive agreement" are both ways for the country to enter into international arrangements.[16] Yet there is a clear distinction between the two, in that executive agreements are only governed by domestic laws. Therefore, most of the US preferential trade agreements (PTAs)—which are by definition executive agreements—are not registered with the UN because they are simply not considered treaties by the USA and thus are not subject to the governance of the international legal system.

Nevertheless, UNTC still provides valuable information. This research project constructs a panel data set of 186 countries and all their treaties (both bilateral and plurilateral) through 1945–2014. Our data set does not include open multilateral treaties such as the Convention on the Elimination of All Forms of Discrimination against Women, as they are global treaties seeking to create GPGs.

The sample in our study incorporates the vast majority of the nation-states in the current world system. Besides countries, international organizations also have treaty-making capacity. Consequently, the treaties in UNTC are conducted between:

1 States;
2 States and treaty-making international organizations;[17] and
3 Treaty-making international organizations.[18]

However, the main unit of analysis in this research is the nation-state. In other words, the data set includes treaties in the above-listed categories (1) and (2) but not in (3). Compared to international organizations, states constitute the basis of the international system and therefore are a good starting point to examine international cooperation and RPGs. Additionally, the process and objectives of treaty making solely between international organizations may be very different from those involving national governments.

Variable construction

The data set downloaded from UNTC originally contains over 100,000 observations (the number of treaties). It includes some duplicate values and blank treaties,[19] which were eliminated in the variable construction process. Besides, many international treaties also entail subsequent amendments. As important as these amendments are, including them could lead to double counting, so amendments were removed from the data set. After this cleanup procedure, the number of observations was reduced to approximately 89,000. There were two main steps in constructing the "RPG cooperation" variable:

1   Separate ODA from RPG cooperation; and
2   Code RPG cooperation by functional areas.

Within our framework, RPG cooperation and ODA are differentiated based on the level of interdependence and mutuality of benefits.[20] First, ODA is a one-way flow of assistance from donors to developing country beneficiaries, and must, in the case of financial assistance, take the form of concessional funding (or soft loans[21]) with a grant component of at least 25 percent. In contrast, RPG cooperation involves two or more parties acting together to achieve development outcomes. In this process, the parties rely on each other to contribute funds, technical expertise, and human resources.

Further, producing mutual and relatively equal benefits is another key characteristic of RPG cooperation.[22] The benefits of ODA are mainly channeled to recipients/developing countries. In comparison, the benefits of RPG cooperation should accrue to all parties involved, whether they are developed or developing countries. For example, funding and technical assistance provided by a donor agency to cure animal diseases is clearly ODA, in that it only benefits the recipient country. However, collaboration between countries on controlling animal diseases in the frontier region is RPG cooperation.[23]

In order to better analyze the scope of RPG cooperation, a system of functional categories pertaining to international development is needed. UNTC has coded each treaty document with subject terms. However, this UNTC classification is neither concise nor analytically useful. There are a large number of subject terms (787 in total), and they are not organized in a coherent manner. While some subject terms correspond to functional categories such as education and energy, others simply are names of geographic locations, organizations, and even of academic disciplines. Therefore, to facilitate analysis, we have devised a new system of classification.

This project constructs and analyzes the variable "RPG cooperation" across six functional areas, as shown in Table 2.1. This taxonomy is based on a variety of sources: the OECD aid statistics codes;[24] UN Sustainable Development Goals;[25] RPG projects financed by the IDB; and Sandler (2007).[26] The synthesis of these sources provides a relatively complete picture of matters important to sustainable development and peace. These issues lie in the environmental, economic, social, and political spheres. Some of them can be solved within national borders, while others (e.g. communicable diseases, climate change) permeate across countries and need resolution through international cooperation. We therefore argue that nations cooperate and create public goods to tackle challenges in relation to such issues.

Table 2.1 Six Main Public Goods Functions

Functions	Examples
1 Natural Resources and Environment	Energy, environmental protection
2 Economic Cooperation and Integration	Trade, taxation, customs regulation
3 Human and Social Development	Education, culture, science, health
4 Governance and Institutions	General cooperation, legal issues
5 Peace and Security	Military alliance, crime control
6 Connectivity	Transportation network, visa, infrastructure

The first function is concerned with environmental governance, pertaining to matters such as energy, conservation, and pollution management. For instance, Brazil, Peru, and Colombia have established treaties with each other on conserving the Amazon rainforest.[27] The second function includes trade agreements[28] and bilateral investment treaties, which have been extensively studied in economic integration literature. However, our framework is more holistic as it also considers taxation, customs, intellectual property rights, and cooperation in agriculture, industry, and services.

The third and fourth functions focus on the social and governance dimensions of sustainable development. International public goods relating to social protection and human capital include mutual recognition of education certificates,[29] public health in border regions,[30] and insurance provision for migrant workers.[31] The fourth function is the most general category of the taxonomy. Many treaties in the UNTC do not have substantive provisions and their titles are often noted with keywords such as "general cooperation" and "treaty of friendship." However, these treaties may help create RPGs such as favorable institutional regimes. This function also encompasses judicial cooperation, diplomatic relations, and political consultation.

The fifth function involves cooperation over matters of security at both the macro and micro levels. Regional defense umbrellas and general military cooperation are typical examples of RPGs in this function. In addition, nations also cooperate in extradition, crime control at borders, and combating drug trafficking networks. "Connectivity" is likely one of the most unique features of RPG cooperation. In this area, nations become more interlinked through border management, communication and logistics networks, transportation infrastructure, and rules of international migration. One may argue that building connectivity is a means to an end (e.g. trade). However, increasing connectedness itself is a goal of regionalization and globalization. Compared to economic cooperation, connectivity issues have received far less scholarly attention. By establishing connectivity as a category, this study purports to bring this issue to the forefront of discussions on integration and RPG cooperation.

Thus, determining the functions of RPG cooperation is a critical component of the process of constructing the variable—each RPG cooperation/treaty can only be assigned to one function to render precise analysis in the results section.

Due to the large number of observations, it would be difficult to analyze each treaty and its original texts in detail. The coding process thus largely relies on the titles of treaties, most of which are very descriptive in terms of treaty functions. For instance, one treaty is entitled the Convention for the Avoidance of Double Taxation and the Prevention of Fiscal Evasion with Respect to Taxes on Income and on Capital.[32] Based on the title, we infer that this treaty deals with taxation matters, which correspond to the second function, "Economic Cooperation and Integration." Because there are many tax-related treaties like this, it is easier to code them together based on the keyword "taxation" than doing so treaty by treaty. In other words, we bundle treaties based on keywords and code them as groups. While this approach is efficient, it does have limitations. First, the depth and quality of treaties are not assessed. Besides, while the titles are informative, misinterpretation may have occurred due to ambiguous wording.[33]

It is important to acknowledge that certain treaties may have multiple functions. In fact, in the process of constructing the variable, this type of dilemma often arises. We thus have established the following assessment criteria:

1 Differentiate between the means and the end (i.e. function);
2 Choose the immediate and direct goal of the agreement (rather than the intangible and indirect goal); and
3 If an agreement has multiple goals/functions, select the one that carries the most weight.

It is also worth emphasizing that this empirical study follows a more holistic framework than the classic definition of public goods (as something nonrivalrous and nonexcludable). In other words, our data set includes cooperation in pure public goods, impure public goods, and club goods. Sandler (2007, p.5) defines "impure public goods" as having properties of "partial rivalry or partial excludability or both," and "club goods" as being "fully excludable and partially rival." For example, Belgium and the Netherlands have an agreement on reciprocally accumulating adequate oil stocks as their petroleum markets are closely connected.[34] The consumption of oil commodities is rivalrous, rendering this agreement impure RPG cooperation. Examples of cooperation over club goods include power networks, roads, and bridges connecting countries. Finally, we assume that national governments' behaviors have a certain degree of publicness. This means that decisions such as treaty making typically affect a large portion of their constituents, thus qualifying as public goods provision. Due to these assumptions, the data set does not eliminate any treaties based on the strict definition of pure public goods. Consequently, the variable "RPG cooperation" is calculated at gross.

Results framework and discussion

The previous sections describe what the variable "RPG cooperation" is, the sources and characteristics of the data used, and how it was constructed. This section presents some results of the data set and, equally importantly, how it may be utilized for future research. The analyses in this section include intensity mapping, the process of sequencing, and top RPG cooperators. Most importantly, the concept of "region" is deconstructed by functions of public goods, through the examples of the United States and Brazil.

As noted in the previous section, there is a great need to conceptually and empirically separate RPGs from ODA. In the existing database, the number of unique agreements for ODA provision is 18,816, and the number for RPG cooperation is 29,740. The figure of RPG cooperation is 58 percent greater than that of ODA. In other words, countries are likely to cooperate more in order to create RPGs than ODA. In development studies literature, the lack of clear division between ODA and RPGs may have contributed to the underestimation of the latter, which further demonstrates the need to examine RPG cooperation much more specifically.

Mapping

Figure 2.1 is an intensity map of RPG cooperation (bilateral and plurilateral) throughout the world between 1945 and 2014. The darker the shade, the greater the number of RPG cooperation efforts a particular country has—as the map illustrates, RPG cooperation is unevenly distributed at the global level. As Figure 2.2 shows, the USA undertakes RPG cooperation disproportionately more than any other country.

RPG cooperation by function

Analyzing the functional areas where nations participate extensively may illustrate the incentives for international cooperation. Figure 2.3 shows that economic incentives seem to be the driving force behind RPG cooperation. Interestingly, connectivity is the second largest area in which RPG cooperation occurs. This is an important finding: very often issues such as transportation and information technologies are treated solely as tools of integration. However, increasing connectivity *is* a critical goal of RPG cooperation and a type of public goods, as the result suggests.

Following the economic and connectivity functions is human and social development. This suggests that nations are concerned with the wellbeing of their citizens within and beyond borders, as is revealed by cooperation on issues such as international education, combating communicable disease, and the sharing of science and knowledge. The numbers of RPG cooperation efforts in "Governance and Institutions" and "Peace and Security" are very similar, although the latter is slightly greater. Environmental issues seem to have received the least attention in RPG cooperation. Nevertheless, the RPG cooperation variable only measures the quantity of cooperation efforts, but not the quality or final impact of these. Further analysis is thus needed before we can argue that environmental RPG cooperation is the most inadequate of all the issues covered.

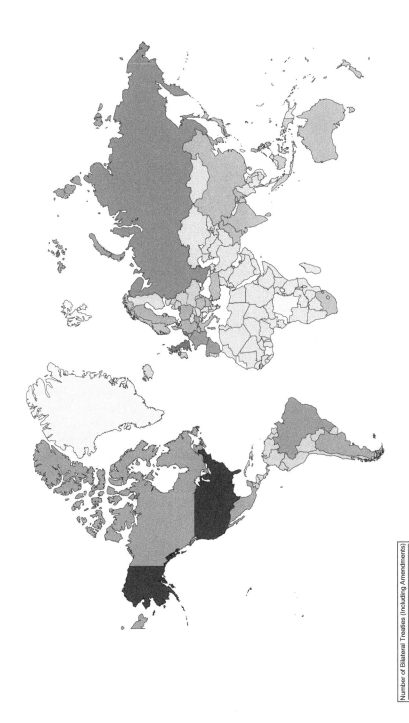

Figure 2.1 Intensity Map of RPG Cooperation (Bilateral and Plurilateral, 1945–2014).

Source: United Nations Treaty Collection (UNTC).

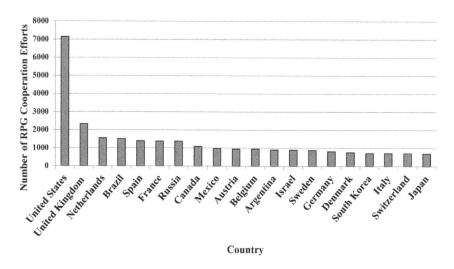

Figure 2.2 Top 20 Participants in RPG Cooperation (Bilateral and Plurilateral, 1945–2014).

Source: United Nations Treaty Collection (UNTC).

RPG cooperation over time

RPG cooperation also needs to be examined over time in order to illustrate sequencing processes. As the cumulative graph (Figure 2.4) shows, between 1945 and 1950 RPG cooperation on all functions occurred at very similar frequencies. Since then, however, these frequencies started to diverge from each other very quickly: RPG cooperation efforts on economic and connectivity issues are always ahead of other functions, indicating their importance for nations. Cooperation on matters of human development, peace, and governance advanced at similar rates until the 1960s, when RPG cooperation on human development accelerated. Finally, cooperation on environmental issues has always fallen behind the other areas.

Top RPG partners and regionality (bilateral)

As Figure 2.2 illustrates, the USA and the United Kingdom are the top two nations involved in RPG cooperation efforts, and Brazil is the developing country that is involved in the highest number of efforts. For the USA, European countries such as Germany and the UK are critical partners, and it also cooperates on RPGs extensively with its neighbors Canada and Mexico. The RPG cooperation network for Brazil is very different. While the top three partners are all developed countries (Germany, the USA, and France), most of the remaining ones are developing countries located in Latin America. It is worth noting that China also ranks high as a partner. Through these

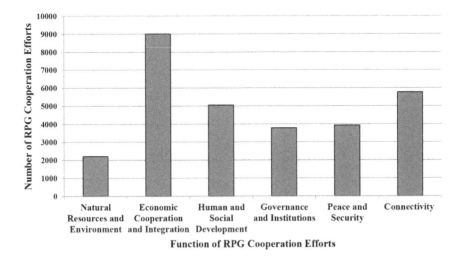

Figure 2.3 RPG Cooperation by Function (Bilateral and Plurilateral, 1945–2014). Based on unique records of treaties (does not include country pairs).

Source: United Nations Treaty Collection (UNTC).

preliminary analyses, it seems that the USA, the UK, and France have played important roles in constructing RPG cooperation networks, as they are consistently among the top partners. Brazil, in contrast, is less prominent despite its large number of treaties.

To deconstruct the concept of "region," we must go beyond traditional geographical and geopolitical categories. "Region" is a relative concept, and regionalization is as much a process of *exclusion* as it is of *inclusion*: if every nation-state was part of this process, it would then constitute globalization. If we apply this assumption to the data set, it is possible to examine which countries in a bilateral or plurilateral group may create a "region" based on the functional areas in which they cooperate with each other. However, this does not mean that if a group of countries cooperate on connectivity RPGs, they then constitute a connectivity "region" per se. Rather, their cooperation around a particular function needs to be so extensive and intensive that it has resulted in a substantially larger number of agreements than any other functions *and* country partners. While this criterion is in need of further development, it may serve as a useful way of analyzing regionality and quantifying regionalization.

For example, Canada, the UK, Mexico, Japan, and Germany are the top five RPG partners for the USA, and it is worth applying the aforementioned criterion of intensiveness and extensiveness to them. Figure 2.5 illustrates these five countries' RPG cooperation activities with the USA: it is striking that Germany (including the former West Germany) outperforms the

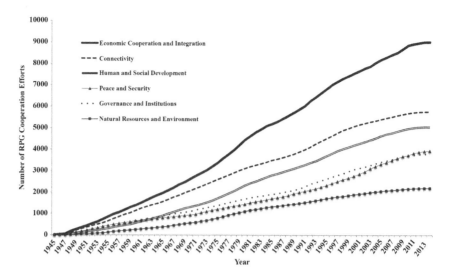

Figure 2.4 Cumulative Graph of RPG Cooperation.

Source: United Nations Treaty Collection (UNTC).

other four countries in terms of peace and security—Germany and the USA likely constitute a large security bloc. Canada is the most important partner in environmental, human development, and connectivity issues.[35] In the case of Brazil, however, the distribution of functions across its top five partners is more evenly distributed. Compared to Brazil's other partners, Germany does not have substantially more agreements in any particular functional area. If areas of cooperation between Germany and Brazil are examined horizontally, no single functional area clearly dominates all others in terms of numbers of cooperation efforts. Consequently, it is difficult to conclude that Brazil and Germany clearly constitute a "region" of a particular kind.

A direct comparison of Figures 2.5 and 2.6 also shows that the USA and Brazil may have differing priorities with regard to RPG cooperation. Brazil's RPG cooperation is skewed toward the left: it cooperates heavily on matters relating to natural resources and the environment, economic cooperation and integration, and human and social development. In comparison, US cooperation is skewed to the right, or is simply concentrated around peace and security RPGs. This suggests that the cooperation incentives of a developed country and a developing country may be very different. As part of its development process, Brazil needs to improve its human capital, utilize its advantages in natural resources, and establish economic connections. It is likely that the USA has a greater need to establish a worldwide security network, having already achieved relatively high levels of economic and human development. We are not necessarily trying to privilege a teleological view of development, but such comparisons provide another way of understanding the sequencing of RPG

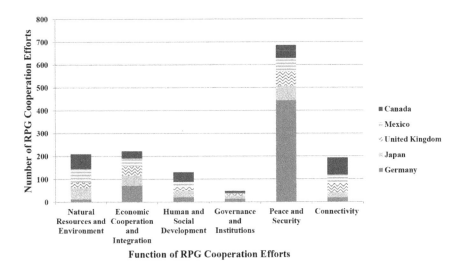

Figure 2.5 Regionality of the US by RPG Function (Bilateral, 1945–2014).

Source: United Nations Treaty Collection (UNTC).

cooperation. Again, before reaching a definitive conclusion, the data for both these and other countries would need to be examined further.

The section thus far has presented some of the results generated from the RPG cooperation database. The goal of this paper is not necessarily to offer a

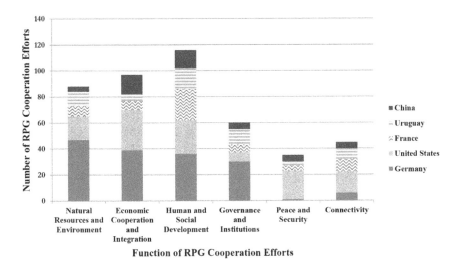

Figure 2.6 Regionality of Brazil by RPG Function (Bilateral, 1945–2014).

Source: United Nations Treaty Collection (UNTC).

comprehensive view of these database results, or to reach definitive conclusions about RPG cooperation and RPGs themselves. In fact, the research potentials of this database require ongoing exploration. As such, we hope that this paper and the database that accompanies it will be a starting point for the endeavor of measuring and understanding RPGs.

Conclusions

This chapter has presented a new dataset on the production of RPGs. The methodology employed is informed by various difficulties in defining and measuring RPGs, as well as the problematic nature of the concept "region" itself. As a result of these challenges, the jurisdiction and coverage of RPGs are murkier than those of local public goods and GPGs. In some existing studies on international public goods, moreover, ODA and RPGs are lumped together, further complicating measurement efforts. But this does not mean that no good tools or data exist.

By sourcing data from the UNTC, we have measured nation-states' inputs into RPG creation through formal treaties across time and coded this data based on functional areas. While this approach admittedly leaves certain important issues unaddressed, we contend that we first need to better understand the concept of regionality and the inputs into RPG creation before we can understand how they are implemented and their impact.

The resulting database provides an overview of the universe of RPGs. While the results are preliminary, some points are clear. First, RPG cooperation is unevenly distributed, with developed countries like the USA dominating the landscape. Second, RPG cooperation on economic matters outweighs other functions both in terms of number of efforts and sequencing. Third, while the geographic sense of "region" still matters, nations may cooperate and constitute a region based on a particular function.

Most importantly, the database that underlies this paper has considerable research potential. Further exploratory analysis and graphing of the data may offer a relatively comprehensive view of RPG inputs through institutional arrangements. From the perspective of data analytics, it is no different from conventional economic databases. In the consolidated version, "RPG Cooperation" is a panel data set that describes the numbers of pertinent agreements, which can be organized by country, year, and/or by function. It could serve a source for formal hypothesis testing using network analysis and regression. Moreover, case studies and qualitative analyses may be developed using the nonconsolidated version, which includes more detailed information about the contents of treaties. Finally, the RPG cooperation data set is expandable so as to incorporate trade agreements from the WTO and treaties between multilateral organizations, among others. Once published on the IDB website, this data set will be a valuable tool for researchers interested in RPGs, regional integration, and/or international cooperation in general.

Notes

1 Estevedeordal (2004, p.107); Sandler (2007, p.3)
2 Examples of such work include Anand (2002), Raffer (1999), and Reisen et al. (2004).
3 The Organisation for Economic Co-operation and Development (OECD) defines ODA as financial flows to recipients that are "administered with the promotion of the economic development and welfare of developing countries as its main objective," and are "concessional in character and conveys a grant element of at least 25 per cent (calculated at a rate of discount of 10 per cent)."

  http://www.oecd.org/dac/stats/officialdevelopmentassistancedefinitionand coverage.htm

4 This definition is given in Sandler (2006) and Estevadeordal (2004), although Sandler (2001, 2004) also acknowledges the ambiguous nature of regions.
5 See for example Bergstrom and Goodman (1973) and Reiter and Weichenrieder (1999), whose approach is based on a crowding function that measures whether population size affects the usefulness of a good for individuals. Note that the publicness of a good is a separate question from which public goods are truly regional in their extent of benefits.
6 Club goods are nonrivalrous but excludable, and examples include telecommunications networks; common goods are nonexcludable but rivalrous, such as fisheries or common resource stocks.
7 Other possible aggregation technologies include weighted summation, where the contribution of each country's efforts to the total is weighted by some factor; threshold, in which the benefits of the public good only come about once a given cumulative quantity is reached; and better shot and weaker link, which are less extreme versions of best shot and weakest link, respectively.
8 This specific form of coordination mechanism could vary from a supranational body such as the EU to a one-off agreement among countries to produce a particular RPG. It is important to note that even in the case of best-shot aggregation, in which the most capable national government should provide the RPG, an efficient level will not be attained unless there is some mechanism to account for the preferences of individuals in the region who receive benefits but are not citizens of the providing nation. On the other hand, some authors have argued that, *pace* subsidiarity, global actors such as multilateral institutions may enjoy economies of scale or economies of scope in the provision of RPGs that might compensate for the inefficiencies associated with overprovision (Kanbur 2001, others cited in Anand 2002 and Sandler 2007).
9 See Ostrom and Ostrom (1978).
10 "Regional public good" has not been widely adopted by governments and organizations as an analytic category or an expenditure item (with exceptions such as the IDB and Asian Development Bank).
11 Scholars have been documenting the creation of international treaties. One notable example is the World Treaty Index (WTI) that Peter Rohn started in the 1970s. WTI strives to collect the population of international agreements in the 20th century using sources including the UN and unregistered treaties. See Poast, Bommarito, and Katz (2010).
12 The main goal of Estevadeordal and Suominen (2008) was to empirically test propositions regarding sequencing of cooperation agreements and their geographic distribution, motivated by the literature on regional integration. The authors found that economic cooperation generally precedes cooperation in other policy areas.

13 One implication of our agnosticism on the boundaries of regions is that cooperation agreements between geographically distant partners such as the United States and Japan are included in the dataset. We believe this approach provides a simple and consistent, if not perfect, solution to ambiguity surrounding regionness. In addition, the recent rise of nonregional blocs such as BRICS suggests that geographic proximity need not be a prerequisite for RPG production.

14 See https://treaties.un.org/home.aspx

15 In the UNTC taxonomy, a bilateral treaty is conducted between two participants, and a multilateral treaty is between three or more participants. A "party" encompasses a national government, a regional grouping, or a regional or global organization. This creates ambiguity when counting treaty numbers in cases where a participant is a regional or international organization. For example, a scientific agreement (I-47953) between the European Union and China is classified as a bilateral agreement when in fact it involves multiple countries and could be analyzed as a multilateral treaty. While acknowledging this ambiguity, our RPG database follows the definitions employed by the UNTC.

16 http://www.state.gov/s/l/treaty/faqs/70133.htm

17 For example, "Argentina–International Atomic Energy Agency. Agreement for the Application of Safeguards" (I-16206).

18 For example, "Financing Agreement (Institutional Development for Education Project) between the United Nations Interim Administration Mission in Kosovo and the International Development Association" (II-1312).

19 There are instances in which a treaty has country information and a registration number but nothing else—possibly due to entry errors at UNTC.

20 The distinction between ODA and RPG cooperation is less clear-cut in practice. OECD has specific criteria determining whether an item is reportable as ODA or not. In fact, our distinction between RPG creation and ODA is partially based on the OECD classification.

21 That is, funding for which the interest rates incurred are below the market average.

22 OECD, "Official Development Assistance – Definition and Coverage."

23 I-7084

24 OECD "Purpose Codes: sector classification" http://www.oecd.org/dac/stats/purpose codessectorclassification.htm

25 UN "Open Working Group proposal for Sustainable Development Goals" https://sustainabledevelopment.un.org/focussdgs.html

26 In Rohn's WTI, treaties are coded by nine topics: diplomacy, welfare, economics, aid, transport, communications, culture, resources, and administration. Unlike Rohn's taxonomy (created in the 1970s), the RPG database excludes aid agreements and includes one classification specifically for security issues.

27 For examples, see treaties registered as I-15938 and I-24121 at the UNTC.

28 These exclude preferential trade agreements (PTAs) undertaken by the US, such as the North American Free Trade Agreement (NAFTA).

29 For example, I-43464

30 For example, I-50359

31 For example, I-13558

32 UNTC registration number I-33995

33 In fact, for certain treaties with ambiguous titles, we referred to original documents to ensure the accuracy of the coding.

34 UNTC registration number I-23628

35 As this data set does not include many US trade agreements, Germany may not necessarily be the largest economic RPG partner for the US, despite what the figure shows.

References

Adhikari, Ramesh, and John Weiss. 2004. "A Methodological Framework for the Economic Analysis of Sub-Regional Projects." In *Regional Public Goods: From Theory to Practice*, edited by Antoni Estevadeordal, Brian Frantz, and Tam Robert Nguyen. Washington, DC: IDB.

Anand, P. B. 2002. "Financing the Provision of Global Public Goods." UNU/WIDER Discussion Paper No. 2002/110.

Bergstrom, Ted, and Robert P. Goodman. 1973. "Private Demands for Public Goods." *American Economic Review* 63, no. 3: 280–296.

De Lombaerde, P., F. Söderbaum, L. Van Langenhove, and F. Baert. 2010. "The Problem of Comparison in Comparative Regionalism." *Review of International Studies* 36, no. 3: 731–753.

Estevedeordal, Antoni, Brian Frantz, and Tam Robert Nguyen, eds. 2004. *Regional Public Goods: From Theory to Practice*. Washington, DC: IDB.

Estevadeordal, Antoni, and Kati Suominen. 2008. *Gatekeepers of Global Commerce: Rules of Origin and International Economic Integration*. Washington, DC: IDB.

Genna, Gaspare M., and Philippe De Lombaerde. 2010. "The Small N Methodological Challenges of Analyzing Regional Integration." *Journal of European Integration* 32, no. 6: 583–595.

IDB. 2015. "Can Regional Standards Be Above the National Norm? Steps into the Potential Impact of Generating Regional Public Goods in LAC." Presentation at the Inter-American Development Bank. Washington, DC, June 23.

Kanbur, Ravi. 2001. "Cross-Border Externalities, International Public Goods and Their Implications for Aid Agencies." Working Paper. Ithaca, NY: Cornell University.

Kaul, Inge, and Katell Le Goulven. 2003. "Financing Global Public Goods: A New Frontier of Public Finance." In *Providing Global Public Goods. Managing Globalization*, edited by Inge Kaul. New York: Oxford University Press.

Kaul, Inge, and Ronald U. Mendoza. 2003. "Advancing the Concept of Public Goods." In *Providing Global Public Goods. Managing Globalization*, edited by Inge Kaul. New York: Oxford University Press.

Laffont, Jean-Jacques, and David Martimort. 2005. "The Design of Transnational Public Good Mechanisms for Developing Countries." *Journal of Public Economics* 89: 159–196.

Oates, Wallace E. 1972. *Fiscal Federalism*. New York: Harcourt.

Ostrom, Vincent, and Elinor Ostrom. 1978. "Public Goods and Public Choices." Workshop in Political Theory and Policy Analysis, Indiana University.

Poast, Paul, Michael James Bommarito, and Daniel Martin Katz. 2010. "The Electronic World Treaty Index: Collecting the Population of International Agreements in the 20th Century." SSRN Scholarly Paper ID 2652760. Rochester, NY: Social Science Research Network.

Portney, Paul R. 1994. "The Contingent Valuation Debate: Why Economists Should Care." *The Journal of Economic Perspectives* 8, no. 4 (autumn): 3–17.

Raffer, Kunibert. 1999. "ODA and Global Public Goods: A Trend Analysis of Past and Present Spending Patterns." UNDP Office of Development Studies Background Paper.

Reisen, Helmut, Marcelo Soto, and Thomas Weithöner. 2004. "Financing Global and Regional Public Goods through ODA: Analysis and Evidence from the OECD Creditor Reporting System." OECD Development Centre Working Paper No. 232.

Reiter, Michael, and Alfons J. Weichenrieder. 1999. "Public Goods, Club Goods, and the Measurement of Crowding." *Journal of Urban Economics* 46, no. 1 (July): 69–79.

Sandler, Todd. 2001. "On Financing Global and International Public Goods." Policy Research Working Papers. World Bank Economic and Prospects Group.

———. 2004. "Demand and Institutions for Regional Public Goods." In *Regional Public Goods: From Theory to Practice*, edited by Antoni Estevadeordal, Brian Frantz, and Tam Robert Nguyen. Washington, DC: IDB.

———. 2006. "Regional Public Goods and International Organizations." *The Review of International Organizations* 1, no. 1 (March): 5–25.

———. 2007. "Regional Public Goods, Aid, and Development." Unpublished manuscript available at https://www.researchgate.net/publication/228901145_Regional_public_goods_aid_and_development

Te Velde, Dirk Willem, Oliver Morrissey, and Adrian Hewitt. 2002. "Defining International Public Goods: Conceptual Issues." In *International Public Goods: Incentives, Measurement, and Financing*, edited by Marco Ferroni and Ashoka Mody. Dordrecht: Kluwer Academic Publishers.

UN Treaty Section of the Office of Legal Affairs. 2012. *Treaty Handbook*. New York: UN.

World Bank. 2001. *Global Development Finance 2001*. Washington, DC: World Bank.

Part II

Regional leadership, alliances, networks, and outcomes

3 Regionalism in the evolving world order

Power, leadership, and the provision of public goods

Amitav Acharya

Introduction

Regionalism is a key element of the emerging world order and potentially a major channel for the provision of public goods. *Potentially*, because the regional approach to public goods has been overshadowed and overlaid by the dominant global economic and security order (which may be called the American World Order), underpinned by the power and purpose of the United States and its Western allies since World War II. But as that order wanes (Acharya 2014a), the need for mechanisms for regional public goods (RPGs) is becoming greater and ever more relevant.

The decline of the American World Order is not leading to multipolarity, as many traditional pundits assume, but to *multiplexity*. Multiplexity, or the idea of a multiplex world, has the following main features (Acharya 2014a and 2014b):

- Whereas the traditional conception of multipolarity (derived from Europe) assumed the primacy of the great powers, actors (or agents) in a multiplex world are not limited to being great powers or indeed states (both Western and non-Western), but also include international institutions, nongovernmental organizations, multinational corporations, and transnational networks (good and bad). As with a multiplex cinema, or living room variants such as streaming and Netflix, a multiplex world gives audiences a wider choice of plots, actors, producers, and directors.
- Some of these plots—or ideas and ideologies—and ways of realizing them, differ from and challenge the cultural and political narratives and instruments of the American-dominated liberal international order. As Thomas Friedman (2005) put it, the world is not "flat," but is of enduring diversity. There is no "end of history" here, except in terms of the relatively short history of Western dominance, bearing in mind that China was also the world's number one economy until the early 19th century.
- It is marked by complex global linkages that include not just trade but also finance and transnational production networks, which were scarce in pre-World War European economic interdependence. While that interdependence was mostly intra-European, with the rest of the world being in a dependent (colonial) relationship with Europe and the United States,

today's interdependence is truly global and increasingly reciprocal. It binds players all around the world, as exemplified by G20 membership, a product of global financial interdependence. Moreover, interdependence today goes beyond economics and also covers many other issue areas, such as the environment, disease, human rights, and social media.

- It has multiple layers of governance, including global, interregional, regional, domestic, and substate levels. Regionalism is a key part of this, but regionalism today is open and overlapping, a far cry from the imperial blocs of the 19th century, which are unlikely to reappear.

Regionalism occupies a central place in the multiplex world. But its nature and role, which are central to understanding the provision of RPGs, differ from that found in traditional forms of regionalism under bipolar or unipolar international systems. The dominant theories and understandings of regionalism up to now have derived from a European and US policy context and approach. They tend to privilege the role of powerful actors in the creation and maintenance of regionalism, and/or hard legalistic institutional forms of regionalism. This has led in the past to an emphasis on two generic types of regionalism, which may be termed hegemonic and integrationist. Yet regionalism has been a much broader and more complex phenomenon encompassing a variety of purposes, approaches, and outcomes. No one size fits them all. The EU centrism of theories about regionalism had already been questioned even before Brexit dealt a major blow to the European Union's claim to be a universal model of regionalism (Acharya 2002, 2014a: Chapter 5). Now, it is imperative that ideas about and mechanisms for RPGs must take this diversity among regions and regional institutions into account. To capture that diversity, as well as the changing nature of regionalism since the end of the Cold War and the relative decline of US power, this chapter offers an alternative conceptualization of regionalism, called "multiplex regionalism," which is based on the idea of a multiplex world. After briefly examining the characteristics of hegemonic, integrationist, and multiplex regionalisms, the paper reflects on regional leadership mechanisms and styles that can affect the provision of public goods.

The issue of regional leadership is key to how regions may provide public goods. Leadership is not the same as power. In this chapter, I argue that there are different types of regional leadership: hegemonic, accommodationist, and communitarian. They differ not in terms of the material power of the leader, but the degree of legitimacy the leader enjoys from those he or she seeks to lead. In a multiplex world, legitimacy achieved through a communitarian approach might be the most effective and durable approach to the provision of RPGs.

Two understandings of regionalism: hegemonic and integrationist

An important source of thinking—and hence a useful starting point for this theoretical discussion—about regions and how they provide public goods is the hegemonic stability theory (HST). At its core, the HST holds that "cooperation and a well-functioning world economy are dependent on a certain kind of political structure, a structure characterized by the dominance of a single actor . . . Both Great Britain in the nineteenth century and the United States after World War II helped bring about an interdependent and overall peaceful world" (Grunberg 1990, p.431). Although the HST is a theory of world politics, echoes of the theory—at least its underlying emphasis on the role of a hegemonic actor providing public goods—can be found in the analysis of regionalism and regional order. Powerful actors enjoy important advantages over others as providers, directly or indirectly, of RPGs. They command greater resources—such as economic aid, capital for investment, and the ability to project power—which can be used to protect allies and impose sanctions to ensure compliance. Another public good is provision of market access, if the powerful actor happens to have a large domestic economy. Hegemonic regionalism can be undertaken by both nonliberal and liberal powers. Examples of the former include the role of Nazi Germany and Imperial Japan before World War II in creating regional economic blocs in Europe (*Mitteleuropa*) and East Asia (Greater East Asia Co-Prosperity Sphere), respectively. The most important example of liberal regional hegemony is the role of the USA in Europe and East Asia after World War II. This role was more direct in Western Europe, where it offered its allies not only large-scale aid through the Marshall Plan, but also protection through NATO. In East Asia, the USA played a less direct, but still significant role. The rapid postwar economic growth of East Asia can be attributed to the US military presence (mainly through bilateral alliances rather than a NATO-like structure). Other public goods provided by the US included access to its huge market and investments in the region.

But hegemony, whether global or regional, is neither necessary nor sufficient as a condition of successful regionalism. Regionalism has been possible in some parts of the world despite, rather than because of, US policy. The USA was not a player behind the formation of the League of Arab States in 1945 and the Organisation of African Unity in 1963. The latter's replacement by the African Union (AU) in 2000 had nothing to do with the USA; if anything, the AU was born out of the collective frustration of African countries over the failure of the USA and UN to engage in Africa after the US debacle in Somalia in 1992. In Asia, where the USA counts itself as a "resident power," its most successful regional grouping, the Association of Southeast Asian Nations (ASEAN), was formed as an indigenous alternative to the US-backed Southeast Asian Treaty Organization (SEATO), created in 1954 (Acharya 2009).

Because they often serve the interests and goals of a dominant actor, the hegemonic approach to RPGs is often at cross-purposes with the "nonrivalrous" and "nonexcludable" criteria that defines the concept of public goods. The key for proponents of RPGs is to keep regionalism "open," inclusive, and interactive with other regions and the global system at large. In this context, fears on the part of some Western analysts that the decline of US hegemony might lead to competitive regional economic blocs may be somewhat far-fetched. John Ikenberry (2011) sees regionalism, unless conceived and directed by the US, as a force for the fragmentation and destabilization of the world order, marking the reappearance of competitive regional blocs of the type that existed in 19th- and early-20th-century Europe. But an argument can be made against this view that the US decline may create new opportunities for RPGs by weakening the overlay of US domestic and international preferences and that the economic and security norms and conditions of the 21st-century world discourage such past practices. To be sure, hegemonic regionalism is far from dead. Both the Trans-Pacific Partnership (TPP) and the Trans-Atlantic Trade and Investment Partnership (TTIP) fall into this category. Both, especially the TPP, are conditioned by US power and purpose, with the TPP having a greater security importance as an integral part of the US "rebalancing" strategy in Asia. But the growth of domestic sentiments against free trade in the USA, if it dooms or significantly undermines these two initiatives, would support the emergence and consolidation of multiplex regionalism.

A second approach to RPGs that has acquired a great deal of prominence in international relations is represented by the European Union (EU), formerly the European Economic Community (EEC). This approach is not directly linked to a hegemonic player, although some argue that the EEC/EU would not have come about or survived without the US-crafted Marshall Plan and NATO. What is distinctive about the EEC/EU approach is the goal of "integration," understood as a process and outcome involving the progressive erosion of sovereignty and the emergence of a supranational authority acting as the main channel for the provision of public goods.

The EU approach to RPGs is also distinguished by a high degree of legalization and institutionalization. In regionalism studies, it is the EU model of integration that has acquired hegemonic status. To quote Richard Higgott (2006, p.23), the EU project acquired "paradigmatic status . . . against which all other regional projects are judged." But this view is increasingly being challenged. Although parts of the developing world have created regional institutions inspired and on occasion directly supported by the EU, none has succeeded in achieving a comparable level of integration. It is hard to find examples in the non-Western world where economic regionalism based on the earlier EEC model, involving market centralization and generation of welfare gains, produced the desired spillover effect, leading to cooperation over security issues.

Differences between Western European and non-Western regionalisms are explained by gaps in resources and capabilities, but also in terms of domestic politics and normative beliefs. Peter Katzenstein (2005) contrasts the more "formal and political" character of EU regionalism and its greater reliance on "state bargains and legal norms" (p.27) with Asia's "informal and economic, and greater reliance on "market transactions and ethnic or national capitalism" (p.219). The EU and Asian regional groups also differ in terms of their attitudes towards sovereignty: "Europe's regionalism is more transparent and intrusive than Asia's" (Katzenstein 2005, p.219); "[a]bsent in Asia are the pooling of sovereignty and far-reaching multilateral arrangements that typify Europe's security order" (p.125). State power and regime types are another distinguishing factor (Katzenstein 2005, p.220). EU membership requires a democratic political system and it started as a regionalism among relatively equal neighbors (although the latter aspect has changed with its enlargement since the 1990s). Intra-Asian relations are more hierarchical. Asian political regimes differ widely and Asian states are "non-Weberian" in the sense that "rule by law" rather than "rule of law" is more commonplace. Despite these insights, Katzenstein's distinction between EU and Asian regionalism, as already noted, gives a central place to the role of the USA and Japan and, like the Realist view, underplays the value of small power leadership.

The first draft of this chapter was written before Brexit. It is too early to determine the full impact of Brexit on the EU; the prognosis is very much a mixed one (Politico, 2016). But Brexit lends further support to this chapter's argument against EU centrism, and the difficulties in applying the EU model to other regions. Some analysts think that the EU will not be seriously affected by Brexit, or may even be strengthened by it. In this view, the departure of Britain, which was frequently a drag on EU integration, leaves France and Germany more room to lead the EU into even greater unity. Other scenarios are more pessimistic, pointing to the possibility of other EU members following Britain's lead. Whether this happens or not, Brexit is already undermining the EU's global prestige and credibility as a model of regional integration for the rest of the world. To quote Maros Sefcovic, a vice president of the EU, "If a country like Britain exits, it must be perceived by the outside world as weakening the Union and as a demonstration of the crisis that the EU is undergoing" (Economic Times, 2016). Moreover, as the *Economist* noted, Brexit could also make the EU "less outward-looking" (Economist, 2016). If this turns out to be the case, it would mean the weakening of the EU's inter-regional cooperation, which has been a key medium for it to influence other regional organizations.

Multiplex regionalism

The two dominant conceptions of regionalism are based on a predominantly Western (US and Western European) context and are a poor fit for non-Western regionalisms desiring to replicate or emulate these. As a result, their utility as analytic frameworks is diminishing in view of the major shifts taking place in world politics and the world order.

To begin with, there has been growth in the scope of regional institutions' activities beyond their traditional concerns, which include trade liberalization or the management of interstate conflicts. In the economic arena, regional trade arrangements continue to proliferate, especially as doubts grow over the future of the liberal international economic order. Some examples include the emergence of new trade groupings in South America—MERCOSUR, UNASUR, and the Pacific Alliance. Regional trading arrangements or initiatives to create these have also emerged in South Asia, with the creation of the ASEAN Economic Community (AEC) in 2015 and the South Asia Free Trade Area (SAFTA). The same is true in East Asia, with the Free Trade Area of the Asia-Pacific (FTAAP), an Asia-Pacific Economic Cooperation (APEC) initiative, and the Regional Comprehensive Economic Partnership (RCEP), more inclusive than the US-backed TPP, which might be considered a more traditional hegemonic and legalistic approach to public goods. While old problems associated with regional integration in the developing world remain, especially the difficulty of ensuring an equitable distribution of benefits, these new regional groupings are inspired by a desire to use regionalism as a mechanism for the generation and supply of public goods, especially in the economic arena.

In the area of security and politics, entirely new RPG mechanisms have emerged both through the adaptation of these by existing regional bodies and the creation of new bodies. The most important example here is in Africa. In the 1990s, even the normally sovereignty-bound Organisation of African Unity (OAU) went beyond its traditional mandate to deal only with interstate conflicts and recognized the need to address internal conflicts, including those dealing with human rights violations.[1] As a result, it adopted a policy framework to isolate regimes that come to office through military coups. African regional organizations are also now more receptive to humanitarian intervention. The replacement of the OAU with the AU in 2000 removed the former's aversion to intervention and allowed subregional groupings such as the Economic Community of West African States (ECOWAS) and the Southern African Development Community (SADC) to undertake numerous humanitarian and political interventions in Africa. African regional groups have also embraced the Responsibility to Protect (R2P) norm. The New Partnership for African Development (NEPAD) combines development and security goals in the form of three core initiatives: peace and stability, democracy and political governance, and economic and corporate governance.

In the Americas, the 1991 Santiago Declaration (Andersen 1994, p.2; Farer 1996) and the 2001 Inter-American Democratic Charter (IADC) expanded the role of the Organization of American States (OAS) in democracy promotion. Following the end of the Cold War and decolonization, Asia was the only continent not to have a macroregional security grouping (ASEAN was a subregional body). The founding of the ASEAN Regional Forum (ARF) in 1994 filled this gap. The ARF is to some extent a unique regional organization, in that it is the only regional group to bring together all the great powers of the contemporary international system. However, it is at the same time led by ASEAN, a group of weaker members of the society of states. While realists see this as a structural flaw, institutionalists draw attention to the role of soft and ideational power in the making of regional security arrangements that may promote international order. Although APEC was originally created to liberalize trade and manage economic interdependence, it has also developed a role in security consultations, such as during the East Timor crisis in 1990 and in the aftermath of the 9/11 attacks. Asia later saw the emergence of the East Asia Summit (EAS), which engages in discussions over regional conflicts and nontraditional security threats.

While traditional RPG frameworks were mostly limited to trade liberalization, collective defense, and dispute settlement, regional groups in a multiplex world have to deal with an increasingly wider menu of issues, including financial volatility, drugs, refugees, pandemics, natural disasters, humanitarian crises, and environmental degradation.[2] The important feature of these transnational, or "intermestic" (international + domestic) challenges is that they cannot be addressed alone by the traditional great powers such as the USA and/or the EU through their global or regional public goods frameworks. Moreover, they do necessitate a departure from the principle of nonintervention. As noted, the AU has undertaken a variety of humanitarian initiatives, including military action, which would have been inconceivable until the 1990s. Other important examples of RPGs dealing with transnational challenges can be found in Asia, but this trend is by no means confined to this region. The creation of the ASEAN Political-Security Community in 2003 was partly a response to transnational dangers: terrorism, piracy, infectious diseases such as the Severe Acute Respiratory Syndrome (SARS), and air pollution (haze forest fires in Indonesia). The strongest new initiative in regional cooperation against financial crises is found in Asia, in the form of the ASEAN Plus Three (APT) forum and the Chiang Mai Initiative (CMI), which include both bilateral currency swaps and a multilateral lending facility. While these arrangements do not replace the IMF, they certainly create important independent avenues for the provision of RPGs in the critical area of finance.

The growing salience of transnational challenges has contributed to another trend that features prominently in multiplex regionalism: its departure from the strict Westphalian notion of state sovereignty in the provision of RPGs. Although by no means comparable to the EU's supranationalism, this trend involves at least a dilution of the principle of nonintervention. As noted, the AU represents the most dramatic example of this through its shift from nonintervention to nonindifference. NEPAD, an economic framework (with some political underpinnings) that is strongly backed by South Africa, has also sought to move beyond Westphalian sovereignty by adopting a peer review mechanism. In Southeast Asia, the retreat from the nonintervention mindset has been slower. Whereas African regional bodies have embraced the R2P norm and undertaken multiple collective interventions, no Asian regional organization has undertaken a collective intervention, humanitarian or otherwise. But even here there are emergent forms of cooperation against transnational threats and for human rights promotion that at the very least dilute the principle of nonintervention.

Next, multiplex regionalism is more flexible and expansive in terms of institutionalization than traditional regionalism. The role of the earlier macroregional regional groups (like the OAS or OAU), regional security alliances (SEATO), and regional integration organizations (East African Community,

Andean Pact), all embodied a conception of regionalism in which formal and institutional patterns of interaction were considered to be the crucial yardstick of effectiveness. The regional integration theories derived from the EEC "remained closely tied to the study of formal organizations, missing a range of state behaviour that nonetheless appeared regulated and organized in a broader sense" (Haggard and Simmons 1987). But as a wide variety of regionalist enterprises showed, regionalism could no longer be identified with formal, organized collective action. A more useful conception of regionalism is provided by Puchala and Fagan (1982, p.47), for whom regionalism is "a collection of procedures and techniques" both formal and informal, to facilitate interactions and cooperation among regional actors who "maximise mutual positive payoffs by exploiting their interdependence." Or, as Paul Taylor (1990, p.151) put it, regionalism "is a concern with that particular scale of geographical area which is best fitted to the performance of tasks judged crucial for the welfare of individuals, or for the advantage of governments." In recent studies of regionalism, as Weatherbee (1984, p.19) notes in the context of ASEAN, the "absence of explicit organizational arrangements and formally articulated regional structures becomes less important than the attitudinal underpinnings that support 'a recognized pattern of practice around which expectations converge.'"

Another important trend in regionalism today is the creation of new mechanisms for RPGs by the emerging powers. Some emerging powers in the multiplex world require legitimation through RPGs as a prop for their global leadership ambitions (Acharya 2011). Perhaps the most important example here is the China-initiated Asian Infrastructure Investment Bank (AIIB). The AIIB is seen by some observers as a form of hegemonic regionalism under China. Even those countries which have joined it—such as India, Australia, the UK, Germany, France, and Italy—are apprehensive that they might have directly or indirectly contributed to an initiative that might enhance China's authority and feed into its geopolitical ambitions, which are not always welcome. But the AIIB may also be understood as a Chinese response to its de facto exclusion from the US-led TPP and to the slow process of reform of existing multilateral institutions, such as the IMF and the World Bank, which remain under US and Western control. Moreover, the AIIB poses no risk of Chinese hegemony, while putting China's leadership capacity to its most severe test to date. In other words, it is in keeping with the notion of "open regionalism." Participation is open to any country in Asia, but also to others outside the region: as mentioned above, Germany, France, UK, and Italy, all G7 members, have already signaled their participation. Having proposed the AIIB, Beijing will be under intense international observation to see whether it delivers results. China has to ensure that it does not usher in a Chinese Asian fiefdom, but instead conforms to international norms and standards of transparency for such institutions. If the AIIB fails, China's image and potential clout as an emerging global power will be seriously damaged. But if China succeeds—and success here requires China making significant adjustments to its regional policy by abandoning its expansive territorial claims and enhancing its military and economic transparency—Asia and the West, including the USA and indeed the entire system of global governance, will be the big winners.

Regionalism in the multiplex world is marked by important differences between the EU style of regionalism and non-European varieties that have already been discussed, and also among these non-EU regionalisms. East Asia's regionalism is more focused on transnational production (Acharya 1995b), the extent and degree of which is not found anywhere else in the world, including the Middle East, Africa, and Latin America. The trend to dilute nonintervention and the move towards "intrusive regionalism"[3] is most pronounced, as already noted, in Africa, and the least so in the Middle East. Somewhere in between are the Americas, although through the aforementioned IADC the OAS has developed new norms and practices to undertake collective action in the case of coups and antidemocratic and unconstitutional "backsliding" by elected rulers. Asia remains further behind the Americas.

Comparing regionalism in Africa and Asia also suggests another important difference between regionalisms. The role of regional powers, especially South Africa and Nigeria, is a fact of life driving African regionalism; the AU was the brainchild of both powers. In Asia, regional or global hegemons are the targets of socialization (they are the *socializee* rather than the socializer) on the part of weaker states, especially members of ASEAN. Asian regionalism is more functionally differentiated than in Africa and the Middle East. Asia's regional bodies have different, if overlapping, membership and functions. Thus ASEAN is multi-purpose; the ARF deals with security, APEC is concerned with trade, the APT and CMI with financial flows, and the EAS with political and strategic issues (there is some overlap here with the ARF, but the EAS meets at the summit level, whereas the ARF is a foreign ministers' body). In African regionalism we see more convergence and less separation among functional areas. Even the NEPAD is closely linked to the AU; the latter is supposed to be the umbrella body that coordinates subregional economic communities, even though the subregional groups may act as voting or lobby blocs. ASEAN's level of direct engagement involvement with outside powers is not matched by any other regional body, including the EU. Asia and Africa display different ways of dealing with outside powers. Africa deals with outside powers like China and India on a one-to-one basis (e.g. Africa Plus One), while Asia deals with outside powers multilaterally, that is, by including them all in one forum (ARF and EAS). This gives Asia a better chance of balancing the influence of different outside powers.

A final feature of multiplex regionalism that is relevant to the provision of RPGs is interregionalism. While much of the recent theoretical and policy attention to interregionalism is given to the EU's elaborate efforts to project a global normative influence, interregionalism is also evident elsewhere. Apart from the revived Asia-Africa cooperation, there have emerged groupings such as the Asia-Europe Meeting (ASEM), and the Forum for East Asia-Latin American Cooperation (FEALAC), which are clearly interregional. Even some of the Asia Pacific and East Asian regional groupings such as APEC,

ARF, and EAS may be regarded as interregional, since their membership include countries that are normally seen to be from distinctive regions: Asia, Europe, and the Americas. Thus the EU is a member of the ARF; Australia, New Zealand, and several North and South American countries belong to APEC; while Australia, New Zealand, the US, and Russia are among the EAS members.

Such interregionalism offers several benefits to world order. It plays a key role in keeping regionalism "open" and interactive, preventing rivalry and conflict among regions. It also gives regional institutions additional means for managing their security concerns and projecting their influence on world affairs. It expands the avenues for engaging all the major powers to complement the functions of global bodies like the UN. Interregionalism also helps to prevent the intrusive dominance of any power—be it an individual country or a regional body—in another region, by offering a mechanism for maintaining equilibrium. This has been the case with APEC as well as the ASEM; the former was seen by the Asia Pacific countries as a counter to the EU's increased clout after the announcement of its single market, while the latter was a response to fears of excessive US dominance of Asia Pacific economic cooperation. Another contribution of interregionalism lies in mitigating the dangers of a culture clash, or a clash of civilizations. The sharing of common global and regionally constructed norms through localization, emulation, and learning are a useful basis for the intercivilizational dialogues that have become increasingly commonplace since 9/11. Finally, interregionalism helps the management of transnational issues such as climate change, illegal migration, drug trafficking, natural disasters, and financial meltdowns, which call for responses that no single regional institution can offer on its own. With global institutions facing a crisis of legitimacy because their hitherto Western-dominated leadership and decision-making structures are being challenged by the redistribution of power in the global system, interregionalism has an important role to play in devising responses that could address the gap between purely global and purely regional responses to transnational issues.

Regional leadership

A key issue in deciding how regions may provide public goods relates to the position, perception, and leadership styles of regional powers and institutions. But leadership should not be conflated with power. "States lacking structural power," contends David Rapkin (1994, p.109), could "exercise entrepreneurial and/or intellectual leadership to activate—by establishing settings, framing issues and forming coalitions—cooperation that induces the structural leadership of those that possess it." Rapkin's view reflects a revisionist or "posthegemonic" approach to international institutions. Snidal (1985) argued that a small group of rising powers may sustain regimes and assume responsibility for cooperation and provision of collective good in a posthegemonic setting. Subsequently, Oran Young (1991) made a further contribution to the "pluralization" of leadership in institution building by differentiating between three kinds of leadership: "structural," "intellectual," and "entrepreneurial." He describes this in more detail:

> The structural leader translates power resources into bargaining leverage in an effort to bring pressure to bear on others to assent to the terms of proposed constitutional contracts. The entrepreneurial leader makes use of negotiating skill to frame the issues at stake, devise mutually acceptable formulas, and broker the interests of key players in building support for these formulas. The intellectual leader, by contrast, relies on the power of ideas to shape the thinking of the principals in processes of institutional bargaining.
>
> (Young 1991, p.307)[4]

Such pluralization of leadership is a hallmark of the multiplex world. Accordingly, regional leadership styles can fall into three broad categories. The first one may be called hegemonic/domineering. This kind of leadership is usually obtained within the framework of hegemonic regionalism, as outlined earlier, and conforms to Young's (1991) notion of the "structural leader." More extreme examples of this style can be found in the US Monroe Doctrine in the Western hemisphere during the 19th and early 20th centuries and Japan's Greater East Asia Co-Prosperity Sphere concept around World War II. Today, this style can be seen in Russia's conception of its "Near Abroad" (including Ukraine, Caucasus, and Central Asia) and now to the Eurasian Union. A less extreme version, one that is domineering if not outright hegemonic, may apply to India's role in South Asia until recently, and China's in Southeast Asia over the past few years. Nigeria's role in ECOWAS is also relevant as a possible example of the domineering approach.

Structural power can also be found in regional groups that have emerged from the break-up of empires in which the former colonial power provides support to the regional group. This is exemplified in France's role in West and Central African regionalisms. The Union économique et monétaire de l'ouest africain (UEMOA) and the Communauté économique et monétaire d'Afrique centrale (CEMAC) were initially developed as monetary unions using the French franc, which was controlled by France (Bach 1999, Bilal 2013), and they still maintain substantial economic and security links with France. Other examples are regionalism in East Africa (the East African Community, which came about as the break-up of the British Empire) and Southern Africa (the precursors to SADC, which was fostered by Apartheid South Africa), the Commonwealth of Independent States, and the Collective Security Treaty Organization, created after the break-up of the Soviet Union.

Structural leadership relies heavily on physical and material capabilities. Although the provision of public goods through a regional institution can help to legitimize structural leadership, the use or threat of use of sanctions and coercion is never far removed from the picture. Sometimes, the recipients accept a hegemon's public goods out of fear of the coercive capacity of the leader. Even if direct force is not used, the fear of sanctions (including denial of military and economic aid, investment, transportation, and market access) might lead small states to accept a leader's public good offered bilaterally or through regional mechanisms, as has been the case with China in Myanmar; China and India in Nepal; Russia in its area; and the US in Asia, the Caribbean, and Africa.

A second style of regional leadership may be termed "accommodation-ist." It describes the approaches of Brazil, South Africa, and Japan today. It is hierarchical, rather than hegemonic. The neighbors still fear dominance or interference by the leading power, whether due to material power disparities or some memories of the past. But the leading powers have gone some way in reassuring their neighbors by pursuing cooperation and providing some public goods while avoiding pressure and coercion. All the same, there may not be the kind of "we feeling" found in a communitarian organization. Cooperation is sometimes induced because of the perceived dangers of noncooperation rather than positive mutual identification. This kind of grouping is better described as "consociational" rather than communitarian.[5] Leadership is not structural, but relies heavily on entrepreneurship and ideas/norms. Usually, accommodation-ist leadership is found within multiplex regionalism. It is relatively rare within hegemonic or integrationist regionalisms.

A third regional style may be termed "communitarian." This can be found in both integrationist and multiplex regionalisms, but they emerge and work in different ways. Communitarian leadership in the EU is heavily institutionalized and distinctly supranational. Although the leadership role of individual countries like France and Germany—the traditional major players in EU—remain important, they are subsumed by the role of the European Commission in Brussels and the EU's three presidencies (i.e. the Presidency of the European Commission, the Presidency of the European Council, and the Presidency of the Council of the EU). By contrast, leadership in ASEAN, while communitarian in nature (Acharya 1995a), is much more flexible, nonlegalistic, has less of a supranational dimension, and is shared and pluralized. Indonesia, the largest ASEAN member in population and overall gross economy (not in per capita terms, however), is often called the leader of ASEAN, but this is not accurate. Indonesia's role in ASEAN has been likened to that of being in a "golden cage": Jakarta's restraint towards its smaller neighbors, such as Singapore and Malaysia, has led the latter to express a degree of deference to Indonesia as being "first among equals" within ASEAN. There has been no war between Indonesia and its immedi-ate neighbors since ASEAN was founded in 1967, just after Indonesia's war against Malaysia had ended. However, in reality, ASEAN has a plural leader-ship. Indonesia has mostly led on regional security issues, whereas Singapore has led in economic cooperation, and the Philippines in the area of human rights and civil society engagement. In fact, the three countries were the proposers of the ASEAN Political-Security Community (APSC), the AEC, and the ASEAN Socio-Cultural Community (ASCC), respectively.

The "ASEAN Way" is a *process* of regional interactions and cooperation featuring informality, consensus building, and nonconfrontational bargaining styles which are often contrasted with the adversarial posturing, majority vote, and other legalistic decision-making procedures in Western multilateral negotiations (Boyce 1973, p.175).[6] The ASEAN Way has been described as "consultation on the basis of equality, tolerance, and understanding with overtones of kinship and common interests." Long before Nye (1990) developed his idea of "soft power," the ASEAN Way was described as a form of "soft diplomacy as contrasted to saber-rattling, gunboat diplomacy of the colonial and Big Power variety" (Elizalde and Beltran n.d., p.39). Consensus building requires a nonhostile psychological setting of consultations. The idea of consensus in ASEAN represents a pragmatic way of advancing RPGs that was initially applied to ASEAN industrial joint ventures and tariff reductions. As Lee Kuan Yew observed in the context of ASEAN economic cooperation (at a time when ASEAN consisted of only five members: Indonesia, Malaysia, Thailand, the Philippines, and Singapore): "When four agree [to a certain scheme] and one does not, this can still be considered as consensus and the five-minus-one scheme can benefit the participating four without damaging the remaining one." (Cited in Irvine 1982, p.62.) This process is now known as the "ASEAN minus X" approach. Consensus as understood in the ASEAN context is not to be confused with unanimity. In a consensus situation, "not everyone would always be comfortable," but they tend to "go along so long as their basic interests were not disregarded" (cited in The Straits Times 1994, p.17). It should be noted that such flexibility is far more evident in Asian regionalism than in the EU—where decision making is often influenced by the big powers like Germany and France, and which is a little feared by its smaller members for its rigid, binding, legalistic, and bureaucratic formulas and approach, backed by economic or political sanctions—and the Eurasian Union being developed by Russia, which is not shy of applying outright coercion.

ASEAN offers an important example of regional cooperation for public goods in a multiplex world. ASEAN's approach is in direct contrast to the North American hegemonic or the European integrationist models for RPGs in world politics. Its communitarian leadership structure and nonexclusionary, comprehensive approach to public goods encompassing economic, security, and social elements should be examined closely for possible emulation and adaptation by other parts of the world. Although the ASEAN Way is undergoing some changes due to new developments such as the US's highly legalistic TPP and ASEAN's own slow but steady turn towards institutionalization, it continues to inform ASEAN's decision-making style and process and does represent an alternative point of reference for how regional bodies may make collective decisions for the provision of public goods.

Conclusion

Regionalism is an integral feature of the multiplex world, which is defined by both intra- and interregional interdependence interacting closely with global interdependence. Regionalism in a multiplex world is neither US- nor EU-centric. This is no longer just a theoretical possibility. Brexit and the growing domestic pressures in the USA against free trade initiatives such as the TPP and TTIP are challenging the older models of hegemonic and integrationist regionalism. They underscore the need for regions to provide public goods without hegemonic leadership like that of the USA and without strongly formal and supranational institutions and rules like those of the EU. Overall, RPG mechanisms encompass a variety of pathways, and no one size is likely to fit all regions. Regional governance and public goods do not displace bilateralism, universalism, and other mechanisms, but in some parts of the world, including Asia and Africa, they are becoming more important. Old regional mechanisms for RPG provision are evolving towards wider and more complex functions, and new mechanisms are emerging. Some but not all of these would be under the influence of the emerging powers. New institutions initiated by non-Western nations, such as the New Development Bank and the AIIB, increase pressure on global institutions to speed up their own reform, and embrace a more shared leadership, which is vital to their legitimacy and longevity. These trends might create short-term institutional uncertainty or even chaos, but will also generate opportunities for crafting better regional and global governance structures.

Notes

1 The development of African mechanisms to "prevent or at any rate to resolve, any conflict situation that arises on the continent . . . especially in the area of internal conflicts" is outlined in OAU (1992, p.9).
2 For examples of the merit of regional approaches to transnational issues, see Mathews (1994, p.287) and Dewitt and Acharya (1995).
3 For a more detailed discussion, see Acharya (2002).
4 For further contributions to nonhegemonic leadership, see Cooper, Higgott and Nossal (1993).
5 On consociational and communitarian regional orders, see Acharya (2014c).
6 The first of these features, a disposition to summitry, may seem to go against what many think to be another key aspect of the ASEAN Way—aversion to institutionalization. But until the 1990s, ASEAN summits had been an irregular and informal affair. Mere gatherings of leaders/officials should not be confused with "institutionalization," as the latter involves a degree of bureaucratization and resorting to formal procedures and mechanisms.

References

Acharya, Amitav. 1995a. "A Regional Security Community in Southeast Asia?" *Journal of Strategic Studies* 18, no. 3: 175–200.
——. 1995b. "Transnational Production and Security: Southeast Asia's Growth Triangles." *Contemporary Southeast Asia* 17, no. 2: 173–185.

———. 2002. "Regionalism and the Emerging World Order: Sovereignty, Autonomy, Identity." In *New Regionalisms in the Global Political Economy*, edited by Shaun Breslin, Christopher W. Hughes, Nicola Phillips, and Ben Rosamond. London and New York: Routledge.

———. 2009. *Whose Ideas Matter? Agency and Power in Asian Regionalism*. Ithaca, NY: Cornell University Press.

———. 2011. "Can Asia Lead? Power Ambitions and Global Governance in the Twenty-first Century." *International Affairs* 87, no. 4: 851–869.

———. 2014a. *The End of American World Order*. Cambridge, UK: Polity.

———. 2014b. "From the Unipolar Moment to a Multiplex World." *YaleGlobal*, July 3. http://yaleglobal.yale.edu/content/unipolar-moment-multiplex-world

——— 2014c. "Power Shift or Paradigm Shift: China's Rise and Asia's Security Order." *International Studies Quarterly* 58, no. 1: 158–73.

Andersen, Robert B. 1994. "Inter-IGO Dynamics in the Post-Cold War Era: The OAS and the UN." Paper prepared for the 1994 Annual Convention of the International Studies Association, Washington, DC, March 28–April 1.

Bach, Daniel C. 1999. "The Revival of Regional Integration in Africa." In *Transfrontier Regionalism*, A.I. Asiwaju and Daniel C. Bach, 43–77. Ibadan, Nigeria: Institut français de recherche en Afrique IFRA-Nigeria. http://books.openedition.org/ifra/592

Bilal, Sanoussi. 2013. "External Influences on Regional Integration in West Africa: The Role of Third Parties." In *Regional Trade and Monetary Integration in West Africa and Europe*, edited by R. Sohn and A. Konadu Oppong. WAI-Zei Paper 6. Bonn: University of Bonn. http://ecdpm.org/wp-content/uploads/2013/11/2012-Regional-Integration-West-Africa-role-third-parties-.pdf

Boyce, Peter. 1973. "The Machinery of Southeast Asian Regional Diplomacy." In *New Directions in the International Relations of Southeast Asia: Global Powers and Southeast Asia*, edited by Lau Teik Soon. Singapore: Singapore University Press.

Cooper, Andrew F., Richard A. Higgott, and Kim Richard Nossal. 1993. *Relocating Middle Powers: Australia and Canada in a Changing World Order*. Vancouver: University of British Columbia Press.

Dewitt, David, and Amitav Acharya. 1995. *Refugees, Security and International Politics: The Principles and Practices of Burden-Sharing*. York University: Centre for Refugee Studies.

Economic Times. 2016. "Brexit will greatly weaken EU: Maros Sefcovic." *The Economic Times*, June 27. http://articles.economictimes.indiatimes.com/2016-06-27/news/74051143_1_brexit-eurosceptics-british-referendum

Economist. 2016. How Others See It. *The Economist*, April 30. http://www.economist.com/news/britain/21697825-european-union-would-suffer-brexitwhich-why-it-could-not-be-kind-britain.

Elizalde, Fred J., and Luis D. Beltran. n.d. *Of Kingdoms and Brothers: ASEAN Dawn*. Quezon City: University of the Philippines.

Farer, Tom. 1996. "Collectively Defending Democracy in the Western Hemisphere." In *Beyond Sovereignty: Collectively Defending Democracy in the Americas,* edited by Tom Farer, pp. 1–25. Baltimore and London: The Johns Hopkins University Press.

Friedman, Thomas. 2005. *The World Is Flat*. New York: Farrar, Straus, and Giroux.

Grunberg, Isabelle. 1990. "Exploring the Myth of Hegemonic Stability." *International Organization* 44, no. 4 (Autumn).

Haggard, Stephan, and Beth A. Simmons. 1987. "Theories of International Regimes." *International Organization* 41, no.3 (summer).

Higgott, Richard. 2006. "The Theory and Practice of Region." In *Regional Integration in East Asia and Europe: Convergence or Divergence*, edited by Bertrand Fort and Douglas Webber. London: Routledge.

Ikenberry, John. 2011. *Liberal Leviathan*. Princeton and Oxford: Princeton University Press.

Irvine, Roger. 1982. "The Formative Years of ASEAN: 1967–1975." In *Understanding ASEAN*, edited by Alison Broinowski. New York: St. Martin's Press.

Katzenstein, Peter J. 2005. *A World of Regions: Asia and Europe in the American Imperium.* Ithaca, NY: Cornell University Press.

Mathews, Jessica Tuchman. 1994. "The Environment and International Security." In *World Security: Challenges for a New Century*, edited by Michael T. Klare and Daniel C. Thomas. New York: St. Martin's Press.

Nye, Joseph. 1990. *Bound to Lead: The Changing Nature of American Power.* New York: Basic Books.

Organisation of African Unity (OAU). 1992. *Resolving Conflicts in Africa: Proposals for Action.* Addis Ababa: OAU Press and Information Service.

Politico. 2016. "How Brexit Will Change the World." *Politico*, June 25. http://www.politico.com/magazine/story/2016/06/brexit-change-europe-britain-us-politics-213990

Puchala, Donald J., and Stuart I. Fagan. 1982. "International Politics in the 1970s: The Search for a Perspective." In *Globalism Versus Realism: International Relations' Third Debate*, edited by Ray Maghroori and Bennett Ramberg. Boulder, CO: Westview Press.

Rapkin, David. 1994. "Leadership and Cooperative Institutions." In *Pacific Cooperation: Building Economic and Security Regimes in the Asia-Pacific Region*, edited by Andrew Mack and John Ravenhill. St. Leonards, NSW: Allen and Unwin.

Snidal, Duncan. 1985. "The Limits of Hegemonic Stability Theory." *International Organization* 39 (autumn).

The Straits Times. 1994. November 13, p.17.

Taylor, Paul. 1990. "Regionalism: The Thought and the Deed." In *Frameworks for International Co-operation*, edited by A.J.R. Groom and Paul Taylor. New York: St Martin's Press.

Weatherbee, Donald. 1984. "ASEAN Regionalism: The Salient Dimension." In *ASEAN Security and Economic Development*, edited by Karl D. Jackson and M. Hadi Soesastro. Berkeley: University of California, Institute of East Asian Studies.

Young, Oran R. 1991. "Political Leadership and Regime Formation: On the Development of Institutions in International Society." *International Organization* 45, no. 3 (summer).

4 Transnational policy networks and regional public goods in Latin America

Jacint Jordana

Introduction

Regionalism can take different forms. In recent decades, we have witnessed important waves of regionalism amid globalization across the world, but the drivers of these waves have been very different. In Europe, the main driver has been institutionalization and the establishment of formal rules (and often informal ones, too) to arrange the provision of regional public goods (RPGs). In South Asia, regionalism has moved forward thanks to economic integration, often privately driven. In Latin America, however, there has been no clear driver. For decades, the region has been characterized by constant failure in its attempts to advance institutionalization, as well as by weak advances in economic integration beyond the pressures of globalization.

In discussing this challenging situation, this paper will argue that a particular and distinctive driver for regionalism has been emerging in Latin America. The driver that I suggest has been operating strongly in the region is socially shaped and is particularly rooted in the dynamics of myriad nonhierarchical policy networks that operate across countries and sectors throughout the region. As I will explain, this network-based mode of regional integration has been firmly on the rise over the last three decades, and has become capable of providing some level of RPGs, while also contributing to many successful processes of policy diffusion in the region. Unfortunately, these networks do not yet fulfill most of the promises of the "new world order" suggested ten years ago by Anne-Marie Slaughter (2004).

Regional policy networks are probably not an alternative to institutions for political integration. Instead, they represent a different itinerary for providing some RPGs, with their particular intricacies. Networks are located in multiple places and spheres, and do not show a well-designed structure or logic of cohesion: they can be embedded within international organizations, or explicitly promoted for policy coordination purposes; they can be the result of professional associations at the regional level (e.g. LASA, CLAD, LACEA among others); they can be government-based networks under the umbrella of particular intergovernmental or transnational entities; and they can also be promoted by interest groups and civil society organizations operating at the regional level. In fact, these are only a few examples that show where such networks are located and remain active over time. Networks do not require large budgets, formal organizations, or hierarchic management; but of course they can benefit from these resources if they are available.

Transnational networks in Latin America are valuable for developing social and professional communities, for facilitating mobility and mutual support when needed, and for managing training and transmitting information (Fernández-i-Marín and Jordana 2015). Aided by weak language barriers, Latin American transnational networks have contributed to the diffusion of policy innovations and the transmission of political ideas. In a way, they contribute to promoting a soft version of regionalism, which is also very convenient for establishing linkages with networks, platforms, and international organizations related to global governance. However, the major obstacle to constructing a network-based regionalism in Latin America is that these setups cannot fully tackle the problem of underprovision of regional or transnational public goods. Networks often suffer from a serious collective action problem due to the free-rider effect and the lack of selective incentives or coercive mechanisms, and this limits their potential. However, such limitations do not undermine their ability to provide some RPGs effectively.

In this paper, I concentrate on the governance of regulation at the regional level by means of networks, as an example of public good provision, to exemplify and develop the arguments previously outlined. I explore some of the reasons behind the weakness of regulatory networks in providing RPGs, while recognizing their contributions to a basic level of provision. The primary outputs of regulatory networks are, as identified by Berg and Horrall (2008, p.188): "(1) events and meetings; (2) data for benchmarking; (3) public pronouncements; (4) material for stakeholders; (5) capacity building for professional staff; (6) best practice laws, procedures and rules; (7) regulatory network news; and (8) technical studies." Some of these are club goods, while others are pure or impure (excludable) public goods that fulfill the purposes of the network's members, in particular its sponsors or leading members. Governance functions that I expect can be activated by such networks include norm and agenda setting, consensus building, policy coordination, knowledge production, exchange and dissemination, and also the use of international reputation for domestic purposes. I will also discuss the potential for developing more hybrid modes of governance, in which networks and other forms of such markets or hierarchies could merge into synthetic and polymorphic innovative governance structures.

This is important as networks have played important roles in Europe during the 2000s and also in forging public–private trust-based structures in some Asian cases. In addition, networks and their related hybrid forms have great potential for articulating interregional connections, adapting their shape and profile to specific geopolitical constraints and becoming temporal constructions without major path-dependence consequences. In this sense, network-driven policies appear to be extremely relevant for the fragmented and changing circumstances of contemporary global governance.

Based on several examples drawn from the areas of finance and telecommunications, I will discuss the logic of regional regulatory networks in Latin America. The reason for selecting these areas is connected to the different conditions of global governance in each case. In finance and banking regulation there are many global governance shortages due to the lack of well-established international organizations capable of playing an authoritative role in these areas (Abdelal 2007; Angeloni 2008; Major 2012; Tsingou 2009; Underhill and Zhang 2008). In contrast, a large number of international organizations are involved in the governance of telecommunications at the global level—from the longstanding International Telecommunications Union (ITU) to the new Internet Corporation for Assigned Names and Numbers (ICANN) (Archer 2014; Kim and Barnett 2000). The next section develops a conceptual framework for the analysis of transnational regulatory networks in regional environments, while the following sections examine networks in the selected policy areas. The final section provides conclusions, including some considerations on the potential role of policy networks for the provision of RPGs.

A framework for studying regional governance by transnational regulatory networks

Network-based transgovernmental actors are increasingly present in international arenas, both global and regional, in particular in specialized sectors with significant technical components, such as pharmaceuticals, telecommunications, data privacy, standard setting, or human rights, among many others (Djelic and Quack 2010; Kahler 2010). These networks may take multiple organizational forms and also adopt different functions in regulatory policy making, including rule making, rule taking, and rule intermediation. Professionals and civil servants working in governmental or quasi-governmental organizations from different countries are the agents that constitute these networks, and the interactions between these individuals frequently take place in a plurality of international settings and venues which their countries are members of. In fact, shared membership in international settings has been identified as a powerful mechanism for policy diffusion, fostering the introduction of policy and institutional innovations at the domestic level (Fernández-i-Marín and Jordana 2015; Holzinger et al. 2008). These interactions are often articulated and convened by international associations and organizations not based on international treaties, but on soft structures of mutual collaboration, information circulation, and informal coordination. It has been observed that the activity of such international structures, which usually operate in a nonbinding fashion, retains most of the characteristics of network governance (Kahler 2010; Levi-Faur 2012; Risse 2004).

A network mode of global—or regional—governance is "based on shared or pooled authority and on repeated, enduring, and reciprocal relations among actors in different national jurisdictions [. . .] (even if one member of the network has a more central position or more influence over outcomes than others)" (Kahler and Lake 2009, p.248). As stated, by means of diffusion mechanisms related to the network environment, their activities may also involve substantive impacts on the development of domestic policies, despite their having no formal authority (Bach and Newman 2010; Brust and McDermott 2012). Regulatory conventions, managerial and policy best practices, and procedures for establishing policy instruments are typical examples of informal norms and models circulating within such transnational network circles, which are then processed and adopted by domestic government authorities in their specific domains.

Together with international organizations, regulatory agencies are major players in regulatory networks. Their global spread across many policy areas over the last few decades (Jordana et al. 2011) has brought many changes to the domestic policy arena in diverse sectors. Regulatory agencies have become important actors, often bringing together high visibility and enough technical resources to intervene in domestic policy making, while also being well connected to similar institutions in other countries. Beyond their specific tasks, with their strong professional patterns, regulatory agencies can also be understood as institutional solutions to the problems related to the management of regulatory capitalism (Jordana and Levi-Faur 2005). They have been expanding significantly in Latin America and the Caribbean (LAC) (Jordana 2012) and constitute nodal institutions capable of articulating interactions between global and local actors, as well as between public and private ones (Bianculli et al. 2015). For this reason, regulatory agencies would be expected to engage in transnational regional networks, to promote them, and also to obtain benefits from their involvement in policy making at multiple levels of government (Berg and Horrall 2008; Djelic and Sahlin-Andersson 2006).

Network structures may effectively facilitate the intermediation of regulatory concepts and practices from the international to the national level, or from one country to another (Levi-Faur and Starobin 2014). They establish spaces in which regulatory innovation and policy change come up against potential regulatory compliance. In contrast to marketplaces, in which the exchange of interests predominates, networks are places in which deliberation, value formation, and policy learning are also possible. This means that processes of regulatory diffusion often have complex and uncertain outcomes, but ones that are often more promising than formal trade agreements in terms of overcoming difficulties and gridlocks. Network-level outcomes may involve the introduction of screening systems that most members of the network will consent to and accept, thus legitimizing them. In fact, actors involved in transnational regulatory policy networks may include, among others, rule makers, rule takers, and rule intermediaries. The involvement of these three kinds of actors represents an opportunity to promote or also establish formal or informal systems of regional regulatory governance.

However, the governance of these networks may present distinct structural properties, and each particular form of network governance can create very different situations that are capable of shaping the activity of regulatory intermediaries. Networks are not formal organizations, nor do their members share legal ties; in fact, their connections are usually based on mutual trust and repeated contacts. Provan and Kenis (2007) identify three types of network governance. First, "participant governance," which involves the direct participation of members without any specialized structure of governance. Second, "lead organization governance," a model in which a particular organization operates as a leader by administering the network and supporting the other members in their efforts related to the goals of the network. Finally, "network administrative organizations (NAO)" governance, based on the existence of a separate entity designed specifically to govern the network, or which simply becomes the network facilitator or the network broker.

I suspect each form of network governance would be articulated through a different framework. While participant governance would require high consensus in selecting and accepting actors, lead organization governance would not require more than the implicit understanding of network members. Also, the NAO form of network governance would allow the acceptance of certain participants to be specified and suggested to the network members, without the requirement of high levels of consensus. These expectations are useful for better understanding the diversity of modes of governance that emerge in transnational regulatory domains, and how they are selected and recognized as valuable by rule takers at the national level.

Transnational networks in banking in Latin America

In this section I examine regional policy networks in banking in Latin America as an example of a regulatory context in which there are multiple global governance shortcomings. Globally, the main rule maker in banking is the Basel Committee, while national regulatory agencies also play an important role. Within this context, states decide "voluntarily" whether or not to adopt certain pieces of regulation (as rule takers). However, I am curious about the role that regional networks may play in connecting the global and domestic levels (including networks of agencies, rating agencies, consultants, and experts), and how they contribute to facilitating decisions on rule adoption.

Financial regulatory institutions in Latin America were surrounded by a turbulent environment during the 1980s and 1990s, coping with banking crises and domestic fiscal crises. Economic developments and policy reactions in the region have been intensively researched and extensively discussed in the literature (for example, Lora 2007; Ocampo and Ros 2011; Rojas-Suárez and Weisbrod 1995). However, this paper takes a different approach to public intervention into banking policy in Latin America. Focusing on the transnational dimension, I discuss how banking regulators in the region were capable of establishing new governance arrangements following the crisis at the regional level, which in some way contributed to greater financial stability in recent years. The section scrutinizes the architecture of Latin American international organizations and transgovernmental networks within the banking regulatory space and assesses how far their institutionalization has contributed to a more effective form of regional regulatory governance and RPG provision in more recent times.

Regional networks in banking play a significant role in the absence of a worldwide organization of banking regulators, in contrast to other financial sectors, such as insurance or securities and exchange, where a more articulated system of global governance exists. In fact, the European Union exemplifies a different response to these shortcomings. In 2003, it established the Committee of European Banking Supervisors (CEBS), aiming to create an independent advisory group on banking supervision that was capable of articulating a network mode of governance in banking regulation within the EU. This network, however, enjoyed very few resources, and was instead solely focused on the coordination of national authorities (Quaglia 2007). Several years later, a more hierarchical structure was introduced with the creation of the European Banking Authority (EBA), which started operations in 2011. EBA inherited all the tasks and responsibilities of CEBS, but also obtained some powers to overrule national banking supervisors, particularly in cases of competitive behavior among countries regarding banking regulation that might undermine common regulatory standards. More recently, the European Central Bank (ECB) obtained more relevant responsibilities to supervise those large banks in Europe that are able to create systemic risks. Compared to Latin American initiatives, however, those in Europe were proposed and also driven by the EU and involved a hierarchical logic of regional integration that was not present in the Latin American context.

Network governance forms in Latin American banking

There are several transnational structures in Latin America that relate to the governance of banking at the regional level. Some of these structures are international associations that all the countries in the region are members of. These were not created by international treaties but instead evolved from the very informal network arrangements that began several decades ago. They now have a certain degree of formal organizational structure, but their members still work largely as a network for coordination and information exchange. These structures are complemented by public–private dialogue networks articulated by multilateral organizations, fundamentally the Inter-American Development Bank (IDB). In addition, there are two international associations operating at the subregional level, one related to the MERCOSUR and the other to Central American countries, and both of which undertake their activities within the framework of subregional integration initiatives with specific institutional structures.

The most relevant transgovernmental structure for network governance in banking in LAC—but that also encompasses North America—is the Association of Supervisors of Banks of the Americas (ASBA, *Asociación de Supervisores Bancarios de las Américas*). This association has gained a preeminent position in the regional governance of banking issues, particularly after the banking and debt crises that many countries in the region suffered in the 1980s and 1990s. It is a clear case of the NAO form of network governance, one that evolved from a simpler participant governance form at its origins.

One factor to be taken into account when assessing the relevance of banking agencies in the region is that they were first introduced in many countries in the

1920s (Jordana and Levi-Faur 2006). At the time, their initial design was strongly influenced by North American models, partly as a result of the missions led by Edwin Walter Kemmerer, a Princeton University professor who acted as a consultant for many governments at that time (Drake 1989). In subsequent decades, these banking agencies went through a long history of institutional development and occasional crises (see Nogales 2000 on Bolivia, and Garavito and Fernando 2003 on Colombia). As can be observed in Figure 4.1, these agencies expanded quite rapidly across the region (Jordana and Levi-Faur 2005). More recently, they underwent massive reforms in order to obtain more autonomy vis-à-vis the executive (Jordana and Ramió 2010). Except in Argentina and Brazil, designs of banking regulatory agencies in Latin America are much more homogeneous than in Europe, where central banks are involved in banking regulation in a large number of countries. Within this context, it is no surprise that the first meeting of banking regulators in Latin America took place in 1981, when the Commission of Latin American and Caribbean Banking Supervisory and Inspection Organizations (*Comisión de Organismos de Supervisión y Fiscalización Bancaria de América Latina y el Caribe*) met for the first time in Mexico, after being

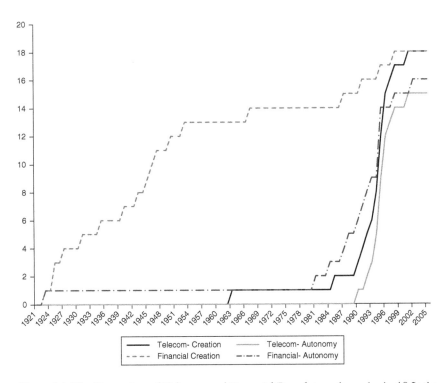

Figure 4.1 The Expansion of Telecom and Financial Regulatory Agencies in 18 Latin American Countries (1920–2005): Creation and Autonomy (Fixed-Term Tenure).

Source: Jordana and Ramió (2010).

convened by the Center for Latin American Monetary Studies (CEMLA, *Centro de Estudios Monetarios Latinoamericanos*).[1]

The Commission of Latin American and Caribbean Banking Supervisory and Inspection Organizations held meetings almost every year during the 1980s and adopted a formal organizational design as early as 1982, during its second meeting, held in Lima, when its statutes were approved. Membership reached 27 countries by 1984, and meetings were open to experts and representatives from different international organizations. Representatives were also frequently invited from extraregional supervisory authorities, like the USA or Spain. In addition to these general meetings of agency heads or presidents, a number of technical committees started to operate on specific issues during the 1980s. During the ninth meeting, held in 1992 in Santa Cruz, Bolivia, it was decided that the organization would change its name to Association of Banking Supervisory Organizations of Latin America and the Caribbean (ASBALC, *Asociación de Organismos Supervisores Bancarios de América Latina y el Caribe*). Organizational support from CEMLA remained in place until the late 1990s, when ASBALC became more self-sufficient and established its own permanent secretariat in Mexico, DF. This also led to changes in its network governance form, which evolved towards the NAO type, with a specialized organization responsible for coordination, administrative services, and service provision to members. It was at this time that the organization was renamed ASBA, partly to signify the full inclusion of North American banking regulatory agencies.

In recent decades, ASBA's main task has been to disseminate the regulatory requirements of the Basel Committee on Banking Supervision through the region, helping with their implementation, explaining their contents, and facilitating a space for the exchange of information and experiences among members. One major instrument for achieving this aim has been a large-scale training program with guest teaching staff from the United States, Canada, Spain, and also from within the region itself. A second instrument is the working groups (and subgroups) on multiple regulatory issues. These include one representative per country who exchange experiences, elaborate common positions, or revise the implementation of Basel-based regulations in the region. The secretariat provides support to all high-level meetings of ASBA members, manages the training program, and also implements modernization programs. Two successive technical cooperation programs established by the IDB have supported ASBA's efforts to propagate the Basel regulatory frameworks, and have also provided technical support to countries when needed (Gutierrez and Caraballo 2011).

Regulatory regimes in most countries in the region were focused on microprudential regulation until 2008, and banking agencies and their networks usually promoted more intense adoption of international regulatory standards. Currently, levels of implementation of Basel I and Basel II regulatory requirements are very high in most countries in the region, reaching about 80% in 2010 (De la Torre et al. 2012). Furthermore, ASBA is also allowed to participate in some Basel Committee meetings so as to obtain information directly and provide views from LAC. This is very useful for small countries, which do not have alternative channels, but not for larger ones, as these have their own seat on the Basel Committee.

In this sense, it can be argued that the main information circulating in the regional network relates to the diffusion of the international standards that are commonly accepted as correct or adequate at a given time, including assessments of their adequacy, practicality, and other details of their implementation. This can be understood as a valuable club good for national supervisors, particularly for small countries. However, larger countries also obtained public good compensations from membership: one the one hand, they enjoyed increased influence in defining region-wide regulatory positions and, on the other hand, they benefited from some level of regional regulatory harmonization and by avoiding dumping on the part of their smaller neighbors.

Subregional networks of regulators in financial governance

There are other financial regulatory networks in the region, such as the Central American Council of Superintendents of Banks, Insurance, and other Financial Institutions (CCSBSO, *Consejo Centroamericano de Superintendentes de Bancos, de Seguros y de Otras Instituciones Financieras*). This network was created in 1976 and includes regulatory agencies from Honduras, Guatemala, El Salvador, Nicaragua, Costa Rica, and the Dominican Republic. The CCSBSO initially operated as a network, convening annual meetings, but in 2000 it established itself formally as an international association, showing a similar pattern of moving towards an NAO form of governance. During the 2000s, the CCSBSO became very active, establishing many technical committees to deal with regulatory harmonization or accounting standardization and other issues. In 2011, it decided to establish a permanent secretariat in Panama with the aim of achieving a stable organizational structure while moving beyond the network approach that characterized its operations at its beginnings. This is a clear case of a transnational network providing club goods by means of developing organizational capabilities—and establishing strong connections with rule takers at the national level within the subregion. Finally, it is also important to note that CCSBSO is directly represented within ASBA, in addition to its national members.

In addition, the MERCOSUR also emerged as an active cluster for coordinating financial regulation at the subregional level, in a similar way to CCSBSO countries. Working Subgroup 4, which deals with financial issues, is made up of representatives from central banks, banking authorities, and insurance and securities agencies, and articulates different technical teams focusing on specific areas of financial regulation (insurance, capital markets, money laundering, and financial services), which meet relatively frequently. However, their activities are based more on negative coordination and information exchange than on advancing regulatory harmonization and the integration of financial systems and regulatory supervision. In this sense, the structure of the body's network governance has remained a participant governance form of network. In this sense, its capacity to play an active role in providing subregional public goods is weak, but it is nonetheless capable of reaching some decisions by consensus. It has made, in fact, some advances towards reaching certain levels of harmonization in technical areas (i.e., accounting criteria) and also in developing common criteria for the implementation of Basel II and Basel III standards.

Multilateral international organizations and transnational banking networks

Networks promoted by multilateral organizations are clear cases of lead organization governance networks, which usually require less coordination and cooperation in order to operate. The IDB established a research network called the Latin American Financial Network in the early 2000s, with the purpose of promoting high-level policy discussions on financial issues in Latin America. The new network also aimed to foster personal bonds among the academic community, regional policymakers, and the IDB research team, to facilitate policy exchange and, eventually, policy diffusion. The network's main activity is a yearly workshop that brings together top researchers, policymakers, and financial regulators from the North and the South to discuss recent theoretical and empirical advances in the economics of corporate finance in a two-day brainstorming session, and to coordinate a common agenda.

Around the same time, the IDB also launched a series of regional policy dialogues in different areas, including banking supervision. In 2003, this network started as a public–private conference on the implications of Basel II for Latin America, convened by the IDB in Washington, DC, with high-level representatives from domestic regulatory institutions, major banking associations, and also regional or subregional associations. These meetings continued each year in different places, as a venue at which bank representatives and supervisors could engage in dialogue with a regional perspective. This network includes 25–50 members at each meeting, and is also supported by major regional associations and networks in the area (ASBA and CCSBSO for regulators, and FELABAN for banks). Since 2010, this initiative has been integrated into the IDB's regional policy dialogues and is also becoming better articulated within the IDB's development strategy. In general, the governance form of this network is based neither on self-organization or consensus making, but provides some benefits for participants, such as information exchange and consensus building, without any commitments on their part.

Transnational networks in telecommunications in Latin America and the Caribbean[2]

International organizations as regional network promoters

There is no shortage of international organizations in the area of telecommunications worldwide. It is thus no surprise that they are among the most important sources of support for governance in this sector in Latin America. In this sense, two organizations that aim to act as lead organization governance in the region are especially important. First, there is a broad-purpose, territorially based international organization that focuses on regional integration goals: the Organization of American States (OAS), which was established in 1948 for pancontinental purposes and is headquartered in Washington, DC. Second, there is the sector-based Latin American branch of the ITU, an intergovernmental organization affiliated with the United Nations that is one of the oldest intergovernmental organizations in the world, as it was originally established in 1865.

Among the regional networks connected to these international organizations, the most important is the Inter-American Telecommunication Commission (CITEL, *Comisión Interamericana de Telecomunicaciones*; CITEL 2005), which aims to perform in the NAO mode. Created by the OAS in 1994, the high point of the sector's commitment to market competition and privatization, it is a subunit specializing in the regional governance of telecommunications. CITEL has two types of members: representatives from the public sector (who now come from 33 countries), who may come from any type of public body, and often include sector ministers; and associate members from different areas of the private sector, mainly regulated firms.

CITEL's main governance purpose, however, is to focus on pure public goods, promoting agenda and rule setting on the technical and regulatory side of telecommunications, in order to establish common norms, network interoperability, joint use of the radio-electric spectrum, and so forth. In the 1990s, it began work on the *Blue Book on Telecommunications Policy for the Americas* (2005), published jointly with the ITU's branch in the Americas. Its contents aimed to suggest policies and rules to be developed in the region after the liberalization of the sector in the early 1990s. During the 2000s, CITEL became less stringent in terms of its policy suggestions, and increasingly turned into a space where government positions for forthcoming ITU conferences were negotiated, with the aim of eventually reaching consensus for regional strength in different global telecom forums. This is particularly true for the United States and Canada, which usually look to conclude hemispheric agreements at CITEL, while striving to establish common regional standards, a process which is strongly contested by several Latin American countries.

CITEL has a complex structure including a rotating board of directors and two specialized Permanent Consultative Committees within which detailed discussions take place. There are a number of other working groups, which include representatives from several countries. In addition to these regular gatherings, CITEL is very active in providing specialized training: it has established a number of training centers in most Latin American countries, offers a large number of courses, provides grants for course participants, and coordinates these tasks with the regional branch of the ITU, which is also involved in providing specialized training.

The abovementioned ITU branch, which was opened in 1992, is active in launching programs to provide technical support and promote the advance of telecommunications in the less developed countries in the region. In addition to government participation, the regional ITU branch has also expanded its membership to form a network-like structure involving 115 organizations, which include firms, NGOs, scientific units, and regional organizations. The network is employed to disseminate information, facilitate meetings, and provide specialized training. In fact, the ITU office is strongly focused on developing policies in the area of telecommunications in the region, providing technical advice on the telecoms governance of less developed countries, and also coordinating some ICT development projects. This initiative represents a move towards establishing a hybrid mode of regional governance, taking advantage of the characteristics of network-based procedures within a more traditional institution.

In addition to CITEL and the regional branch of ITU, there are a number of subregional organizations with a similar operational logic. These subregional initiatives have a public nature, taking the form of an international treaty or sectoral initiatives that form part of subregional integration processes. For example, a group of Central American countries established the Telecommunications Regional Technical Commission (COMTELCA, *Comisión Técnica Regional de Telecomunicaciones*) in 1966. Originally a network of public operators, COMTELCA is an association of different Central American regulatory agencies that is a common space for subregional governance involving national authorities and regulatory agencies. Also at the subregional level are other structures that serve some governance functions, mainly consensus building and policy coordination, such as the MERCOSUR Committee for Communications, SGT-1, established in 1995, or the Andean Committee of Telecommunications Authorities (CAATEL, *Comité Andino de Autoridades de Telecomunicaciones*), established in 1991. In addition to its regular interactions, CAATEL was also active in joint decision making regarding the regulation of some technical areas (e.g. satellite communications) during the 1990s and early 2000s.

Regulatory agency networks in telecoms

Established in 1998 as a forum to facilitate policy coordination in the region among the new regulatory agencies in most Latin American countries, the Latin American Forum of Telecommunications Regulators (REGULATEL, *Foro Latinoamericano de Entes Reguladores de Telecomunicaciones*) began operating after almost all countries in the region had already created regulatory agencies (see Figure 4.1). This initiative represents a participant governance mode, where members take care of coordination, but without a robust structure. The origins of REGULATEL are strongly related to a critical juncture when all Latin American countries sought to take a common position regarding international call termination costs, in opposition to US and Canadian interests that were seeking to quickly reduce their payments for call termination. This cleavage created the need for a separate forum from CITEL, one that centered on regulatory agencies instead of ministerial representatives. This was a serious dispute that forged interests that would be defended jointly by Latin American agencies, which were all in some way responsible for this issue. REGULATEL rapidly brought together 20 telecommunications regulatory agencies in Latin

America (three European agencies from Portugal, Spain, and Italy later joined as observers, but Caribbean regulatory agencies were not invited).

By the time the termination cost dispute was over, the network was already in operation, and the member agencies—most of which were then still young, expanding organizations—have since continued to perform some governance activities and tried to keep the network structure functioning under certain limited internal rules. For example, the REGULATEL presidency rotates annually among the heads of the 20 regulatory agencies that form the network. REGULATEL is a participant organization, and members did not agree to make financial contributions to sustain the network. Resistance in several countries has stifled continued support for this initiative, limiting the possibility of its becoming a lead organization in the sector and developing a stronger transnational platform.

A significant obstacle to the REGULATEL network becoming more institutionalized and better able to produce more public and club goods is related to the widely varied formal status of telecom regulatory agencies in Latin America. The network operates only as a coordinating body, sharing tasks and responsibilities among its members through a minimal organizational structure; but it does not operate as an international organization. Its members see the network as a forum, a common space in which to manage knowledge and build consensus: "the Forum operates through an organization that takes advantage of the infrastructure of the regulator of each member country, to carry out exchanges of information and experiences" (REGULATEL 2009). However, they do not perceive it as providing authoritative guidance. Its main objectives are to facilitate the exchange of information and policy coordination, to promote the harmonization of regulation in the region (thus contributing to regional integration), and to identify and defend regional interests as a whole, seeking to define common positions to be defended in international forums. But only the first of these has really been achieved.

In spite of its limited governance capabilities and shortage of public goods provision, REGULATEL has become very active in organizing annual meetings in the region. To some extent, these periodic exchanges of information are believed to contribute to the harmonization of regulation in Latin America, facilitating the emergence of learning mechanisms (Peña 2006). Some club goods are also provided by REGULATEL, such as data for benchmarking, technical studies, or regulatory network news, which particularly benefit small countries. A parallel network involving Caribbean utility regulators exists as well: the Organisation of Caribbean Utility Regulators (OOCUR) was created in 2002 and includes agencies dealing with telecommunications regulation. This is not a formal organization, but a network of regulatory agencies which exchange information, promote joint activities, and facilitate their interactions, and so is similar to REGULATEL but on a smaller scale.

Conclusions

Following my comparison of the structures of regional network governance in the two policy areas examined, I have found many differences, but also some similarities. On the one hand, the lack of a well-established and inclusive regime of global governance in banking has obviously triggered uncertainty and increased the relevance of regional settings as alternative spaces for interaction and information exchange, while the fragmentation and polarization of global governance in telecoms has produced an increasing number of competing regional networks for sector governance, and fewer incentives for regulatory harmonization. On the other hand, both cases show that norm definition and norm setting has not occurred at the regional level, but rather in countries outside the region or at the global level. The role of regional transnational networks emerges as a critical one, in particular for smaller countries, in order to obtain information, advice, and technical support without taking on strong obligations as rule takers. In this sense, I have observed that some policy network patterns are very similar: small countries perceive their outputs as public goods or club goods, while larger countries do not require these, but obtain indirect benefits from their involvement in networks.

Another difference lies in the type of regional network governance predominating in each sector. Given the absence of alternative options, the evolution of ASBA in the banking area shows the transformation of regional network governance from a participant governance to an NAO form over the course of more than 30 years, a process supported by other actors that function as lead organizations for more politically sensitive issues. In the case of telecoms, I have observed how CITEL acted in the 1990s as an NAO for the governance of the sector, but was unable to integrate emerging networks of regulatory agencies, which also developed alternative participant governance network modes, although these were not strong enough to build an alternative NAO that was capable of increasing the offer of RPGs for the sector. Both cases, however, have come up against the same problem of the involvement of countries outside the region, creating more difficulties for collective action, although they provide resources and better information channels for network operations.

For decades, regional governance networks in both sectors have created a sustained pattern of intense information exchange and common understanding for regulatory harmonization in the region, which almost certainly contributed—to different degrees of intensity according to each sector and each country—to the adoption and further adjustment of new rules in national settings. However, these networks have not been capable of enlarging the provision of public goods (or club goods) in their policy areas, nor of evolving towards stronger institutional forms. New ideas circulate through these networks that affect agenda setting at the national level, but only when certain opportunity windows are present are they able to influence policy developments to explicitly harmonize countries' regulatory frameworks, for example.

Regulatory governance networks allowed the emergence of informal mechanisms of regional cooperation, or a rapid diffusion of regulatory innovations, beyond formal institutions, regional summits, and multiple attempts to move forward political integration. However, these networks showed many shortcomings, in particular their inability to act intentionally to pursue relevant objectives, due to weak institutionalization and scarce resources. As a result, however, a novel but limited offer of regional public and club goods—such as stronger cooperation, rapid information exchange, and sustained trust among regulators and policymakers—emerged in the region.

It is probably not to be expected that regional policy networks will provide more public goods, but they can improve the quality of the collective goods they provide in regulatory governance through better coordination, stronger trust formation and increased information exchange. This may produce regulatory convergence through diffusion nurtured by transnational network activity. They also may expand into many other sectors in which regulatory harmonization gains at the regional level are possible. The successes and failures of this network mode of regional governance, however, clarify the existing limitations and opportunities for the provision of RPGs. In this sense, promoting regulatory governance networks may well contribute to providing the region with more benefits, but also it is clear that this mode of governance cannot be the solution to most of the region's integration problems.

More promising are hybrid modes of governance that, given the particularities of Latin American integration, have the potential to promote regulatory harmonization. For example, establishing political links within the same area between regional regulatory networks and initiatives relating to "hard" public goods (such as infrastructure provision), provided by different institutions, may help to overcome some weaknesses in collective action. An advantage of networks is that they do not compromise sovereignty, nor oblige participation in decision-making processes, nor require sunk costs or long-term investments. They are simply *ad hoc* working arrangements which can be adapted to many different geographies and moving sector-specific borders. In sum, experimentation and originality in regional governance is necessary for Latin American integration, as each region must find its own mode of integration and its own connection to global governance. A larger supply of different types of RPGs could be provided by a multiplicity of hybrid modes and polymorphic structures of governance, involving innovative combinations of institutions and networks.

Notes

1 CEMLA was created by a network of economists from Latin American central banks as early as 1952 to provide training and technical advice from within the region itself. When central bank governors from LAC started to meet in 1964, CEMLA became its permanent secretariat (CEMLA 1993).
2 This section is based on a previous study by Jordana and Levi-Faur (2014).

References

Abdelal, Ravi. 2007. *Capital Rules. The Construction of Global Finance*. Cambridge, MA: Harvard University Press.
Angeloni, Ignazio. 2008. *Testing Times for Global Financial Governance*. Bruegel Essay and Lectures Series. Brussels: Bruegel.

Archer, Clive. 2014. *International Organizations*. London: Routledge.

Bach, David, and Abraham L. Newman. 2010. "Trans-governmental Networks and Domestic Policy Convergence: Evidence from Insider Trading Regulation." *International Organization* 6, no. 3: 505–528.

Berg, V. S., and J. Horrall. 2008. "Networks of Regulatory Agencies as Regional Public Goods." *Review of International Organizations* 3, no. 2: 179–200.

Bianculli, Andrea C., Jacint Jordana, and Xavier Fernandez-Marin (eds.). 2015. *Accountability and Regulatory Governance*. Basingstoke, UK: Palgrave Macmillan.

Brust, Lazlo, and Gerald A. McDermott. 2012. "Integrating Rule Takers: Transnational Integration Regimes Shaping Institutional Change in Emerging Market Democracies." *Review of International Political Economy* 19, no. 5: 743–778.

CEMLA. 1993. *Cuarenta Años del Centro de Estudios Monetarios Latinoamericanos 1952–1992*. México, DF: CEMLA. www.cemla.org/old/pdf/cemla-080001.pdf

CITEL (Comisión Interamericana de Telecomunicaciones). 2005. *Libro Azul: Políticas de Telecomunicaciones para las Américas*. Washington, DC: CITEL-ITU.

De la Torre, Augusto, Alain Ize, and Sergio L. Schmukler. 2012. *Financial Development in Latin America and the Caribbean: The Road Ahead*. Washington, DC: World Bank.

Djelic, M. L., and K. Sahlin-Andersson (eds.). 2006. *Transnational Governance: Institutional Dynamics of Regulation*. Cambridge: Cambridge University Press.

Djelic, M. L., and Quack, S. (eds.). 2010. *Transnational Communities: Shaping Global Economic Governance*. Cambridge: Cambridge University Press.

Drake, Paul W. 1989. *The Money Doctor in the Andes. U.S. Advisors, Investors, and Economic Reform in Latin America from World War I to the Great Depression*. Durham, NC: Duke University Press.

Fernández-i-Marín, Xavier, and Jacint Jordana. 2015. "The Emergence of Regulatory Regionalism: Transnational Networks and the Diffusion of Regulatory Agencies within Regions." *Contemporary Politics* 21, no. 4: 417–434.

Garavito, López, and Luis Fernando. 2003. "Una visión del desarrollo institucional de la Superintendencia Bancaria de Colombia, 1923–2003." In *80 años de Superintendencia Bancaria en Colombia*. Bogotá: Superintendencia Bancaria.

Gutierrez, Eva, and Patricia Caraballo. 2011. *Survey on Systemic Oversight Frameworks in LAC: Current Practices and Reform Agenda*. Washington, DC: ASBA/The World Bank.

Holzinger, Katharina, Christoph Knill, and Thomas Sommerer. 2008. "Environmental Policy Convergence: The Impact of International Harmonization, Transnational Communication, and Regulatory Competition." *International Organization* 62, no. 3: 553–587.

Jordana, Jacint. 2012. "The Institutional Development of Latin American Regulatory State." In *Handbook on the Politics of Regulation*, edited by David Levi-Faur. Cheltenham: Edward Elgar.

Jordana, Jacint, and David Levi-Faur. 2005. "The Diffusion of Regulatory Capitalism in Latin America: Sectorial and National Channels in the Making of New Order." *Annals of the American Academy for Political and Social Sciences* 598: 102–24.

———. 2006. "Towards a Latin American Regulatory State? The Diffusion of Autonomous Regulatory Agencies across Countries and Sectors." *International Journal of Public Administration* 29, no. 4–5: 335–366.

———. 2014. "Regional Integration and Transnational Regulatory Regimes. The Polycentric Architecture of Governance in Latin American Telecommunications." In *Leveling the Playing Field: Transnational Regulatory Integration and Development*, edited by Laszlo Bruszt and Gerald A. McDermott. Oxford: Oxford University Press.

Jordana, Jacint, David Levi-Faur, and Xavier Fernández-i-Marín. 2011. "The Global Diffusion of Regulatory Agencies: Channels of Transfer and Stages of Diffusion." *Comparative Political Studies* 44 no. 10: 1343–1369.

Jordana, Jacint, and Carles Ramió. 2010. "Delegation, Presidential Regimes, and Latin American Regulatory Agencies." *Journal of Politics in Latin America* 2 no. 1: 3–30.

Kahler, Miles (ed.). 2010. *Networked Politics. Agency, Power and Governance*. Ithaca, NY: Cornell University Press.

Kahler, Miles, and David A. Lake. 2009. "Economic Integration and Global Governance: Why So Little Supranationalism?" In *The Politics of Global Regulation*, edited by Walter Mattli and Ngaire Woods. Princeton, NJ: Princeton University Press.

Kim, K., and G. Barnett. 2000. "The Structure of the International Telecommunications Regime in Transition: A Network Analysis of International Organizations." *International Interactions* 26, no. 1: 91–127.

Levi-Faur, David. 2012. "From 'Big Government' to 'Big Governance?'" In *The Oxford Handbook of Governance*, edited by David Levi-Faur. Oxford: Oxford University Press.

Levi-Faur, David, and Shana M. Starobin. 2014. "Transnational Political and Policy: From Two-Way to Three-Way Interactions." Working Paper no. 62. *Jerusalem Papers in Regulation and Governance.*

Lora, Eduardo (ed.). 2007. *The State of State Reform in Latin America*. Palo Alto, CA: Stanford University Press.

Major, Aaron. 2012. "Neo-liberalism and the New International Financial Architecture." *Review of International Political Economy* 19, no. 4.

Nogales, Xavier. 2000. "Superintendencia de bancos y entidades financieras en Bolivia." CLAD-IDB. www.clad.org.ve/nogales.html

Ocampo, José Antonio, and Jaime Ros (eds.). 2011. *The Oxford Handbook of Latin America Economics*. Oxford: Oxford University Press.

Provan, Keith, and Patrick Kenis. 2007. "Modes of Network Governance: Structure, Management and Effectiveness." *Journal of Public Administration Research and Theory* 18: 229–252.

Quaglia, Lucia. 2007. "The Politics of Financial Services Regulation and Supervision Reform in the European Union." *European Journal of Political Research* 46 no. 2: 269–290.

REGULATEL. 2009. "Foro latinoamericano de entes reguladores de telecomunicaciones. 11 años promoviendo el intercambio de información y las experiencias reguladoras en la región."

Risse, Thomas. 2004. "Global Governance and Communication Action." *Government and Opposition* 39, no. 2: 288–313.

Rojas-Suárez, Liliana, and Stefen R. Weisbrod. 1995. *Financial Fragilities in Latin America. The 1980s and 1990s*. Washington, DC: World Bank.

Slaughter, Anne-Marie. 2004. *A New World Order*. Princeton, NJ: Princeton University Press.

Tsingou, Eleni. 2009. "Regulatory Reactions to the Global Credit Crisis: Analysing a Policy Community under Stress." In *Global Finance in Crisis. The Politics of International Regulatory Change*, edited by E. Helleiner, S. Pagliari, and H. Zimmermann. London: Routledge.

Underhill, Geoffrey, and Xiaoke Zhang. 2008. "Setting the Rules: Private Power, Political Underpinnings, and Legitimacy in Global Monetary and Financial Governance." *International Affairs* 84, no. 3: 535–554.

5 Can regional standards be above the national norm?

Impact evaluation issues for regional public goods

Joaquim Tres and Paulo Barbieri

Introduction

Countries across the globe face challenges and opportunities that are often better addressed through regional cooperation and collective action to produce public goods. Some examples include regional regulation to reduce water pollution in a multinational sea, lake, or watershed; a common prevention and preparedness strategy in a seismic region; a regional arrangement of small countries to collectively procure medicines at lower prices and at higher quality, a regional free trade agreement to reduce trade costs; or a joint export promotion scheme by small economies to target distant markets. Throughout history, examples of regional cooperation such as these abound, ranging from defense agreements to trade and economic development policies and investments. There has consequently been a great deal of research that charts and analyzes regional cooperation. In recent years, assessment studies have been carried out through more systematic network analysis to shed light on the interactions, flows, and relations in regional cooperation. However, with the rare exception of trade and investment agreements, regional cooperation seldom has been assessed using methodologies that measure the effectiveness of its execution and implementation and the specifics of its development impact, especially in Latin America and the Caribbean (LAC).

In a nutshell, this chapter proposes the use a range of impact evaluation methods to assess the development impact of regional cooperation projects and to attempt to transfer learning from one context to another to design better regional public goods (RPGs) projects. The need for LAC to do this is the result of: i) the international community's adoption of principles that emphasize the measuring of development cooperation results;[1] ii) the growing interest in and social pressure toward increasing accountability for development cooperation in developed countries in general; iii) the consolidation of South-South cooperation (SSC), which increases the need to show its development effectiveness; and iv) declining development cooperation flows to most LAC countries as a result of their economic and social progress leading to their "graduation" from traditional donors' programs. Thus, there is an overdue need for LAC countries to find new ways of continuing to engage with traditional donors. Showing the development impact of their SSC, most of it bilateral, may attract the interest of traditional donors to engage LAC countries in triangular cooperation both within LAC and in other geographical contexts. But LAC countries' SSC is also regional, including the horizontal, bottom-up, country-driven generation of RPGs that can benefit from traditional donors as key strategic partners, as long as their benefit spillovers are above the national norms.

This chapter begins by presenting the Inter-American Development Bank's (IDB) Regional Public Goods Initiative[2] because for over a decade it has been one of the largest and most innovative instruments providing support for horizontal regional SSC in LAC; also because many of the supported projects produce regional standards that are reported to be above the national norms and that intuitively show strong results and sustainability beyond the IDB funding phase. We believe that the results achieved by the IDB-supported RPG projects can only be partially captured by network analysis and that they require a range of impact analysis methods to be undertaken if we are to fully capture their development impact, draw lessons for other horizontal SSC interventions in LAC and other regions, and leverage new forms of engagement with traditional donors. This section also reviews the relevant definitions of public goods that underpin the IDB RPG Initiative against the backdrop of the aggregation technologies used to characterize RPGs, so as to later explain why the definition used in the IDB RPG Initiative includes the collective regional production of public goods, an aspect which is usually neglected.

The following section discusses whether regional standards created by regional cooperation can be above national norms. More specifically, this chapter challenges the notion that regional cooperation is mainly based on the "weakest link" aggregation technology of production (whereby the smallest/weakest contribution determines the good's aggregate level) or a sort of "race to the lowest common denominator." Instead, it supports the idea that countries' policy makers quite often resort to creating and converging to higher transnational standards characterized by a "better shot" aggregation technology of production (whereby the largest/strongest contribution has the greatest influence on the good's aggregate level) or a sort of "race to the top." To do this, they embark on challenging policy reforms that need to pool stronger technical capacity, want to make national backtracking more difficult, and often try to overcome domestic political economy resistance to reforms. Despite the potential and actual positive development outcomes of such "higher" regulatory convergence as a result of the generation of those RPGs, development impact analysis and national regulatory enforcement are surprisingly scant in LAC.

This chapter will continue by acknowledging the importance of network analysis while still stressing the importance of adopting a range of impact evaluation methodologies that can shed light on the actual development impact of RPGs. Empirical evidence, either qualitative or quantitative, is needed to determine the results and potential impact of those RPGs. Furthermore, the chapter proposes the use of a range of impact evaluation methods as this goes one step beyond customary monitoring and evaluation of development cooperation by focusing on causality and isolating other effects and potential selection bias. It thus may allow us to explain why and in what contexts regional cooperation projects can be expected to succeed. Among the experiences generated by the IDB RPG Initiative's projects, this chapter focuses on the Central American Pharmaceutical Protocol Project to illustrate the relevance and importance of measuring the development impact of regional cooperation because it may pave the way to assessing regional cooperation beyond documenting the wealth of exchanges among partners. This case study, together with other briefly cited examples, can also show traditional donors the usefulness of partnering in horizontal SSC, even if participating agencies are from middle-income countries that will soon "graduate" as development cooperation recipients, so as to spur on triangular cooperation in other contexts.

Mindful that sometimes supranational regulation leads to weak implementation in the absence of penalties, in this chapter we insist that in many instances of regional cooperation, regional standards can indeed be above the national norm because the generation of RPGs can:

- pool limited national technical capacity to produce a new, higher regional standard,
- lower costs by realizing economies of scale (as in the Central American Pharmaceutical Protocol presented in this chapter),
- reduce the costs of navigating country-specific regulatory environments,
- curtail attempts at regulatory capture in cases of limited market competition,
- prevent backtracking due to the difficulty of persuading partner countries to break the regional standard, and
- prevent backtracking due to implementation costs.

This chapter concludes that, after analyzing the project inventory for the IDB RPG Initiative, it is evident that regional standards can be above the national norm, but only in limited circumstances. It also concludes that there is a need to develop an impact evaluation agenda focusing on RPGs because it will be important to further assess ex-post results and to focus on national regulatory enforcement. If regulatory convergence to higher regional standards is happening as part of the implementation of RPGs in the region, studying the national enforcement of the new legal arrangements is an important endeavor to undertake.

Generating development solutions through collective regional action

At the turn of this millennium, the international community began to come together around the UN Millennium Development Goals.[3] The debate around providing global public goods picked up considerable momentum, and later moved on to include RPGs. Some drilled down through that debate to show that "the potential benefits of global public goods were actually 'regional' in nature and a promising way to supply such goods might lie in regional solutions" (Estevadeordal, Frantz, and Nguyen 2004, p.1).

Beyond that assertion, others like Sandler (2005 and 2013) highlighted additional factors promoting RPGs such as the favorable characteristics of publicness (nonexcludability, nonrivalry, and aggregation technologies of public supply); fewer nations involved than in global public goods (thus reducing the disincentives of cross-border collective action); and past and ongoing interactions among regional countries (both positive and negative such as peace-building efforts and wars). The rest of the factors promoting RPGs identified by Sandler (2013) bear a special significance in the light of developments in LAC countries since the 1990s in relation to the rise of new regionalism and customs unions and thus deserve additional comment. Countries in LAC have been especially active in signing regional trade agreements (RTAs), which account for over 70 of the 270 RTAs worldwide and regulate two-thirds of trade in the region; and there is cultural and spatial propinquity among spillover recipients. The dominance of the Spanish language in Latin America and its compatibility with Portuguese spoken in Brazil (which is mirrored by similar affinities in the English-speaking Caribbean), together with similar political and legal systems among countries in the region, all bode well for reducing the cost of regional coordination and collective action to promote RPGs.

However, RPGs are also subject to factors inhibiting their generation and face challenges that are harder to overcome than those faced by national or global public goods. With regard to national public goods, countries have the proper incentives for providing these, and global public goods are promoted through their far-ranging benefit spillovers because donor countries stand to gain through their efforts to underwrite recipient countries' provision of such goods (Sandler 2013). The IDB's experience in managing the RPG portfolio concurs with Sandler (2013) that the main factor inhibiting the generation of RPGs is less donor spillover as a result of a limited range of benefits to the region in question. This, for example, is the case of the Central American Pharmaceutical Protocol presented in this chapter, for which there are no spillover benefits outside the participating Central American countries. Other inhibiting factors include the fact that nations must form (complex) coalitions to gain finance or provide collateral (as is the case of EU countries that are part of a Trans-European Network transportation corridor and want to collectively access concessional financing from EU entities such as loans, guarantees, and grants); regional rivalry (which may stem from ideological and policy diversity); and an insufficient culture of support for regional development banks (which is also due to limited funds as a result of supporting the generation of global public goods through entities with global reach in the form of international organizations, as is the case of the support several donors have given the WTO to implement its 2013 Bali Trade Facilitation Agreement).

Thus, in the context of such insufficient support from traditional donors due to limited spillover benefits and the "graduation" of LAC countries from their aid programs, resorting to the subsidiarity principle may help us understand and determine which institutions should be involved in the provision of RPGs. Kanbur, Sandler and Morrison (1999) assert that there should be a close match between the providing institution's jurisdictional authority and the range of benefit spillovers of the public good, thus they identify the IDB as the most appropriate such institution when the spillover range for the public goods in question is Latin America or its subregions. Based on the factors promoting and also inhibiting the generation of RPGs as well as the application of the subsidiarity principle highlighted above, the IDB established its RPG Initiative in 2005.

The IDB RPG Initiative has so far invested over US$100 million in grants to 140 RPG projects executed by over 100 LAC organizations and in which over 700 entities participated, most of which were public but which also included private not-for-profit agencies. The initiative used the IDB's own resources earned through LAC countries' loan repayments. IDB-supported RPGs have so far had an average of eight participating countries from LAC with the frequent engagement of strategic partners from traditional donor countries or international and regional organizations. Figure 5.1 shows histori-cal data on the number of projects and total amounts per sector for the IDB's RPG portfolio. The initiative has funded projects in different sectors, including climate change, education, energy, public institutions, and trade. The amounts

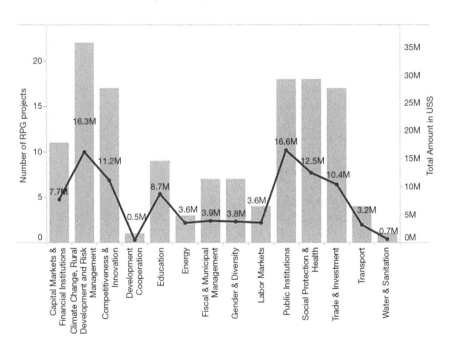

Figure 5.1 Number of RPG Projects Funded by the IDB (in US$ and by Sector).

Source: Author, based on historical data for IDB RPG Initiative.

disbursed have varied from US$500,000 to almost US$2 million per project (see Annex for project details). In line with the properties of nonexcludability and nonrivalry for public goods and bearing in mind aggregation technologies (from summation to better shot), additional countries from the region can join a project once it has started (thus enhancing scale spillovers).[4] The average amount disbursed for a project is US$820,000. The projects included in the IDB RPG Initiative have been some of the most structured, demand-driven efforts among LAC countries to generate RPGs. These projects allow countries both to produce and reap the benefits of the RPGs that were generated, thus engaging them in horizontal, regional, SSC and offering a platform from which to leverage triangular cooperation and explore potential new ways of meaningfully engaging the dwindling traditional donors in LAC.

The IDB RPG Initiative is based on the rationale that LAC countries share many development challenges and opportunities that can be addressed more effectively and efficiently at the regional level. However, that assertion does not imply that all LAC countries share the same challenges or opportunities, and thus countries form collectives or coalitions of those willing to generate RPGs. Sandler's categories (2013) are used below with examples of real IDB-supported RPGs because they are helpful for understanding LAC's often revealed preferences. Countries form *ad hoc* coalitions for the following reasons:

- geology (El Salvador, Guatemala, and Honduras in Central America's Northern Triangle share the Lempa River and generated an RPG to improve management of its watershed),
- geography (countries in Central America decided to adopt an International Transit of Merchandise system and reduce physical inspections of cargo containers at border crossings when cargo was only in transit in the country),
- country proximity (MERCOSUR countries coalesced to eradicate the cattle screwworm), and
- shared policy values (Caribbean countries established a joint FDI investment map and an association of investment promotion agencies).

These examples illustrate the diversity of factors that lead LAC countries to establish coalitions to generate RPGs that can address their challenges and opportunities.

Promoting those regional/subregional coalitions was and still is deemed to add more value than purely national interventions that seek to address many kinds of regional issues. Take the example provided in this chapter's introduction of regional regulation to reduce water pollution in a multinational sea, lake, or watershed. In such a case, a purely national intervention would be insufficient and also quite ineffective because while one country would limit or control its polluted water discharges, the rest of the countries sharing the same ecosystem would continue to pollute with only overall marginal progress in reducing pollution. This example and others presented so far illustrate that many issues to be addressed are regional in nature and that national public goods are unable to address them efficiently or effectively, thus requiring collective regional action mechanisms to generate the adequate range of spillover benefits.

With this rationale, the IDB RPG Initiative adopted a practical definition that guides the annual approval of projects. The definition stems from the two properties of nonrivalry and nonexcludability that define public goods, that is, that the use (or consumption) of the available good by one or more countries does not generally preclude other eligible countries from using it, and that no eligible country can be reasonably excluded from its use. On that basis, the IDB RPG Initiative defines RPGs as products, services, or resources that are consumed and produced collectively by the public sector and, if appropriate, by the private sector in a minimum of three countries.[5]

The production element in the IDB's definition, however, requires some explanation as it represents a departure from the standard definition of public goods. In the case of the IDB RPG Initiative, the production element matters almost as much as the consumption factor because it underpins the regional cooperation dimension that the IDB wants to promote in the generation of RPGs. As RPG practitioners, we concur with Nordhaus's (2005) conclusion that the debate on public goods focused on nonrivalry and nonexcludability in their consumption and neglected the nature of the production of public goods underlying the indivisible benefits. This is an additional reason for proposing in this chapter that a range of impact evaluation methods be undertaken so as to also focus on why and in what institutional contexts RPG production can be expected to succeed, thus allowing for learning from other RPGs.

The definition also allows for not-for-profit private-sector entities to participate in the generation of RPGs and for public–private partnerships since private-sector entities require the nonobjection of governments to participate. This inclusion is due to the increasingly blurred boundaries between the public and private spheres and the growing number of privately regulated entities in LAC countries that serve public purposes and generate national public goods, as is the case of export promotion agencies or voluntary certification standards entities. The inclusion of private-sector entities also recognizes that the new regionalism is multidimensional and entails the active cross-border engagement not just of states, as in the old regionalism, but also of multilevel government entities and nonstate actors such as entities from the private sector and civil society in general that take form as asymmetric networks and *ad hoc* coalitions.[6]

To strengthen the cooperation element, the IDB requires the participation of entities from at least three countries at any government level, as long as they are responsible for public policy in their field of interest. The main reason for stipulating that three countries be involved is that the IDB RPG Initiative is also an instrument for supporting regional horizontal cooperation. It attempts to create a critical mass of countries for two main reasons. First, coordination beyond two countries is more complex and costly due to more severe coordination failures that act as roadblocks to the generation of RPGs. Countries often find their own domestic resources for addressing binational public bads such as the local spread of foot-and-mouth disease among cattle or for generating new opportunities through a public good such as a shared international airport or a binational border control. Second, the IDB RPG Initiative attempts to promote RPGs that in many instances rely on economies of scale to produce tangible shared benefits, such as those that focus on pooling knowledge from participating countries.

Since the initiative attempts to promote regional cooperation, it also stresses that public goods are to be produced by means of horizontal, collective regional action. It accepts proposals that fit into a broad range of public goods aggregation technologies, including summation, weighted sum, weakest link, threshold, and better shot but tending to exclude clearly apparent best shot production, whereby the largest contribution determines the good's aggregate level. Participating countries thus collectively decide the size of their contribution and how to achieve their goals, develop their own agendas, adopt their own working mechanisms, establish project governance, select their executing agencies and strategic partners, and decide which commitments they are willing to undertake together. The involvement of public agencies is a requirement because the initiative concentrates on RPGs that are related to the coordination of public policy design and reform, such as regulatory upgrades, institutional strengthening, and capacity development, which have significant potential for development impact.

The IDB RPG Initiative places a premium on goods that have the potential to generate significant spillover effects in terms of scope when the spillover benefits extend beyond the sector that was originally targeted, as is the case of the Central American Pharmaceutical Protocol that ministries of health in the subregion in question want to use to procure hospital supplies.[7] The IDB RPG Initiative also places a premium on those goods with the potential for generating spillover effects in terms of scale when the benefits extend beyond the original group of countries, as was the case with the Central American Pharmaceutical Protocol Project when Guatemala joined it in 2015.[8]

The key features of the IDB RPG Initiative worth highlighting in this chapter are its:

- demand-driven nature, which means that countries themselves get together to identify the development challenge or opportunity, then generate consensus to develop and present a project proposal to the IDB to produce the public good deciding on the spillover benefit range;
- competitive allocation of funds through an annual call for proposals that is highly competitive;
- laboratory of ideas role that countries use to share the risks of innovation and pool their best capabilities to attempt higher regional standards; and
- promotion of SSC and triangular cooperation to allow for knowledge and technology transfer and horizontal institutional strengthening.

The initiative is open to all areas of work in which the IDB is active and has thus become its main instrument for supporting regional cooperation and collective regional action.

In addition to funding the annual call for proposals (which results in the approval of an average of ten RPG projects), the IDB provides several types of support for the specific groups of countries that produce the RPGs. These types of support are worth highlighting, as they are gradually becoming key to understanding the institutional factors for successful RPG generation. The IDB acts as a knowledge broker to bring together state-of-the-art knowledge, regional and international lessons learned, and good practices from outside the region in order to inspire the production of RPGs. The IDB leverages its international social capital by offering to bring in strategic partners, often from outside the region, and also plays an honest-broker role among the countries participating in the project.

A close examination of the IDB RPG project inventory has made it clear that a large number of projects aim to create regional regulatory summits that are higher than national standards, often resorting to "better shot" projects. Given the relatively large inventory of RPG projects in question, it is worth conceptualizing, documenting, and evaluating their development impacts and also assessing whether these RPGs are subsequently enforced at the national level, so as to draw development cooperation-related conclusions that will be useful for the countries of the region and beyond in the context of SSC. This chapter now turns to explaining and discussing these higher regional regulatory summits that policy makers are attempting to make and which have been observed in many IDB-supported RPG projects.[9]

Toward higher regional regulatory summits

Regional cooperation outcomes are quite frequently characterized by weakest link aggregation technology, whereby countries that have fewer installed institutional and financial capacities set the aggregate outcome level. This is actually documented in many instances and it is quite intuitive, thus the perception that regional cooperation only converges downwards to that "minimum common denominator" in the good's overall production, or a race to the bottom, is quite widespread. In such common cases, regional cooperation does not result in the optimal potential outcome, especially for countries with stronger capabilities. Nevertheless, the more capable countries in a given cooperation endeavor may still be interested in participating so as to benefit from other spillovers such as contributing to peaceful neighborhood relations that prevent conflict.

However, more often than is actually documented, countries' regional cooperation outcomes produce RPGs in the best shot/better shot range, whereby the highest-quality contribution determines the good's aggregate level or has the greatest influence on this. In such contexts, regional cooperation tends to produce higher regulatory standards than would be generated individually at the national level or higher than in the summation or weighted sum aggregation technologies, generating high regional regulatory summits, or a race to the top.[10] The following paragraphs will discuss such higher regulatory outcomes with specific cases that show the establishment of coalitions that converge to best shot regulation (Figure 5.2) or that push the boundaries of regional best shot regulation above the national norms of any of the participating countries (Figure 5.3).

A recent IDB RPG project on LAC's financial integration established that the first challenge in an integrated economic space is to avoid the trend toward the weakest link because firms and professionals would seek countries with better (more stable) regulatory environments and because lower quality regulation was also a source of macroeconomic instability. Zooming in from financial integration to stock exchange regulation, Larrain (2014) points out that when national regulatory standards are low in some countries in a given region, a regional segment of stocks could be developed and voluntarily adopted by countries with lower regulation, so as to aim for a higher regulatory summit—in other words, a race to the top, or best shot logic—as shown in Figure 5.2.[11]

The gray-shaded areas of Figure 5.2 represent national stock exchange regulations in three different countries, while the white tops represent the highest-quality national regulations that govern specific asset classes in those same countries. It has been documented that in many instances, countries' policy makers would like their highest-quality regulation (white tops in the figure) to converge to the best shot case represented by country 2 because

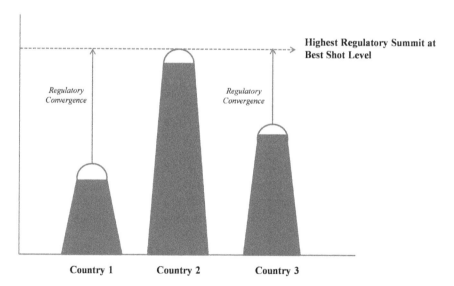

Figure 5.2 Higher Regulatory Summits: Converging to Best Shot Public Goods.
Source: Larrain (2014).

their country would be closer to or would match the highest international regulatory standards. That race to the top for a stock exchange market segment is the opposite of the weakest link logic and prevents firms and professionals from migrating to country 2 in the integrated or converging zone. Many similar cases similar can be found in the IDB RPG Initiative's portfolio in which coalitions of countries in several public policy sectors strive for higher regional regulatory summits.

A closer examination of the project inventory shows that countries attempt to create superior regulation even beyond the highest regional summit represented by the best shot, as shown in Figure 5.3, where a new regional standard is created. In some instances, regional cooperation may produce public goods beyond the better shot/best shot higher regulatory environments when regional resources are pooled and strategic partners are attracted that may not necessarily share spillover benefits. We believe that this is the case for the Central American Pharmaceutical Protocol RPG that is explained in detail in the next section.

Policy makers often use regional coalitions or use global standards to undertake national reforms to improve national regulation. For example, Ecuador is leading an IDB RPG project that aims to support countries in the adoption of an international vehicle standard that focuses on safety and environmental protection.[12] The harmonization of regulation in this particular case would produce both economic gains in relation to car exports and also significant improvements in road safety in the countries that participate in generating the

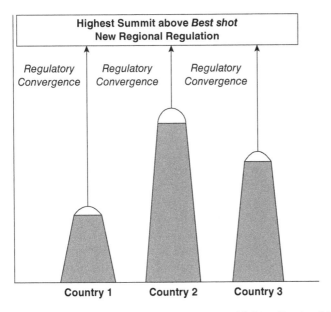

Figure 5.3 Highest Regulatory Summits: Establishing Regional Public Goods Above Best Shot.

RPG. Decision makers often establish regional coalitions when they embark on challenging policy reforms so that they can: (i) pool stronger regulatory capacity, benefiting from knowledge economies of scale from several countries; (ii) make national backtracking on reforms more difficult as is the case in partner countries' RTAs; and (iii) try to overcome domestic political economy-related resistance to reforms. One effective way of addressing developing countries' limited regulatory capacity is by pooling technical knowledge and capacities across countries, as is suggested by Estache and Wren-Lewis (2009) and as is the case in several IDB-supported RPG projects that also benefit from strategic partners outside of LAC or regional bodies.

A body of evidence-based research supports the race to the top notion and shows that it can be achieved in different ways as a result of SSC to generate RPGs. This is shown in Figures 5.2 and 5.3 for stock exchanges or the Central American Pharmaceutical Protocol. Other case studies show, for example, how countries are working together to improve their school infrastructure by establishing regional standards and regulations for the construction, use, and administration of school spaces. Ten Latin American countries with diverse regulation on education were part of the project from its beginnings, and two more joined later. Many of those countries established goals that included improving their school construction laws, and some of them are on the way to implementing a jointly developed school survey instrument to better identify their needs. As a result, school construction in some participating countries such as Chile, Honduras, and Panama is undertaken using the RPG that represents the highest regulatory summit, one that is above the participating countries' best shot.

Other cases show how signing an RTA with economies that have stronger regulation promotes such regulatory convergence toward the top. For example, RTAs that include environmental provisions foster convergence around reductions in CO_2 emissions. Baghdadi, Martinez-Zarzoso and Zitouna (2013) found that the gap in emissions per capita is about 18% lower for pairs of countries that signed RTAs with environmental harmonization policies. Those RTAs are global and are not necessarily between developed and developing countries. Dewan and Ronconi (2014) studied the enforcement of labor law in LAC countries that have either signed or have not signed an RTA with the United States and concluded that the number of labor inspectors increased by 20% and the number of inspections rose almost 60% on average for those countries with such RTAs.

Other cases show how a national public good expanded its range of benefit spillover into an entire region due to one of the countries' market power. One example of this is a carbonated drinks company that removed an additive from all its products being distributed in Central American countries after Costa Rica banned it as a suspected carcinogen. The cost of two separate production runs, one solely for Costa Rica and one for the rest of the Central American market, was prohibitive. In that case, the rest of Central American countries enjoyed the spillover benefits of higher-quality national preventive health regulation (a best shot scenario) via a private firm response, without having to change their own regulations.

The cases presented above show different ways of racing to the top, some of which entail clear national enforcement, but is this always the case? Despite the potential and actual positive development outcomes of such convergence to higher regional regulatory environments as a result of the generation of the RPGs reviewed above, there is a surprising scarcity of development impact analysis and rigorous assessment of national regulatory enforcement so as to ascertain why RPG projects work and which institutional contexts success takes place in.

In the context of the "graduation" of some LAC countries from traditional donors' OECD eligibility list of aid recipients, documenting those impacts and demonstrating the broad benefit spillovers from regional cooperation would represent a step forward in strengthening the case for SSC within LAC, offering it as a platform for triangular cooperation, and may also become a key asset for LAC countries to engage in the development effectiveness dialogue more meaningfully. We now turn to a widely disseminated IDB-supported RPG in Central America, as it may pave the way to answering many of the questions on impact analysis and the national regulatory enforcement of RPGs posed in this chapter and shared by many LAC development cooperation practitioners.

The Central American pharmaceutical procurement mechanism

In 2007, with the support of the IDB, eight Central American countries designed the Central American Protocol for Drug Procurement and Quality Control RPG project.[13] Led by the Council of Ministers of Health of Central America and the Dominican Republic (COMISCA), the project aimed to set up a coordinated regulatory framework for medicine procurement through a joint price negotiation process in order to provide the subregion with common regulation, procedures, and quality control standards for the medications used in public hospitals. The IDB ended its financial support for this RPG in 2012, and the Central American countries and their regional institutions, led by COMISCA, have continued to benefit from lower prices and higher-quality medicines.

The joint negotiation process (the actual RPG) established by the project consists of two stages. The first stage is centralized and has a region-wide scope. In it, COMISCA's executive secretariat acts as the executing agency and leads a five-step process: (i) planning; (ii) event publicizing and tender reception; (iii) legal and technical assessment of tenders; (iv) price negotiation; and (v) allocation of medicines according to each country's demand and needs.[14] The second stage takes place at the national level, as each country's health ministry, having previously estimated the quantities of medication to be procured, will purchase them through this regional mechanism via collective bids and at the prices and quality standards agreed on by the region.

Joint negotiations take place via reverse auctions,[15] where the winners are the companies that offer the highest-quality medications at the lowest cost. To be eligible for the auction, suppliers must meet several requirements and obtain a prequalification certificate from COMISCA that allows them to participate in negotiation events. This is a highly competitive process in which only the suppliers that are capable of meeting high quality standards are prequalified. The eligibility of suppliers and the selection of medicines to be acquired are based on existing regional pharmaceutical regulations and international quality norms, including those issued by the World Health Organization.[16] Through these procedures, Central American countries benefit from a transparent system that optimizes public health resources and selects only the best drugs and supplies.

In terms of quality control standards and common procedures for acquiring drugs, the system operates around a single harmonized list for the entire region that includes all the medications that countries are interested in purchasing. This allows countries to avoid duplicating efforts and to reduce purchase times and costs while promoting the faster introduction of cutting-edge and priority medications into their public hospitals.

Between 2010 and 2015, five joint negotiation events were carried out, signifying estimated regional savings of around US$36 million, as is shown in Table 5.1. Cost reductions for each round ranged between 20% and 30%, and for some specific drugs reductions were as high as 1,000% (COMISCA 2016). It is important to note that the IDB's investment in this RPG project was US$800,000, which represents 2.2% of the total estimated savings for the 2010–2015 period. This RPG business model is a clear example that could inspire triangular cooperation, whereby traditional donors request that COMISCA become the executing agency, for a fee, in a different geographical context. The question, however, is whether the Central American institutional context can be replicated and whether the initial success of the project can be scaled up in other contexts through learning from this experience. In broad terms, what are the institutional underpinnings of what appears to be a successful regional cooperation project? Would these allow us to spread the use of the mechanism and explain why and in what context similar projects can be expected to work, as observed by Deaton (2009)?

Readers not familiar with Central America may be unaware that an institutional structure for regional integration and cooperation has existed in the area since the early 1950s, though with important subsequent institutional reforms. The current institutional setting, which dates from the early 1990s, is led by a supranational body called the Central American Integration System (SICA) and its sectoral bodies, which include the intergovernmental political and policy mechanism run by member countries' ministers (COMISCA), which is served by an executive secretariat. COMISCA generates mandates through regional political will, and its secretariat provides general support, seeks international cooperation, and, most importantly, generates technical capacity and follows up on the implementation of the mandates. In our view, those institutional

Table 5.1 Joint Negotiation Results 2010–2015

	2010	2012	2013	2014	2015 (estimated)	2010–2015
Number of Medications Subject to Negotiation	37	66	16	22	21	
Number of Procured Medications	15	19	6	13	18	
Regional Savings (US$)	$10,340,000	$7,993,716	$1,606,214	$2,900,993	$12,900,000	**$35,740,923**

Source: COMISCA (2016).

underpinnings were fundamental to the success of this RPG project and in distributing the RPG's benefits. We wonder whether the generation of an RPG of this caliber would be possible with only a network of countries' policy makers with the support of *ad hoc* experts. We need to know more to explore the external validity of the lessons offered by this RPG for other contexts.

Beyond the accumulated and current savings due to this effective procurement system, higher drug quality, and the contribution of requisite institutions, it would be interesting to apply impact evaluation methodologies to assess the project's real impact and draw lessons from the protocol itself for future RPG projects, being mindful, however, of the limitations of scaling up (Deaton 2009; Nadel and Pritchett 2016). Specifically, we propose a comparative study be conducted that includes treatment and control groups. Those drugs that have been included in the negotiation would be part of the treatment group, and similar medicines that have not been included in the agreement would be part of the control group. This counterfactual would allow one to assess what would have happened in terms of drug prices and savings in the absence of the protocol. The internal validity provided by this type of randomized control trial (RCT) analysis will provide robust arguments for continuing to engage traditional donors in such projects though it may not be sufficient for learning why it is working, as demanded by RCT skeptics. Figure 5.4 provides a graphic illustration of the proposed impact evaluation in parallel with network and institutional analysis.

There are several reasons for undertaking this type of evaluation. First and foremost, it is important to ensure that the RPG improves Central Americans' wellbeing through medicine procurement savings in the region's

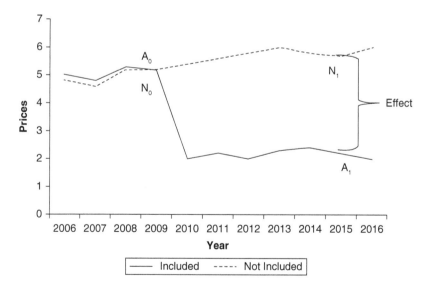

Figure 5.4 Proposed Impact Study.

public hospitals. This would also free up budget resources to buy either larger quantities of medicines or procure other goods or services for the subregion's health systems. Second, the IDB needs to know the real impact of its investment beyond the protocol and assess the institutional underpinnings so it can draw lessons for the formulation of future RPG projects in LAC. As explained in the introduction to this chapter, four reasons stand out to carry on such evaluations: the adoption of measuring development results by the aid community; social demand for them; consolidation of SSC; and the decline of aid to LAC countries.

There is thus an overdue need for LAC countries to find new, innovative ways of continuing to engage with traditional donors. Showing the development impact of their SSC may attract the interest of traditional donors to engage LAC countries in triangular cooperation both in LAC itself and in other geographical contexts. Additionally, if RPG projects show high development impact they could benefit from traditional donors as key strategic partners, provided that the benefit spillovers of the RPG projects are above national norms and their potential and actual development impact can be demonstrated. This chapter now proposes the most salient issues for assessing RPG development impact, starting with network analysis but including further steps such as robust project monitoring and evaluation, as well as ways of measuring actual development impact through RCTs and beyond to find out why RPG projects work and in which contexts.

Main issues in the impact evaluation of regional public goods

Network analysis has been broadly used in the social sciences as a methodology derived from the physical sciences that focuses on interactions, flows, and relationships between different actors inside a network (Borgati et al. 2009). Network analysis has indeed been very useful for the understanding and practice of international relations and regional cooperation. Network research has mainly focused on the consequences of networks and uses graphic language to represent individuals (or aggregations of individuals) as "nodes" (points in the network) and their relationships or links with other individuals as lines (Vera and Schupp 2006). Berg and Horrall's (2008) work on applied network analysis techniques for the study RPGs will be particularly relevant to the proposed exercise since the authors explore how networks of sector regulatory agencies create RPGs to provide a variety of goods, such as data for benchmarking, handbooks on regulatory best practices, studies, and sponsored meetings. Jordana and Sancho (2005) found, among other conclusions, that network analysis cannot, however, explain the political decisions taken but it places decision-making processes in context by setting out why some policy options were eventually adopted while others were not even contemplated. This type of approach to network analysis may prove useful as a necessary step for evaluating RPGs but, in our view, it will not be sufficient.

Although the outcomes of network studies provide a powerful tool for graphically representing variables and scenarios, they have been criticized by skeptics for being merely descriptive and for lacking an explanation of the causality mechanisms that connect the independent and dependent variables that we deem important to assessing why RPG projects work. The same question of causality sets impact evaluation apart from other monitoring and evaluation approaches. The case of the Central American Pharmaceutical Protocol presented above, however, seems to concur with such skeptical views on the limits of network analysis and on the ability of networks alone to assess high development impact projects such as the protocol. Most RPG projects in the IDB inventory, beyond the wealth of interaction assessment shown by network analysis, also require a focus on progress indicators for evaluating project outcomes and assessing the effectiveness of implementation and execution, as outlined by Khandker, Koolwal, and Samad (2010). The following cost-benefit analysis conducted by a smallpox eradication program coordinated by the World Health Organization (WHO) illustrates the point. Once the smallpox was eradicated, the impact study showed that the ratios of benefits to costs were impressive.[17] The total expenditure on eradication was around US$298 million, and the total annual benefit was estimated to be US$ 1,420 million. These benefits are not only the prevented number of deaths but also vaccination costs and the cost of illness (Fenner et al. 1988; Barrett 2007).

However, to assess the full range of benefits at the national scale during the implementation of an RPG, one final step needs to be added. Banerjee and Duflo (2012) argue that in order to assess the effectiveness of a policy or program, the behavior of comparable groups facing different levels of exposure to the program or subsidy need to be observed. To do so, they suggest adapting RCTs conducted by medical science to test new drugs. Impact evaluation can be implemented with both quantitative and qualitative methods as well as with ex-ante and ex-post methods. Nevertheless, the evaluation work carried out by Banerjee, Duflo, and the MIT Poverty Action Lab associates tends to focus on the impact of national public goods. For RPGs, it would be necessary to zoom in from the RPGs themselves to their national implementation, as RPG impact evaluation aimed at measuring benefits at the national level is still quite scarce. Having said that, however, Deaton's (2009) and Nadel and Pritchett's (2016) caveats to RCTs apply when assessing why an RPG is successfully applied in some countries and not in others. Barrett (2007) points to cases that include tsunami warnings, disease eradication (malaria, for example), and climate change adaptation that could be addressed through a global public goods approach that may be instrumental when applying the proposed evaluation exercise to RPGs.

Perhaps one of the few RPGs in developing countries that was a result of regional cooperation and that conducted an impact evaluation within its results framework was the Asian Development Bank's project to combat dengue in the ASEAN subregion of Cambodia and Lao PDR in 2009, using pilot strategies for mosquito larval control and source reduction. One of the main components of the project was the introduction of a larvae-eating guppy fish in domestic water containers within a strategy of health education and community mobilization. The project design established a treatment group (where project activities were conducted and indicators measured) and a control group (where no intervention took place but the same indicators were measured) in each country, including monthly visits and four quarterly surveys. The evaluation found that 88% of surveyed containers in Cambodia and 76% in Lao PDR had at least one guppy fish, 80% of all district health staff and primary school teachers were trained, and by the end of the intervention, less than 3% of containers in Cambodian households contained larvae.[18]

Nevertheless, moving toward rigorous empirical evaluation/experimentation would not necessarily mean that results can be easily scaled up, as mentioned above. An "external validity" problem can arise when trying to generalize results to other settings (Deaton 2009; Nadel and Pritchett 2016; and Rodrik 2008). In the case of RPG projects, the external validity problem is relevant in two dimensions. The first concerns learning from countries that successfully applied and sustained the national implementation of an RPG, and the second concerns the generation of new RPGs in other sectors or regions.

Concerned about learning "what works" by using RCTs, Nadel and Pritchett (2016) point out that "the devil may really be in the details," meaning that systematic project reviews do not tend to take into account the high variability of project design or the "high dimensional space" between programs and thus the possibility of having many different outcomes. In other words, every RCT exercise faces the challenge of a broad variability in project design leading to many possible outcomes of that program. Therefore, these possible differences within the same kind of program (for example, conditional cash transfers) could pose construct validity issues when trying to learn from the RCT exercises to learn from their results and scale up the program or implement it in other similar contexts.

These methodological concerns are not against the idea of taking a step further on RPG impact evaluation, and shedding the light on what kind of programs work, but instead should be taken into account in the evaluation design when trying to learn from why the work and in what contexts.

Conclusions

This chapter posed the question of whether regional standards could be above national norms. The answer is mixed. On the one hand, regional cooperation has a tendency to take place at the weakest link level when countries converge to the limited institutional and financial capacities of the weakest contribution to the production of an RPG. On the other hand, and more often than is documented, regional cooperation outcomes are also generated in the best shot/better shot range, whereby the highest-quality contribution determines the good's aggregate level or has the greatest influence on the outcome. These RPGs are above the national norm, at least for most of the countries participating in specific regional cooperation efforts. An examination of the project inventory for the IDB RPG Initiative initially shows that countries' policy makers establish transnational coalitions in order to pool regional knowledge to overcome their countries' capacity limits, prevent backtracking from regulatory reforms, or overcome national political economy-related resistance to them.

After assessing the IDB RPG Initiative against the backdrop of the properties of public goods and aggregation technologies in their production, this chapter showed that, in many instances, countries' policy makers also engage in regional cooperation to reach higher regulatory summits. Those summits may be achieved through convergence to best-shot standards in specific market segments or through innovative environmental and labor standards in RTAs. They may also aim higher altogether by establishing new regional standards that are above the national norms of the countries contributing to RPGs.

To illustrate a case of a "higher regulatory summit" that is above the national norms of the contributing countries, the chapter presented the Central American Protocol for Drug Procurement and Quality Control, an RPG supported by the IDB between 2008 and 2012 that remains in full operation to this day and that has generated estimated regional savings of around US$36 million, among other achievements. Such positive regional cooperation outcomes pose the question of whether this experience can be replicated, due to the specific intergovernmental and supranational mechanisms that underpin it. They also encourage evaluation efforts, not just for this protocol but also for a selection of other projects from the IDB RPG inventory, so that lessons can be drawn regarding the implementation of RPGs in national contexts and the future generation of RPGs within LAC and in other regions.

To initiate the RPG evaluation efforts we propose that impact evaluation techniques be used to assess the development impact of regional cooperation building on existing methodologies such as M&E and network analysis. This empirical research agenda should also focus on the national enforcement of regional regulatory convergence, as well as on its potential national spillovers. The evaluation endeavors are needed to position regional cooperation within the mainstream of development results assessment utilized by the international development cooperation community, and to respond to the growing social interest for accountability of development cooperation in general as well as the need to show the development effectiveness of SSC.

Annex

Table 5.A1 IDB-Funded RPG Projects: Capital Markets and Financial Institutions

Project Name	Field	Current Approved Amount (in US$)	Status	Participating Countries
Strengthening and Harmonization of the Resolution Banking Process in CA	Capital Markets and Financial Institutions	737,376.73	Completed	CR, DR, ES, GU, HO, NI, PN
Broadband Development for Competitiveness and Integration	Capital Markets and Financial Institutions	724,879.12	Completed	CR, ES, GU, HO, PN
BPR 27: Improvement of the Public Debt Management and Knowledge	Capital Markets and Financial Institutions	500,000	Completed	AR, BA, BE, BH, BO, BR, CH, CO, DR, ES, GU, GY, HA, HO, JA, MX, NI, PE, PN, PR, SU, TT, UR, VE
BPR 19: Strengthening of the Regional Stock Market	Capital Markets and Financial Institutions	189,880.92	Completed	AR, BO, BR, CH, CO, CR, EC, ES, MX, PE, PN, UR, VE
Generación de conocimiento y fortalecimiento de capacidades institucionales para el manejo de riesgos asociados al financiamiento de naturaleza público-privada en países de América Latina y el Caribe	Capital Markets and Financial Institutions	850,000	Disbursement	BR, CO, CR, GU, HO, PE, PR, UR

(continued)

Table 5.A1 (continued)

Project Name	Field	Current Approved Amount (in US$)	Status	Participating Countries
Cumplimiento regional de los Principios Globales para Entidades del Mercado Financiero	Capital Markets and Financial Institutions	306,815.35	Disbursement	AR, BA, BO, BR, CH, CO, CR, DR, ES, GU, JA, ME, PE, PN, PR, UR
Financial Integration Latin America: Realities, Challenges, Strategic Proposals	Capital Markets and Financial Institutions	850,000	Disbursement	BR, CH, CO, PE
MILA: Challenges for the Consolidation of a Broader and Inclusive Stock Market	Capital Markets and Financial Institutions	1,100,000	Disbursement	CH, CO, PE
Broadband Infrastructure and Public Awareness in the Caribbean	Capital Markets and Financial Institutions	840,000	Disbursement	BA, DR, GY, HA, JA, SU, TT
Public Debt Management in LAC Countries (LAC Debt Group)	Capital Markets and Financial Institutions	500,000	Disbursement	AR, BA, BH, BR, CH, CO, CR, DR, ES, GU, GY, JA, NI, PE, PN, PR, SU, TT, UR
Financial Stability and Development Group	Capital Markets and Financial Institutions	1,150,000	Disbursement	BO, BR, CO, PE, UR

Table 5.A2 IDB-Funded RPG Projects: Competitiveness and Innovation

Project Name	Field	Current Approved Amount (in US$)	Status	Participating Countries
Strengthening CLARA Academic Network	Competitiveness and Innovation	567,483.32	Completed	AR, BO, BR, CH, CO, CR, EC, ES, GU, HO, MX, NI, PE, PN, UR, VE
Micro SME Regional System for the Public Policy Design	Competitiveness and Innovation	537,721.9	Completed	AR, BR, CH
Development of a Caribbean Broadband Network c@ribNET	Competitiveness and Innovation	596,068.87	Completed	BA, BH, DR, GY, HA, JA, SU, TT
Regional Regulatory Policy to Consolidate Telecommunications in the PPP	Competitiveness and Innovation	1,110.14	Completed	BE, CO, CR, ES, GU, HO, MX, NI, PN
Accreditation of Architecture and Engineering Programs in CA	Competitiveness and Innovation	375,671.26	Completed	BE, CR, ES, GU, HO, NI, PN
Entrepreneurship and Technological Innovation Regional Program	Competitiveness and Innovation	707,559.12	Completed	AR, BR, CH, UR
Regional Protocols on Telehealth Public Policy	Competitiveness and Innovation	841,867.59	Completed	AR, BO, BR, CH, CO, CR, EC, ES, GU, GY, MX, PE, PN, SU, UR, VE
Plan of Action for Roaming Services in Mobile Telecommunications	Competitiveness and Innovation	730,950	Completed	AR, BO, BR, CO, MX, PE, UR
Cooperation System on Operational Information and Industrial Property	Competitiveness and Innovation	712,947.83	Completed	AR, BR, CH, CO, EC, PE, PR, SU, UR

(continued)

Table 5.A2 (continued)

Project Name	Field	Current Approved Amount (in US$)	Status	Participating Countries
Institutional Framework for Scientific Publications	Competitiveness and Innovation	591,234.22	Completed	AR, BR, CH, CO, EC, MX, PE, VE
Regional Program of Using of Satellite Information for Agricultural Production	Competitiveness and Innovation	650,000	Completed	AR, CH, PR, UR
Micro SME Regional Information for Central America	Competitiveness and Innovation	982,023.46	Completed	BE, CR, ES, GU, HO, NI, PN
Strengthening National Metrology Institutes in the Hemisphere in Support of Emergencies	Competitiveness and Innovation	700,000	Disbursement	BA, BO, BR, CH, CO, CR, DR, EC, GU, PE, PN, PR, SU, TT, UR
Building an Innovation and Entrepreneurship Ecosystem	Competitiveness and Innovation	700,000	Disbursement	CH, CO, PE
Sistema integral regional de información satelital para mejorar la productividad y la prevención de riesgos productivos y ambientales	Competitiveness and Innovation	700,000	Disbursement	AR, CH, EC, ME, PE, PR, UR
Caribbean Regional Entrepreneurial Assets Commercialization Hub	Competitiveness and Innovation	900,000	Disbursement	BA, BE, BH, GY, HA, JA, SU, TT
Strengthening of Cooperation between IP Offices in South America PROSUR II	Competitiveness and Innovation	900,000	Disbursement	AR, BR, CH, CO, EC, PE, UR

Table 5.A3 IDB-Funded RPG Projects: Education

Project Name	Field	Current Approved Amount (in US$)	Status	Participating Countries
Evaluation and Development of Regional System of Citizen Competitions	Education	1,529,323.39	Completed	CH, CO, DR, GU, MX, PR
Regional Engineering Accreditation System for the Greater Caribbean Region	Education	563,124.93	Completed	DR, JA, PN
Common Framework for a Literacy Survey	Education	575,239.85	Completed	BA, BE, BH, GY, HA, JA, SU, TT
Learning in the Schools of the 21st Century	Education	1,398,072.91	Completed	AR, BA, CH, CO, CR, DR, HO, MX, PR
BPR 35: Latin American Network of Education Portals	Education	2,121,144.68	Completed	AR, BO, BR, CH, CO, CR, EC, ES, GU, HO, MX, NI, PE, PN, PR, UR, VE
Innovation and Research Laboratory in Education for Latin America	Education	950,000	Disbursement	BR, CO, EC, PE, UR
School Learning in the Twenty-First Century—Second Phase	Education	1,000,000	Disbursement	AR, BA, CH, CO, CR, DR, GU, HO, JA, TT
Action Plan to Develop Citizen Competencies for the Schools in LAC	Education	600,000	Disbursement	CO, CR
MERCOSUR Higher Education Accreditation System	Education	0		AR, BO, BR, CH, PR, UR, VE

Table 5.A4 IDB-Funded RPG Projects: Energy

Project Name	Field	Current Approved Amount (in US$)	Status	Participating Countries
Regional Information System for Energy	Energy	705,884.92	Completed	AR, BR, CH, CO, CR, DR, EC, ES, GU, GY, HO, JA, MX, NI, PE, PN, PR, UR
Programa para el fortalecimiento de la gestión y difusión de información energética para el desarrollo sostenible en América Latina y el Caribe	Energy	850,000	Disbursement	AR, BE, BO, CO, CR, DR, EC, HO, PN, PR, UR
Caribbean Hotel Energy Efficiency and Renewable Energy Action—Advanced Program	Energy	2,000,000	Disbursement	BA, BE, BH, DR, GU, HA, JA, SU, TT

Table 5.A5 IDB-Funded RPG Projects: Climate Change, Rural Development, and Risk Management

Project Name	Field	Current Approved Amount (in US$)	Status	Participating Countries
Climatic Information Applied to Management of Risk in Agriculture for Andean Community	Climate Change, Rural Development and Risk Management	785,000	Completed	BO, CH, CO, EC, PE, VE
Regional Disaster Risk Management for Sustainable Tourism in the Caribbean	Climate Change, Rural Development and Risk Management	757,959.31	Completed	BA, BE, BH, DR, GY, HA, JA, SU, TT
Regional Information System for Agriculture Development of Southern Cone Countries	Climate Change, Rural Development and Risk Management	679,009.82	Completed	AR, BO, BR, CH, PR, UR
Management of the Trinational Selva Maya Ecosystem (ME-GU-BE)	Climate Change, Rural Development and Risk Management	800,000	Completed	BE, GU, MX
Central America Climatic Data Base	Climate Change, Rural Development and Risk Management	423,718.19	Completed	BE, CR, ES, GU, HO, NI, PN
Program to Eradicate the Cattle Screwworm in MERCOSUR Countries	Climate Change, Rural Development and Risk Management	991,965.59	Completed	AR, BR, PR, UR
Monitoring and Evaluation Biodiversity Program for Central America	Climate Change, Rural Development and Risk Management	642,208.73	Completed	BE, CR, ES, NI, PN
Capacities to Improve the Competitiveness of Caribbean Agricultural Sector	Climate Change, Rural Development and Risk Management	399,341.95	Completed	BA, DR, GY, SU, TT
Management System Fishery Resources in the East Tropical Pacific Marine Corridor	Climate Change, Rural Development and Risk Management	727,562.46	Completed	CO, CR, PN

(continued)

Table 5.A5 (continued)

Project Name	Field	Current Approved Amount (in US$)	Status	Participating Countries
Central American System for Disaster Management	Climate Change, Rural Development and Risk Management	767,713.71	Completed	BE, CO, CR, ES, GU, HO, MX, NI, PN
Harmonized System of Bovine Traceability in Central America, Belize, Panama, and Dominican Republic	Climate Change, Rural Development and Risk Management	1,167,405.36	Completed	BE, CR, DR, ES, GU, HO, NI, PN
Monitoring and Evaluation Framework for Disaster Risk Management in Tourism Sector	Climate Change, Rural Development and Risk Management	342,781.65	Completed	BA, BE, BH, DR, GY, HA, JA, SU, TT
Climate Change and Biodiversity Information in the Tropical Andes	Climate Change, Rural Development and Risk Management	477,713.69	Completed	BO, EC, PE
Incentives for the Conservation of Natural Grazing Lands in the Southern Cone	Climate Change, Rural Development and Risk Management	750,000	Completed	AR, BR, PR, UR
Regional Forest Health System for the Southern Corn Countries	Climate Change, Rural Development and Risk Management	628,297.48	Completed	AR, BO, BR, CH, PR, UR
Database Management System for a Regional Integrated Observing Network for Environment	Climate Change, Rural Development and Risk Management	600,000	Completed	BA, BE, BH, GY, HA, JA, SU, TT

Project	Category	Amount	Status	Countries
BPR 38: Sustainable Management of Amazon Biodiversity	Climate Change, Rural Development and Risk Management	1,859,257.18	Completed	BO, BR, CO, EC, GY, PE, SU, VE
BPR 13: Plan Trifinio Trinational Commission	Climate Change, Rural Development and Risk Management	826,240.05	Completed	ES, GU, HO
Instrumentación del Sistema Mesoamericano de Información Territorial (SMIT) para la gestión de riesgos de desastres—Red Mesoamericana para la Gestión Integral del Riesgo (RM-GIR)	Climate Change, Rural Development and Risk Management	600,000	Disbursement	BE, CO, DR, ES, GU, HO, ME, PN
Institutional Strengthening for Improving Competitiveness of Fruit Production in CA and DR	Climate Change, Rural Development and Risk Management	655,000	Disbursement	CR, DR, ES, GU, HO, NI, PN
Ampliación de los municipios atendidos por el mecanismo regional para la gestión integral del riesgo y adopción del blindaje climático en la infraestructura pública	Climate Change, Rural Development and Risk Management	700,000	Disbursement	CR, ES, GU, PN
Regional Mechanism to Adopt Climate Protection in Public Infrastructure	Climate Change, Rural Development and Risk Management	700,000	Disbursement	ES, HO, PN

Table 5.A6 IDB-Funded RPG Projects: Fiscal and Municipal Management

Project Name	Field	Current Approved Amount (in US$)	Status	Participating Countries
Regional Strategy of Advanced Formation in Applied Economics	Fiscal and Municipal Management	354,432.63	Completed	CR, DR, ES, GU, HO, NI, PN
Governmental Purchases Policy	Fiscal and Municipal Management	650,000	Completed	AR, BA, BE, BH, BO, BR, CH, CO, CR, DR, EC, ES, GU, GY, HA, HO, JA, MX, NI, PE, PN, PR, SU, TT, UR, VE
Decentralization and Subnational Fiscal Management Network	Fiscal and Municipal Management	600,000	Disbursement	BO, BR, CH, CO, DR, GU, HO, PE, PN, UR
Metropolitan Management and Investment Capacity of Local Governments	Fiscal and Municipal Management	500,000	Disbursement	CO, ES
Strengthening the Regional Public Procurement Marketplace in the Caribbean	Fiscal and Municipal Management	600,000	Disbursement	BA, BE, BH, JA
Regional Network to Support the Housing and Urban Development Sectors in LAC	Fiscal and Municipal Management	700,000	Disbursement	BO, CH, PE
Platform for Knowledge and Innovation in Public Financial Management	Fiscal and Municipal Management	530,000	Disbursement	CR, ES, PR

Table 5.A7 IDB-Funded RPG Projects: Gender and Diversity

Project Name	Field	Current Approved Amount (in US$)	Status	Participating Countries
Conservation of the Environmental Patrimony of the Great Chaco	Gender and Diversity	153,389.32	Completed	AR, BO, PR
Natural and Cultural Aymara Heritage	Gender and Diversity	647,858.35	Completed	BO, CH, PE
Regional Framework Against Trafficking of People	Gender and Diversity	600,000	Completed	CR, ES, GU, HO, NI
Regional Strategic Framework for Protection of Non-Contacted Indigenous People	Gender and Diversity	800,000	Completed	BO, BR, CO, EC, GY, PE, PR, SU
Indigenous Peoples in the Border Region of ACTO	Gender and Diversity	500,000	Disbursement	BO, CO, EC, GY, PE, SU, VE
Coalición Latinoamericana y Caribeña contra el racismo, la discriminación y la xenofobia	Gender and Diversity	400,000	Disbursement	CO, EC, ME, UR
Protect the Traditional Ecological Knowledge of the Intellectual Property located at the border of Honduras and Guatemala	Gender and Diversity	700,000	Disbursement	GU, HO

Table 5.A8 IIDB-Funded RPG Projects: Public Institutions

Project Name	Field	Current Approved Amount (in US$)	Status	Participating Countries
Regional System of Standardized Citizen Security and Violent Prevention Indicators	Public Institutions	2,550,000	Completed	AR, BO, BR, CH, CO, CR, DR, EC, ES, GU, GY, HO, JA, MX, NI, PE, PR, UR
Trafficking of Children and Adolescents for Sex Exploitation in MERCOSUR	Public Institutions	941,177.09	Completed	AR, BR, PR, UR
Mechanism for the Professional Accreditation in Fiscal Public Control	Public Institutions	242,408.06	Completed	AR, BO, BR, CH, CO, CR, DR, EC, ES, GU, HO, MX, NI, PE, PN, PR, UR, VE
Operational Framework for Statistics	Public Institutions	973,637.46	Completed	BR, CH, CO, DR, EC, ES, HO, MX, PE, PR, UR
Regional Mechanism for Peace and Conflict Resolution	Public Institutions	471,811.59	Completed	CO, CR, ES, GU, PN
Caribbean Regional Tourism Satellite Account (TSA) Implementation Initiative	Public Institutions	396,521.51	Completed	BA, BE, BH, GY, JA, TT
BPR 33: Improving Public Administration through E-Government Best Practices	Public Institutions	199,667.69	Completed	AR, BA, BE, BH, BO, BR, CH, CO, CR, DR, EC, ES, GU, GY, HA, HO, MX, NI, PE, PN, PR, SU, TT, UR, VE
BPR 17: Improvement of Statistics for Measuring Living Conditions	Public Institutions	1,799,675.69	Completed	AR, BO, BR, CH, CO, CR, DR, EC, ES, GU, HO, MX, NI, PE, PN, PR, UR
BPR 7: Single-based Social Security for MERCOSUR	Public Institutions	1,284,664.73	Completed	AR, BR, PR, UR

Project	Type	Amount	Status	Countries
Regional Adaptation of New International Guidelines for Measuring Labor Statistics	Public Institutions	650,000	Disbursement	EC, ES, PE, UR
Protocolos de uso de datos masivos para la eficiencia del Estado y la integración regional	Public Institutions	850,000	Disbursement	AR, CH, CO, ME, UR
Development of Methodology for the Implementation of Agricultural Statistics	Public Institutions	1,150,000	Disbursement	BR, CO, PR
Population and Property Statistics Using Administrative Records in Andean Countries	Public Institutions	700,000	Disbursement	BO, CO, EC, PE
Development and Strengthening of Official Environmental Statistics	Public Institutions	1,300,000	Disbursement	BA, CO, CR, DR, JA, MX, PN, SU, VE
Mechanism for Regional Cooperation on Public Software	Public Institutions	500,000	Disbursement	AR, BR, CO, CR, DR, EC, ES, PR, UR, VE
Regional Evaluation System of the Impact of Public Policies in Security for LAC	Public Institutions	1,250,000	Disbursement	AR, CH, CO, CR, ES, HO, MX, UR
Common Framework for Population Census in CARICOM	Public Institutions	473,925.47	Completed	BA, BE, BH, GY, HA, JA, SU, TT
Crecimiento económico y productividad en América Latina: LA-KLEMS	Public Institutions	850,000	Disbursement	BR, CH, CO, CR, DR, ES, ME, PE

Table 5.A9 IDB-Funded RPG Projects: Labor Markets

Project Name	Field	Current Approved Amount (in US$)	Status	Participating Countries
Regional Framework Protection, Monitoring and Registration of Migrant Workers in LAC	Labor Markets	417,194.53	Completed	AR, BO, BR, CH, CO, CR, DR, EC, ES, GU, GY, HO, NI, PE, PN, PR, UR
Longitudinal Social Protection Survey (LSPS)	Labor Markets	1,163,580.49	Completed	CO, CR, EC, ES, HO, MX, PR, UR
Consolidation of the Longitudinal Social Protection Survey	Labor Markets	1,000,000	Disbursement	BR, CO, EC, ES, PR, UR
Regional Strategy for a Citizenry with a Culture of Social Security	Labor Markets	1,000,000	Disbursement	AR, BE, BH, BO, BR, CH, CO, CR, DR, EC, ES, GU, HA, HO, MX, PE, PN, PR, UR

Table 5.A10 IDB-Funded RPG Projects: Development Cooperation

Project Name	Field	Current Approved Amount (in US$)	Status	Participating Countries
Sistema de información para la cooperación internacional	Development Cooperation	500,000	Disbursement	CH, CR, PN

Table 5.A11 IDB-Funded RPG Projects: Social Protection and Health

Project Name	Field	Current Approved Amount (in US$)	Status	Participating Countries
Regional Program Control of the Disease of Chagas in LA	Social Protection and Health	661,165.88	Completed	AR, BO, CO, EC, ES, GU, HO, NI, PR, UR
Central American Protocol for Procurement and Quality Control of Medicines	Social Protection and Health	607,383.57	Completed	BE, CR, DR, ES, GU, HO, NI, PN
Regional Non-Communicable Diseases Surveillance System	Social Protection and Health	593,400.52	Completed	BA, BE, BH, GY, JA, TT
Environmental Health Surveillance System in the Amazon Region	Social Protection and Health	865,825.39	Completed	BO, BR, CO, EC, GY, PE, SU, VE
Regional Framework to control Youth Contagious Diseases	Social Protection and Health	267,857.22	Completed	AR, BR, PR, UR
Food Fortification with Folic Acid and Other Micro-Nutrients	Social Protection and Health	1,296,754.02	Completed	BE, CR, DR, ES, GU, HO, NI, PN
Regional Collaboration Initiative for the Management of Integrated Health Network	Social Protection and Health	650,000	Disbursement	CH, CO
Regional Tourism Health Information, Monitoring and Response Systems and Standard	Social Protection and Health	800,000	Disbursement	BA, BH, GY, JA
Proyecto para la creación de un Programa regional de gestión estratégica de emergencias epidemiológicas	Social Protection and Health	600,000	Disbursement	BO, CH, CO, PE

Project	Sector	Amount	Type	Countries
Fortalecimiento de competencias y capacidades para la seguridad sanitaria regional en el Caribe	Social Protection and Health	500,000	Disbursement	BE, GY, JA
Regional Cooperation for the Management of High-cost Medications	Social Protection and Health	543,279	Disbursement	CH, CR, ES, PE
Network for the Development of Electronic Medical Records (EMR) in LAC	Social Protection and Health	700,000	Disbursement	CH, CO, UR
Prevention and Control of Micronutrient Deficiencies in Central America	Social Protection and Health	600,000	Disbursement	CR, DR, ES, GU, HO, NI, PN
Regional Framework to Promote Interventions for At-Risk Youth	Social Protection and Health	900,000	Disbursement	BR, PR, UR
Regional Instruments for Adaptation to Climate Change by the Health Sector	Social Protection and Health	900,000	Disbursement	BO, BR, CO, MX, PR
Regional Observatory to Improve the Efficiency in Managing Pharmaceuticals	Social Protection and Health	500,000	Disbursement	CO, EC
Information and Knowledge System for the Design of Public Policy	Social Protection and Health	750,000	Disbursement	AR, CH, UR
Regional Protocol of Epidemiology in Border Zones	Social Protection and Health	800,000	Disbursement	AR, PR, UR

Table 5.A12 IDB-Funded RPG Projects: Trade and Investment

Project Name	Field	Current Approved Amount (in US$)	Status	Participating Countries
Advisory Facility on Investor-State Dispute Settlement	Trade and Investment	297,913.21	Completed	CO, CR, DR, ES, GU, HO, MX, NI, PE, PN
Common Framework for Statistics Production in CARICOM	Trade and Investment	349,294.89	Completed	BA, BE, BH, GY, HA, JA, SU, TT
Central America Competitiveness Program for Fruits	Trade and Investment	799,546.59	Completed	BE, CR, DR, ES, GU, HO, NI, PN
Institutional and Normative Framework for a Regional Competence Policy	Trade and Investment	443,925.42	Completed	CR, ES, GU, HO, NI, PN
Regional Strategy for Management and Trade of Chemical Products	Trade and Investment	296,256.1	Completed	AR, BR, CH, PR, UR
Reg. strategy for regulation and supervision of the Central American stock market	Trade and Investment	290,165.2	Completed	CR, ES, PN
Regional System of Methodical Information for the LAD Services Sector	Trade and Investment	497,574.02	Completed	AR, BO, BR, CH, CO, CR, EC, ES, GU, MX, NI, PE, PN, PR, UR
Observatory of Firm Entrepreneurship and Regional Productive Integration	Trade and Investment	752,378.36	Completed	AR, BR, PR, UR
Latin American Regional Network To Strengthen Competition Policy	Trade and Investment	1,180,000	Completed	AR, CH, CO, CR, DR, EC, ES, GU, HO, MX, NI, PE

Estrategia regional para promover las inversiones en América Latina, medir el impacto de las Organizaciones de Promoción Comercial en promoción de exportaciones e inversiones y desarrollar herramientas regionales para promover las exportaciones	Trade and Investment	500,000	Disbursement	CO, EC, UR
Support to Promote Interoperability of Foreign Trade Single Windows	Trade and Investment	900,000	Disbursement	CH, CO, CR, PE
Greenhouse Gas Inventory for Exporting Companies in Central America	Trade and Investment	500,000	Disbursement	CR, GU, NI
Support to Foreign Direct Investment in the Caribbean	Trade and Investment	900,000	Disbursement	BA, DR, GY, HA, JA, TT
Regional Platform to Coordinate and Promote the Export of Audio-visual Services	Trade and Investment	430,000	Disbursement	BO, CO, EC, PE, UR
Regional Strategy of Export Promotion and Investment Attraction	Trade and Investment	700,000	Disbursement	AR, BO, BR, CH, CO, CR, DR, EC, ES, GU, MX, NI, PE, PN, PR, UR
Unleashing the Potential of Diaspora Direct Investment in Central America	Trade and Investment	750,000	Disbursement	CR, DR, ES, NI
Continuous Monitoring System for Regional Integration in LAC	Trade and Investment	850,000	Disbursement	BR, CH, DR, EC, PE, PR, UR

Table 5.A13 IDB-Funded RPG Projects: Transportation

Project Name	Field	Current Approved Amount (in US$)	Status	Participating Countries
Mesoamerican Observatory on Freight Transport and Logistics	Transportation	723,201.31	Completed	BE, CO, CR, DR, ES, GU, HO, MX, NI, PN
Transport GenderLab: Banco de iniciativas para integrar la perspectiva de género	Transportation	600,000	Disbursement	AR, CO, EC, ME
Implementation Support for Vehicle Safety Standards in Latin America and the Car	Transportation	1,250,000	Disbursement	AR, BR, EC
Comprehensive Strategy for the Use of Bicycles in Latin America Cities	Transportation	650,000	Disbursement	AR, BR, CO

Table 5.A14 IDB-Funded RPG Projects: Water and Sanitation

Project Name	Field	Current Approved Amount (in US$)	Status	Participating Countries
Nodo tecnológico para la competitividad regional: cadena de valor para la gestión integral de residuos sólidos	Water and Sanitation	650,000	Disbursement	CR, GU, HO

Notes

1 Paris Declaration on Aid Effectiveness (2005), Accra Agenda for Action (2008) www.oecd.org/dac/effectiveness/parisdeclarationandaccraagendaforaction.htm; The Busan Partnership for Development Cooperation (2011) www.oecd.org/development/effectiveness/busanpartnership.htm; and The Sustainable Development Goals (17) www.globalgoals.org/global-goals/partnerships-for-the-goals/
2 IDB Regional Public Goods Initiative: www.iadb.org/en/topics/regional-integration/what-is-the-regional-public-goods-program,2803.html
3 www.unmillenniumproject.org/goals/
4 For a helpful review of aggregation technologies and typologies with the examples see Sandler (2005), Table 5.1.
5 www.iadb.org/en/topics/regional-integration/what-is-the-regional-public-goods-initiative,2803.html
6 For a useful distinction between the old and new regionalism, see Hettne and Soderbaum (2006) and Table 5.1.
7 The COMISCA (2016) report proposed expanding the use of the Central American Pharmaceutical Protocol to other sectors.
8 The eight SICA member countries took part in the negotiation rounds of 2015. See also Pérez (2015).
9 The concept of the "summit" is often used in international relations, where it builds on Galtung's definition of "important meetings, events and other sort of diplomacy between two or more head of states" (Galtung 1964) to illustrate regulation that is of a higher quality than national standards in determined groups of countries, as is used in Larrain (2014).
10 Summation aggregation technology describes the overall level of the public good as being equal to the sum of countries' contributions, while the weighted sum describes the overall level of the public good as being equal to the weighted sum of countries' contributions (Sandler 2005, Table 5.1).
11 Guillermo Larrain was the senior advisor to the IDB-supported RPG on financial integration led by Brazil Investimentos e Negocios (BRAiN).
12 These standards were defined by the World Forum for Harmonization of Vehicle Regulations, and are referred to as WP.29. WP.29 is a permanent working party in the institutional framework of the United Nations (UN) with a specific mandate and rules of procedure. It works as a global forum allowing open discussions on motor vehicle regulations. Any member country of the UN and any regional economic integration organization set up by member countries of the UN may participate fully in the activities of the World Forum and may become a contracting party to the agreements on vehicles administered by the World Forum.
13 Belize, Costa Rica, Dominican Republic, El Salvador, Guatemala, Honduras, Nicaragua, and Panama.
14 The COMISCA Subregional Technical Commission on Drugs (CTSM) also takes part in the process.
15 This means that companies start offering at a reference price, and then subsequently offer a lower price, until the lowest price wins.
16 In many developing countries, drug quality is a public health issue due to insufficient quality enforcement controls, and Central America was no exception. The protocol established minimum quality standards to ensure the medicines would be medically effective in public hospitals.
17 The benefit-cost ratio was 159:1 if all costs are included and 483:1 if international finance only is counted (Barrett 2007).

---

18 The per person cost of the project was US$2–5 (training and dissemination activities), and US$0.2 for guppy fish breeding and management. Additional information about this project can be found at ADB (2012).

References

ADB (Asian Development Bank). 2012. "Regional Public Goods for Health: Combating Dengue in ASEAN." Technical Assistance Completion Report, ADB Human and Social Development Division. www.adb.org/sites/default/files/project-document/74703/42190-012-reg-tcr.pdf

Baghdadi, L., I. Martinez-Zarzoso, and H. Zitouna. 2013. "Are RTA Agreements with Environmental Provisions Reducing Emissions?" *Journal of International Economics* 90, no. 2: 378–390.

Banerjee, A., and E. Duflo. 2012. *Poor Economics: A Radical Rethinking of the Way to Fight Global Poverty*. New York: Public Affairs.

Barrett, S. 2007. *Why Cooperate? The Incentive to Supply Global Public Goods*. Oxford: Oxford University Press.

Berg, S. V., and J. Horrall. 2008. "Networks of Regulatory Agencies as Regional Public Goods: Improving Infrastructure Performance." *The Review of International Organizations* 3, no. 2: 179–200.

Borgatti, S., A. Mehra, D. Brass, and G. Labianca. 2009. "Network Analysis in the Social Sciences." *Science* 323, no. 5916: 892–895.

COMISCA. 2016. Negociación Conjunta de Precios y Compra de Medicamentos para Centroamérica y República Dominica: Una Mirada desde la perspectiva de Salud Internacional. El Salvador: COMISCA.

Deaton, A. S. 2009. "Instruments of Development: Randomization in the Tropics, and the Search for the Elusive Keys to Economic Development." NBER Working Paper 14690. Cambridge, MA: NBER.

Dewan, S., and L. Ronconi. 2014. "US Free Trade Agreements and Enforcement of Labor Law in Latin America." IDB Working Paper Series No. IDB-WP-543. Washington, DC: Inter-American Development Bank.

Estache, A. and L. Wren-Lewis. 2009. "Toward a Theory of Regulation for Developing Countries: Following Jean-Jacques Laffont's Lead." *Journal of Economic Literature* 47, no. 3: 729–770.

Estevadeordal, A., B. Frantz, and T. R. Nguyen. (2004). *Regional Public Goods: From Theory to Practice*. Washington, DC: IDB and ADB.

Fenner, F., D. A. Henderson, I. Arita, Z. Ježek, and I. D. Ladnyi. (1987). *Smallpox and Its Eradication*. Geneva: WHO.

Galtung, J. 1964. "Summit Meetings and International Relations." *Journal of Peace Research* 1: 36–54.

Hettne, B., and F. Soderbaum. 2006. "Regional Cooperation: A Tool for Addressing Regional and Global Challenges." In *Meeting Global Challenges: International Cooperation in the National Interest. Final Report*, edited by Ernesto Zedillo and Tidjane Thiam. Stockholm: Secretariat of the International Task Force on Global Public Goods.

Jordana, J., and D. Sancho. 2005. "Policy Networks and Market Opening: Telecommunications Liberalization in Spain." *European Journal of Political Research* 44, no. 4: 519–546.

Kanbur, R., T. Sandler, and K. Morrison. 1999. *The Future of Development Assistance: Common Polls and International Public Goods.* Washington, DC: Overseas Development Council.

Khandker, S. R., G. B. Koolwal, and H. A. Samad. 2010. *Handbook on Impact Evaluation: Quantitative Methods and Practices.* Washington, DC: World Bank Publications.

Larrain, G. 2014. "Integración financiera en América Latina: realidades, desafíos y propuestas estratégicas." Iniciativa para la Promoción de Bienes Públicos Regionales, mimeo. Washington, DC: Inter-American Development Bank.

Nadel, S., and L. Pritchett. 2016. "Searching for the Devil in the Details: Learning about Development Program Design." CDG Working Paper 434. Washington, DC: Center for Global Development.

Nordhaus, W. D. 2005. "Paul Samuelson and Global Public Goods." In *Samuelsonian Economics in the Twenty-First Century,* edited by M. Szenberg, R. Lall, and A. A. Gottesman. Oxford: Oxford University Press.

OECD. 2011. Busan Partnership for Development Cooperation. www.oecd.org/development/effectiveness/busanpartnership.htm

Paris Declaration on Aid Effectiveness (2005), Accra Agenda for Action (2008) www.oecd.org/dac/effectiveness/parisdeclarationandaccraagendaforaction.htm (both references retrieved from same PDF).

Pérez, L. M. 2015. "Experiencias y oportunidades de compras conjuntas de medicamentos en Guatemala." Strengthening Health Outcomes through the Private Sector Project. Guatemala: USAID.

Rodrik, D. 2008. "The New Development Economics: We Shall Experiment, But How Shall We Learn?" HKS Faculty Research Working Papers Series. Cambridge, MA: John F. Kennedy School of Government, Harvard University.

Sandler, T. 2005. "Regional Public Goods and International Organizations." Mimeo.

Sandler, T. 2013. "Public Goods and Regional Cooperation for Development: A New Look." *INTAL Journal* 36, no. 17 (January–June).

UN Millennium Development Goals, www.unmillenniumproject.org/goals/

UN Sustainable Development Goals (17) www.globalgoals.org/global-goals/partnerships-for-the-goals/

Vera, E. R., and T. Schupp. 2006. "Network Analysis in Comparative Social Sciences." *Comparative Education* 42, no. 3: 405–429.

Part III

New frontiers in functional cooperation

6 Regional public goods
The case of migration

Uri Dadush

Introduction

The provision of public goods—activities which most people can enjoy at little or no additional cost and from which few can be excluded—are a natural province of governments. Examples of pure public goods include investments in national defense and regulations that assure clean air, and examples of partial public goods include roads and the electricity grid. These public goods can be provided at many levels, by a city, a nation, or through a regional or global arrangement involving many countries. Throughout this chapter, by "regional" I mean approaches coordinated across countries in geographic proximity to each other. What, specifically, is the role of regional arrangements in the provision of public goods? How is this role changing against the background of an ever-deepening globalization?

This chapter aims to provide an initial answer to these questions, and in so doing, it will look more closely at the example of migration as a public good—the set of institutions and policies that allow free movement of people across borders, and so make it easier to work or reside in other countries. As with trade, much migration takes place at the regional level, but while regional trade agreements (RTAs) have proliferated, the international coordination of migration has fallen far short of what might be expected. Since most migration originates in the South, the focus of the chapter is mainly on developing regions. The prospects for increased cooperation in two regions with large South–North migrant flows, the Middle East and North Africa (MENA) and Latin America and the Caribbean (LAC), will be examined in some detail.

An important message of the chapter is that, across a broad spectrum and not just in the case of migration, the ability of developing regions to provide public goods is actually quite limited and confined to very specific areas. Clearly, to fight climate change or prevent the propagation of banking crises and macroeconomic instability, a globally coordinated approach is needed, and neither a national nor a regional approach are sufficient. On the other hand, the provision of education and policing can be done at the local or national level, without much need to resort to regional approaches. If one can be clear about what the comparative advantage of regions is in relation to other levels of governance, then one can also define the conditions under which the regional provision of public goods is most likely to succeed. With rising incomes and deepening international integration, the demand for public goods is likely to increase at all levels of governance, including at the regional level, although it is unclear whether the "market share" of regions in the provision of public goods is likely to rise or decline relative to the local and global levels.

There is an obvious need for regional public goods in some contexts, such as border management, transportation, and water and energy infrastructure. There are also clear opportunities for harmonizing regulations and for striking RTAs (Perry 2014). However, there is also a tendency to hype the potential for regional cooperation. For example, in trade, recent research has found that the average preference margin in RTAs is in the vicinity of 1% (Carpenter 2011). Though there is occasionally talk of closer coordination in regional macroeconomic policy, research suggests that such coordination is difficult to achieve and that the benefits to be derived from it are small (Fischer 1987). Too often, the tendency is to unnecessarily delay necessary domestic reforms to await the conclusion of international agreements. This provides an alibi for inaction, as in the case of agricultural subsidies, where the impasse in the WTO Doha negotiations is being used to delay cuts that are needed anyway. Furthermore, there are many instances, such as trade facilitation (custom and border logistics reforms) in which by far the greatest gains emanate from domestic reforms, while reforms by regional partners represent only a secondary source of benefits.

The role of regions in providing public goods

In examining the role of regions, it is useful to think of the provision of public goods that encompass a smaller or greater share of the world's citizens. Start with a small group. Today, a critical role in providing public goods is played by cities. Cities such as São Paulo or Berlin provide those who live there—with varying degrees of success—security against theft and violence, clean streets, most business regulations, and in many instances, public utilities such as water and gas, and health and education services—altogether a compelling list of necessities. For this reason, some experts have come to think of cities as the main determinant of a competitive business climate: it is not nations, the argument goes, so much as cities that compete internationally for trade and investment or to attract the best available talent. Cities easily connect to *citi*zens: they are seen as legitimate and are also potentially the most effective way to provide many essential public goods. However, cities are not the natural providers of public goods such as security against the encroachment of hostile nations, protection against global terrorism and crime, or infrastructure to connect with the wider economy. The provision of many such public goods requires reaching across a broader space of economic activity, and so remains the role of nations or associations of nations rather than cities.

At the other end of the spectrum from cities, and involving all the world's inhabitants, is the provision of global public goods. Undertaking this role are the WTO, IMF, the UN agencies, and dozens of other universal or near-universal organizations. These institutions aim with greater or lesser degrees of success to safeguard the citizens of all their member countries against arbitrary restrictions to international trade, macroeconomic instability and financial crises, and catastrophic climate change. The role these institutions play is crucial, and, in fact, it is difficult to imagine the operation of today's increasingly interdependent world economy without them. However, compared to cities or nations, global institutions confront enormous problems of coordination, and their legitimacy is more easily challenged, especially by groups who see the provision of a public good such as free trade or financial regulation as a direct threat to their interests.

There are many layers of governance and provision of public goods in between Berlin, which addresses the needs of perhaps 5 million people, and the WTO, which addresses the needs of almost 7 billion. In between Berlin and the WTO, there is state government, national government, various bilateral arrangements, regional associations such as the European Union (EU), and links between the EU and other regional groups. Increasingly prominent are plurilateral agreements among a large subset of nations that are not necessarily contiguous and coalesce around a specific issue or interest and that extend beyond regions but do not encompass the globe. In the sphere of trade, for example, such plurilateral agreements take two forms—comprehensive, as is the case of the proposed Transatlantic Trade and Investment Partnership (TTIP) between the United States and the EU, or issue-based, such as the proposed Trade in Services Agreement (TiSA).

The different levels of governance at which public goods are provided, from the local to the regional to the global, interact constantly and can complement or substitute each other. For example, the control of carbon emissions, a global public good, requires regulation and implementation at the local and national level; national macro-prudential regulation and sound macroeconomic policies are an essential complement to global mechanisms that assure macroeconomic stability; and effective national policies and institutions can guard against instability even in the absence of international agreements or a lender of last resort.

In providing public goods, all levels of governance are required to be both effective and legitimate. The United States of America, which can be seen as the ultimate example of a long-standing and successful regional agreement and one which eventually evolved into the world's superpower, is a case in point. The US Federal government is perceived as being quite effective in providing some public goods, such as defense, but it is also seen as ineffective in others, such as in providing adequate infrastructure and a valid framework for managing immigration, which are some of the reasons that the US Congress has an approval rating of less than 10%. If anything, the European Commission, which is at the center of a federation in the making, is viewed as even less effective. A lack of effectiveness, if it persists, eventually erodes legitimacy.

Regional arrangements in a changing world

The world economy is characterized today by three well-known and closely related trends: rapid growth and a deepening globalization of developing countries; a shift in economic and political power away from the industrialized economies towards China and the large developing countries; and cumulative advances in technology, especially ICT, which are being quickly adopted throughout the world and causing a progressive intensification of these trends. To quote a few numbers, according to the World Bank, over the 20 years prior to 2012 developing countries grew in excess of 5%, about 3% faster than advanced countries, and now account for nearly half of world output at purchasing power parity exchange rates. Likewise, the world trade/GDP ratio increased from 32% to 51% over this period; and the share of the population of developing countries using the internet rose from 0% to 26%, and using cell phones from 0% to 81% (Dadush and Shaw 2010).

These seismic shifts carry implications for governance at all levels. Most clearly, global institutions are called upon to do more and better at regulating an increasingly integrated world, even as the increased dispersion of power is making coordination more difficult. But, perhaps less obviously, the pressure on institutions at the local or city level to provide high-quality public goods is also increasing. The intensification of international competition, which is an integral part of globalization, means that failure to provide adequate schools, efficient logistics, or sound business regulation has become costlier than in the past in terms of both foregone market and investment opportunities and in averting competitive threats.

The provision of public goods at the regional level is also being affected. Globalization and the spread of ICT creates new demands, such as for regional broadband networks and harmonization of e-commerce regulations, and for more effective border management. However, the new world order also creates major challenges in the provision of regional public goods, and these challenges apply quite differently across developing regions and can be examined through various dimensions.

Political and security challenges to regional cooperation have become more prominent with rapid shifts in economic power. Territorial disputes between a burgeoning China and the Philippines, Vietnam, and Japan clearly complicate the provision of public goods in the East Asian region. So does rivalry between a rising India and a lagging Pakistan in South Asia. The intensifying political turmoil across the MENA region, combined with traditional rivalries between Saudi Arabia and Iran, or Morocco and Algeria, greatly reduces the potential for collaboration in that region. The perceived fading or withdrawal of the USA as hegemon and the increasingly polycentric nature of the current system is making politics at the regional level more fluid, less predictable, and more acrimonious. This is currently most obvious in the neighborhood of Russia. However, even in Latin America, a continent where international conflicts are noticeably absent, the rise of China and the BRICS grouping, together with diminishing US influence, has strengthened the hand of those inclined to adopt heterodox policies and essentially eliminated any likelihood of a long-mooted region-wide trade deal with or without the United States.

Shifts in the structure of economies are affecting the capacity of developing regions to integrate differently and, by reflection, the demand for regional public goods is progressing at very different speeds across regions. For example, increasingly commodity dependent countries in Sub-Saharan Africa, the MENA region, and LAC have become more reliant on China and tend to buy relatively little from each other. On the other hand, large parts of the East Asia region have diversified into manufacturers and have become increasingly integrated with each other as part of global and regional value chains. A similar process of diversification and integration, but one with much stronger political underpinnings in the form of the EU, has been bringing together Western Europe and its neighbors to the east. Accordingly, the demand for trade deals and cross-border infrastructure and regulations has increased more rapidly in Eastern Europe and in East Asia than in Latin America and other developing regions.

The large technological gap that persists between developing and advanced countries and the rapid pushing out of the knowledge frontier makes development today more dependent than ever before on being in close touch with the state of the art through trade, investment, and movement of people. This makes Mexico's connections with the United States and Romania's connection with Germany, to give two examples, disproportionately more important than relations with nations that are close and of similar incomes—even large nations. Moreover, it has become easier to connect to this state-of-the art knowledge anywhere in the world. Consequently, among developing countries, the need for global connectivity in its various forms (trade, FDI, movement of people, broadband, transport infrastructure, etc.) has become as or more compelling than that for regional links.

At a time of such rapid change in technology, markets, and competition, the provision of public goods is also facing great administrative and collaborative challenges, as well as the need to respond quickly and not get bogged down in coordination problems such as demand shifts. Comparing the different levels of governance, this gives a greater advantage to institutions at the local, city, or national level even when the ideal would be to provide public goods at the global or regional level. For example, to avoid hub-and-spoke effects, ideally trade integration between MENA and the EU or between LAC and the USA would take the form of concurrent integration within MENA and LAC. However, the complexity of negotiating such intraregional agreements makes it much simpler for Morocco to negotiate directly with the EU or for Colombia to negotiate directly with the United States. Nations or cities can also respond more nimbly to demands for regional public goods by crafting bilateral agreements among themselves, or by addressing themselves to the large growing markets outside their region, bypassing this altogether.

This cursory examination makes it quite evident that the demand for regional public goods is rising much faster in some regions and sectors than in others. In the remainder of this chapter, I examine the role of regions in providing frameworks that enable workers and their families to move freely across national borders. I will argue that there are very considerable opportunities in fostering migration, but that they will most likely be captured by shifts in policies in the country of origin or by bilateral deals between the country of origin and the country of destination along major migration corridors such as Morocco–France or Mexico–United States, and that region-wide migration agreements will play a limited role at best.

Regions, migration, and development

I am interested in migration and the diaspora, defined as "the movement, migration or scattering of a people away from an established or ancestral homeland" because they can play an important role in the development and welfare of the country of origin and destination (World Bank 2006; Dadush 2014). Currently, some 214 million people reside in countries that are not their place of birth, representing about 3.1% of the world's population. Public goods in this space include agreements that allow people to move permanently or temporarily, protection of the rights of migrants, facilitation of their investments in and remittances to the country of origin, border management, and so on.

People residing outside their country of birth serve as the narrowest measure of the diaspora. For the purposes of economic analysis, a more appropriate measure of the diaspora could include all people residing abroad but likely to have strong links to their ancestral place of origin, including knowledge of its language and customs, and so might extend at least to the immediate offspring of migrants, easily doubling or even trebling the narrowest measure. Moreover, it should be recognized that the roots of the diaspora run deep and wide in the country of origin through the family and friends left behind: in countries such as Morocco—where migrant estimates vary but may represent 10%–15% of the native population—most people will have a son or daughter, sibling, cousin, or close friend who resides overseas.

The considerable capacity to network across borders that such large diasporas imply—especially now, in the age of social media and low-cost travel and communication—is what makes them potentially important facilitators of all forms of international exchange. By far the most prevalent motive for migration, initially, is economic, as distinct from forced migration resulting from political upheaval or persecution. Subsequent waves of migration can be driven more prominently by a desire for family reunification. This helps explain why some two-thirds of migration occurs from less developed economies to advanced ones (Crespo Cuaresma et al. 2013), so a large diaspora can, in addition to remittances, often facilitate access to more sophisticated and larger markets, deeper capital markets, state-of-the art technologies, and management know-how. At a time when the productivity gap between advanced and low-income economies is typically in the range of 20 to 1, and between advanced and middle-income economies 5 to 1, the opportunities to learn from the frontier have never been more important. The diaspora can significantly facilitate this process of convergence.

In examining the impact of the diaspora, the spotlight has naturally been placed on migrant remittances, which reached US$436 billion in 2014, given their enormous importance as a source of foreign exchange in developing countries and of sustenance for tens of millions of poor families (see Figure 6.1).

As has been widely documented, reducing the cost of transferring these funds, which can amount to several percentage points of the value of smaller remittances, is an obvious opportunity for government action (World Bank 2006). By enhancing competition in funds transfer and supporting the adoption of new fund-transfer technologies, such as through cell phones, credit cards, and Web-based systems, governments can make remittances easier and more convenient as well as increase their flow directly.

However, important as they are, remittances constitute far too narrow a prism through which to view the effect of diaspora on development and poverty alleviation in the country of origin. Compared to a country that has a

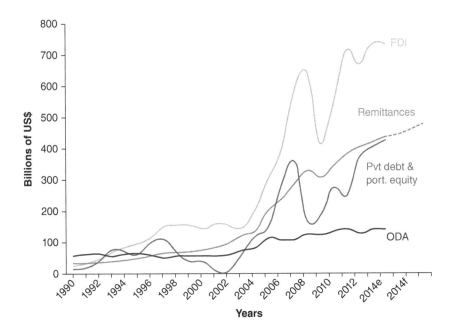

Figure 6.1 Remittances to Developing Countries (1990–2016).

Source: World Bank.

small and disconnected diaspora, a country that interacts closely with its large diaspora can not only rely on their help when times at home are hard (remittances, for example, tend to be a stable source of foreign exchange) but may also experience a multiplier effect in the form of increased trade and investment links when reforms succeed or when times are good.

The recent and growing literature on the diaspora provides considerable evidence for it playing an important role in international integration. One study shows a significant association between a large diaspora and a higher intensity of bilateral trade between the country of origin and destination (see Figure 6.2), and that the effect is much more pronounced in the case of trade in heterogeneous or differentiated products than in homogenous products such as primary commodities (Rauch 2002).

This suggests that links to the diaspora can help overcome the information asymmetries and nontariff barriers that are known to play a large role in inhibiting trade. Along similar lines, diasporas are found to be significantly associated with the intensity of international investment flows, and more especially with bilateral FDI flows than with (more homogenous and less information-intensive) portfolio flows (Leblang 2010). Figure 6.3, which refers to Sub-Saharan Africa, shows that in some countries, such as Nigeria and Kenya, real estate and business investments account for over half of total remittances.

Moreover, numerous studies identify a large diaspora as the single most important determinant of bilateral migration flows (Crespo Cuaresma et al. 2013), demonstrating the importance of networks in migration, and their cumulative effect.

These systematic empirical studies are supported by numerous anecdotes which illustrate the importance of the diaspora in helping develop export industries. The most frequently cited example is the development of the Indian

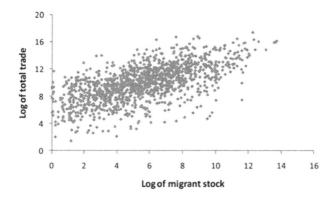

Figure 6.2 Bilateral Trade (2007) and Migrant Population (2010) between OECD and Africa. Note: Each dot represents a migrant corridor (Kenya–UK, Morocco–France, etc.).

Source: http://blogs.worldbank.org/peoplemove/migration-and-trade-go-hand-in-hand-for-africa-and-the-us

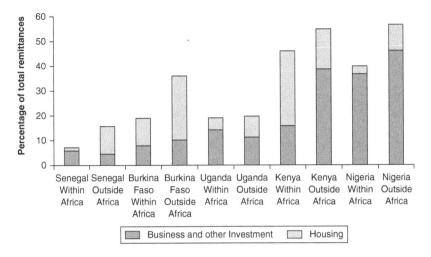

Figure 6.3 Investments in Business and Housing.

Source: World Bank (2011); http://siteresources.worldbank.org/EXTDECPROSPECTS/Resources/476882-1157133580628/Plaza_Navarrete_Ratha_MethodologicalPaper.pdf

IT industry, which now employs some 3.5 million people and represents a large share of India's exports, and which has relied greatly on the two-way flow of talent, money, ideas, and contacts between Bangalore and the Indian diaspora in Silicon Valley as well as other technology corridors in the United States. A notable feature of the Indian IT industry's development and of its diaspora links is the absence of any significant government involvement, except in terms of the public funding for prominent educational institutions such as the Indian Institute of Technology. But perhaps the most important diaspora links in terms of their effect on international trade comes from China, with its large expatriate communities throughout East Asia, the United States, and, increasingly, Africa and large parts of the developing world (Rauch and Trindade 2002). Hong Kong and Singapore, with their large concentrations of overseas Chinese, are the largest sources of FDI into China.

There is much that the government can do to strengthen links to the diaspora, but this would nearly always entail viewing the relationship through the prism of the needs of the diaspora rather than, as is customary, primarily through that of the needs of the country of origin and its need to attract remittances. As already discussed, the diaspora want to continue to belong, influence, and help, as well as to invest when the opportunity is ripe. Many in the diaspora also entertain the possibility of return and want to keep that option open, and many eventually do fulfil this. The challenge is to find win-win opportunities in fostering the diaspora relationship.

The Philippines, for example, has what is probably the most elaborate and sophisticated approach to diaspora relations of any country. Over 10 million

Filipinos reside overseas, of whom some 1.1 million are irregular migrants. These migrants remit US$28 billion a year to the Philippines. The Philippines manages its relations with the diaspora through a cabinet-level secretary of state, and the engagement is systematic, including diaspora philanthropy (remittances etc.), tourism initiatives, diaspora investment and business advisory circles, technology sharing and "brain gain," the encouragement of return migration or exchange on the part of the highly skilled, global legal assistance and advocacy, and cultural exchange. Community programs at the provincial level help prepare workers for migration though education and training (Pernia 2006). The Philippines allows dual citizenship, and makes provisions for overseas voting. It also has worker mobility agreements with some 80 countries. Regional agreements with which the Philippines is associated, such as the Association of Southeast Asian Nations (ASEAN), play only a modest role in fostering worker mobility, as do the Mode 4 provisions for the temporary movement of skilled workers under the WTO.

I shall now briefly review the state of migration and migration policies in two regions which are the source of large numbers of migrants.

Migration and diaspora: the case of the MENA region

At least 18 million migrants hail from MENA, representing over 5% of the population of that region, a much larger proportion than the world average. The largest diasporas in absolute terms originate in Palestine (3.64 million people), Egypt (3.47 million), Morocco (2.85 million), Iraq (2.32 million), and Algeria (1.72 million) (see Figure 6.4).

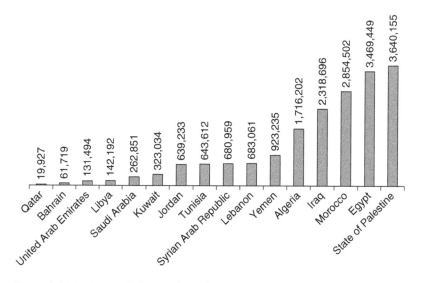

Figure 6.4 Numbers of Migrants from the MENA Region.

Source: Author calculations based on www.un.org/en/development/desa/population/migration/data/estimates2/estimatesorigin.shtml

The diaspora originating in the oil-rich Gulf countries, by contrast, is tiny—these states instead attract migrants from the rest of the MENA region.

It is estimated that migrants from the MENA region sent home some US$53 billion in remittances in 2014 and that countries such as Lebanon and Jordan received remittances in excess of 10% of GDP (see Figure 6.5), well in excess of what those countries spend on education, health care, and defense combined.

Migrants are especially important as a vehicle for international integration in the MENA region, given its relatively low integration through the trade channel. Moreover, migration provides a crucial exit route for the legion of young unemployed. While policies that facilitate international trade and investment are not high on the agenda at present on account of the region's political and security crisis, there is clearly much more that governments in the MENA region can do to facilitate emigration and draw support from the diaspora, including though internal reforms and bilateral deals with destination countries.

Links to the diaspora are, or should be, a two-way street. An online survey of the diaspora of the MENA region, the first of its kind, was recently conducted by the World Bank, yielding some 800 valid responses on the general issue of what the diaspora need and how they could support their country of origin's development. The overwhelming message of the survey is that the diaspora want to help and remain engaged with their country of origin, especially their region or city of origin: 85% of those surveyed responded positively to the statement "giving back to my country of origin is important to me." Respondents looked not just to maintaining their ties with families and friends, but also to helping more broadly,

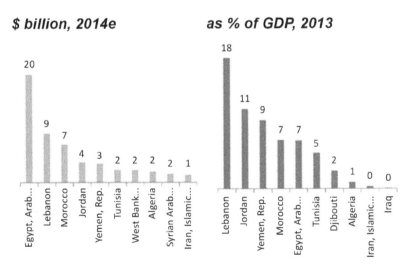

Figure 6.5 Top Recipients of Remittances (2013).

Source: https://siteresources.worldbank.org/INTPROSPECTS/Resources/334934-1288990760745/MigrationandDevelopmentBrief24.pdf

and 44% responded affirmatively to the statement "I feel more attached to my country of origin than where I live now." Migrants expressed a strong interest in sharing the skills they have acquired, but were also willing to invest, using their network and business contacts.

Some countries in the MENA region make a systematic effort to engage their diaspora. Morocco, which has a long-standing and articulated program to support its diaspora, coordinates its activities through a ministry dedicated to Moroccans overseas and a Royal Foundation that focuses on enhancing engagement with the diaspora. It also has negotiated bilateral treaties with France, Belgium, and other countries of destination covering circular migration, including border controls and portability of pensions and health benefits. The website "Marocains du Monde" is intended as a one-stop venue to engage the diaspora with its country of origin. Dedicated agencies aim to promote knowledge and technology transfer and investments on the part of overseas Moroccans. Likewise, Tunisia has a secretary of state in its Ministry of Social Affairs dedicated to diaspora engagement. Both countries allow double nationality and overseas voting. In Algeria, the Ministry of Foreign Affairs and of Information and Technology take the lead in diaspora relations. However, in comparison to the systematic approach to migrants adopted by the Philippines and the significant resources it dedicates to this effort, MENA countries, with one or two exceptions, do relatively little, and their efforts appear not infrequently to lack vision and visibility. For example, communications with the diaspora are often focused on pleas for help instead of on the diaspora's needs and the broader opportunities for cooperation.

The key question is why more is not being done to engage with the diaspora, given the considerable benefits to be derived from it. A number of obstacles appear to stand in the way of more systematic engagement. In most MENA countries, the diaspora has little voice or representation, reflecting the nature of the political regime or a lack of organization, or both. Depending on the nature of the regime, the government may be fearful of the influence of the diaspora and of its relative freedom of expression. Limited resources and a lack of coordination among the many parts of the government concerned (Ministry of Finance, the Central Bank, Ministry of Foreign Affairs, Ministry of Social Affairs, Ministry of Internal Affairs and/or of Regional Development, etc.) are also an important part of the problem. There has to be clear ownership of the migration and diaspora agenda. Among the diaspora, there is also a great deal of mistrust of the government and its capacity and willingness to help—in particular, any effort to channel or tax remittances is viewed with suspicion. Given the political sensitivity of migration in the countries of destination, the government of the country of origin must tread a fine diplomatic line in assisting its diaspora overseas. Last but not least, there is a serious lack of information about the diaspora and great difficulties in finding out who is part of it, where they are, what they are doing, and how best to reach them.

There has been little attention to the public debate on the role that governments in countries of destination can play in supporting enhanced links between the diaspora and the country of origin. Yet, the role of the country of destination is also crucial, for example in ensuring that the rights of migrants are observed, and in facilitating circular migration by—for example—allowing dual citizenship, permitting portability of pensions, and adopting appropriate labor permit and tax regimes. Insofar as tighter diaspora links with the country of origin can enhance its development, the country of destination benefits from growth and stability in its area, and, by encouraging return and circular migration, it can avoid some of the political complications and tensions associated with large permanent migration. In this context, too, there are clear win-win opportunities for the governments in the countries of origin and destination and the diaspora itself to arrive at cooperative solutions.

This creates an environment ripe for bilateral deals, but it is unclear how much more regional coordination can add beyond exchanges of information or joint advocacy initiatives. Since nearly all MENA countries have direct links with the countries of destination and, unlike trade in goods, the movement of people does not require the operation of a complex value chain of inputs, the easiest route is for the countries of origin and destination to negotiate directly. While our criteria for successful provision of regional public goods (political will, complementarity, technology transfer, and nimble responses) can be fulfilled in the case of a bilateral North–South deal, the conditions are mainly lacking for broader regional agreements.

Migration and the diaspora: the case of LAC[1]

Latin America, for centuries a magnet for migrants from Europe and a destination for the slave trade, has only recently seen large-scale emigration. The debt crisis of the 1980s marked the turning point, after which emigration accelerated up until the outbreak of the Great Recession, and has stabilized at low levels since. Today, some 30 million people born in Latin America reside outside their country of origin, about 5% of the native population, a proportion some 60% higher than the world average. Some 85% of LAC migrants reside in high-income countries, with the United States being the dominant destination, followed by Canada and Spain; only around 13% of LAC migrants reside in other Latin American countries.

Of the ten largest migration corridors, Mexico–United States is by far the largest, and seven others are between individual Latin American countries and the United States. Two other relatively small corridors are Ecuador–Spain, and Colombia–Venezuela, which is the only top-ten corridor that is intraregional. Within the region, historically only Venezuela, Argentina and, more recently, Costa Rica, have been countries attracting significant intraregional migration. During its short-lived recent economic boom, Brazil became a magnet for illegal migrants from Haiti and Central America. Like migration anywhere, movement within and out of Latin America has ebbed and flowed with economic fortune, which means that—with Argentina and Venezuela in crisis—intraregional migration is currently at a low point.

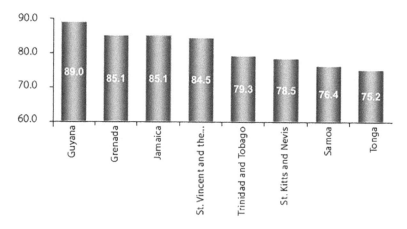

Figure 6.6 Emigration Rate (as a Percentage) of High-skilled Population with Tertiary Education from Small States in LAC.

Source: World Bank (2011).

The small economies of Central America and the Caribbean have derived proportionally the greatest benefits from remittances (they often exceed 10% of the GDP of small economies) but have also experienced a very large outflow of their skilled population, often half or more.

Mexico, whose US- and Canada-based diaspora dwarfs all others, including over 5 million undocumented migrants, is a large and diversified economy that is only modestly dependent on remittances and retains proportionally large numbers of its skilled workers. However, Mexico's links with its migrants to the north are extensive and politically significant. In recent years, Mexico has seen a large increase in transit migrants from Central America destined to the United States, raising the political stakes of migration policies in both Mexico and the United States and calling for a more coordinated approach.

Migration pressures out of Latin America and towards the United States are widely expected to escalate over the next decade or two—a reflection of persistent wage gaps, aging in the north, continued rapid growth of the working age population in the poorest countries, especially in Central America, ease of communication, and the increased pull of migrant networks. The United States became heavily dependent on less-skilled immigrants from Latin America decades ago, a situation that is expected to continue and intensify. The reform of the broken immigration system in the United States took a significant turn with President Obama's executive order intended to protect many undocumented migrants from deportation, but this is now being severely challenged by the courts. Whatever the outcome, Obama's initiative has certainly helped place immigration policy at the center of the political debate, and the issue is likely to feature prominently in the 2016 presidential election.

The immediate prospects for increased migration inside Latin America and from Latin America to Spain, Italy, and other European countries are dim on account of the economic weakness in these destination countries. But, given the demographic pressures in Europe and the security and integration tensions associated with Muslim immigrants from North Africa, it still is a fair guess that, five or ten years from now, migration from Latin America towards Europe will accelerate once again.

At this stage, it is difficult to be optimistic about increased intraregional migration in Latin America both in the short- and medium-term. An interesting question is how much structural complementarity there is between labor markets within Latin America. At first glance, it would appear that the opportunities for movement of unskilled labor within Latin America are limited. The opportunities for movement of skilled labor may be greater, but are bound to vary substantially across disciplines and countries—medical doctors from Cuba migrating to Venezuela are one example of this specificity.

In contrast, the economic gains from migration towards the United States, Canada, and Europe are potentially huge, outweighing those from trade or any other form of integration by a wide margin (World Bank 2006). These gains would accrue predominantly to the migrant and his family through remittances, but would also benefit origin and destination countries in numerous ways (Dadush 2014). However, the nation-state defines itself by who lives within its borders, and the forces standing in the way of increased migration—xenophobia and the (largely misplaced) perception that migrants reduce the job opportunities of natives—are extremely powerful. This is true even in countries that have traditionally been a haven for migrants and have been built by them.

In contrast to trade and FDI, international agreements designed to ensure freedom of movement of labor and fair treatment of migrants remain among the least effective aspects of international coordination, a situation which is true of most regions, including LAC (Martin and Martin 2014). The EU, a political project where movement of people ranks at the same level as the other three freedoms (movement of goods, services and capital), is the most notable exception to this rule. At the global level, there is nothing resembling a multilateral institution such as the WTO to regulate migration flows.

The scarcity and ineffectiveness of international worker mobility agreements is in part the result of the inauspicious political economy of such negotiations, where the migrant is the largest gainer, but the country of origin is typically ambivalent about facilitating emigration, and also has little to offer in return to the country of destination, which, as is the case of the United States, can draw migrants from around the world. Within countries of destination, the business community (and, interestingly, the Catholic Church) are typically important lobbies in favor of immigration. However, agreements have typically been confined to temporary movement of workers and struck during periods of acute labor shortage in the country of destination and in the absence of realistic alternatives. The Bracero programs struck by the full-employment United States of the 1960s with Mexico and other countries in Latin America are the most prominent example, but they were eventually discontinued as growth slowed and it became evident that temporary movement tended to become permanent settlement. An interesting recent development is the worker mobility and visa-free travel agreements concluded or envisaged as part of the Pacific Alliance—a far-reaching trade agreement among Chile, Colombia, Mexico, and Peru. The South American Conference on Migration has long provided a useful forum for exchange, information, and analysis.

In recent years, restrictions on immigration in advanced countries have tightened considerably. Yet, historically, draconian restrictions on immigration have suffered the same fate as controls on capital outflows, sky-high tariffs, or prohibitive sin taxes: they proved largely ineffectual. When the demand for migrants is high or when migrants are forced to leave their home for economic or political reasons, restrictions do not prevent migration. Instead, they slow it to some degree but also change its nature—from documented to undocumented, from high- to low-skilled—and create large costs and risks for the migrants and rents for those who know how to facilitate illegal migration.

The challenge of arriving at migration regimes and regional migration agreements that satisfy the growing labor needs of the United States, Canada, and other destination countries as well as the needs of origin countries in Latin America to provide better livelihoods for their people—without undermining the rule of law and exposing the migrant to a multitude of risks—remains unmet. But neither the opportunities inherent in migration nor the problems caused by a dysfunctional system are going away—more likely, they will become more and more pressing in coming years. As in the case of the MENA region, the needs and opportunities for intraregional coordination of migration regimes are currently limited. The biggest needs are for reforms of the immigration regime in the United States, tighter links between countries of origin and their diaspora, and for bilateral agreements covering the spectrum of the mobility agenda between the countries of origin and the main destinations, namely the United States and Canada.

Conclusion

This chapter has argued that, to achieve legitimacy and effectiveness, the provision of a regional public good, like the provision of any good, should be the subject of a competitive process: what is the best way of providing it? The design and ambition of regional arrangements among developing countries must accurately evaluate the opportunities, recognize the risks and limitations, and ensure that—of all the other mechanisms that exist to provide such goods—regional arrangements are the most likely to prove legitimate and effective. As the global economy becomes more integrated and new sources of demand and competition arise, the demand for the provision of public goods at all levels of government has increased. The provision of regional public goods is most likely to succeed if the criteria identified above hold true: political will, complementarity of economic structure, ability to learn from each other, and effective coordination. In the important area of migration, the biggest needs are in domestic reforms and bilateral negotiations between partners in the largest migration corridors, which nearly always entail movement from a developing to an advanced country, as well as increased engagement with the diaspora. The contribution of intraregional processes involving a broader group of countries is likely to remain modest, as they do not, by and large, fill the criteria outlined above. In the area of migration, broad regional provision of public goods is likely to be limited to information exchange and joint advocacy, or in some instances, to agreements that facilitate the transit of migrants.

Note

1 The literature on migration in Latin America is extensive. See, for example, Orozco (2009 and 2014) and the websites of the Princeton University Latin American Migration Project (http://lamp.opr.princeton.edu/); the South American section of the Migration Policy Institute website (www.migrationpolicy.org/regions/south-america); and the Inter-American Dialogue website (www.thedialogue.org/).

References

Carpenter, Theresa, and Andreas Lendle. 2011. "How Preferential Is World Trade?" *Vox EU* (March).

Crespo Cuaresma, Jesús, Mathias Moser, and Anna Raggl. 2013. "On the Determinants of Global Bilateral Migration Flows." WWWforEUROPE Working Paper no. 5. Vienna: WIFO.

Dadush, Uri. 2014. "The Effect of Low-Skilled Labor Migration on the Host Economy." World Bank KNOMAD Working Paper Series, No.1. Washington, DC: World Bank.

Dadush, Uri, and William Shaw. 2010. *Juggernaut: How Emerging Markets Are Reshaping Globalization*. Washington, DC: Carnegie Endowment for International Peace.

Fischer, Stanley. 1987. "International Macroeconomic Policy Coordination." NBER Working Paper 2244. Cambridge, MA: National Bureau of Economic Research.

Leblang, David. 2010. "Familiarity Breeds Investment." *American Political Science Review* 104.

Martin, Philip, and Susan Martin. 2014. "Migration in the South Atlantic Basin. Patterns, Governance, and Development." OCP Policy Center.

Orozco, Manuel. 2009. "Migration and remittances in times of recession: Effects on Latin American economies." Washington, DC: Inter-American Dialogue.

———. 2014. "Economic Status and Remittance Behavior Among Latin American and Caribbean Migrants in the Post-Recession Period." Washington, DC: Inter-American Dialogue.

Pernia, Ernesto. 2006. "Diaspora, Remittances and Poverty RP's Regions." Mimeo.

Perry, Guillermo. 2014. "Regional Public Goods in Finance, Trade, and Infrastructure: An Agenda for Latin America." CGD Policy Paper 037. Washington DC: Center for Global Development.

Rauch, James, and Vitor Trindade. 2002. "Ethnic Chinese Networks in International Trade." *Review of Economics and Statistics* 84, no. 1 (February).

World Bank. 2006. *Global Economic Prospects: Economic Implications of Remittances and Migration.* Washington, DC: World Bank.

———. 2011. *Migration and Remittances Factbook 2011.* Washington, DC: World Bank.

7 Connectivity and infrastructure as 21st-century regional public goods

Jayant Prasad

Introduction

The global landscape is being changed by new geo–economics, with trade and investment flows shifting from the North to the South. Commercial exchanges among developing countries today account for half of world trade, and global foreign direct investment (FDI) flows more to countries of the South rather than the North. About three-fourths of FDI from the South goes to developing countries, with a growing proportion of such investments directed toward greenfield projects rather than existing businesses and mergers and acquisitions. Despite these dynamic trends, and the increasing role of developing countries in the global economy, they are challenged by poverty, low per capita incomes, employment-neutral growth, and the unmet demand for public education and health, livelihood, and social security.

Developing countries can accelerate their ongoing transformation and achieve their development goals quicker and more effectively through regional collective action. Improved connectivity and infrastructure can help them reap potential synergies and externalities, including by promoting trade and investment across contiguous countries. Such actions have the natural advantage of developing supply chains through the facilitation of border transactions and establishing compatible regulatory regimes within a region. Collaborative initiatives have increased already over recent decades to establish regional economic, social, and developmental institutions whose scope, reach, and perceived utility continue to increase across different parts of the world.

Connectivity and infrastructure are at the very core of regional cooperation and integration, as their key enablers. Regional integration, in turn, promotes social development and sustainable and better-distributed growth across a given region. The pursuit of these objectives involves creating a range of regional public goods (RPGs), including investment in inter- and intraregional connectivity projects, in five distinct clusters: trade, transportation, information and communication technologies (ICTs), energy, and people.

All these together, underpinned by appropriate infrastructure, facilitate the free and unfettered flow of goods, services, investments, persons, ideas, and technology. The permeation of know-how and technology through various connectivity networks has a direct bearing on people's lives by facilitating their access to education, health, and social insurance and improving state support for dealing with the negative consequences of climate change and natural disasters. A particular feature of connectivity-related RPGs that develop unhindered regional linkages are the improvements these bring about in people's living conditions, including those of the most impoverished and disadvantaged social strata.

In this respect, RPGs could be promoted more effectively through an approach conceptualized around connectivity and infrastructure, instead of the conventional discourses on regional integration. The latter have been modeled, historically, on the European experience, which started with free trade arrangements and culminated in the formation of a common currency zone through closer economic and monetary unification. Regional cooperation institutions worldwide, therefore, traditionally consider growing trade and capital flows among their members as the stepping stones to regional integration. The South Asian Association of Regional Cooperation (SAARC) is no exception.[1] The 1998 Group of Eminent Persons, a meeting of the heads of state of governments of constituted by SAARC member states, for instance, proposed a three-stage vision for regional cooperation in South Asia: a South Asia free trade area in phase I; a customs union in phase II; and a broader economic union in phase III, by the year 2020. Cooperation within SAARC has not kept pace with the ambition of its proponents, nor have the experiences of other regional groupings with similar blueprints, with the exception of the European Union (EU).

Scholars of subaltern economics and dependency theorists levied heavy criticism on this linear, largely market-led, model. They blamed it for causing large inequalities both within and between countries and a culture of dependency of the periphery on the core, and of smaller countries on their larger and more powerful neighbors. RPGs with a focus on publicly available connectivity and infrastructure assets, created through partnerships, might instead appeal more as a socially constructive way to invest in regional development. The least developed countries (LDCs) and landlocked developing countries (LLDCs) generally join regional cooperation initiatives aspiring for connectivity with their contiguous countries, not for integration into the region, even if that might remain for them an important, if distant, goal. When Afghanistan became SAARC's newest member in 2007, it did so with the hope of becoming the land bridge connecting South Asia, Central Asia, Eurasia, and the Middle East and a regional trade, transportation, minerals, and energy hub. President Karzai spoke of his expectation that Afghanistan would gain from investments, integrate itself with regional railways and road networks, become an important partner in regional energy markets, and eliminate the narcotics trade. This, he added, would result in what he described as "huge economic opportunities" for Afghanistan, including "as a wheeler of electricity from Central Asian Republics to Pakistan and through Pakistan to India and other South Asia countries."[2]

SAARC's challenges might illustrate the impediments to integration efforts among other regional cooperation initiatives among developing countries. The borders of South Asia were redrawn in 1947, with the Partition of India, and in 1971, with the Indo-Pakistan War and the creation of Bangladesh. The peoples of South Asia diverge in many ways, most of all politically, despite their cultural closeness and shared history and geography, including the common civilizational space that anchors their relations. Rather than bringing people together, speaking the same language or belonging to the same ethnicity or religion on both sides of a given border have had the effect of reinforcing a sense of distinctiveness vis-à-vis one another. Other factors exacerbating this include the unevenness of countries' developments and disproportionate distribution of resources, population, and land area. The shared inheritance provides, at best, for ease of interaction, an important but insufficient condition for promoting regional cooperation and integration. These require mutual trust and political entente, as much in South Asia as in other parts of the world.

Regional integration that threatens national sovereignty cannot attract support. Integrative activities are pursued by stealth in many regions of the world, including South Asia—that is, through activities below the horizon that duck the sovereignty issue, in contrast to the case of the EU, where the sovereignty problem was successfully overcome to achieve a common purpose. Regional integration is often hampered by hostilities, the prevailing asymmetries within regions, absence of economic complementarity, and the lack of political will and traction from local communities. The resulting trust deficit is exacerbated by the perception of differential gains from integration, which evokes the idea of hegemony, for instance in the case of India in South Asia, or China in Asia.

In contrast, connectivity and infrastructure as RPGs can spur greater regional cooperation and integration in significant ways, since RPGs ingrain the idea of the "common good," of making the region a better place, and of joint and equal access to the various commons for productive social use. This will help overcome resistance from local interests that drive governmental planning and budgeting processes. The act of drawing resources away from highly competitive allocation politics at the local level, driven by sectional interests, to a nonlocal, regional level, requires a different kind of constituency building that straddles borders, including the borders of federal units within states. The South Asian border regions, interestingly, are densely populated, and cross-border development linkages are therefore likely to invigorate growth in these lagging regions. Such an approach will require fostering collaboration among actors who have their social and political base in the border regions, for which the RPG vocabulary might help in winning converts, as cross-border connectivity does not normally enter the mindset of local political elites. For South Asia, this will be a novel experiment.

RPGs that are related to connectivity and infrastructure projects can be free from the confines of a formal regional architecture or treaty arrangements. These RPGs can be produced nationally, bilaterally, regionally, and plurilaterally; their scale can range from small to large; and they can encompass subregional to multinational economies. RPGs can be built without following the equal-cost, equal-benefit principle. While RPGs cannot be developed without coordinated efforts among the countries concerned and cannot be an agglomeration of individual, *ad hoc* efforts, they can evolve and operate at various levels. Overarching and all-encompassing projects can develop later once these first, more modest efforts have become established. Moreover, gains from such RPGs, even when nonexcludable and nonrivalrous, can be unequal, as can the investments made to create them, for such investments must necessarily be proportionate to the capacities of the states involved. Cooperation in producing RPGs can also have positive externalities, in terms of a payoff in increased security. These intangibles can contribute to regional peace and stability, without which securing rapid growth and prosperity would become more difficult.

RPGs can be distinguished from the conventional idea of regional integration while being organically linked to it. The production of transnational RPGs is different from integrating national, subregional, and regional markets, businesses, or transportation and energy networks. It requires a conceptual leap that entails politically calibrated flexibility around the idea of sharing national assets, for instance by allowing a dedicated national railway freight corridor to be used for trade between two neighboring countries. The functional efficiency of purpose-built RPGs clearly surpasses the cobbling together of national assets normally pursued under regional integration projects. Unless RPGs are designed in this way, local sectional or rent-seeking interests could impede implementation. RPGs also require national development plans to put regional connectivity, infrastructure, and economic integration at the core of their growth strategies, rather than leave them to their facilitative margins. For this, leadership and responsibility would be important drivers.

Political outcomes

Connectivity based on regional contiguity will help nations overcome political differences by conceiving of their borders as bridges, not barriers; by better leveraging their geographic proximity for mutual benefit; by optimally utilizing resources of the region; and by enhancing their capacities and competitiveness to more effectively engage with the international system. RPG investments in commerce, transportation, ICTs, energy, and people-to-people connectivity projects will enlarge the basket of tradable benefits. Looking at all five clusters has the advantage of compensating in one of these for the losses in another. Regional connectivity linked public goods can meanwhile attenuate conflicts between states and raise the threshold below which bilateral relations will not fall. Increasing integration—the natural consequence of increased regional connectivity, entailing interwoven interactions and interdependence—might reduce tensions and stabilize the region by raising the costs of noncooperative behavior.

Roadmap for connectivity and infrastructure RPGs

The strategic objectives of connectivity linked RPGs are well established. Trade and transportation connectivity entails facilitation, dismantling of nontariff barriers, and infrastructure development of air, rail, road, and waterway transportation. As RPGs, these go hand-in-hand with the development of "soft infrastructure"—improvements in transboundary crossings and regional transportation and logistics services. Power grids, pipelines, and nonconventional sources of energy will enhance access to commercially available energy to communities presently deprived of it. Knowledge generation and sharing can transform regions with modest investments and quick returns. Attendant benefits include improved public health and environmental management.

All states seek to create a conducive international environment for their growth and regeneration, a process which RPGs should logically help. The relevant question is that if connectivity and infrastructure gains are so well accepted, why is there a deficit of such projects in the regions that most need them? This might be the case because, their evident economic benefits notwithstanding, the decision to invest in them is politically driven. It would be logical, therefore, to prioritize consideration not of *what* has to be done—since that is largely known—but rather of *how* to do it.

Building infrastructure for better regional connectivity in the form of RPGs will require that four core aspects be addressed: institutional design, financing, sequencing, and measurement. These are examined in detail in the following sections.

Institutional design

Conventionally, comprehensive regional strategies for developing critical connectivity networks are driven by regional cooperation organizations. Not all initiatives, however, need to be regional. It might actually be better, initially, to proceed with cooperative ventures discretely, and to do so bilaterally, subregionally, and regionally, as building blocks for a wider regional architecture of cooperation and integration. Beginning with smaller steps and fewer members might take nations further, as much by overcoming political obstacles as by demonstrating the success of low-gestation, quick result-oriented connectivity and infrastructure projects.

SAARC's free trade initiative, the South Asia Free Trade Agreement (SAFTA), has failed to propel intraregional trade and investment toward double-digit percentage figures, largely because of the size of its other constituents relative to that of India, and also because of the absence of political consensus among its members concerning the pace of its progress. South Asia continues to be among the least economically integrated areas in the world, with its states connected more to the outside world than to each other. A comparative analysis indicates that South Asia lags behind all other regions in Asia in terms of regional trade integration indices, as Table 7.1 demonstrates. Regional trade accounts for a high percentage of the total trade of the smaller

Table 7.1 Intraregional Trade Share Percentages in Asia

	Regions	2000	2005	2010	2011	2012	2013	2014
Intraregional	Southeast Asia	22.74	24.86	24.62	24.26	24.56	24.31	24.22
Trade	Central and West Asia	6.22	7.52	6.92	6.40	6.25	6.66	7.07
Share (%)	East Asia	36.82	39.88	36.86	35.47	34.87	36.16	35.51
	South Asia	4.41	5.46	4.55	4.25	4.29	4.52	5.31

Source: Asian Regional Integration Centre, Asian Development Bank.

South Asian economies, such as Afghanistan, Bhutan, and Nepal, as shown in Table 7.2. For the largest country, India, the opposite is true.

The political blockages impeding region-wide cooperation initiatives might be circumvented by following bilateral and subregional approaches, as Bangladesh, Bhutan, India, and Nepal have decided by reviving the South Asia Growth Quadrangle (SAGQ). SAGQ, now known as the Bangladesh, Bhutan, India, Nepal Initiative (BBIN), is estimated to account for about 80% of the potential energy trade for the whole of South Asia. BBIN has accelerated subregional cooperation by concluding, within a year, a framework agreement on passenger transportation and personal vehicles, and identified sites for multicountry hydropower projects.[3] While demonstrating their determination to pursue regional cooperation at a variable speed within SAARC, member countries have not shut the door on wider cooperation with other interested countries. A recent World Bank study indicates that South Asian electricity coordination and trade could generate average savings of US$9 billion per year.[4]

The main rationale for the grouping is that the subregion has the world's largest and deepest concentration of poverty, with a high potential for rapid poverty reduction through growth.[5] Other similar subregional groupings in Asia that have already begun to realize their promise include the Greater Mekong Subregion (GMS) and the Central Asia Regional Economic

Table 7.2 SAARC Intraregional Imports and Exports in 2011.

SAARC Members	Imports from SAARC (US$ million)	Exports to SAARC (US$ million)	Regional imports as percentage of total imports	Regional exports as percentage of total exports
Afghanistan	983	251	6.63%	66.80%
Bangladesh	5,666	606	13.75%	2.49%
Bhutan	767	371	72.92%	81.92%
India	2,501	12,937	0.54%	4.29%
Nepal	3,779	647	63.87%	71.24%
Maldives	228	11.5	16.14%	13.84%
Pakistan	1,953	4,235	4.48%	16.71%
Sri Lanka	4,730	702	24.01%	7.01%
Total	**20,607**	**19,760**		

Source: International Trade Center Statistics.

Cooperation (CAREC).[6] All three partnerships are engaged in building regional connectivity and infrastructure projects to reach out to newer markets within the region and beyond. The embedded idea shared by the participating countries is threefold: that the structured, subregional approach be used in a way that, whatever coverage is feasible, is quickly adopted; nonstructured approaches at national or various international levels be used to supplement these; and the extent of the subregion be taken as a moving concept, in that the scope of the region may continue to change, depending on what regional grouping is being worked out.

Like China, India is involving itself in new regional partnerships. To the east, these include the Mekong-Ganga Cooperation between India and five Southeast Asian countries: Myanmar, Thailand, Laos, Cambodia, and Vietnam. Even more promising is the Bay of Bengal Initiative for Multi-Sectoral Technical and Economic Cooperation (BIMSTEC), bringing together Bhutan, Nepal, Bangladesh, Sri Lanka, India, Myanmar, and Thailand. Looking to its western flank, and taking account of the slow movement toward engagement with Central Asia and Iran through Pakistan and Afghanistan, India unveiled its Connect Central Asia initiative in 2012.[7] This includes synergy of joint efforts through the Shanghai Cooperation Organization (SCO), the Eurasian Economic Community (EurAsEC), and the Eurasian Economic Union (EEU), with which India has proposed a Comprehensive Economic Cooperation Agreement.[8] India is seeking to integrate its markets with those of Eurasia, making Central Asia a long-term partner in energy and natural resources, and reactivating the International North-South Transport Corridor (INSTC), which will go north through Iranian ports.

A new feature of cooperation among countries in the South is triangular cooperation—when a traditional northern donor from the ranks of the Development Assistance Committee (DAC) of the Organisation of Economic Cooperation and Development (OECD) or an international organization forms an association with a donor from the South to work together in another country of the South. Notably, while this idea has occupied a prominent place within the UN, World Bank, and OECD since 2009–10, India's practical experience in triangular cooperation predates this. In 2008, India collaborated with the World Bank and the Asian Development Bank (ADB) to bring Uzbek electricity to Kabul by building a 202-kilometer transmission line and a power distribution substation with 300 MW capacity. The dynamics of the trilateral cooperation between USAID and Indian and Afghan companies involved Afghan engineers being trained in Indian facilities while being financed by the United States, thereby enabling them to manage the entire project from the day the power station was commissioned.

DAC's 2015 Survey of Triangular Cooperation (STC) indicates that the average budget for projects under survey was US$1.8 million, while eight percent of them had a budget in excess of US$5 million. The World Food Programme (WFP) has been identified as one of the most dynamic organizations in this field. In this light, India's assistance to the WFP's School Nutritional

Programme in Afghanistan—supplying high protein biscuits in 32 out of 34 Afghan districts—amounted to US$87 million in 2014–15.[9]

Institutional design also includes the process of envisioning and implementing connectivity related RPGs, which must include members of the informed public, particularly civil society organizations and think tanks. The idea for creating a new multilateral development bank operated by the BRICS states (Brazil, Russia, India, China, and South Africa), known as the New Development Bank BRICS (NDB BRICS), was aired publicly for the first time in 2012 at the BRICS Academic Forum hosted by a New Delhi-based think tank, Observer Research Foundation. The forum recommended that the leaders, who were to meet later that year at their annual summit, study "the establishment and operational modalities of financial institutions such as a development bank and/or an investment fund" (Jha 2014).[10] The Shanghai-based NDB BRICS, with an initial share capital of US$50 billion and a contingency reserve arrangement of US$100 billion, is authorized to lend up to US$34 billion for infrastructure projects annually and began its operations in early 2016.

Another example of how a think tank–led Track One initiative was placed on a Track Two rail is provided by the evolution of the Bangladesh–China–India–Myanmar (BCIM) Forum for Regional Cooperation, first proposed in a conference in 1999 in Kunming. The initiative was conceived to revive China's southwestern Silk Route, which once connected the Bay of Bengal and India's northeastern states to the Chinese province of Yunnan.[11]

Finally, the institutional design for RPGs must provide adequate space for businesses, which tend to be more interconnected across national frontiers, more inclined to seek mutual benefits, and more opportunistic than governments. They operate on the basis of a balance of interests and not a balance of power. They also tend to be bolder and more results-oriented. A greater measure of support from the business community and civil society can help orient the political system to support RPGs.

Financing

Financing is arguably the most critical element of connectivity and infrastructure, in that several well-conceived initiatives have been kept on the shelf simply for lack of funding. Although international financial institutions and regional development banks, such as the ADB, the African Development Bank (AfDB), and the Inter-American Development Bank (IDB), have played a role in financing global public goods and RPGs, the gap between regional investment needs and the available public and private funding has been growing.[12]

RPGs cannot flourish unless they are propelled by the more prosperous economies. More developed states should take on larger commitments and contribute more meaningfully to regional projects as their special responsibility, for they have much to gain from the creation of a larger economic space. Indeed, in proportion to their economic weight within the given region, RPGs should be an obligatory, not an optional, charge on their national budget. According to a recent McKinsey estimate, over the next ten years Asian infrastructure projects will require financing of US$8 trillion, of which over 80% is slated for the transportation and energy sectors (Tahilyani, Tamhane, and Tan 2011).

It is the Asian states that must mobilize the required financing, first from their own resources. While Asia's share in world GDP is 31% in constant US dollars, its share in global savings and reserves, including gold, is 51% and 59%, respectively (Akhtar 2014). The largest of the surplus Asian economies, those of China and Japan, are now beginning to set aside a higher percentage of their available resources for financing infrastructure development in other parts of Asia. Indeed, in November 2014, President Xi Jinping committed to contributing US$40 billion for a Silk Road Infrastructure Fund to "break the connectivity bottleneck in Asia" (Carsten and Blanchard 2014). The Japan Bank for International Cooperation is contemplating an increase in infrastructure funding in Asia, in conjunction with ADB, of up to 25% of its present commitments over the next five years (Iwamoto and Shimodoi 2015). Without competing with China in this respect, India too is planning a special-purpose facility to fund roads, bridges, and power plants across South Asia for infrastructure investment and trade facilitation in the region. Sovereign funds from nonregional states, particularly the Gulf States, are also expected to invest in these projects.

China proposed the creation of the Asian Infrastructure and Investment Bank (AIIB) to partially fill the prevailing infrastructure funding gap in Asia. Twenty-one nations signed the agreement establishing the AIIB on October 24, 2014. As of 2016, it is expected that China and India will be the two largest shareholders in the AIIB, with India also expected to be one of its biggest future borrowers.

In June 2016, AIIB announced four loans totaling US$509 million for projects ranging from power distribution in Bangladesh, highway construction in Pakistan, slum development in Indonesia, and improving border roads in Tajikistan (Bloomberg 2016). Three of these projects will be co-financed with other multilateral development banks. Meanwhile, the New Development Bank set up by BRICS had approved four renewable energy projects by April 2016, with a combined capacity generation of 2,370 MW in India, China, Brazil and South Africa, worth US$811 million.[13] The Indian project entails a US$250 million loan for generating 500 MW of renewal energy, which will result in savings of 800,000 tonnes of carbon emissions.

A significant proportion of the connectivity and infrastructure projects it funds are likely to be public–private partnerships, which could help absorb some costs. Many projects, however, might not be sustainable without viability gap funding by way of outright grants, which might be provided by the states concerned as they do within their own national territories. Institutional reforms—such as the unbundling of the generation, transmission, and distribution of electricity—and the creation of market instruments—such as commercial grid connectivity, power trading, and retail sales mechanisms—could create a regional electricity market, obviate the need for government subsidy, and help in regional energy security.

Sequencing

Sequencing, conceived as an incentive structure in terms of immediate accessibility of benefits, is an equally significant factor in promoting regional connectivity. Giving priority to projects that might have the most optimal results in terms of readily accruable mutual benefits might in some regions lower the cost of cooperation and build confidence in the process. Moreover, a step-by-step approach in preference to pursuing a "grand" overall design of regional integration might overcome the traditional constraint of sovereignty in accepting cooperative obligations. Making these attractive to the more disadvantaged and less developed countries will be a special challenge for the more prosperous ones. Smart sequencing, in terms of quick distribution of benefits through low-risk projects, could serve as an incentive to communities and governments.

A good example of this is how India, itself energy deficient, decided to connect Bangladesh with the 71-kilometer Baharampur-Bheramara high-voltage direct current transmission line, which now carries 500MW of electricity to Bangladesh, a supply that will soon double. Since then, partnership in energy has been a two-way process. Bangladesh facilitated the transportation, by the riverine route, of the two 300-tonne gas turbines for the Palatana power project in Tripura, along with 88 other packages of over-dimensional cargo that would have been virtually impossible to carry along the serpentine, single-lane roads of northern Bengal, Assam, Meghalaya, and Tripura.[14] Some 100MW of power is soon expected to flow to Bangladesh from Palatana. When additional hydropower becomes available from Bhutan and, later, from projects in India's northeast, Bangladesh will benefit from these. In return, Bangladesh has agreed to wheel electricity through its territory for supply to other Indian provinces. This electricity supply could conceivably be extended to Pakistan, making the grid connectivity within Bangladesh and across its borders with India a public good for the South Asian region as a whole.

Regional power grids and pipelines connecting a small number of countries are typically seen as club rather than public goods (Sandler 2003, p.11). In regions where mutual suspicions run high, the pursuit of mutual benefit in building such grids and pipelines provides the base on which region-wide public goods could be erected in the future. Such beginnings may sometimes be modest, but their eventual outcomes can potentially change regional configuration. The decision by ADB, World Bank, KfW, JICA, and the Government of India to pool their resources for building Afghanistan's North East Transmission System has been instructive in this regard. India contributed US$110 million for the construction of Afghanistan's largest substation in Chimtala in the outskirts of Kabul, and 202-kilometer stretch of transmission lines from Pul-e-Khumri to

Kabul, which brought Uzbek electricity to Kabul in January 2009. A portion of the grid goes over the Salang Pass, at a height of over 3,700 meters.

This extraordinary initiative, if seen in isolation in the context of Afghanistan alone, might appear to be of limited regional value. However, it must be seen in conjunction with two sustainable energy projects to promote a region-wide energy exchange: the Turkmenistan–Afghanistan–Pakistan–India (TAPI) gas pipeline, and the Central Asia–South Asia Electricity Transmission and Trade Project (CASA-1000), expected to bring Tajik and Kyrgyz hydropower to Afghanistan and Pakistan. This, in turn, is expected to evolve into the Central Asia–South Asia Regional Energy Market (CASAREM), once the planned Central Asian hydro potential comes onstream. The energy resource reserves of the five Central Asian states—Kazakhstan, the Kyrgyz Republic, Tajikistan, Turkmenistan, and Uzbekistan—consists of 3.2 billion tons of oil, 38 billion tons of coal, and 6,717 billion cubic meters of gas (Shah 2013, p.102). In contrast, all South Asian states are energy hungry in terms of their natural resource endowment, except Bhutan and Nepal. Thus, with Afghanistan's membership of SAARC, it has become possible, in theory, to envision another arc of advantage—a new Silk Route connecting the Ferghana Valley to the Mekong Delta—should peace and stability return to the region.

Smart sequencing can also boost connectivity immediately without a sudden outflow of resources. For instance, in South Asia, regional transportation connectivity can be instantly augmented by integrating existing national networks regionally, restoring their pre-1947 linkages, requiring minimal financing. This could logically be followed by extending carriage capacities, such as by more frequent and regular airline, rail, road, and coastal shipping services, broadening roads, and dredging existing inland waterways to improve navigable draft for their optimal use. New cross-border transportation infrastructure covering alternate and quicker routes and cost-reducing multimodal systems linking manufacturing hubs in the hinterland to urban markets and ports could follow, after exhausting the lower-cost options.

Measurement

Finally, measurement will be the key to promoting regional connectivity by documenting and demonstrating how it could enhance the capacities of the participating states for their social and economic development in ways that would not have been possible otherwise. This is important since the lack of propulsion at the political level for greater regional connectivity, could be attributed to incomplete knowledge of its benefits, besides indifferent and inimical relationships. It was the awareness of the high cost of noncooperation that helped transform Europe and create the EU as we know it today. The negative opportunity cost of the nonintegration of South Asian economies could amount to forgoing an estimated 2% of additional GDP growth annually. Moreover, measurement of potential gains could also offset notions about the "trade diverting and hence welfare-reducing" impact of regional integration (Das 2009, p.2).

Gains from connectivity in terms of increased employment, productivity, manufacturing capacity, and reductions in import and export costs and greenhouse gas (GHG) emissions might be easy to measure. In the area of transportation, improved measurements might help establish priorities among alternate routes or modes of transportation. Measurement could assist both in sequencing and in ensuring that regional assets, once created, are kept in good repair. These could cumulatively contribute to avoiding the negative consequences of cross-border initiatives. An important measurement to obtain commitments for RPGs would be to ascertain how a connectivity linked RPG could promote national planning objectives. Regional development banks could also play a role in this context by providing a relatively neutral forum for assessing relative costs and benefits of RPGs, thereby assisting national decision making and preparing the ground rules for operationalizing the connectivity infrastructure.

Priority areas in connectivity clusters

The following subsections make up an illustrative listing of priorities with particular relevance to South Asia.

Trade connectivity

Connectivity is an important driver for regional trade and growth. The development of local and regional markets provides a cushion against economic slowdowns. Optimal levels of commercial exchanges and the creation of forward and backward economic linkages are not possible without it. In South Asia, notwithstanding the fact that trade and growth rates are running significantly ahead of global averages, local businesses are largely cut off from regional and global production processes and value chains, with the exception of India's exporting of fabric to Bangladesh and Bangladesh's exporting of garments worldwide.

Within South Asia, for increased trade connectivity, states must make a greater effort to reduce the number of products in their negative lists by removing from the list products of export interest to others; to address nontariff barriers such as onerous testing requirements for natural products produced in similar, neighboring geo-climatic conditions; to improve suboptimal trade facilitation at land customs stations by adopting common tariff nomenclatures, customs procedures, and methods of valuation; to harmonize or mutually recognize standards; to provide more liberal and accessible transit facilities, including by facilitation of transshipments; and to undertake common measures for regulating trade to prevent smuggling of third-country goods.

Transportation connectivity

The development of air, rail, road, and waterway transportation increases trade and reduces logistic costs. The high cost of and time taken for imports and exports, particularly for LDCs and LLDCs—across three different regional groupings ranging from Central to Southeast Asia, spanning CAREC, GMS, and SAGQ—are depicted in the comparative graphs in Annexes I and II. In each of these regions, the LLDCs—Laos in GMS, Nepal and Bhutan in BBIN, and Afghanistan, Azerbaijan, Kazakhstan, the Kyrgyz Republic, Mongolia, Tajikistan, Turkmenistan, and Uzbekistan in CAREC—have substantial cost and time disadvantages compared to the coastal countries. These make it impossible for them to adhere to the just-in-time schedules required for manufacturing value chains, from which they find themselves excluded.

The absence of transit and inadequacies of regional logistics hampers even normal trade in South Asia. Shipments of Assam tea to Europe via Kolkata have to traverse a distance of 1,400 kilometers through the "Chicken's Neck," the narrow 23-kilometer strip of territory officially known as the Siliguri Corridor, through which the bulk of India is connected to its eight northeastern provinces, instead of traveling directly through Bangladesh, a distance of about 400 kilometers. Similarly, a container traveling from Dhaka to Lahore has to be shipped 7,162 kilometers by sea instead of being sent 2,300 kilometers across India by land. Container traffic between Delhi and Dhaka moves even more strangely, by a 35-day maritime route via Mumbai and Singapore or Colombo to Chittagong, instead of by railway, which would take a fraction of this time (Rahmatullah 2010, pp.176–78).

It stands to reason that the creation of cross-border infrastructure, such as the construction of integrated check posts in order to connect air, rail, road, and waterway links, and improvements to trade facilitation can reduce significantly trade and transactions costs. India has commenced building the 1,839-kilometer Eastern Dedicated Freight Corridor (a freight-only railway line) between Ludhiana and Kolkata, which will dramatically improve the movement of goods from northern to eastern India, significantly reducing GHG emissions and, ultimately, helping freight movement between Dhaka and Lahore.[15] The improvement in physical infrastructure must be complemented by improved management of shipments and customs compliance, agreements on cross-border movement of transportation vehicles, and "behind-the-border" legal and policy improvements, including the removal of red tape and spanning both "hard" and "soft" infrastructure.

For South Asia, the three new transportation connectivity proposals on the table include the Great Asian Highway project, which comprises 32 countries and includes the Asian Highway and the Trans-Asian Railways; the 5,272-kilometer Afghanistan–Pakistan–India–Bangladesh–Myanmar (APIBM) Transport Corridor connecting Kabul to Yangon; the Bangladesh–China–India–Myanmar (BCIM) Economic Corridor connecting Kunming, the capital of Yunnan Province, to Kolkata, the capital of West Bengal Province, through Myanmar and Bangladesh; and the INSTC connecting the Indian Ocean and Persian Gulf to the Caspian Sea via Iran, and then to St. Petersburg and northern Europe via the Russian Federation.[16]

Information and communication technology connectivity

The dissemination of ICTs improves productivity, facilitates trade and investment, and helps remotely located communities to be reached and integrated into the regional and global economies. ICTs are also vital for effectively leveraging transportation connectivity and promoting greater sharing of knowledge and technology within the region, leading to LDCs saving on their research and development costs.

In South Asia, India is the best-connected country at the international level, served by "the world's two largest undersea optic fiber networks owned by Indian investors," and "11 major interregional submarine systems and multiple terrestrial links," [17] placing it in a good position to provide a range of RPGs to its neighbors. These are supplemented by an array of Indian communication satellites, one of which is to be made available to the SAARC countries by the end of 2016. India could extend free or subsidized access to public facilities to its own universities. International call rates could also be dramatically reduced in the region by providing international communications gateways through India, which would benefit businesses and the general public. Nationally, India is riding its fiber optics network on the infrastructure frame of the fixed assets of its railways, such as towers, ducts, bridges, and right of way. In the same way, the basis for the Asia-Pacific Information Superhighway Initiative could be provided by the Asian Highway and the Trans-Asian Railway (United Nations ESCAP 2014, pp.28 and 56). India has launched a major program called Digital India,[18] which has counterparts in some other South Asian countries, such as Bangladesh. Countries within the region could exchange experiences and provide assistance for upgrading capacities to address common objectives and constraints.

Energy connectivity

In Asia energy demand is expected to double by 2050 (United Nations ESCAP 2014, p.9) as a result of the continent's high growth rates. Even so, two in five South Asians do not have access to commercially available energy. The cost of installing a permanent electricity connection for a newly constructed warehouse relative to per capita income is inordinately high in South Asia, ranging from 488% in India to 3,890% in Bangladesh. A particular problem for South Asia is that, like China, it is heavily dependent on fossil fuel imports, and coal remains its primary captive energy resource.

Bhutan, Nepal, and northeastern India have considerable untapped hydropower potential. Nepal alone has the potential to generate 83,000MW of hydropower, at least half of it from run-of-the-river projects that avoid ecological surprises in the fragile Himalayan region. The development of Nepal's hydropower would lead to the energy security of both Nepal and South Asia in general, creating jobs, businesses, and industry, and redressing the acute imbalance in Nepal's external trade account. Hydropower is available, affordable, reliable, and sustainable. It can contribute to climate change mitigation in South Asia generally, and especially in the Himalayan region, by reducing dependence on carbon-based fuels. Besides, through river-basin initiatives, transmission networks, and the creation of power pools, hydropower infrastructure can augment water security, flood mitigation, and irrigation, thereby increasing food security as well. If Nepal were also to build the Sapta-Koshi and Kosi high dam, currently undergoing prospection, this could ensure the availability of navigable waters along the channels connecting Nepal to the Ganges, which could help free Nepal from its landlocked status by gaining access to the Bay of Bengal through India's national waterway system, currently being used for ferrying Indonesian and Australian coal upstream to fire a series of new super-thermal power projects.

People-to-people connectivity

South Asia has done well in reducing absolute poverty from over 50% in the late 1970s to less than 30% today. Even so, besides harboring the majority of the world's poor peoples, who are water-stressed and increasingly vulnerable to environmental risks, the region has high infant and maternal mortality and child malnutrition rates, and low social investment in school education and public health (Sachs 2009, pp.43–47). Furthermore, its population is expected to rise from 1.68 billion in 2010 to 2.22 billion by 2040 (Price 2014, p.vii). Given these challenges, when designing regional projects the concerned states must ensure outcomes that are more people friendly in their welfare impact. Sustainable infrastructure services are both public goods and a form of physical and social capital, whose provision endures over time. Nationally, these would include urban renewal through smart city construction, community renovation through social housing, rural modernization through extension services and greater access to credits and markets, and improved basic services through delivery of education, public health, potable water, sanitation, and waste renewal. Regionally, these could encompass control of communicable diseases, planning for coping with pandemics, natural disaster management, and sustainable development.

The areas of cooperation listed above will require interventions from public authorities, the private sector, and civil society organizations. For instance, the Self Employed Women's Association (SEWA)—the largest trade union of unorganized women workers in the world—has mooted several people-centric initiatives in South Asia. Together with Homenet South Asia, SEWA has created a company for home-based women's workers of South Asia, the SAARC Business Association of Home Based Workers (SABAH). The Mahila Housing SEWA Trust (MHT) is working with South Asian women from slums in seven cities to combat climate change-related risks such as flooding, waters security, heat waves, and water-borne diseases. SEWA has followed a strategy to promote gender equality, employment, and augmentation of family incomes by connecting people, sharing best practices, and organizing them. Although efforts by such nongovernmental organizations can sometimes have fleeting or ephemeral impacts on the big challenges that developing countries face, the example of their success is inspirational and sometimes leads to subsequent government-led initiatives.

Conclusions

A people-centric approach could help accelerate progress on those connectivity and infrastructure projects that are most congruent with the development strategies of the states in the region.

Regarding connectivity, it might also be useful to shift the emphasis away from transit corridors, which do little to transform the transited territories, and economic corridors, which are primarily focused on ensuring a flow of investments and building manufacturing clusters, to the idea of development corridors, which consciously seek to avoid employment-neutral growth models and might ensure a more equitable distribution of benefits. This would be the surest way to gain regional traction and popular support for building the new connectivity and infrastructure RPGs needed by developing country regions all over the world.

Finally, ensuring RPG-related investments in connectivity in national development outlays will require the countries concerned to view connectivity as a key engine for sustainable growth, beginning with connectivity within these countries, such as building dedicated freight carriage railway lines, and extending it to connectivity across national borders. Even if such an approach were to be embraced at the policy level, mobilizing the means for connectivity infrastructure would still remain a challenge, and local resources would not suffice for the massive investments needed. This is where a strategic understanding among key donors and lenders, bilateral and multilateral, might prove useful in mainstreaming connectivity in development planning in individual countries, and in bringing together an international coalition for this greater purpose.

Annex I

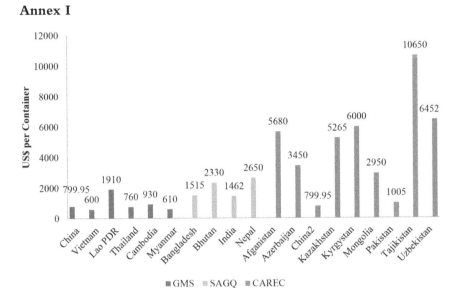

Figure 7.A1 Cost of Imports.

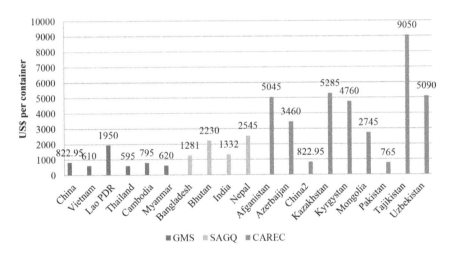

Figure 7.A2 Cost of Exports.

These graphs were created using the data from the Doing Business 2015 Database created by the World Bank Group. For more information, see www. doingbusiness.org/data/exploretopics/trading-across-borders

No data was available for Turkmenistan, hence only nine member countries of CAREC were included in the comparative graphs.

Annex II

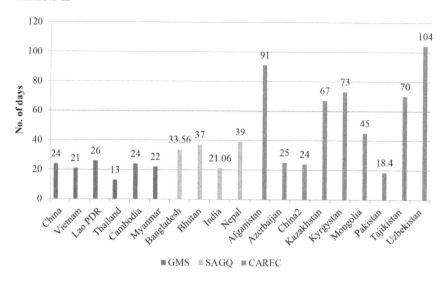

Figure 7.A3 Time for Imports.

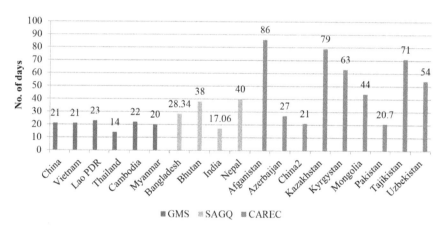

Figure 7.A4 Time for Exports.

Notes

1 SAARC comprises Afghanistan, Bangladesh, Bhutan, India, Maldives, Nepal, Pakistan, and Sri Lanka.
2 Statement of President Hamid Karzai at the 14th SAARC Summit Meeting, New Delhi, April 3, 2007. www.saceps.org/upload_file/recommendation_pdf/afghanistan_pres_hamid_karzai.pdf
3 Joint Press Release, The Third Joint Working Group Meeting on Sub-regional Cooperation between Bangladesh, Bhutan, India, and Nepal, Dhaka, January 19–20, 2016.
4 See Toman and Timilsina (2015).
5 Sudipto Mundle, emeritus professor and member of the board of governors of the National Institute of Public Finance and Policy, New Delhi, provided this insight.
6 The countries constituting the GMS include Cambodia, the People's Republic of China (PRC, specifically Yunnan Province and Guangxi Zhuang Autonomous Region), Lao People's Democratic Republic (Lao PDR), Myanmar, Thailand, and Vietnam. Those comprising CAREC include Afghanistan, Azerbaijan, PRC, Kazakhstan, Kyrgyz Republic, Mongolia, Pakistan, Tajikistan, Turkmenistan, and Uzbekistan.
7 This initiative was announced by India's Minister of State for External Affairs, A. E. Ahmed, at the first India-Central Asia Dialogue, Bishkek, June 12, 2012.
8 The SCO comprises Kazakhstan, Kyrgyz Republic, PRC, Russia, Tajikistan, and Uzbekistan. The EurAsEC is made up of Belarus, Kazakhstan, Kyrgyz Republic, Russia, Tajikistan, and Uzbekistan. The members of the EEU are Belarus, Kazakhstan, Kyrgyzstan, Armenia, and Russia.
9 OECD. "Triangular Co-operation" Findings from a 2015 Development Assistance Committee Survey. www.oecd.org/dac/dac-global-relations/Updated%20Triangular%20co-operation%20fact%20sheet.pdf. India committed food assistance of one million tonnes of wheat to Afghanistan in 2002, a part of which is being converted into high-protein biscuits for their School Feeding Programme for supply through the WFP.
10 In developing the idea of the New Development Bank, the BRICS Academic Forum had a degree of synergy in their interactions with government.
11 The Joint Statement issued at the end of the Chinese Premier, Li Kequiang, to New Delhi on May 20, 2013, stated that the two countries had agreed to hold consultations "with a view to establishing a Joint Study Group on strengthening connectivity in the BCIM region for closer economic, trade, and people-to-people linkages and to initiating the development of a BCIM Economic Corridor."
12 For information on the financing of RPGs, see Ferroni (2002, pp. 12–17). For a summary of the growing contribution by the ADB, AfDB, and IDB to RPG projects, see Hu (2012).
13 Press Information Bureau, Government of India, April 15, 2016 at http://pib.nic.in/newsite/PrintRelease.aspx?relid=138899
14 A special feature of the eight northeastern Indian provinces is that 97% of their borders are with Bangladesh, Bhutan, China, and Myanmar.
15 An environmental impact study has shown that this dedicated rail-freight corridor will generate 10.48 million tonnes of GHG emissions up to 2041–42, compared to 23.29 million tonnes in its absence—a 55% reduction in GHG emissions. See World Bank (2014, pp. 121–23).
16 The original Memorandum of Understanding for the International North-South Transport Corridor (INSTC) was signed on September 12, 2000, in St. Petersburg

by India, Iran, and the Russian Federation. Since then, 11 new members have joined: Azerbaijan, Armenia, Belarus, Bulgaria, Kazakhstan, the Kyrgyz Republic, Oman, Syria, Tajikistan, Turkey, and Ukraine.
17 "Submarine Cable Map," *Tele Geography*, www.submarinecablemap.com/
18 Digital India is a Government of India plan designed to transform the country into a digitally empowered society and knowledge economy. Its focus is on making technology central to enabling change.

References

Akhtar, Shamshad. 2014. Speech given at the United Nations Economic Commission for Asia and the Pacific, China Institute on International Studies Forum, Beijing. June 5. www.unescap.org/speeches/asia-pacific-regional-connectivity-and-integration

Bloomberg. 2016. "China-Led AIIB Announces First Loans," Bloomberg.com, June 24. www.bloomberg.com/news/articles/2016-06-24/china-led-aiib-announces-first-loans-in-xi-push-for-influence

Carsten, Paul, and Ben Blanchard. 2014. "China to Establish $40 Billion Infrastructure Fund." *Reuters*. November 8. www.reuters.com/article/2014/11/08/us-china-diplomacy-idUSKBN0IS0BQ20141108

Das, Ram Upendra. 2009. "Regional Economic Integration in South Asia: Prospects and Challenges." Research and Information System for Developing Countries (RIS) Discussion Paper No. 157, New Delhi.

Ferroni, Marco. 2002. "Regional Public Goods: The Comparative Edge of Regional Development Banks." Paper given at the Conference on Financing for Development: Regional Challenges and the Regional Development Banks, Institute for International Economics, Washington, DC. February 19. www.iie.com/publications/papers/ferroni0202.pdf

Hu, Xinglan. 2012. "Provision of Regional Public Goods: Best Practices and Role of Regional Development Banks." Policy Brief, No. 3. ADB Office of Regional Economic Integration.

Iwamoto, Masaaki, and Kyoko Shimodoi. 2015. "Japan Boosts Asia Infrastructure Outlays as China Champions AIIB." *Bloomberg Business*. May 21. www.bloomberg.com/news/articles/2015-05-21/japan-boosts-asia-infrastructure-outlays-as-china-champions-aiib

Jha, Prashant. 2014. "BRICS Bank: How PM Got Big Powers to Accept India's Idea." *Hindustan Times*. August 9. www.hindustantimes.com/allaboutmodisarkar/bank-on-modi-what-pm-got-for-india-from-brics-summit/article1-1240877.aspx

Price, Gareth. 2014. *Attitudes to Water in South Asia*. Chatham House Report. London: Royal Institute of International Affairs. www.chathamhouse.org/sites/files/chathamhouse/field/field_document/20140627WaterSouthAsia.pdf

Rahmatullah, M. 2010. "Transport Issues and Integration in South Asia." In *Promoting Economic Cooperation in South Asia: Beyond SAFTA*, edited by Sadiq Ahmed, Saman Kelegama, and Ejaz Ghani. New Delhi: SAGE Publications India.

Sachs, Jeffrey D. 2009. "South Asia Story of Development: Opportunities and Risks." In *Accelerating Growth and Job Creation in South Asia*, edited by Ejaz Ghani and Sadiq Ahmed. Oxford: Oxford University Press. http://siteresources.worldbank.org/SOUTHASIAEXT/Resources/223546-1192413140459/4281804-1192413178157/4281806-1255623211158/fulltextjobcreation.pdf

Sandler, Todd. 2003. "Demand and Institutions for Regional Public Goods." In *Regional Public Goods: From Theory to Practice*, edited by Tam Nguyen, Antoni Estevadeordal, and Brian Frantz. Washington, DC: Inter-American Development Bank and Asian Development Bank. https://publications.iadb.org/handle/11319/260?locale-attribute=en

Shah, Ghulam. 2013. "Energy Cooperation between Central Asia and South Asia: Prospects and Challenges." In *Perspectives on Bilateral and Regional Cooperation: South and Central Asia*, edited by Rashpal Malhotra. Chandigarh: Centre for Research in Rural and Industrial Development.

Tahilyani, Naveen, Toshan Tamhane, and Jessica Tan. 2011. "Asia's $1 Trillion Infrastructure Opportunity." McKinsey and Company. www.mckinsey.com/insights/financial_services/asias_1_trillion_infrastructure_opportunity.

Toman, Michael, and Govinda Timilsina. 2015. "The Benefits of Expanding Cross-Border Electricity Cooperation and Trade in South Asia," World Bank, June. http://pubdocs.worldbank.org/en/271291458180265540/pdf/South-Asia-Electricity-Trade.pdf

United Nations ESCAP. 2014. "Bridging Transport, ICT and Energy Infrastructure Gaps for Seamless Regional Connectivity." Paper presented at the Second United Nations Conference on Landlocked Developing Countries. Vienna, Austria. November 3–5. www.unescap.org/sites/default/files/LLDCs%20paper.pdf

World Bank. 2014. "Government of India and World Bank Sign $1.1 Billion Agreement for the Eastern Dedicated Freight Corridor Project." World Bank. December 11. www.worldbank.org/en/news/press-release/2014/12/11/sign-billion-agreeement-eastern-dedicated-freight-corridor

8 Open borders

A regional public good

Johanna Mendelson-Forman

Introduction

If there are two words that define the history of the Americas, then "borders" and "sovereignty" would be near the top. Since the Treaty of Tordesillas (1494) divided the New World between Spain and Portugal, boundaries have characterized the way sovereignty has been perceived. In reality, however, lines on maps were often disregarded as settlers and traders expanded their reach across boundaries.[1] The Treaty of Madrid (1750) between the Spanish and Portuguese crowns ended an armed conflict over what constituted the borders between these two empires in South America, with Spain ceding much of what is present-day Brazil to the Portuguese.

When parts of the Americas became independent from Spain at the beginning of the 19th century, borders were also very much on the minds of liberators. New countries were carved out of the old viceroyalties and captaincies general of the Spanish Empire. Geography was also a factor in retaining the old borders of the former colonies since the Andes, a formidable natural barrier, limited the scope for cross-continental engagement.

Brazil did not become an independent nation until 1822. Its territory encompassed much of the land given to Portugal with the drawing of the 15th-century Tordesillas line, and it remains a vast nation, the largest in South America. Ten other nations border Brazil from the forests of the Amazon to the Atlantic. Brazil's western borderlands still remain largely ungoverned spaces, due to the natural barrier of the Amazon. Brazil has tended to look toward the Atlantic and only in recent years has it seemed to engage more with the potential for looking west toward the Pacific Coast.

Why all this history? If borders were real barriers to economic and political engagement until the end of the 20th century, in the 21st century they have become enablers of a wide range of regional public goods (RPGs). In an age of globalization, where both opportunities and threats to peace and security respect no boundaries, it is important to consider borders as more than territorial markers. Today, borders are less a cause of conflict than a means to build peace. Borders create opportunities to harmonize the rule of law across boundaries, to ensure access to trade, and to jointly address threats arising from climate change.

By analogy, when borders between states are open, there is greater mobility of people, knowledge, and goods. South America, one of the world's most peaceful regions, also has the capacity to become a source of food and water security in a more hostile world if its borders were to become fully open. This is not to diminish the challenges of transnational criminal activities in the region—these are the strongest cases against opening borders in South America. These challenges are a cause for concern, especially since they take advantage of the lack of infrastructure and investments needed to connect the continent.

The potential for South America to emerge as a region that can work multilaterally to become part of the solution to its own problems is an opportunity that cannot be squandered. If regionalism is used wisely this century, South American nations could lead the way in creating greater energy and environmental security, greater global trade in products that can feed the world, while also addressing some of the thornier problems of security that are ever-present in this vast continent.

This paper makes the case for considering whether open borders in South America should be considered an RPG. If we add open borders to the list of RPGs, can this promote greater security, economic growth, and development? While sovereignty remains a defining feature in the politics and diplomacy of the region, there is a growing recognition that there is a greater need to work collectively to address issues that are no longer limited to single states. Disagreement is often over who the appropriate partners are for such collaborations.

By using examples from the region, and also from other parts of the world that have experienced a decline in state sovereignty resulting from borderless threats, there may be a basis for the countries of South America to redefine their collective action in terms of open borders being an RPG. If borders are viewed as public goods, they can be used positively to address common challenges, from the harmonization of customs rules to the identification of joint infrastructure needs among neighboring states. Open borders can also facilitate a greater sense of continental integration that has been hard to achieve, but yet remains important to increase economic growth. More effective regional collaboration that takes economic integration seriously can also help collective responses to such transnational threats as climate change, environmental threats, migration, and all forms of illicit activities. Section 2 of this paper examines the evolving concepts of RPGs and the application of these to the reality of South America.

Section 3 reviews examples of other approaches to open borders and also looks at some cases in the region that have provided benefits from cross-border integration. Some of the examples from within South America arose from situations where regional governance was weak. Others were the result of geography that made defense of national territory difficult. More recent efforts to deploy military units to borders in places like Brazil do not provide adequate security to ensure that cross-border threats in largely uninhabited areas can be easily managed.

Section 4 takes the case of Brazil and its neighbors as a first step in examining the practical application of borders as an RPG in terms of the threats and challenges faced by such a large country with so many neighbors. Brazil's geopolitical situation shares common transnational challenges with its neighbors, from environmental issues and illicit activities to gaps in governance, due to the vast and uninhabited regions within its territory that create a political space for nonstate actors to operate in.

Section 5 examines how the new multilateralism in South America impacts the concept of open borders. In section 6, I also suggest some possible measures to evaluate the way borders in South America may be transforming other RPGs. Lessons learned can provide important applications for investment, prevention of transnational criminal activity, and controlling climate and environmental change.

The evolving concept of borders as public goods

Territoriality as an organizing principle of international relations has been challenged time and again since the end of the Cold War. Globalization has ended the nation-state's monopoly over internal sovereignty, which in earlier times was guaranteed by territory. Economic integration and interdependence have been the basis for a globalized economy by creating this transformation in thinking. Open borders are a manifestation of this change and have contributed to reducing internal sovereignty when it comes to promoting trade, infrastructure, and migration in some parts of the world (Reinicke 1997).

In the 21st century, open borders have become a form of RPG precisely because the nature of globalism has shifted from a world solely inhabited by nation-states to a world where nonstate actors are engaging in actions that were once the sole domain of sovereign actors. States in Latin America were once wary of violating the sovereignty of other states by crossing geographic boundaries, but this is no longer the case. When nonstate actors no longer respect boundaries, be they guerrillas, paramilitaries, gangs, or other illicit actors, governments are less concerned about the legalities of pursuing criminals across frontiers.

Anne Clunan and Harold Trikunas (2010, p.18) call this an era of "softened sovereignty," in which nonstate actors, both good (international organizations, nongovernmental organizations, transnational corporations) and bad (terrorist groups, transnational criminal networks) impinge upon the sovereignty of the state. The fact that one nation's border policies on everything from trade, migration, and illicit activity might impact security and development throughout an entire region is evidence of softened sovereignty.

The existence of the borderless threats that United Nations (UN) Secretary General Kofi Annan cited in his 2005 report helped to recalibrate thinking about the limits of sovereignty when it comes to economic growth and development in many multilateral institutions. Central to this thinking was the notion that only collective actions by groups of nations would suffice to address this new world without traditional boundary lines (Annan 2005; United Nations 2004).

A decade later, we are still trying to manage the ever-growing number of transnational threats that impact peace and security.

In a region whose history has been one of wars fought over borders since the days of independence, South America in the 21st century is becoming a borderless space where transnational threats to regional security can no longer be thought of in terms of lines between countries. The ongoing threats of illicit flows of narcotics, money, arms, and people are also giving new meaning to creating policies that collectively address transnational challenges to peace and security. Brazil has been especially interested in finding regional solutions by working together with its neighbors on these types of issues.[2]

There still exists a residue of distrust among many countries of South America when it comes to completely embracing the notion of open borders. A long history of earlier border conflicts, like the one between Chile and Bolivia or the rekindling of the one between Venezuela and Guyana, suggest that confidence building is essential to advance cross-border collaboration around economic and social issues. These disputes, however, all point to the nexus of security and development, as these involve ongoing issues of trade and access to natural resources and markets that require a delicate balance between the role of regional organizations that facilitate opportunities and bilateral confidence-building measures that require careful, delicate, diplomatic solutions.

Regional governance is affected by transnational threats such that borders can no longer be used as a barrier to action. This is especially the case in the post-9/11 environment, as Andres Serbin (2014) observed: since 9/11, Latin American regionalism has shifted, prioritizing transborder threats over national security. The ongoing threats of illicit flows of narcotics, money, arms, and people are also giving new meaning to creating policies that collectively address transnational challenges to peace and security. In 2005, the Organization of American States (OAS) created the Secretariat for Multidimensional Security, a direct response to the increasingly transboundary nature of threats in the region.[3]

As the region's largest country and one that borders ten other states, Brazil has the greatest interest in ensuring that its borders are secure and are not barriers to greater economic development. The evolving policies of both Rousseff governments, which advocated for policies strengthening borders, demonstrate a growing awareness of what is at stake at the farthest outposts of its territory. Managing transnational criminal activities in the 28 twin cities that are located on the borders between Brazil and Peru, Bolivia, and Uruguay has presented the government of Brazil with new challenges managing cross-border law enforcement and customs. The interconnectedness of these twin cities blurs the national borders running through them and fuels high levels of informal economic and criminal activity.

Precedents for open borders

The idea and practice of open borders as RPGs has strong international precedent—either *de jure,* as in the Schengen Area—a borderless zone in

Europe consisting of 28 countries with no border checks and a common visa policy—or *de facto*, such as the border between the Hong Kong SAR and the rest of China, which has relatively unchecked cross-border movement of goods and people.

The European Union (EU) "experiment" and concurrent development of the open border Schengen Area established an international precedent for the overhaul of traditional border management in favor of open borders as RPGs. The Schengen Area and the EU created a common passport to facilitate ease of travel between member states, developed a predictable trade system, and intensified information sharing on transborder threats.

To promote integrated border management across the expansive Schengen Area, which spans 1.6 million square miles and has a population of 400 million people, participating countries created infrastructure such as the Schengen Information System, which facilitates rapid communication for law enforcement in all states. Furthermore, with 37% of Europe's population living in border areas along 38 international borders made up of geographic and linguistic barriers, many of which bear the scars of European wars, the EU created the European Territorial Cooperation program, better known as Interreg, to promote harmony and cooperation across borders.

As the first policy of its kind, the benefits and challenges of the Schengen Area provide good lessons learned for others heading down the open border route. The positive results of open borders for participating states are varied and include increasing migration and mobility of people, increasing ease of trade, and making states more robust trading partners in the international arena (Davis and Gift 2014). Some of the biggest challenges Schengen countries face today include the negative effect of strict visa regimes on tourism and surging numbers of illegal immigrants, which are putting pressure on a relatively young collective border management system. The Schengen Area is the strongest case of *de jure* open borders today and provides a framework for other regions to emulate when pursuing open borders for RPGs.[4]

Hong Kong, on the other hand, represents an interesting case study for the value of *de facto* open borders without the official infrastructure. Since the transition of Hong Kong's sovereignty from the United Kingdom to China in 1997, the economically laissez-faire city-state has attracted high volumes of trade, migrants, and daily workers from the neighboring Chinese city of Shenzhen. Facilitating this level of border crossing are extraordinarily relaxed border policies creating a "blurred" border between the two sides. While border and visa checks remain in place, and the border is still considered heavily guarded (Chen 2005, p.86), the process is largely symbolic and often very fast—most individuals cross within 30 minutes.

This *de facto* open border has allowed both adjoining areas to experience rapid economic growth, and is "intimately linked with the miraculous growth of Shenzhen from a tiny farming and fishing border town to a large modern metropolis over the last two decades" (Chen 2005, p.86). Integrated border management helps manage the blurring of the Guangdong–Hong Kong border.

Examples of this integrated border management are dual Guangdong–Hong Kong license plates for cars commonly traversing the border, and the Working Meeting of the Hong Kong/Guangdong Co-operation Joint Conference (also referred to as the Guangdong–Hong Kong Liaison Annual Working Meeting), a joint committee established in 1987 which facilitates cross-border police cooperation (Wong 2012, p.126).

The beginnings of an open border framework also exist within the Union of South American Nations (UNASUR)[5], which has raised the question of a common South American currency and citizenship, integrated defense policies, and a single market, inspired by the EU (Flannery 2012; Kašpar 2011). On December 5 2014 the leaders of UNASUR met in Mérida, Venezuela. The 12-nation organization proposed a framework for South American integration approving the concept of South American citizenship. According to UNASUR Secretary General Ernesto Samper, "this should be the greatest register of what has happened" (Robertson 2014). Included in this proposal was the creation of a single passport and a homologate university degree in order to give South Americans the right to live, work, and study in any UNASUR country. It also gave legal protection to migrants—similar to the freedom of movement rule for EU citizens. While Samper's declaration did not constitute a total commitment to open borders, he spoke of the convergence of citizens and similarities, all with the goal of greater integration (Robertson 2014). Former Brazilian president Lula da Silva noted at the meeting where Samper gave his statement that "today we construct an integration project that is more daring, that takes advantage of our rich history, goods, and culture" (Robertson 2014).

At UNASUR's February 2015 meeting, Ecuadorian President Rafael Correa announced his support for this unity framework, stating that a united South America would be the fourth-largest economy in the world, accounting for 6% of global GDP (Sputnik News 2014). This factor alone will in the end only be measured by the ability to continue to attract increased foreign investment and willingness by each of the UNASUR member states to participate in more open trade arrangements going forward.

Brazil's evolving border policies: making the case for a regional public good

The strip of land along Brazil's ten-nation border, the "*faixa de fronteira*," is a remarkable space that embraces large parts of the Amazon and areas of more populated regions in the south.[6] After those of Russia and China, Brazil has the world's longest frontier, totaling more than 10,400 miles, and these adjacent areas account for 27% of its national territory. Ten million people live along the border areas, including many of Brazil's protected indigenous groups. The security dimensions of such a vast frontier are manifold—not least of which are due to the ungoverned spaces of borderlands.[7] Transnational crime—drug trafficking, arms trafficking, natural resource exploitation, illegal migration, and environmental challenges such as deforestation from land grabs for agriculture and illegal logging, disruption of biodiversity, and managing the insurgency from Colombia—all present a complex set of issues that the Brazilian government is compelled to address (Lyons 2014).

In 2005, Brazil started a process of rethinking its borders with a focus on integration, cooperation, articulation of specific issues, and collaboration with its neighbors on shared security and development issues. It established the Ministry of National Integration, with its Secretariat for Regional Programs (Ministério da Integração Nacional 2005). In 2011, President Dilma Rousseff unveiled the Strategic Border Plan, the main objective of which is prevention, surveillance, and prosecution of cross-border crimes. As part of this new strategy, the Development Program for the Frontier Strip (PDFF) was established, targeting a strip 150 kilometers wide along the length of the border. This frontier strip is now considered a priority area for regional development instead of just an area of national defense.

Under the revised policy, the border has been divided into three zones—north, central, and south. Each area has its own specific characteristics with challenges for security. For example, most of the drug trafficking comes through the central zone, but it has more recently become a hub of illegal migration, especially from Peru and Ecuador. The smuggling of arms, cigarettes, and other contraband comes through the south, in the region close to Paraguay and the Triple Frontier (the tri-border area between Argentina, Brazil, and Paraguay). The north is also a zone of illicit arms transfers where armed insurgents frequently operate.

Having such a large frontier makes it difficult to secure national territory, as the Brazilian Army alone is not able to cover all of the terrain. Brazil's Integrated Border Monitoring System, known as SISFRON, is a radar network managed by the Ministry of Defense that will create an electronic fence with the country's ten neighbors (Moura 2013). It is already operational in the southern arc, but is not expected to be completed until the end of 2019 (Szklarz 2014). In the last few years, the Brazilian Army has been deployed to the northern frontier, with 35 brigades and 49 platoons operating along the border. SISFRON will help the Brazilian military detect smuggling, terrorism, and drug-trafficking activities by enabling coordination with all organizations and government agencies responsible for monitoring and surveillance of the land borders. Over the last 30 years, Brazil has also complemented its military presence with technical support, radar, and other forms of observation to deal with homeland security.

Since 2011, the challenge for Brazil's military is that increased responsibility at the border has given the armed forces a traditional policing role. That same year, the Brazilian government implemented military operations Ágata I, II, and III, to combat illegal activities such as illicit drugs, weapons, and contraband in border areas. The three operations required more than 15,000 soldiers and spanned borders with Argentina, Paraguay, Uruguay, Colombia, Bolivia, and Peru. Since 2011, operations Ágata IV, V, VI, and VII have been put into place, the latter involving over 30,000 members of the armed forces and covering the entire border, focusing on the northern region (Muggah and Diniz 2013). This mission has not been well received by some civilian politicians, although the military is reported to be performing well. This reflects a deep-rooted distrust on the part of some Brazilians toward the military, whose border policing functions reach up to 150 kilometers into the country. Ironically, the average citizen has no idea of the connection between borders and crime (Muggah and Szabo 2014).

Of the many twin cities along Brazil's extensive border, there are 28 that the Ministry of Regional Integration has identified as entailing specific, separate challenges. Mostly located in the southern part of the country, these are places where two cities operate independently on either side of the border, one in Brazil and the other in Uruguay, Bolivia, or Peru (Duarte de Castro 2011). Both sides have separate police forces, and necessary coordination of policies to address transnational crimes is difficult because there are no formal border agreements in many cities. There is an ongoing effort to rectify this situation, especially as Brazil seeks to support economic development and regional integration with its neighbors. It is in these twin cities that these borders could generate RPGs if policies could be harmonized to give both countries some sense of confidence that both countries would gain from such coordination.

Experts on border policy note that Brazil's transition from a security-only approach to one that includes development has not been easy, and some have offered harsh analyses in this regard (Muggah and Diniz 2013). The lack of interagency coordination makes the implementation of projects very difficult, mainly because the National Integration Commission relies on the willingness of other ministries to engage in a country where a strong tradition of independence of action characterizes the way ministries operate. Similarly, the Border Caucus that operates in the National Congress of Brazil lacks strong influence in border management because its members represent states, not cities. Action only takes place at the mayoral level since these are the officials with the resources to implement meaningful actions in border zones.

The Ministry of National Integration and Commerce often attempts to address cross-border questions, but national legislation is needed to create a strategy for better coordination. For example, the ministry asked for the creation of a Regional Border Fund, but this has yet to be funded by Congress. In the meantime, Brazil's greater funds and capacities, compared with its neighbors, create additional problems in terms of governance of border city regions, particularly when it comes to the question of managing transnational threats. Among the economic priorities at the border is electricity, where there are opportunities for investments in hydroelectric power plus wind and solar energy.

In light of phenomena such as those discussed above, scholar Alcides Vaz (2014) has drawn the following seven conclusions about Brazil's border strategy:

1　Integration must take place at the local level, not on a national platform.
2　There is no relationship between border policy and broader national development objectives.
3　There is no mandate to work the development side of the border, thus initiatives are effectively done piecemeal, rather than through an integrated strategy that brings together security and development.
4　Due to the lack of infrastructure, the private sector is ambiguous about what the borders mean in terms of investment. Some even believe that these areas are a constraint to investment.
5　There has been little effort to integrate the private sector into the policy dialogue—agribusiness, defense, and energy sectors could all play a role, but have not as of the time of writing.
6　There is great potential for triangular cooperation at the border with international cooperation being the missing link in developing the border space.
7　Civil society actors at the local level could be more involved in communities when it comes to discussions about the border. To some extent the Ministry of Justice, through AFRON, is working on this aspect of the problem.

Multilateral forums such as the South American Defense Council, part of UNASUR, have little interest in border security per se. In spite of the opportunity in the region to broadly coordinate border management on security and trade, Brazil prefers to manage its border through country-specific agreements. This tends to limit the opportunities for a more strategic approach that would address the types of transnational issues that affect both Brazil and its neighbors. It does, however, give Brazil the ability to dominate the policy agenda through its large resource base.

As the world's second largest cocaine consumer, Brazil has an interest in managing drug trafficking. Brazil should also be interested in protecting its homeland from becoming a global base for illicit transfers of arms. Building responsive capacity to address these challenges, both domestically in Brazil and internationally through targeted foreign assistance, aids in the prevention of conventional counter-trafficking and in better screening for weapons of mass destruction or related contraband, the irregular movement of people (terrorists), and more widely in building efficiencies at border crossings that facilitate the enhanced movement of legitimate goods and persons.

In sum, while Brazil may currently be an imperfect example of integrated counter-trafficking—much less of coordinated nonproliferation—its internal efforts to better integrate development objectives with security policies is enviable and worthy of further examination by governments across the Global North who seek to press a nonproliferation agenda onto developing states of the South.

Brazil is also a country where the notion of borders as RPGs is highly evolved and worthy of greater study. The fact that there are regional meetings and resources dedicated to addressing common problems, and consultation with a multilateral actor, albeit a weak one (UNASUR), may reflect a growing trend in shared sovereignty. The increasing need for cross-regional infrastructure, the expansion of connectivity in the region, and the deepening of trade relationships no longer makes the actual geographic barriers an excuse for Brazil's policy makers to ignore its borders. In the process of making full use of open borders to enable greater public goods, Brazil has become much more engaged in recognizing the advantages it can gain by pursuing more integrated border policies in South America, both bilaterally and through multilateral organizations such as UNASUR and MERCOSUR.

Finally, what may be overlooked in the case of Brazil is that the rise of UNASUR with its evolving creation of norms, procedures, and commissions may be creating other types of public goods akin to insurance. The creation of regional mechanisms to discuss border issues should be considered a means of conflict prevention at the borders, one that adds great value by insuring that any protracted conflict with Brazil's neighbors is highly unlikely (Domínguez 2000).

New regionalism, competitive multilateralism, and regional integration

South America's rich history of support for multilateral organizations such as the OAS has given way to a new regionalism to create the strong foundation needed to use open borders as a mechanism for regional integration. UNASUR, the Community of Latin America and Caribbean States (CELAC), the part-trade, part-political arrangement that is MERCOSUR,[8] and the newly created Pacific Alliance (PA) all create new demands on regional leaders that go well beyond national borders. These organizations have taken on the challenge of promoting regional dialogue among members, while also providing space for bilateral diplomacy.[9]

As Jorge Domínguez (2000) notes, the "relative insulation" of Latin America from the global economic system, due to factors both political and geographic, allowed for "Latin American governments [to] found [. . .] and foment [. . .] a multilayered international system." Furthermore, these governments fostered the ideology "that countries from all the Americas should engage in conflict containment and conflict settlement wherever conflict emerged." As early as the 20th century, South American nations permitted multilateral organizations to act as external conflict mediators between states. These factors, argues Domínguez (2000), allowed Latin America to create comparatively strong regional conflict mitigation institutions, and bolstered regionalism over globalism.

Early conflicts arose from unresolved border disputes whose roots were deeply enmeshed in the economy and infrastructure of the region. From 1919 to 1995 there were 51 border disputes in the Americas: 30 prior to 1945; 6 after 1945; and 15 that remained active throughout this entire 76-year period. During that same timeframe, these territorial disputes increased the risk of armed conflict between states. The Leticia Border Dispute was the earliest example of multilateralism as an effective peacekeeper and guardian of border management. It centered on a 20th-century territorial dispute between Colombia and Peru over a trapezoid of tropical jungle which connected Colombia to the Amazon River, the port of Leticia, and by extension to the South Atlantic. Leticia was founded by Peruvians in the 19th century but was ceded to Colombia in the 1922 Salomón–Lozano Treaty. In late 1932, an armed band of Peruvian civilians and soldiers (supposedly acting without Peruvian government approval) took Leticia and forced the Colombian residents to flee. The League of Nations was asked to mediate with the support of Brazilian diplomats and eventually oversaw the peaceful return of the area to Colombian control. The process generated an interesting historical precedent: for the first time ever, soldiers wore the armband of an international organization (the League of Nations) as they performed peacekeeping duties. The soldiers were Colombian, and the use of the armbands was primarily a face-saving device to permit the Peruvians to leave without appearing to submit to the Colombians. Nevertheless, the use of these 75 Colombian soldiers as international peacekeepers was an antecedent for UN peacekeeping several decades later (Minster 2016; Huth and Allee 2003, p.27).

Similarly, there is a border dispute between Ecuador and Peru that dates back to the period of independence from Spain and has twice resulted in armed conflict between the two nations: once in 1828 and again in 1995 with the brief Cenepa War, whose end was brokered by four countries—Brazil, Argentina, Chile, and the United States. The creation of the multinational Military Observer Mission Ecuador–Peru (MOMEP) was yet another dimension of how regional security concerns had evolved so that the ultimate disposition of this border area became a source of regional military confidence building in the process of keeping the peace. On October 26, 1998, Ecuador and Peru signed a comprehensive peace accord establishing the framework for ending border disputes. Formal demarcation of these border regions started on May 13, 1999, and the agreement was ratified without opposition by both nations' congresses. Of the process, US President Bill Clinton said: "This signing marks the end of the last and longest-running source of armed international conflict in the Western hemisphere" (BBC News 1998).

Another outcome of this conflict was the creation of an RPG between Ecuador and Peru that remains an example of how a security issue was transformed into a demonstration of the potential for cross-border integration. This RPG took the form of two officially established protected zones governed by the peace treaty between the two countries. These are the 2,540-hectare El Cóndor National Park in Ecuador and the 5,440-hectare Ecological Protection Area in Peru, in addition to which the Peruvian government established the Santiago-Comaina Reserved Zone, with a surface area of 1.64 million hectares. Conservationists commonly call these protected areas "peace parks." These actions created a space for cooperation between both countries and ultimately led to binational initiatives (Alcalde, Ponce, and Curonisy 2004).

Perhaps the most important joint conservation initiative in this region was the Peace and Binational Conservation in the Cordillera del Cóndor, Ecuador–Peru project, which was financed by the International Tropical Timber Organization (ITTO) and included governmental agencies, representatives from indigenous communities, and domestic and international NGOs. This project, which was developed between 2002 and 2004, stood out for its contribution to the peace agreement and overall biodiversity conservation.

Other major regional players include the OAS, which was formed in 1948 as a regional organization that reflected the security needs of the Cold War. Today it has been sidelined by other regional organizations, but still operates as a treaty-based organization with obligations by member states to respect sovereignty in the face of transnational threats. Its strong adherence to the principles of sovereignty in an age of transnational challenges has been both its strength and its weakness.[10]

In South America, the 1947 Inter-American Treaty of Reciprocal Assistance, commonly known as the Rio Treaty, may be the first recognition of security as an RPG in the 20th century. The treaty was promoted by the United States in the lead-up to the Cold War, and propagated the notion of "hemispheric defense." It stated that an attack against any signatory was considered an attack against all, and is credited with having made "a significant impact in preventing and resolving some conflicts in the region, both within and between states" (Serbin 2014). Although several countries have denounced the treaty, noting that it was a vestige of US imperial interests in the region,[11] it still remains in force. Alternative regional security arrangements by the countries of the Bolivarian Alliance for the People of the Americas (ALBA)[12] have become an alternative to US-based security arrangements. Nevertheless, these new configurations still rely on the concept of collective security against threats arising from transnational problems.

Ironically, it was the OAS that actually embraced a much broader definition of security with its Declaration of Multidimensional Security in 2003, three years before the UN noted that collective security could be invoked not only upon the invasion of one country by another, but also as a result of the existence of transnational threats that respected no borders yet represented a threat to peace and security. This declaration recognized that the traditional military approach to security was not sufficient, and that security required the engagement of civil society and the private sector, and that events such as natural disasters also required collective action.

The constitutive articles of UNASUR specify that among the threats the region would have to address was global drug trafficking; endemic corruption that eroded governance; trafficking in persons; arms trafficking; transnational organized crime; terrorism; nonproliferation; ending landmines; countering terrorism; and strengthening regional cooperation on citizen security. Yet addressing these threats would be done with the exclusion of the United States and Canada.

As mentioned above, UNASUR is the first regional institution in South America to explicitly raise the question of common currency and citizenship. At the time of its founding, Brazil's foreign minister, Celso Amorim, proclaimed, "UNASUR has given South America a face" (Nolte and Wehner 2012, p.10). The formation of a South American Defense Council as an organ of UNASUR engendered security cooperation and conflict resolution but was not created as a system of common defense.

UNASUR has become the forum of choice in South America as a mediator for regional disputes. In 2010 it worked to resolved border tensions between Colombia and Venezuela and in 2009 it also negotiated the relocation of US military bases from Ecuador to Colombia. These actions have reinforced UNASUR's ability to replace the OAS as a source for dialogue and mediation, thus changing the regional norms and preferences for dispute resolution going forward (Amorim 2010, p.229).

However, the intention to create an open border policy has yet to be implemented. What has become apparent with the new multilateralism of South America is that there is a growing willingness to recognize the concept of shared sovereignty among members. This has laid a foundation for looking at groups like UNASUR to enable open borders as an RPG. It is an important first step in expanding the potential for greater collaboration around borders and economic development.

Are open borders creating regional public goods?

Estevadeordal et al. (2016) identify six main public good functions: natural resources, economic cooperation and integration, human and social development, governance and institutions, peace and security, and connectivity. Many of these functions require management across a country's borders plus cross-border cooperation for their implementation. They suggest that the appropriate measure of cooperation for each of these functions is the number and quality of treaties between or among a group of countries. These provide the legal basis for the creation of RPGs.

A review of the 16 agreements ratified among Brazil and its neighbors (Table 8.1) show that ten are bilateral and six are multilateral. All, however, demonstrate a high level of engagement over a wide range of issues, underscoring the importance of breadth of public goods functions that these agreements cover. It would be a mistake to look at the history of agreements and think they were examples of Brazil's unilateral security interests alone. These agreements are entry points to the creation of RPGs precisely because they promote greater peace and security for Brazil and its neighbors.

When it comes to peace and security, "all nuclear related and military treaties are considered RPG cooperation" (Estevadeordal et al. 2016). One example of this is the highly successful implementation of the 1968 Treaty of Tlalteloco, ratified by most nations in South America, Mexico, and the Caribbean during the Cold War. The creation of a nuclear-free zone predates UNASUR, but the ongoing regional compliance with the Treaty of Tlalteloco supporting the nonproliferation of nuclear arms from Mexico to Patagonia is a clear example

Table 8.1 Brazil's Border Agreements

Year	Country partner(s)	Title of Agreement	Details	Source*
1979	Argentina, Brazil, Paraguay	Tripartite Agreement Itaipú–Corpus	This agreement ended a long-standing dispute between the three countries on hydroelectric development on the Paraná River. It established rules governing the shared use of hydroelectric projects. The rules were amended for fairer allocation of resources to Paraguay in 2009.	International Water Law
1991	Argentina	Brazilian–Argentine Agency for Accounting and Control of Nuclear Materials (ABACC)	Established under an agreement between Brazil and Argentina to engage exclusively in the peaceful use of nuclear energy, the ABACC is charged with the administration of safeguards ruling all nuclear energy use in both countries.	Nuclear Threat Initiative/
1993	Colombia	Colombo–Brazilian Neighborhood and Integration Commission	Signed initially in 1993 and reactivated in 2003, this commission is designed to facilitate strategic coordination across borders, particularly those of twin cities Leticia and Tabatinga, on issues such as environmental and health regulations and human rights commitments.	Colombia's Ministry of Foreign Affairs
1994	Guyana	Guyana/Brazil Mixed Border Commission	The commission works on maintenance of boundaries, access to cross border commerce, and issues related to defense and border security. The fifth commission meeting took place in 2009.	
1995	Bolivia, Colombia, Ecuador, Guyana, Peru, Suriname, Venezuela	Amazon Cooperation Treaty Organization (ACTO–OTCA)	The ACTO was designed to promote the sustainable development of the Amazon basin. Today it coordinates infrastructure and transportation projects among member states and with UNASUR. Most recently, a 2010 meeting of Ministers of Foreign Affairs held in Lima, Peru, approved the strategic Amazon cooperation agenda which established the way forward for the organization in the coming five years.	Organização do Tratado de Cooperação Amazônica

(continued)

Table 8.1 (continued)

Year	Country partner(s)	Title of Agreement	Details	Source*
1998	Argentina, Paraguay	Tripartite Commission of the Triple Frontier	This commission serves as a security mechanism along the triple border and meets regularly together with the United States on counterterrorism.	US Department of State
2000	Argentina, Bolivia, Chile, Colombia, Ecuador, Guyana, Paraguay, Peru, Suriname, Uruguay, Venezuela	Initiative for the Integration of Regional Infrastructure in South America (IIRSA) for COSIPLAN/UNASUR	This initiative created an action plan on the subject of regional infrastructure integration including telecommunications, transportation, and infrastructure. The Coordinating Committee of the South American Infrastructure and Planning Council (COSIPLAN) of the Union of South American Nations (UNASUR) was founded in 2009 to assist in these continuing efforts.	Initiative for the Integration of Regional Infrastructure in South America
2002	Colombia	Brazilian–Colombian Border Commission	This commission meets only as needs arise and is designed to quickly resolve border issues, and includes public and private parties according to the issue at hand.	Janus.net, e-Journal of International Relations
2004	Colombia, Peru	Memorandum of Understanding between Colombia, Brazil and Peru to Fight Illicit Activities in the Border Rivers and/or Communes	This memorandum establishes multiple forums for coordination including information sharing, joint exercises, and logistical support.	Janus.net, e-Journal of International Relations
2008	Colombia	Agreement for the Establishment of a Special Regime Border Zone for Leticia and Tabatinga	The establishment of a special borders zone is designed to encourage bilateral projects in these twin cities.	Janus.net, e-Journal of International Relations

2009	Colombia	Establishment of the Bilateral Commission	The bilateral commission meets regularly and aims to encourage greater bilateral coordination.	Janus.net, e-Journal of International Relations
2011	Colombia	Bilateral Border Security Plan	This plan allowed for the buildup of troops on both sides of the border, as well as for "hot pursuit", across borderlines of guerrillas and traffickers.	Diálogo Digital Military Magazine (1)
2011	Paraguay	Information sharing agreements	Brazil and Paraguay signed bilateral agreements to improve information sharing and to coordinate anti-trafficking efforts. According to InSight Crime, these agreements allow for greater coordination and exchange of information about drug trafficking in the region.	InSight Crime and Americas Quarterly
2011	Bolivia	Operation Brazil-Bolivia (commonly known as Operation BraBo)	This action plan consisted of three separate agreements on coordinated information sharing, training, and bilateral police cooperation to combat drug trafficking across the border.	Diálogo Digital Military Magazine (2)
2012	Suriname	Bilateral Defense Cooperation	Defense cooperation between the two countries has thus far consisted of overhauling Suriname's military equipment and cooperating on Brazil's border security initiative, Operation Agata 7.	Diálogo Digital Military Magazine (3)
2014	Venezuela	Bilateral agreement to enhance cross-border health interventions to interrupt transmission of onchocerciasis in the Yanomami area	This agreement allows both countries to work across borders to implement the World Health Organization's strategy to eliminate onchocerciasis, primarily through joint surveillance and technical teams.	World Health Organization

(continued)

Table 8.1 (continued)

Sources: Americas Quarterly: www.americasquarterly.org/brune (accessed April 8 2016).

Colombia's Ministry of Foreign Affairs

Diálogo Digital Military Magazine (1): http://dialogo-americas.com/en_GB/articles/rmisa/features/regional_news/2011/07/15/aa-colombia-brazil-security (accessed April 8 2016).

Diálogo Digital Military Magazine (2): http://dialogo-americas.com/en_GB/articles/rmisa/features/regional_news/2011/06/10/aa-bolivia-brazil (accessed April 8 2016).

Diálogo Digital Military Magazine (3): http://dialogo-americas.com/en_GB/articles/rmisa/features/regional_news/2013/08/13/suriname-brazil (accessed April 8 2016).

Fifth Conference of the Guyana/Brazil Mixed Border Commission http://sistemas.mre.gov.br/kitweb/datafiles/Pcdl/pt-br/file/Documenta%C3%A7%C3%A3o%20Oficial/Guiana/Densifica%C3%A7%C3%A3o/5%C2%AA%20Confer%6C3%6AAncia-Ingl%C3%AAs.pdf

Initiative for the Integration of Regional Infrastructure in South America: www.iirsa.org/ (accessed April 8 2016).

InSight Crime: www.insightcrime.org/news-briefs/brazil-paraguay-to-join-forces-against-organized-crime (accessed April 8 2016).

International Water Law: www.internationalwaterlaw.org/documents/regionaldocs/parana1.html (accessed April 8 2016).

Janus.net, e-Journal of International Relations (1): www.redalyc.org/pdf/4135/413536171001.pdf (accessed April 8 2016).

Nuclear Threat Initiative: www.nti.org/learn/treaties-and-regimes/brazilian-argentine-agency-accounting-and-control-nuclear-materials-abacc/ (accessed April 8 2016).

Organização do Tratado de Cooperação Amazônica: http://otca.info/portal/ (accessed April 8 2016).

US Department of State: www.state.gov/documents/organization/31943.pdf (accessed April 8 2016).

World Health Organization: www.who.int/neglected_diseases/onchocerciasis_brazil_venezuela/en/ (accessed April 8 2016).

of transnational needs trumping the older issue of national sovereignty. That this treaty remains in force and is a centerpiece of regional diplomacy speaks to the potential for other agreements that address other contemporary threats including climate change, environmental crimes, and illicit trafficking.[13]

Recent agreements between countries in South America around peace and security cooperation underscore the importance of cooperation through peace-keeper training and support for a South American Defense Council. While this initiative is still being formed, it has produced a new regional training school located at the UNASUR headquarters in Ecuador to teach regional defense doctrine to military and civilian national security experts.

Cooperation within South America, particularly between Brazil and its ten neighbors, is also driven by economic incentives (resources, infrastructure, and connectivity). The announcement that Brazil and China would build a Trans-Pacific Railroad opens greater opportunities for Brazilian businesses to expand commerce with Asia by reducing transportation costs. Even with the current slowdown in China's economy, the demand for Brazilian beef and other commodities will continue. This ambitious project will expand Brazil's trade horizons toward the Pacific and will also open up access to Peru and other markets along South America's Pacific coast (Stuenkel 2015).

Some specific types of indicators come to mind that can help us understand this connection. In the case of natural resource cooperation, it is possible to measure cross-border cooperation for resource development and also whether some types of border disputes arise from the discovery of new high-value resources that rekindle old conflicts. Some types of energy production, especially hydroelectric and wind power, devolve economic benefits to border states and can also help promote investment and growth. These agreements and projects can easily be measured.[14]

Similarly, economic cooperation can be measured by both cross-border trade statistics and by the number of regional and bilateral trade agreements that have been negotiated in support of greater regional integration. The growing willingness of countries to cooperate around trade both regionally and subregionally again helps explain the salience of open borders as a basic RPG enabler. MERCOSUR and the more recent Pacific Alliance and Andean Cooperation Agreement are all examples of public goods created by countries looking beyond borders to develop greater trade and investment.

Conclusions

Whether borders have become an RPG in South America depends on where you sit. Trends in multilateral organizations to consider open borders are a first step toward regional integration. Moreover, in spite of rhetoric to the contrary, many of South America's states are demonstrating that shared sovereignty is an essential factor in managing threats that arise from the environment and public health. What limits the concept of borders as RPGs is the way South American states balance their own security interests, especially with respect to ungoverned spaces, with the broader needs of creating common strategies that protect all nations against the rising transnational criminality that can easily undermine economic gains.[15] If open borders are to enable a wide range of other public goods, then a greater push to harmonize laws, especially in twin cities, must become a priority. The same can be said for creating migration policies that are both humane and respectful of national economic and social integration needs.

While South American leaders had looked to Europe as a model for open borders, the current migration and refugee crisis has actually challenged the successful 1995 Schengen agreement. Both Germany and France suspended their open border policy. Public opinion has turned against this vision of integration in part because of the overwhelming flow of refugees from Syria and elsewhere into Europe since the fall of 2015 (Traynor 2016). If South America is to move toward a European model of open borders it must also be mindful of the potential for things going awry. UNASUR's 2015 proposal to create a South American passport and to provide region-wide academic credentials is just that. It will not get to the bigger question of how regional governance over migrant populations will evolve in the years to come. Yet at the July 2016 UNASUR meeting of the Bureau on Regional Mechanisms for Integration, efforts were being made to consolidate a regional identity through the progressive recognition of the rights of citizens of one member state in any other member state.[16] The expansion of regional multilateralism in the hemisphere, especially through UNASUR, is significant, but remains untested in terms of managing transnational threats to peace and security with the exception of proliferation of nuclear materials. Traditional multilateralism, organizations whose charters are binding and have international legal consequences—that is, the OAS and UN—are still more important in terms of developing policies that have the force of law when it comes to border management. The rise of the South American Defense Council and the various bilateral commissions in Brazil represent more localized forms of governance that may also yield new rules that may be easier and faster to implement. But the ability to enforce these new agreements is still in question. Whether the nations of South America are willing to work with the older charter organizations to guide policy on a wide range of cross-border issues moving forward is a cause for concern. This competitive multilateralism also has deeper implications for border management and regional policies in the long run.

Open borders should be thought of as a threshold issue for the creation of RPGs. While South America is a relatively peaceful zone, it is still a region faced with many transnational threats that impact security, development, and governance. Reliance on a regional power like Brazil to set the agenda for using open borders to generate other public goods is very much a work in progress. Yet Brazil's experience provides both positive and negative lessons for how greater openness and shared sovereignty might lead to greater regional economic integration, increased access to knowledge, connectivity, and more stable and reliable governance.

Notes

1 The Treaty of Madrid, 1750, between the crowns of Spain and Portugal, established a form of *Pax Americana* after both countries fought a war over Portuguese incursions into Spanish colonial territory, specifically the Banda Oriental, most of which constitutes present-day Uruguay. Spain ceded much of its land to Portugal.

2 An example of this type of policy coordination is taking place in Brazil in its work with other neighboring states through its Commission on Macro-Regional Integration, as confirmed in an interview with the coordinator of macro-regional programs from Brazil's Ministry of National Integration (Bastos Peixoto 2014).

3 See Organization of American States website on the Secretariat for Multidimensional Security www.oas.org/en/sms/sms_secretaria.asp and its "Declaration of Security in the Americas" (Organization of American States 2003).

4 The Schengen Agreement, a core principle of European regional unity, is under assault today because of the refugee crisis, which is testing the limits of the principle of open borders. Yet the Schengen Agreement has always contained an exception in times of national emergency for countries to limit free movement. Only time will tell whether the EU will be able to retain the Schengen principles if refugee flows and provision for the displaced are not resolved (Smale and Eddy 2015).

5 UNASUR was founded in 2008 and consists of 12 South American member states: Argentina, Bolivia, Brazil, Chile, Colombia, Ecuador, Guyana, Paraguay, Peru, Suriname, Uruguay, and Venezuela.

6 French Guyana is an overseas territory of France and is thus not recognized as a country.

7 See Kacowicz (2012), who describes the necessary conditions for a safe haven as being "specific geographical features, weak governance, a history of corruption and violence, and poverty and inequality."

8 The creation of MERCOSUR in 1992 was seen as a means of reducing the rivalry between Argentina and Brazil, although the other members, Uruguay and Paraguay, were also beneficiaries of this new common market arrangement.

9 See Trinkunas, Jaskoski, and Sotomayor (2012) for a comprehensive discussion of border issues in the Americas.

10 While this paper does not address the role of the OAS, it is clear from recent history that some efforts, such as the creation of the Democratic Charter in 2001, actually were headed toward recognition of a more reduced emphasis on sovereignty as it related to good governance. The charter, signed on September 11 2001, came at time when there was great emphasis on the need for collective action against not only threats to democracy in the hemisphere, but against nonstate actors attacking sovereign nations. The implication was that there was a sense of shared sovereignty in light of external events, but it was considered by many of the countries to be something that the USA could impose in the face of external transnational threats. This aspect of the charter was ultimately its less effective link to civil society organizations as well as to certain regional governments.

11 Nicaragua denounced the Rio Treaty on September 20 2012; Bolivia on October 17 2012; Venezuela on May 14 2013; and Ecuador on February 19 2014.

12 The ALBA countries are Antigua and Barbuda, Bolivia, Cuba, Dominica, Ecuador, Grenada, Nicaragua, Saint Kitts and Nevis, Saint Lucia, Saint Vincent and the Grenadines, and Venezuela.

13 See "Treaty for the Prohibition of Nuclear Weapons in Latin America," *International Atomic Energy Agency*. https://www.iaea.org/publications/documents/treaties/treaty-prohibition-nuclear-weapons-latin-america-tlatelolco-treaty

14　It should also be noted that the recent Venezuela-Guyana dispute over a border territory that contains potentially important oil deposits is an example of how conflict may arise over these types of territorial boundary issues go unresolved. See Miroff (2015).

15　The World Economic Forum's Open Borders Index, www.worldatlas.com/articles/top-50-countries-on-the-open-border-index.html, noted that only Chile and Costa Rica were among the most open in terms of migration and trade. El Salvador at 61 is also of note. More importantly all three of these countries are inside the top ten for the market access pillar.

16　See www.unasursg.org/en/node/844

References

Alcalde, Martín, Carlos F. Ponce, and Yanitza Curonisy. 2004. "Peace Parks in the Cordillera del Cóndor Mountain Range and Biodiversity Conservation Corridor." Woodrow Wilson Center Working Paper. Washington, DC: Woodrow Wilson International Center for Scholars. www.wilsoncenter.org/sites/default/files/ponce.pdf

Amorim, Celso. 2010. "Brazilian Foreign Policy under President Lula (2003–2010): An Overview." *Revista Brasileira de Política Internacional* 53: 214–240.

Annan, Kofi. 2005. "In Larger Freedom: Towards Development, Security and Human Rights for All." Report presented at the 59th Session of the United Nations General Assembly, New York City, NY. March 21. www.unmillenniumproject.org/documents/Inlargerfreedom.pdf

Bastos Peixoto, Alexandre. 2014. Interview by author. Brasilia, Brazil. May 29.

BBC News. 1998. "Peru and Ecuador Sign Border Treaty." October 27. http://news.bbc.co.uk/2/hi/americas/201442.stm

Chen, Xiangming. 2005. *As Borders Bend: Transnational Spaces on the Pacific Rim.* Lanham, MD: Rowman and Littlefield, 2005.

Clunan, Anne, and Harold Trinkunas. 2010. "Conceptualizing Ungoverned Spaces: Territorial Statehood, Contested Authority, and Softened Sovereignty." In *Ungoverned Spaces: Alternatives to State Authority in an Era of Softened Sovereignty*, edited by Anne Clunan and Harold Trinkunas. Stanford, CA: Stanford University Press.

Davis, Dane, and Thomas Gift. 2014. "The Positive Effects of the Schengen Agreement on European Trade." *The World Economy* 37: 1541–1557.

Domínguez, Jorge I. 2000. *Boundary Disputes in Latin America.* Washington, DC: United States Institute of Peace. www.usip.org/sites/default/files/pwks50.pdf

Duarte de Castro, Sergio. 2011. "Cross-Border and Inter-Regional Cooperation: New Actors and Institutions in Brazil." Presentation at the Secretariat of Regional Development, Ministry of National Integration, Brasilia, Brazil.

Estevadeordal, Antoni, Louis W. Goodman, Theodore Kahn, and Teng Liu. 2016. "Regional Public Goods and Sustainable Development." Unpublished paper. June 22.

Flannery, Nathaniel Parish. 2012. "Explainer: What is UNASUR?" Americas Society/Council of the Americas. November 30. www.as-coa.org/articles/explainer-what-unasur

Huth, Paul K., and Todd L. Allee. 2003. *Democratic Peace and Territorial Conflict in the Twentieth Century.* Ann Arbor, MI: University of Michigan Press.

Kacowicz, Arie M. 2012. "Regional Peace and Unintended Consequences: The Peculiar Case of the Tri-Border Area of Argentina, Brazil and Paraguay." Paper presented at the "Borders and Borderlands in the Americas" workshop, Stanford University, Palo Alto, CA. June 18–19.

Kašpar, Petr. 2011. "The Logic of UNASUR: Its Origins and Institutionalization." Master's Thesis, Aalborg University, Denmark. http://projekter.aau.dk/projekter/files/53154638/The_LOGIC_OF_UNASUR.pdf

Lyons, John. 2014. "Brazil Reaches Across Border to Battle Source of Cocaine." *Wall Street Journal*. December 3.

Ministério da Integração Nacional [Ministry of National Integration, Brazil]. 2005. *Proposta de Reestruturação do Programa de Desenvolvimento da Faixa de Fronteira* [Proposal for the restructuring of the border strip development program]. Brasilia: Ministério da Integração Nacional. www.mi.gov.br/documents/10157/3773138/Introdu%C3%A7%C3%A3o+e+antecedentes.pdf/98476e45-c143-449b-b6c5-1f9287a90553

Minster, Christopher. 2016. "The Colombia-Peru War of 1932." http://latinamerican history.about.com/od/thehistoryofcolombia/p/The-Colombia-Peru-War-Of-1932. htm.

Miroff, Nick. 2015. "Taking Land from Guyana May Be One Thing All Venezuelans Can Agree on." *Washington Post*. July 16. www.washingtonpost.com/news/worldviews/wp/2015/07/16/something-venezuelans-can-all-agree-on-taking-land-from-guyana/

Moura, Paula. 2013. "Brazil Looks to Build a 10,000 Mile Virtual Fence." *National Public Radio*. May 16.

Muggah, Robert, and Gustavo Diniz. 2013. "Securing the Border: Brazil's "South America First" Approach to Transnational Organized Crime." Igarapé Institute. October.

Muggah, Robert, and Ilona Szabo de Carvalho. 2014. "Changes in the Neighborhood: Reviewing Citizen Security Cooperation in Latin America." Igarapé Institute. March.

Nolte, Detlef, and Leslie Wehner. 2012. "UNASUR and the New Geopolitics of South America." Paper prepared for the XXIII World Congress of Political Science, Madrid. July 8–12.

Organization of American States. 2003. "Declaration of Security in the Americas." Declaration presented at the Organization of American States Special Conference on Security, Mexico City, Mexico. October 27–28. www.oas.org/en/sms/docs/DECLARATION%20SECURITY%20AMERICAS%20REV%201%20-%2028%20OCT%202003%20CE00339.pdf

Reinicke, Wolfgang H. 1997. "Global Public Policy." *Foreign Affairs* 76: 131–132.

Robertson, Ewan. 2014. "UNASUR Moves toward Continental Freedom of Movement, Venezuela Makes 'Equality' Call." *Venezuela Analysis*. December 5. http://venezuelanalysis.com/news/11057

Serbin, Andres. 2014. "Squaring the Circle? Transatlantic Relations and New Latin American Regionalism." In *Atlantic Currents. An Annual Report on Wider Atlantic Perspectives and Patterns*, 61–80. Washington: The German Marshall Fund at the United States and OCP Center.

Smale, Alison, and Melissa Eddy. 2015. "Crisis Tests European Core Value: Open Borders." *New York Times*. October 1.

Sputnik News. 2014. "South American UNASUR Summit Calls for Greater Unity, Freedom of Movement." *Sputnik News*. June 12. http://sputniknews.com/latam/20141206/1015559314.html

Stuenkel, Oliver. 2015. "The Politics of China's Amazonian Railway." *Post-Western World*. August 16. www.postwesternworld.com/2015/08/16/politics-amazonian-railway/

Szklarz, Eduardo. 2014. "Sisfron Technology Helps the Brazilian Armed Forces Secure Border Regions." *Diálogo, Digital Military Magazine*. November 21. http://dialogo-americas.com/en_GB/articles/rmisa/features/2014/11/21/feature-03.

Traynor, Ian. 2016. "Is the Schengen Dream of Europe Without Borders Becoming a Thing of the Past?" *The Guardian*, January 5.

Trinkunas, Harold, Maiah Jaskoski, and Arturo Sotomayor. 2012. "Border and Borderlands in the Americas." Report for the US Naval Postgraduate School Center on Contemporary Conflict.

United Nations. 2004. "A More Secure World: Our Shared Responsibility." Report of the Secretary-General's High-Level Panel on Threats, Challenges and Change. www.un.org/en/peacebuilding/pdf/historical/hlp_more_secure_world.pdf

Vaz, Alcides. 2014. Interview by author. University of Brasilia, Brasilia, Brazil. May 29.

Wong, Kam C. 2012. *One Country, Two Systems: Cross-Border Crime Between Hong Kong and China*. New Brunswick: Transaction Publishers.

9 Advancing digitization as a regional public good

Kati Suominen

Introduction

International trade is a regional and global public good with significant development benefits. Studies show that international cooperation in trade, such as the formation of regional trade agreements and harmonization of policies, leads to increased regional trade flows, which in turn advance economic growth and development within regional economies through various mechanisms, such as an increased variety of products, lower prices for consumers and companies, the expansion of scale economies and productivity, and job creation among firms engaging in international trade.

What is more, when carried out in the spirit of open regionalism, increased regional economic activity has been shown to bring positive externalities for nonregional economies, due to the increased demand for goods and services in the regional market—the European Union (EU), for example, has benefited from the North American Free Trade Agreement (NAFTA), just as China is poised to benefit from the Transatlantic Trade and Investment Partnership (TTIP). The literature has also found that in many countries, regional trade cooperation has brought countries together to negotiate trade agreements and consolidate pro-trade business lobbies, paving the way to global, multilateral liberalization and trade.

However, while hugely beneficial, existing regional and global cooperation has yet to be aligned with the dramatic changes in the global economy and trade spurred on by digitization. New disruptive technologies—the cloud, e-commerce, 3D printing, big data, the Internet of Everything, virtual currencies, and other digital technologies—are revolutionizing the economics of global production and trade. In this way, they are opening up great new opportunities for even the smallest businesses and solo entrepreneurs to make, market, and move products; to scale their businesses at lower cost; and to reduce waste and slack. These technologies put the consumer rather than giant retail chains behind the wheel of globalization, expanding access to a wide variety of products and reducing costs. As such, emerging technologies are the 21st-century equivalent of steam engines and containers: they dramatically expand the possibilities of trade to generate economic growth.

These changes are not automatic, however. The Internet has been successful thanks to multilateral, multi-stakeholder dialogues that created the basis from which market forces have been able to spread the Web. However, today's governments face two key challenges in translating digitization into trade, economic development, and inclusive growth: (1) most people and companies have yet to use the Internet regularly, let alone to do so to gain new economic opportunities; and (2) even the companies and consumers that do operate online have yet to fully leverage the Internet and other digital technologies when they do become available to add new value to products and services—such as by streamlining operations, developing new solutions, and making transactions easier and more efficient, including across borders.

Numerous obstacles stand in the way of these two goals. Some are national policy and regulatory barriers in terms of data flows and e-commerce, trade in digital products and services, and government procurement of IT services. Others are disparate national standards, such as different mobile spectra, that result in frictions and welfare losses. Still others involve inadequate investments in digitization. The purpose of this chapter is to propose ways for countries to overcome these obstacles through regional action with their neighbors.

Some might argue that this focus is redundant—that regional action is less relevant as the world becomes digital. Conceived as a global highway for the 21st century, the Internet spans the globe. Likewise, many companies today are fully global, and more and more consumers buy goods and services online from abroad, often from sellers in entirely different regions. Empirical evidence indicates that geographic distance or a common language are less relevant in determining the direction of e-commerce than that of traditional trade. As such, it could be said that multilateralism, not regionalism, is essential in the global digital economy—and also that business interests will call for multilateral action. Furthermore, it is perfectly reasonable to assert that it is national and not regional action that is critical for success in the global digital economy: Estonia, Korea, Finland, Singapore, Israel, and some other economies have become digital powerhouses not because they collaborated with their neighbors, but because they put domestic policies in place to systematically invest in digitization and have a workforce able to take advantage of new technologies.

At the same time, regional action can complement national and global policies in two ways:

- *Creation of regional digital scale economies*. Regions that are fragmented by barriers to the movement of digital goods and services and that lack common interconnection points, interoperable payment networks, fluid cross-border data flows, harmonized mobile spectra, or interoperable Internet laws are not in a position to create the scale economies that have allowed such digital markets such as the United States and China to birth global companies like Facebook, Google, and Alibaba. Common regional regulatory and policy frameworks in such areas as privacy, consumer protection, and cybersecurity help lower operating costs for companies across regional markets and also incentivize investment and the creation of start-ups. The EU is currently taking steps toward a single European digital market precisely by harmonizing national regulatory frameworks. Regionalized digital markets can also stimulate new efficiencies, such as by forcing consolidation among national operators.

*   *Spurring regional digital trade and e-commerce.* E-commerce is about digital marketing and sales and the online purchasing of mostly physical products that then need to be shipped to the end consumer, who often resides in another country. Most companies that sell online also export. Often involving shipments of small parcels that are highly sensitive to the fixed costs of shipping and delivery, e-commerce requires world-class transport infrastructure, fluid customs procedures, and efficient logistics. In addition, given that many actual and prospective participants in e-commerce are small businesses and even solo entrepreneurs with limited capacities for complying with complex trade rules, there is a growing need for new, simplified trade compliance systems. Individual regions can be useful laboratories for such improvements, especially given that, on the one hand, countries within key regions have often achieved similar levels of development and sophistication in these areas, and, on the other, that most regions have carried out extensive work over the last few decades to catalyze "regular" (i.e. nonelectronic) intraregional trade. The Asia-Pacific Economic Cooperation forum (APEC) and the Association of Southeast Asian Nations (ASEAN) have long cooperated precisely to catalyze intraregional e-commerce.

This chapter will propose new regional strategies to drive digital scale economies and regional e-commerce. The chapter is organized as follows. Section 2 reviews the impact of digitization on growth and trade. Section 3 analyzes the state of digitization in different world regions and the extent of digital flows (including data flows and e-commerce) within different regions. Section 4 puts forth strategies and policies for action, while Section 5 contains conclusions.

Digitization as a driver for growth

Digitization drives economic growth and productivity in a number of ways: directly, through the production of ICT goods and services; and indirectly, through the reorganization of the ways goods and services are created and distributed as well as through employment gains in digital industries and new digital applications that help consumers and companies cut costs, establish their business, and engage in trade (Pepper and Garrity 2015). Digitization can be measured in many ways—the most commonly used proxies, Internet usage and broadband penetration, have been found to reflect significant boosts in trade, growth, and productivity.

For example, Riker (2014) finds that growth in broadband use between 2000 and 2011 increased a country's trade-to-GDP ratio by 4.2% on average, with much larger effects in high-income countries (a 10.2% increase on average) than in developing countries (a 1.7% increase on average). Assuming that broadband adoption continues to increase, Riker calculates that the trade-to-GDP ratio will increase by an additional 6.9% on average in high-income countries and by an additional 1.7% on average in developing countries. According to a US International Trade Commission study (USITC 2013), the Internet has been found to reduce trade costs for US imports and exports of digitally intensive goods and services by 26% on average. Also many other scholars such as Vemuri and Siddiqi (2009), Choi (2010), and Liu and Nath (2013) have found the Internet to boost trade.

Connectivity also spurs on macroeconomic growth. Manyika et al. (2013) find that in 2004–2009, the Internet contributed 10% or more to total GDP growth in Brazil, China, and India, and this effect has accelerated. Scott (2012), who analyzed the effect of fixed telephony, mobile telephony, Internet use, and broadband use on economic growth between 1980 and 2011 across 86 countries, shows that a 10% increase in fixed broadband penetration results in a 1.35% increase in GDP growth in developing countries and a 1.19% increase in developed economies. Deloitte (2012) shows that doubling mobile broadband data use leads to a 0.5% increase in GDP per capita growth rates. Jordán and De León (2011) and Mack and Faggian (2013) argue broadband has become a crucial component of national infrastructure similarly to how railroads, roads, and electricity have driven development to date.

It is, of course, lamentable that some 90% of the population in low-income countries and over 60% globally are not online yet, and that even fewer people have broadband. At the same time, it can be argued that the best of digitization is yet to come. For example, to date, the annual economic value generated by the Internet is US$1,488 per capita in developed countries, but only US$119 per capita in developing economies (Nottebohm et al. 2012).

As new Internet-based technologies grow more ubiquitous, these gains can be expected to increase further. For example, new technologies enable companies to make, market, and move products and services at lower costs and tap new scale economies. They expand economic participation, enabling the more marginal participants in the global economy—garage entrepreneurs, small businesses, and individuals from all walks of life—to establish their business, become exporters, and even grow into mini-multinationals running their own supply chains. New technologies also spur growth by enabling consumers and companies to access a wider variety of products and services at lower costs while also reducing search costs. Concrete examples that reflect these notions include the following:

- *3D printing*. With software guiding the printing process, 3D printing revolutionizes manufacturing. It enables items to be made as needed, and made differently without any retooling, leading to savings of as much as 25–50% in component costs. For example, the 130-strong firm ClearCorrect, a maker of invisible orthodontic aligners based in Houston, was previously able to make only one set of aligners at a time before resetting its expensive machinery, which also often broke down (Pullen 2013). Using 3D printing, the company manufactures batches of 60–70 models at a time, taking five minutes to make each one as opposed to the 13 minutes using the previous process. McKinsey calculates that 3D printing could generate US$230–US$550 billion in economic gains per year by 2025, most of them for consumers (Cohen, Sargeant, and Somers 2014).

- *Big data.* Big data has expanded drastically, enabling companies to identify high-quality suppliers, mitigate supply chain shocks, and streamline logistics. For example, the mining giant Rio Tinto taps data from its trucks, drills, process surveillance cameras, control systems, and maintenance system logs from its mines around the planet 100 milliseconds after the data is live. By analyzing this data in Brisbane, Australia, the company is able to cut operational costs and improve the safety and environmental performance of its mines in real time, benefiting employees, host economies, and customers.

- *Radio frequency identification (RFID) and logistics.* DHL and Nike have partnered in Brazil to monitor products at every stage of the warehousing and distribution process through RFID systems that broadcast a signal with information about the product and its location. This enables the companies to monitor workflow in distribution centers and make improvements in real time. By shifting to RFID, Walmart has saved 7.5% on labor costs in warehouses and up to 40% in regional distribution centers (Pisello 2006).

- *E-commerce.* E-commerce enables consumers and businesses to gain access to a wider variety of products and compare prices and facilitates exporting for businesses of all sizes. For example, on surveying 3,250 SMEs in nine developing countries (Brazil, China, India, Kenya, Mexico, South Africa, South Korea, Turkey, and Ukraine) and two advanced economies (France and Sweden), the Boston Consulting Group found that SMEs that are heavy Web users are almost 50% likelier to sell products and services outside of their immediate region and 63% likelier to source products and services from farther afield than light or medium Web users—in other words, the Internet enables them to shop around for the best deal (Figures 9.1 and 9.2) (Zwillenberg, Field, and Dean 2014). Likewise, eBay data indicates that most eBay sellers export—a stark contrast to brick-and-mortar sellers. For example, in Chile 100% of sellers on eBay export, while only 18% of offline firms are exporters; in addition, online sellers reach 28 different world markets, as opposed to the one to two markets of traditional offline exporters (Figure 9.3).

- *Virtual currencies.* Bitcoin has unlocked international peer-to-peer microtransactions that previously might never have been made due to elevated fixed costs. While PayPal is much cheaper than banks for international transactions, it still charges a 3.9% transaction fee plus a fixed fee based on currency received, in addition to hidden currency conversion fees. In contrast, Bitcoin costs less than 1% regardless of how far apart the buyer and seller are.

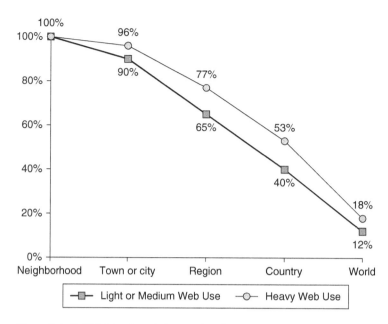

Figure 9.1 SMEs' Sales Reach by Market, by Level of Web Use.
Source: Zwillenberg, Field, and Dean (2014).

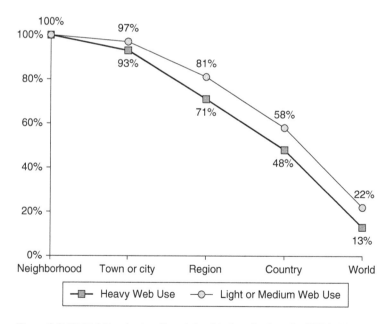

Figure 9.2 SMEs' Purchasing Reach by Market, by Level of Web Use.
Source: Zwillenberg, Field, and Dean (2014).

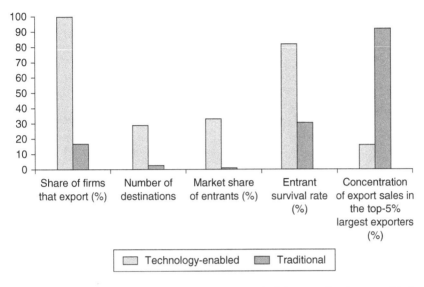

Figure 9.3 Export Participation and Performance of Chilean Technology-Enabled
   SMEs vs. Traditional SMEs, 2013.

Source: eBay (2013).

The state of digitization in world regions

Cloud- and web-based digital technologies and data flows dramatically expand
the opportunities for trade and welfare gains. What, then, is the state of digitization in different world regions? How interconnected are the countries within
specific regions, and how extensive are intraregional cross-border digital flows
and trade? The following sections examine these two questions in turn, with
an eye to generating regional policy recommendations.

How digitized is the world?

Figure 9.4 shows the results of the World Economic Forum's networked readiness index for different regions, which encompasses dozens of digital economy
indicators. African economies are the least digitized, followed by Latin America
and Asia. In most regions, the spread between the top and bottom performers
is not exceedingly wide; however, in Southeast Asia there is a vast gap between
Singapore and Myanmar, and in the Middle East between Israel and Yemen.
   A number of enabling factors drive these results, of which the key ones are:

- **Internet access.** Many regions lag sorely behind advanced economies in
   Internet connectivity. Even though mobile phones have spread explosively
   across the world, Internet penetration and broadband use rates are still very
   low. For example, fewer than 50% of Latin Americans use the Internet

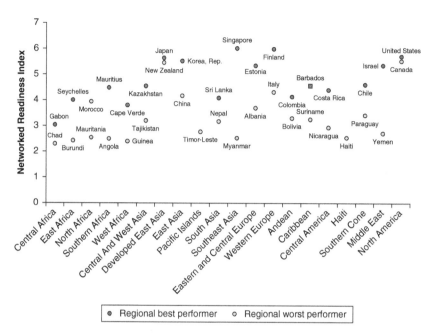

Figure 9.4 Networked Readiness Index in 2015, by Subregion.

Source: Author, based on World Economic Forum data.

(Figure 9.5). While this is more than twice the levels for 2004, it still trails behind Internet use rates in advanced markets. Barely over 10% of people in developing regions have fixed broadband (Figure 9.6). In Africa, this problem affects all countries; in Latin America, countries such as Barbados, Mexico, and Uruguay are doing much better than their neighbors, which tend to be at the level of the least connected African and Asian economies. In regions such as Southeast Asia and Eastern Europe, countries such as Korea and Estonia are among the world's most fully subscribed broadband users, while in these same regions, Mongolia and Ukraine score poorly.

• ***Cost of access***. Low rates of broadband penetration are partly due to high broadband tariffs. Although, globally speaking, incomes are rising and Internet access prices are falling, the cost of connectivity can be excessive to low-income people, who by necessity prioritize food, shelter, clean water, and energy. According to McKinsey (2014), in the 20 countries with the largest number of people offline, low-income individuals account for 50% of the offline population, who together represent 1.6 billion people. Broadband penetration grows rapidly only when the retail price for this service falls below 3% to 5% of the average monthly income for that country (ITU, cited in Rogy 2014). Today, the price of mobile broadband stands at an average 9% of income in the poorer parts of the Middle East and North Africa; in some of these economies, mobile broadband costs more than 40% of disposable income for the poorest.

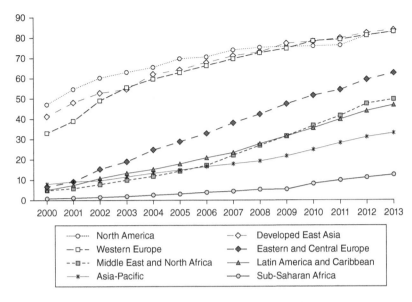

Figure 9.5 Internet Users (per 100 People) in 2000–2013, by Region.

Source: World Bank's World Development Indicators.

- *Adoption and usage by companies and consumers*. Adoption by firms and consumers is critical to the success of the digital economy. Again, many African and Asian economies fall far behind the best performers in their subregions (Figure 9.7). However, firms around the world have yet to adopt e-commerce as a growth driver. Even though many companies use email, most still do not have their own websites, let alone capabilities for potential buyers to order online (Figure 9.8).[1] Several emerging markets in such regions as Southeast Asia and the Southern Cone in Latin America that have relatively good ICT infrastructures and Internet connectivity still struggle to translate their connectedness into economic and social gains (Figure 9.9).

  Assuming that e-business intensity (the extent to which the Internet is integrated into processes within companies) grows as firms adopt digital capabilities (such as using the Internet for internal emails, online banking, and setting up websites with an online store), productivity also surges. One analysis of Asian economies suggests that productivity increases linearly as e-business intensity increases, reaching 10% in services and 5% in manufacturing when intensity reaches 100% (Boston Consulting Group and GSMA 2012). This omits network effects and spillovers, which can be very significant. These findings suggest that there are a number of barriers such as low e-literacy rates, low firm resource bases, low capacities for adopting and absorbing new technologies, and, in the area of e-commerce, obstacles such as poor e-payment systems, and a lack of e-commerce logistics.

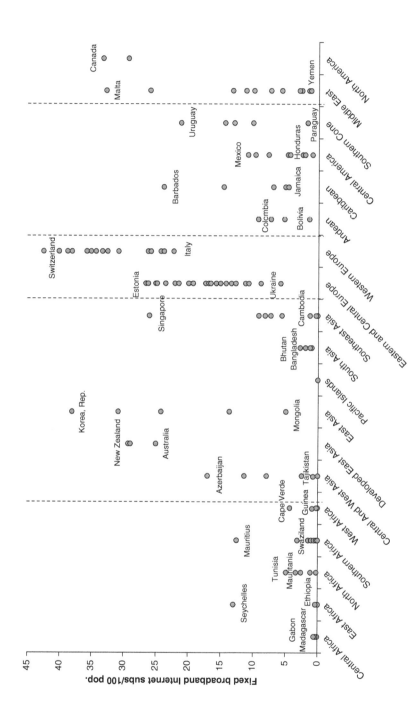

Figure 9.6 Fixed Broadband Internet Subscribers (per 100 people) in 2013, by Region.

Source: Author, based on World Economic Forum data.

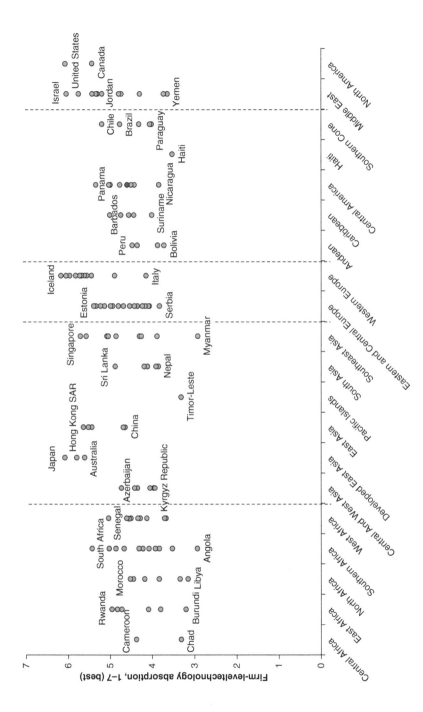

Figure 9.7 Firm-level Technology Absorption in 2015, by Subregion.

Source: Author, based on World Economic Forum data.

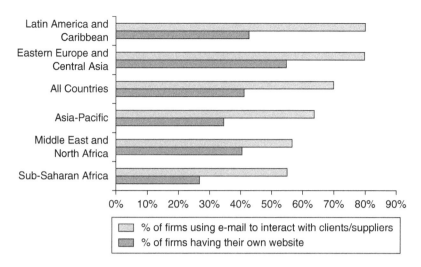

Figure 9.8 Percentage of Firms Using Email and Websites in 2015, by Region.

Source: World Bank's Enterprise Surveys.

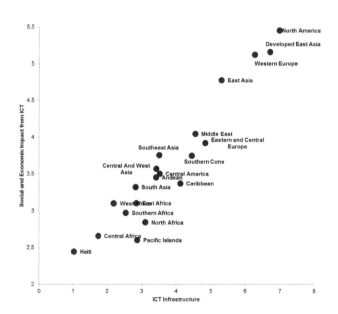

Figure 9.9 ICT Infrastructure and Economic and Social Impacts from ICT in 2015, Selected Regions.

Source: Author, based on World Economic Forum data.

Regional digital trade and economies

How connected are countries to their neighbors digitally? Are there regional digital markets, or are digital flows more global and interregional?

One way to get at this question is to analyze global IP traffic, which has increased fivefold over the past five years and will increase threefold over the next five. According to Cisco, annual global IP traffic will pass the zettabyte (1,000 exabytes) mark by the end of 2016, reaching 2 zettabytes per year by 2019. This is a compound annual growth rate of 23% in 2014–2019—equivalent to 142 million people streaming Internet HD videos simultaneously, all day, every day in 2019. By 2019, global Internet traffic will be 66 times the volume of the entire global Internet in 2005. IP traffic is currently growing fastest in the Middle East and Africa, followed by Asia Pacific (Figure 9.10).[2]

Another measure of the digitization of the world economy is e-commerce. With individuals and businesses of all sizes increasingly engaging in cross-border trade by selling goods and services online, e-commerce is growing explosively around the world. Globally, business-to-consumer (B2C) transactions alone are expected to soar from US$1.5 trillion in 2014 to US$2.4 trillion in 2017 (Figure 9.11). This is approximately 10% of all e-commerce—while data on business-to-business (B2B) transactions is limited, these are estimated to make up some 90% of e-commerce.

The Asia Pacific is the world's leading e-commerce market: transactions in the region have been growing at an annual average of 50% between 2012 and 2017 in the region to make up nearly half of all global e-commerce transactions. The greatest growth is in China, where cross-border transactions are

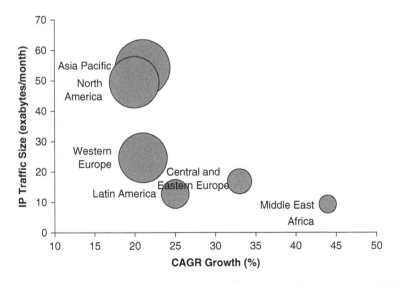

Figure 9.10 IP Traffic in Exabytes per Month by 2019 and CAGR Growth for 2015–2019, by Region.

Source: Cisco.

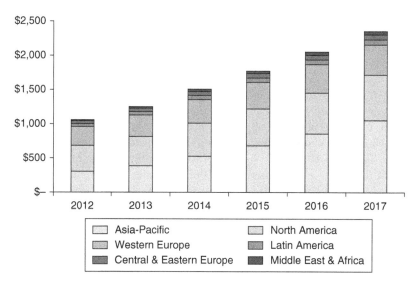

Figure 9.11 Global B2C E-Commerce Marketplace in 2012–2017 (in Billions of US$), by Region.

Source: eMarketer.

expected to make up an estimated US$160 billion in 2018, up from US$43 billion in 2013. China is also the leading e-commerce consumer market: according to the Boston Consulting Group (2012), in 2015 China would have 700 million Internet users, almost twice as many as the United States and Japan combined. Cross-border transactions are an important part of e-commerce: in the six main e-commerce markets—United States, UK, Germany, Brazil, China, and Australia—cross-border e-commerce makes up an average of 16% of all e-commerce transactions (PayPal 2014).[3]

How regional, then, are data and e-commerce? Different sources suggest that intraregional flows are an increasingly important part of global flows (Figures 9.12–9.15). For example, a 2012 report on Internet traffic showed that most European bandwidth is used to connect European countries to each other; the proportion connecting the region with the United States and Canada fell from 30% in 1999 to about 15% in 2011. Similarly, in Asia 90% of broadband traffic in 1999 was with the United States and only about 7% was to other Asian countries, but this figure had increased to 30% by 2011.

Africa connects increasingly to Europe, and only 2% of its flow is within the region. Likewise, most of Latin America's bandwidth is for traffic with the United States, and only 15% is within Latin America.[4] This is caused by a lack of liberalization in regional connectivity that diverts traffic via major IXPs in Europe or the United States. It could, however, be expected that as Internet connectivity expands in the developing world and economic activity grows, intraregional connections will become a stronger element of global flows.

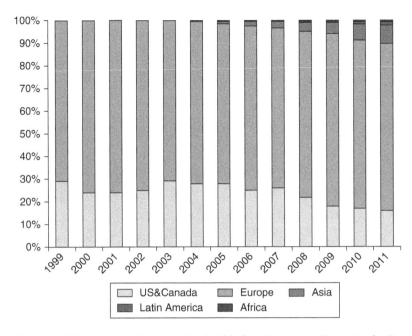

Figure 9.12 International Internet Bandwidth from European Countries, by Region.
Source: Kende (2012).

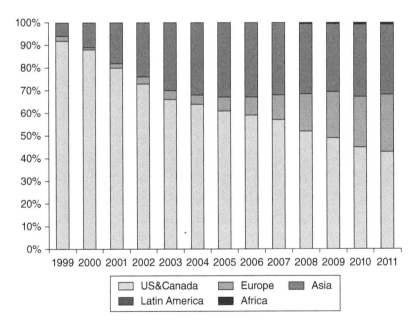

Figure 9.13 International Internet Bandwidth from Asian Countries, by Region.
Source: Kende (2012).

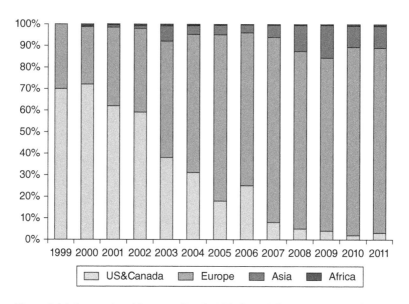

Figure 9.14 International Internet Bandwidth from African Countries, by Region.
Source: Kende (2012).

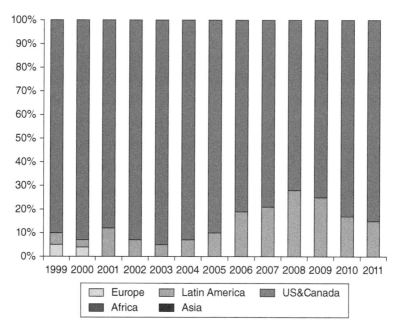

Figure 9.15 International Internet Bandwidth from Latin American Countries,
by Region.
Source: Kende (2012).

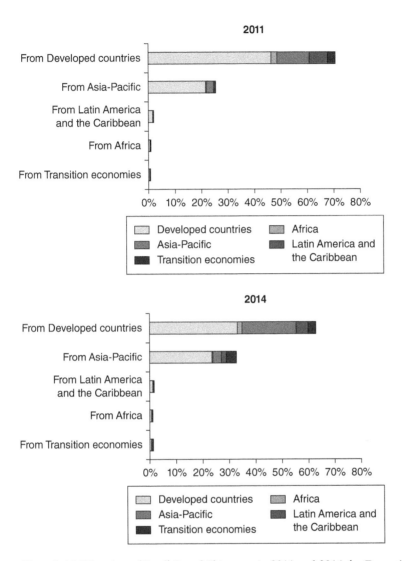

Figure 9.16 Direction of Small Parcel Shipment in 2011 and 2014, by Exporting
        Region.

Source: UNCTAD.

Within e-commerce, intraregional cross-border activity is still in its infancy.
Most global B2C e-commerce is between advanced economies (Figure 9.16).
However, intraregional e-commerce is growing, especially within Asia.

As the 4 billion people that have yet to connect to the web log on over
the next 10–15 years, the prospects for digital flows will expand dramatically.
Yet this potential increase will remain unrealized—as will the trade and shared

prosperity it would create—unless many obstacles are removed. Some of these specific hurdles include:

- **Regional fiber optic cables**. Africa is struggling to create a sufficiently large network of fiber optic cables, the least expensive and highest capacity form of transmitting telephone, Internet, and other data traffic. Access to the global network of submarine cables is today's equivalent of access to sea lanes for landlocked countries, and rates are low in Africa, especially for landlocked countries. The African Development Bank estimates that continental fiber optic submarine cables could reduce Internet and inter-national call charges by 50% (African Development Bank 2010).
- **Regional IXPs**. Regions such as Africa and Latin America have yet to cre-ate regional Internet Exchange Points (IXPs), facilities where all Internet players can interconnect directly with each other. IXPs have played a key role in the development of advanced Internet ecosystems in North America, Europe, and Asia, improving the quality of service and reduc-ing transmission costs (World Economic Forum 2014). In Latin America, the lack of IXPs means that much of the intraregional Internet traffic is rerouted via the United States, a cost of US$2 billion in inefficiencies that is passed on to Latin American consumers (Andean Development Corporation 2014). Overall, transit costs could be reduced by 33%. There are similar opportunities for Africa.
- **Regional mobile spectra**. Mobile phones are the stores and shopping malls for 21st-century consumers. Yet there are frictions in this area: Europe, Asia, and Latin America struggle with divergent mobile spectra. Likewise, 3G and 4G networks operate on different spectrum bands in different countries or in regions within a country—today, 4G networks operate on more than 40 spectrum bands around the world (World Economic Forum 2014). While the United States and China have created a single internal spectrum, the EU has not, which limits regional scale economies and opportunities for the creation of EU-based digital businesses of the scale of, say, Alibaba or Facebook (World Economic Forum 2014). In the Asia Pacific, countries could unlock up to US$1 trillion in GDP growth by 2020 through the harmonized adoption of the 700 MHz spectrum band for mobile services (GSMA and the Boston Consulting Group 2012).
- **Internet and e-commerce legislation**. For regional e-commerce markets to blossom, it is useful for there to be common laws on e-transactions, consumer protection, privacy, and cybercrime. Adoption of such laws is lacking in East and Middle Africa, and Oceania, while it is much more comprehensive in advanced economies and Latin America (Table 9.1). Implementation of laws tends to be weak in these regions, often due to lack of domain expertise among law enforcement officials and courts (UNCTAD 2015). In Europe, mismatches in national regulations and laws have impeded a single digital market: today, only 15% of EU citizens make online purchases from sellers in another EU country, and only 7%

Table 9.1 Laws Related to E-commerce in 2015, by Subregion

	Countries (number)	E-transaction laws (%)	Consumer protection laws (%)	Privacy and data protection laws (%)	Cybercrime laws (%)
Developed economies	42	**97.6**	**85.7**	**97.6**	**83.3**
Developing economies					
Africa	54	**46.3**	**33.3**	**38.9**	**40.7**
Eastern Africa	18	38.9	16.7	27.8	50
Middle Africa	9	22.2	22.2	22.2	11.1
Northern Africa	6	83.3	33.3	50	66.7
Southern Africa	5	60	40	20	40
Western Africa	16	50	56.3	62.5	37.5
Asia and Oceania	48	**72.9**	**37.5**	**29.2**	**56.3**
Eastern Asia	4	75	50	25	50
South-Eastern Asia	11	81.8	81.8	54.5	72.7
Southern Asia	9	77.8	22.2	44.4	66.7
Western Asia	12	91.7	33.3	25	58.3
Oceania	12	41.7	8.3	0	33.3
Latin America and the Caribbean	33	**81.8**	**54.5**	**48.5**	**63.6**
Central America	8	75	87.5	37.5	37.5
South America	12	83.3	75	66.7	75
Caribbean	13	84.6	15.4	38.5	69.2
Transition economies	17	**100**	**11.8**	**88.2**	**70.6**
All economies	194	**74.7**	**47.4**	**55.2**	**60.3**

Source: Information Economy Report 2015, UNCTAD.

of SMEs make cross-border sales. Laws pertinent to ICTs in more general terms have been adopted less in Latin America; Central Africa and select economies in Africa, Asia, and Latin America also lack legal frameworks (Figure 9.17).

- *E-commerce logistics*. In the world of e-commerce where transactions involve millions of small, individual parcels, each with a customized path and delivery, logistics are much more complex than in traditional retail. Warehousing, too, is more demanding: e-commerce warehouses need to handle order fulfilment, sorting, distribution, and returns. African and Latin American economies have relatively long parcel shipping times both as exporters and as importers. For example, in both regions, it takes over twice as long to ship intraregionally (about 20 and 23 days, respectively) as it takes to ship among advanced economies (about 9 days). This adds to the cost at the point of sale and to overall unpredictability, which can become cost prohibitive for small shipments.
- *Barriers to data flows*. Cross-border data flows are critical if companies that manufacture and export are to access digital goods and digital support services—such as logistics, online services, retail, distribution, finance, and professional services—at competitive prices. However, new barriers to this are being created, such as forced localization of data and servers and

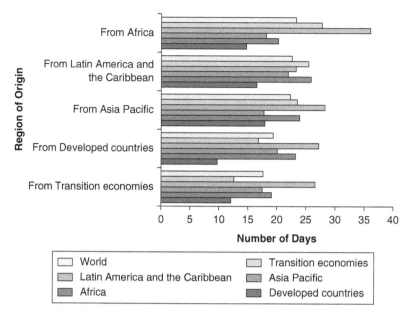

Figure 9.17 Average Shipping Time for Parcels to Various Destinations, Q2 2013 to Q1 2014, Selected Regions.

Source: United Transportation Union (UTU).

stringent data privacy rules (Bauer et al. 2014). According to the think tank ECIPE, data localization and privacy requirements that discriminate against foreign data suppliers and downstream goods and services providers could cost 0.2%–1.7% of national GDPs: specifically, −0.2% in Brazil; −1.1% in China; −0.4% in the EU; −0.1% in India; −0.5% in Indonesia; −0.4% in Korea; and −1.7% in Vietnam.[5]

- *Trade compliance costs.* Surveys show that developing country companies struggle with customs procedures and trade compliance; furthermore, SMEs' trade compliance capacities are poor, even in advanced economies such as the United States. While the costs of non-compliance can include both lost sales and hefty fines, the fixed costs that individuals and small businesses must face in order to meet complex customs regulations risk canceling out the profit they earn from shipping a small parcel. Trusted Trader programs and other similar initiatives that aim to fast-track participating companies' exports through customs are much too elaborate for microbusinesses and individuals. Meanwhile, *de minimis* levels (a ceiling on the value or weight of cross-border shipments below which customs clearance procedures can be simplified and fast-tracked) are still very low in most countries, such as only US$200 in the United States.

- *Interoperable payments.* Fluid and interoperable payment systems are critical for companies selling goods and services online. Interoperability is often a challenge in cross-border or cross-regional payments, especially in Africa and Latin America. However, there has been progress at national levels: for example, Brazil has created uniform standards for mobile payments so as to promote domestic interoperability.

These issues and challenges call for new approaches. The next section turns to possible lines of action regionally and globally.

Regional cooperation in digitization

The Internet has succeeded because of multilateral, multi-stakeholder forums that have guided its governance. The expansion of Internet infrastructure has largely been driven by market forces. Today, however, governments around the world face the challenge of broadening access to the Internet and digital technologies and translating this access into usage by consumers and companies and, further, into trade, economic development, and growth. Regional solutions help lower costs for all economies, expand scale economies, and tap latent markets, and thus can and should be part of governments' policy toolkits. There are grounds for concerted regional action: the countries within particular regions tend to be at similar levels of digitization and share similar problems that could lead to common regulations and connected infrastructures. This is especially true in Africa and Latin America.

In turn, the integration of regional digital marketplaces could enable countries to deepen their cooperation—including in many nontrade areas such as joint development of regional products and services, as well as in terms of further regional harmonization and liberalization pertinent to the digital economy, such as in IP protections, nontariff barriers, competition and procurement policies, cyberspace security, and so on. In addition, the expansion of intraregional opportunities for digital trade could build up pressure in support of domestic reforms, such as for more competitive service provision.

The following points lay out exactly how this could take place and also discuss existing and emerging global practices.

Policy and regulatory liberalization and harmonization

E-commerce and digital trade policy issues are being addressed multilaterally in different ways, via the WTO's Council on Trade in Services, the Information Technology Agreement (ITA), and the Trade in Services Agreement (TiSA). However, concrete progress has come mostly through EU and US free trade agreements, which now include chapters on e-commerce. The Trans-Pacific Partnership (TPP) and the TTIP also are addressing e-commerce in a more comprehensive manner. There are also several examples in different regions of efforts to build regional digital economies by harmonizing laws and regulations:

- ***The EU's Digital Single Market.*** In May 2015, the European Commission unveiled its plan to create a Digital Single Market that aims to tear down national regulatory silos by the end of 2016 (European Commission 2015). It rests on three pillars: (1) improved access for consumers and businesses to digital goods and services across Europe; (2) the right conditions and a level playing field for digital networks and innovative services to flourish; and (3) maximizing the growth potential of the digital economy. According to the EU, a fully functional Digital Single Market could contribute €415 billion per year to the EU economy and create hundreds of thousands of new jobs.

- ***e-ASEAN initiative.*** ASEAN has blazed a trail by creating a harmonized regional legal framework for e-commerce, cooperation on which began in 1999 when all countries endorsed the e-ASEAN initiative (UNCTAD 2013). The e-ASEAN Framework Agreement of 2000 promoted regional development by establishing the ASEAN Information Infrastructure. In 2011, the ASEAN ICT Masterplan 2015 targeted ICTs as an enabler for further social and economic integration. ASEAN legislation has especially focused on electronic transactions, cybercrime, consumer protection, content regulation, data protection and privacy, domain names, and dispute resolution.

- ***APEC's Electronic Commerce Steering Group (ECSG).*** Based on the principles set out in the 1998 APEC Blueprint for Action on Electronic Commerce, APEC's ECSG promotes the development and use of e-commerce through legal, regulatory, and policy environments in the APEC region that are predictable, transparent, and consistent. The ECSG also explores how ICTs can drive economic growth and social development. Furthermore, the ECSG has guided numerous capacity-building projects promoting the development and use of electronic commerce and ICTs within the APEC region.

- ***The APEC Data Privacy Pathfinder.*** This was established in 2007 to secure cross-border flows of personal information within the APEC region. Progress on the implementation of the APEC Privacy Framework includes the application of Information Privacy Individual Action Plans by 14 member economies, and the creation of a study group within the Data Privacy Sub-Group tasked to identify best practices in promoting the cross-border flow of information.

Trade facilitation in the e-commerce era

Trade facilitation is critical for e-commerce to flourish. The WTO's Trade Facilitation Agreement (TFA) opens new opportunities for addressing some of the acutest hurdles facing digital trade, especially small businesses engaged in this activity. However, regions are also relevant units for implementing the agreement, and existing regional examples that could be built upon include:

- **Exporta Fácil**. In South America, 12 countries have adopted the Exporta Fácil program, first implemented by Brazil in 2002, which offers logistics services and facilitates exports through national postal systems. The program has simplified customs clearance for SMEs for shipments weighing less than 30 kilograms and with a value of less than US$5,000. The postal system has also taken on and centralized the tasks of various agencies involved in the export process, such as customs, health and environment agencies, and export agencies. As a result, between 2002 and 2008 10,000 companies started to export. In Peru the program resulted in 6,704 shipments, amounting to US$3 million in sales in 2012.[6]
- **APEC's paperless trading**. APEC's Paperless Trading Subgroup develops projects on the use of paperless trading in B2B and B2C transactions and promotes the use of electronic documents in international trade. APEC is also implementing APEC's Strategies and Actions toward a Cross-Border Paperless Trading Environment to enable the electronic transmission of trade-related information across the region by 2020.
- One new idea is a regional **Trusted eTrader pilot program** discussed in Suominen (2015). This aims to accommodate small online businesses' cross-border trade within the intraregional market, while also protecting intraregional trade from illicit shipments, weapons, and contraband. Such a program would rest on two components:

  o Public-private partnerships in order to work with the big data held by major online platforms such as eBay and Alibaba, which would open up an opportunity for customs to use risk-targeting and predictive analytics in e-commerce. It could be tailored after the Air Cargo Advanced Screening program that the US Customs and Border Protection piloted a few years ago with major shippers such as FedEx, DHL, and UPS.
  o Regional customs agencies and other partners could set up a compliance platform where importers and exporters would be able to quickly access a customized trade compliance form with only 5–6 fields to be filled in. Companies that are consistent and compliant would become Trusted eTraders over time, and would be eligible for expedited entry.

Another quick way to fuel e-commerce is to **raise de minimis *and informal entry programs***, which would expedite the movement of low-value small parcels through customs. In 2016, the United States increased its *de minimis* from US$200 to US$800. A Peterson Institute study in 2011 estimated that the net payoff of an increase of this size in the US *de minimis* threshold for 3.8 million shipments handled by express shipment firms would be US$17 million annually (Hufbauer and Wong 2011). Raising *de minimis* levels also reduces the burden on customs resources, freeing these up to identify serious threats, from terrorism to illegal drugs. In a study of 12 APEC economies (Canada, Chile, the People's Republic of China, Indonesia, Japan, Malaysia,

Mexico, Papua New Guinea, Peru, the Philippines, Thailand, and Vietnam), raising the *de minimis* to just US$200 would generate gains in customs procedures and consumers of US$5.4 billion a year, equivalent to some US$12 billion for all 21 APEC members (Holloway and Rae 2012). The gains would be multiple if the *de minimis* was raised higher, say to US$1,000. To reduce the fiscal and political costs governments associate with a unilateral *de minimis* increase, Suominen (2016) has proposed a plurilateral negotiation on *de minimis* among a coalition of the willing: this would help governments feel they get market access for their SMEs in other member states.

- Regions can also pool resources to mount platforms that enable small businesses to **calculate the total cost involved in e-commerce transactions and shipments**. Often these costs are much more significant than the costs involved in shipping and trade compliance: there are behind-the-border barriers such as value-added taxes and other charges that tend to be invisible to small companies, but raise costs significantly for the unsuspecting end consumer, often causing a loss of future business for the firm in question.

Digital trade and development

Though world trade is increasingly generated bottom-up by thousands of small businesses and entrepreneurs trading online, people in many countries have yet to connect to the Web. New investments and smart technical assistance are needed. This is an area where regional development banks can play a powerful role, given that they tend to have the various sectoral and functional capabilities needed for building digital economies already in place. Regional economies could come together to identify challenges and remove them with the help of development banks and donors, for example as follows:

- Furthering digitization is a place for **public–private partnerships**. For example, companies such as Google and Facebook have openly discussed constructive ideas and made significant investments in spreading Web access around the planet. E-commerce platforms, cloud computing services, social media businesses, financial services, and many, many types of firms have a vested interest in seeing the Web expand and digital economies grow, both regionally and globally.
- One new, big initiative is eTrade for All, a multi-stakeholder effort launched in July 2016 that is aimed at being a resource for developing countries' e-commerce capacity building and for enabling countries to navigate support systems for e-commerce–related capacity building. The initiative also brings together multiple donors and agencies that have prioritized e-commerce development in their development portfolios. It builds directly on the concept **Aid for eTrade** (Suominen 2014, 2015). Donor countries would score immediate benefits: greater use of e-commerce would unlock a giant market of consumers from the developing world

for small business exporters from donor countries. eTrade for All could also incentivize and scale up *indigenous regional solutions*. After all, large providers do not necessarily prioritize all markets or provide solutions appropriate for the contexts of particular developing countries. For example, in Kenya, Equity Bank created an exclusive agreement with PayPal for cash withdrawals, as Kenya's banking infrastructure did not guarantee that buyers could transfer PayPal payments through each local bank.

• Regions could also pool resources for *regional innovation hubs*. Such hubs are typically a community of entrepreneurs that share a space, have reliable Internet access, and work on digital business models for the region. Such regional hubs would also enable entrepreneurs to learn about doing business in the various regional markets, and help them to access investors and resources across regional economies.

Conclusions

Disruptive digital technologies are creating a new wave of growth opportunities. They empower companies to cut costs dramatically and enable even the smallest of businesses and solo entrepreneurs to get into business and engage in trade. At the same time, as is the case with traditional trade, in most world regions majorities have yet to be online regularly and most businesses do not have websites. The Internet, let alone the use of digital technologies, is far from ubiquitous—and in some regions, such as Sub-Saharan Africa, it is nearly nonexistent.

This paper has argued that regional action can be a critical complement to national and multilateral measures. Regionalism can be especially useful in two areas: enhancing opportunities for regional scale economies, especially via regulatory harmonization, as is occurring in Europe; and removing barriers to the flow of data and e-commerce within regions, such as through improved regional Internet infrastructures (common Internet interconnection points, interoperable payment networks, harmonized mobile spectra, and so on), and more fluid customs regulations and trade facilitation, as has been pursued especially in ASEAN and APEC.

Regionalism is also practical: the data indicates that common ground exists in many regions for countries to act together, namely that countries tend to form clusters with their regional neighbors in terms of a number of digitization indicators, and often face very similar challenges. As in trade and many other areas of international cooperation, regional solutions to digital challenges would fuel the global digital economy.

Notes

1 See Enterprise Surveys.
2 By 2019, two-thirds of all IP traffic will originate from non-PC devices—TVs, tablets, smartphones, and machine-to-machine (M2M) modules. In 2014, only 40% of total IP traffic originated from non-PC devices. The number of devices connected to IP networks will be more than three times the global population by 2019. Globally,

smart traffic will grow from 88% of the total global mobile traffic to 97% by 2019. This, in turn, adds to flows: the average smart device generates much higher traffic than a non-smart device. Similarly, technological improvements are enhancing access to any content on any device from anywhere—the Internet of Everything (IoE).
3 For an excellent study of ecommerce in the United States, see USITC (2013).
4 While in 1999, 70% of bandwidth from Africa went to the USA, by 2011 this had fallen to a tiny proportion, and nearly 90% went to Europe as it liberalized its telecom networks and IXPs developed to host the content. This change demonstrates how similar shifts in the future could localize traffic in Africa to further reduce latency and costs.
5 For an industry view of digital protectionism, see, for example, Espinel 2014.
6 "Exporta Fácil registró más de US$ 11 millones en envíos a diversos mercados de destino." *Andina.* April 2, 2013. www.andina.com.pe/espanol/noticia-exporta-facil-registro-mas-11-millones-envios-a-diversos-mercados-destino-453443.aspx#. UsOoyPRDuVI

References

Andean Development Corporation. 2014. "IXP in Latin America: Low cost Internet at Higher Speed." August 11. www.caf.com/en/currently/news/2014/08/ixp-in-latin-america-low-cost-internet-at-higher-speed
Bauer, Matthias, Hosuk Lee-Makiyama, Erik van der Marel, and Bert Verschelde. 2014. "The Costs of Data Localization: Friendly Fire on Economic Recovery," ECIPE Occasional Paper No 3/2014.
Boston Consulting Group and GSMA. 2012. "The Economic Benefits of Early Harmonization of the Digital Dividend Spectrum and the Cost of Fragmentation in Asia-Pacific." www.gsma.com/spectrum/wp-content/uploads/2012/07/277967-01-Asia-Pacific-FINAL-vf1.pdf
Boston Consulting Group. 2012. "Online Retail Sales in China Will Triple to More than $360 Billion by 2015, as the Internet Adds Nearly 200 Million Users." April 12. www.bcg.com/media/PressReleaseDetails.aspx?id=tcm:12-103641
Choi, Changkyu. 2010. "The Effect of the Internet on Service Trade," *Economics Letters* 109, no. 2: 102–104, November, Elsevier.
Cohen, Daniel, Matthew Sargeant, and Ken Somers. 2014. "3-D printing Takes Shape" *McKinsey Quarterly*, January.
Deloitte. 2012. "What Is the Impact of Mobile Telephony on Economic Growth?" www.gsma.com/publicpolicy/wp-content/uploads/2012/11/gsma-deloitteimpact-mobile-telephony-economic-growth.pdf
eBay. 2013. "Commerce 3.0 for Development: The Promise of the Global Empowerment Network." www.ebaymainstreet.com/sites/default/files/eBay_Commerce-3.0-Development.pdf
Espinel, Victoria. 2014. "A Forward-Looking Trade Agenda for the Digital Economy." *BSA TechPost*, January 30. http://techpost.bsa.org/2014/01/30/a-forward-looking-trade-agenda-for-the-digital-economy/#sthash.UkDBYawV.dpuf
European Commission. 2015. "A Digital Single Market Strategy for Europe—COM (2015) 192 Final." https://ec.europa.eu/digital-agenda/en/news/digital-single-market-strategy-europe-com2015-192-final
GSMA and the Boston Consulting Group. 2012. "The Economic Benefits of Early Harmonisation of the Digital Dividend Spectrum and the Cost of Fragmentation in Asia-Pacific." www.gsma.com/spectrum/the-economic-benefits-of-early-harmonisation-of-the-digital-dividend-spectrum-and-the-cost-of-fragmentation-in-asia/

Holloway, S., and J. Rae. 2012. "De-minimis Thresholds in APEC." *World Customs Journal* 6, no. 2: 31–62.

Hufbauer, Gary, and Yee Wong. 2011. "Logistics Reform for Low-Value Shipments." Peterson Institute Policy Brief 11-7, June. www.iie.com/publications/pb/pb11-07.pdf

Jordán, V., and O. De León. 2011. "Broadband and the Digital Revolution." In *Fast-Tracking the Digital Revolution: Broadband for Latin America and the Caribbean*, eds. V. Jordán and H. Galperín, pp. 13–48 Santiago, Chile: United Nations.

Kende, Michael. 2012. "Internet Global Growth: Lessons for the Future." Analysys Mason Knowledge Centre. http://www.analysysmason.com/internet-global-growth-lessons-for-the-future

McKinsey. 2014. "Offline and Falling Behind: Barriers to Internet Adoption." www.mckinsey.com/industries/high-tech/our-insights/offline-and-falling-behind-barriers-to-internet-adoption

Mack, E. and A. Faggian. 2013. "Productivity and Broadband: The Human Factor." *International Regional Science Review* 36, no. 3: 392–423.

Liu, L., and H. K. Nath. 2013. "Information and Communications Technologies (ICT) and Trade in Emerging Market Economies." *Emerging Markets Finance and Trade* 49, no. 6: 67–87.

Manyika, James, Michael Chui, Jacques Bughin, Richard Dobbs, Peter Bisson, and Alex Marrs. 2013. "Disruptive Technologies: Advances that Will Transform Life, Business, and the Global Economy." McKinsey Global Institute. www.mckinsey.com/insights/business_technology/disruptive_technologies.

Nottebohm, Olivia, James Manyika, Jacques Bughin, Michael Chui, and Abdur-Rahim Syed. 2012. "Online and Upcoming: The Internet's Impact on Aspiring Countries." McKinsey & Company, *High Tech Practice*, January. www.mckinsey.com/client_service/high_tech/latest_thinking/impact_of_the_internet_on_aspiring_countries

PayPal. 2014. "Modern Spice Routes: The Cultural Impact and Economic Opportunity of Cross-Border Shopping." www.paypal-media.com/assets/pdf/fact_sheet/PayPal_ModernSpiceRoutes_Report_Final.pdf

Pepper, Robert, and John Garrity. 2015. "ICTs, Income Inequality, and Ensuring Inclusive Growth." In *Global Information Technology Report 2015*. Geneva: World Economic Forum.

Pisello, Thomas. 2006. "The ROI of RFID in the Supply Chain." *RFID Journal*, August 21.

Pullen, John Patrick. 2013. "What 3-D Printing Could Mean for Small Businesses." *Entrepreneur*, March 14.

Riker, David. 2014. "Internet Use and Openness to Trade." US International Trade Commission Working Paper 2014-12C, December.

Rogy, Michel. 2014. "Lowering Barriers to High Speed Internet in the Arab World," *World Bank*, May 2. http://blogs.worldbank.org/arabvoices/lowering-barriers-high-speed-internet-arab-world

Scott, Colin. 2012. "Does Broadband Internet Access Actually Spur Economic Growth?" Paper, December 7. www.eecs.berkeley.edu/~rcs/classes/ictd.pdf

Suominen, Kati. 2014. "Aid for eTrade: Accelerating the Global e-Commerce Revolution." Policy Working Paper, Center for Strategic and International Studies, November. http://csis.org/files/publication/141107_eBay_CSIS_aid_eTrade.pdf

Suominen, Kati. 2015. "Aid for eTrade: Accelerating the e-Commerce Revolution." *E15 Initiative Blog*, March. http://e15initiative.org/blogs/aid-for-etrade-accelerating-the-e-commerce-revolution/

——. 2016. "Silver bullet for Helping Small Businesses Trade: Plurilateral Agreement on de minimis," March. http://e15initiative.org/blogs/silver-bullet-for-helping-small-businesses-trade-plurilateral-agreement-on-de-minimis/

UNCTAD. 2013. "Review of E-commerce Legislation Harmonization in the Association of Southeast Asian Nations." http://unctad.org/en/PublicationsLibrary/dtlstict2013d1_en.pdf

UNCTAD. 2015. *Information Economy Report 2015—Unlocking the Potential of E-commerce for Developing Countries*. UNCTAD: Geneva.

USITC (US International Trade Commission). 2013. "Digital Trade in the US and Global Economies, Part 1." USITC Publication 4415. www.usitc.gov/publications/332/pub4415.pdf

Vemuri, Vijay K., and Shahid Siddiqui. 2009. "Impact of Commercialization of the Internet on International Trade: A Panel Study Using the Extended Gravity Model." *International Trade Journal* 23, no. 4: 458–484.

World Bank. 2010. "Deepening Regional Integration." In *Africa's Infrastructure: A Time for Transformation*, edited by Vivien Foster and Cecilia Briceño-Garmendia. Washington, DC: Agence Française de Développement and the World Bank.

World Economic Forum. 2014. "Delivering Digital Infrastructure: Advancing the Internet Economy." http://reports.weforum.org/delivering-digital-infrastructure/

World Economic Forum. 2014. "Delivering Digital Infrastructure: Advancing the Internet Economy." http://reports.weforum.org/delivering-digital-infrastructure/

Zwillenberg, Paul, Dominic Field, and David Dean. 2014. "Greasing the Wheels of the Internet Economy." Boston Consulting Group. www.bcgperspectives.com/content/articles/digital_economy_telecommunications_greasing_wheels_internet_economy/#chapter1

10 Building regional environmental governance

Northeast Asia's unique path to sustainable development

Suh-Yong Chung

Introduction

Environmental degradation in Northeast Asia has been escalating, causing severe damage to the region. The Yellow Sea is one of the most heavily polluted bodies of water in the world, as intense industrial development along its coastlines has led to the discharge of contaminants into it. Rivers carry water pollutants such as heavy metals to the sea from far inland, which has increased red tides and has diminished fish stocks. In addition, overfishing and expansion of mariculture have intensified environmental stress on the marine ecosystem. Levels of air pollution have recently reached record highs due to fine dust and other air pollutants, and now constitute a grave threat to human lives and health in Northeast Asia. The meteorological phenomenon known as Yellow Dust or Asian Dust has been a problem in the area for hundreds of years but has grown recently due to increased desertification in China and the harmful industrial pollutants produced in industrial and urban areas that are carried eastward, as is fine dust from transportation and industry. As such, the countries of Northeast Asia are wrestling with imminent environmental and health threats.

China has been blamed for much of the environmental damage in Northeast Asia. With its fast-growing economy and population, China has not been effective in controlling and managing the various pollutants (Drifte 2005). However, other Northeast Asian countries are also responsible for regional environmental problems to some extent. Recently, the Republic of Korea (ROK)'s government publicly recognized that environmental damages caused by fine dust were partly due to toxic substances emitted within its territory (Ministry of Environment 2014). Likewise, Japan is contributing to the deterioration of the regional environment: radioactive materials which were produced during the 2011 Fukushima Daiichi nuclear incident became a great concern among neighboring countries as a large volume of radioactive isotopes were released into the seas of Northeast Asia (Fukurai 2012). Other countries in the region such as the Democratic People's Republic of Korea (DPRK) also play a role in creating environmental problems. The DPRK has emitted more air pollutants such as CO_2 than other countries of similar economic development status due to its environmentally unfriendly practices and policies.[1]

Considering the seriousness and interconnectedness of environmental problems in Northeast Asia along with its complex geopolitical situation, the need to build effective regional governance to deal with environmental issues has become vital. In fact, Northeast Asia has been identified as one of the world's most difficult regions for developing regional cooperative institutions (Timmermann 2008), and almost no multilateral treaties have been concluded among the countries of the region. In the case of regional environment issues, however, a relatively good number of regional environmental institutions do exist, although they are not part of legally binding multilateral treaties. These include but are not limited to the following: the United Nations Development Programme/Global Environment Facility Yellow Sea Large Marine Ecosystem Project (UNDP/GEF YSLME); the United Nations Environment Programme (UNEP) Northwest Pacific Action Plan (NOWPAP); the Tripartite Environmental Ministerial Meeting; the North-East Asian Subregional Programme for Environmental Cooperation; and the Acid Deposition Monitoring Network in East Asia (E-Net). Despite the fact that each institution may not be fully effective, they have worked to enhance regional capacity to better address environmental problems. This is largely because their creation and operation were predicated on the uniqueness of Northeast Asia in terms of addressing environmental issues.

Moreover, the recent agreement between the USA and the ROK to deploy Terminal High Altitude Area Defense (THAAD) in the ROK's territory has been met by strong protest from China, which has strained China-ROK relations. This, coupled with the continuing tensions between Japan and the ROK stemming from historical conflicts, has destabilized regional relations in Northeast Asia. Because of these recent security and diplomatic conundrums, cooperation in the environmental realm has become more important in promoting regional stability and sustainability.

Against this backdrop, this chapter discusses, in Part 2, Northeast Asia's unique factors for building environmental governance, especially in comparison with Europe. Part 3 delves into the case of the UNDP/GEF YSLME Project and analyzes the advances that have been made in Northeast Asian marine environment governance through a cooperation-based approach that focuses on soft environmental institution building. Finally, Part 4 summarizes the previous sections and briefly lays out implications that the Northeast Asian process of building environmental governance has for other regions, especially Latin America.

What is unique about building sustainable development governance in Northeast Asia?

The international community's experience in building environmental governance at the global level began in the 1970s, and significant advances were made in the 1980s and 1990s. The growing concern in addressing global environmental problems in a concerted manner has led to a burgeoning of ideas from both scholars and practitioners on how to approach this matter, with discussions around regime formation, institutional design, and the role of nonstate actors. Yet within the realm of global environmental governance, the focus on specific regions and environmental governance building at the regional level has often been conflated with that of the global level, and the importance of regional environmental cooperation was overlooked (Balsiger and VanDeveer 2012).[2] Also, in many cases, the methods and measures used in the success cases of environmental protection, which usually took place in developed countries, were exported to other regions of the world. However, the particularities of a given region—the environmental challenge in question, the geographical and ecological setting, existing institutions, the actors involved, and the level of technological and scientific expertise—are critical to formulating and implementing the most effective system of environmental measures for that region. Therefore, an understanding of specific regional characteristics is necessary to build a unique environmental governance approach that is appropriate and tailored to that region.

This section begins by introducing the European approach to building environmental governance, based on convention protocol. The focus then shifts to the developments of the Northeast Asian approach, based on cooperation and soft institution building.

Europe: The convention protocol approach

Given the various environmental problems in Northeast Asia, one possible development of legally binding treaty mechanisms is worthy of consideration.[3] In Europe, for example, countries have developed a number of regional environmental treaties to deal with environmental problems. In the Mediterranean region, 16 coastal countries in three different political regions of Europe, Asia, and Africa agreed in 1976 on the Convention for the Protection of the Mediterranean Sea Against Pollution (Barcelona Convention), which provides a basic framework on marine environment protection for the region. This was based on the Mediterranean Action Plan, launched in 1975, which was UNEP's first Regional Seas Programme. On the basis of the Barcelona Convention, the countries adopted seven protocols aimed at managing specific marine environment issues. These include protocols on dumping from ships and aircraft, pollution from ships and emergency situations, pollution from land-based sources and activities, specially protected areas and biological biodiversity, pollution from exploration and exploitation, hazardous wastes, and integrated coastal zone management.[4] With the addition of each specific protocol, marine conservation and management efforts in the Mediterranean were expanded from the narrow approach of addressing sources of pollution to a more holistic approach. In 1995, the Barcelona Convention was amended and renamed the Convention for the Protection of the Marine Environment and the Coastal Region of the Mediterranean. This approach of first concluding a framework convention that broadly outlines the common goals to be met, then later adopting specific protocols that are tailored to meet the region's distinct environmental needs was demonstrated as being successful in the Mediterranean region. As a result, UNEP has applied this environmental governance-building approach to other of the world's regional seas. At this time, there are 13 operating Regional Seas Programmes, each with its own legally binding treaty.

As in the case of marine environment protection, European countries also applied the convention protocol approach to the issue of acid rain. Since acid rain had detrimental health implications as well as economic ramifications for countries in Europe in general and Scandinavia in particular, these started negotiations towards creating a framework treaty. Based on strong scientific evidence on the relationship between sulphur emissions in continental Europe and the acidification of Scandinavian lakes, the Geneva Convention on Long-range Transboundary Air Pollution was adopted and signed in November 1979 by 35 countries and the European Community and entered into force in 1983.[5]

Initially, this convention was seen as a forum that could provide opportunities for further negotiations on establishing specific standards on the control and management of air pollutants. In reality, the 1979 Geneva Convention also contributed to interconnecting the various political systems by playing a bridging role and to providing stability and continuity during the political changes that took place during that time in the region. As a result, the 1979 Geneva Convention led the way to the adoption of eight individual protocols.[6] These protocols addressed the various air pollutants as well as new scientific findings. For example, the earlier three protocols (the 1985 Protocol on the Reduction of Sulphur Emissions, the 1988 Protocol on the Control of Nitrogen Oxides, and the 1991 Protocol concerning the Control of Emissions of Volatile Organic Compounds) focus on individual pollutants by imposing uniform emission reduction obligations on members. However, the 1994 Oslo Protocol on Further Reduction of Sulphur Emissions allocates different levels of emission reduction obligations to the members based on so-called cost effectiveness and effect-based principles. Countries negotiated on the basis of a critical loads approach, which facilitated countries' achievement of agreed benefits at minimal cost. Subsequent protocols agreed to include new pollutants in the scope of management, such as persistent organic pollutants, and to create synergies by making linkages between the various air pollutants to be controlled and grouping them. This European way of addressing the problem of transboundary air pollution was seen as a great achievement in mitigating the problem at stake and facilitating intergovernmental cooperation.

In conclusion, successful experiences in addressing both air pollution and marine environment protection in Europe set important precedents on how to address regional environmental problems in a cooperative manner. The main approach for formulating future global environmental institutions—such as UNEP's Regional Seas Programme—was established as two-step institution building based on establishing a legally binding framework convention followed by concluding specific treaties on controlling critical pollutants and/ or implementing sustainable regional development policies and measures.

Northeast Asia: a cooperation-based, soft environmental institution-building approach

In Northeast Asia, there are several outstanding environmental problems. Yellow Dust, fine dust and particulate matters, acid rain, marine pollution, and climate change are a few examples of the environmental issues that exist in the region that remain to be addressed. Currently, there is no multilateral treaty in Northeast Asia that aims to manage regional environmental problems. However, this does not necessarily mean that there are no cooperative mechanisms which address environmental matters there.

In fact, there are a number of regional environmental institutions led by the United Nations in Northeast Asia. In 1994, UNEP launched NOWPAP between China, Japan, the Russian Federation, and the ROK as a component of its Regional Seas Programme. Although this generally follows the approach of UNEP's Regional Seas Programme, which has been advanced through the experience gained from the Mediterranean, NOWPAP has not focused on developing a legally binding treaty. Instead, NOWPAP has stressed creating and implementing practical activities that are more appropriate to meeting the marine environmental challenges that are specific to the region. A Regional Coordinating Unit serves as the permanent secretariat, and four Regional Activity Centers were set up in each of the four member countries. Based on the general guidelines agreed by participating member countries, each Regional Activity Center was assigned distinct tasks. For example, the Marine Environmental Emergency Preparedness and Response Regional Activity Centre (MERRAC), located in the ROK, has developed regional schemes on oil spills.[7] Despite the fact that there is no legally binding instrument governing MERRAC's activities, it was able to establish and operate the Regional Contingency Plan on Oil Spills.

As mentioned in the Introduction, in 2004 UNDP/GEF launched the YSLME Project in the Yellow Sea, which is located between the Korean peninsula and China. Like NOWPAP, YSLME has implemented its activities without deliberating on the creation of a legally binding instrument, at least in the short run. After the successful completion of the first phase, the project aimed to establish an independent regional institution—the YSLME Commission—by 2017. This commission will come to fruition when two participating countries—China and the ROK—endorse the Strategic Action Programme, which the YSLME Commission will oversee.[8] Negotiations for a legally binding agreement in managing the marine environment in the Yellow Sea were not included in this process.

In addition, there are multilateral environment cooperative institutions in Northeast Asia that exist outside the UN system. They include the Tripartite Environmental Ministerial Meeting, North-East Asian Subregional Programme for Environmental Cooperation, the Long-range Transboundary Air Pollutants in Northeast Asia, and the Acid Deposition Monitoring Network in East Asia. The Tripartite Environmental Ministerial Meeting has become the major cooperation body between the environmental ministries of China, Japan, and the ROK. It holds regular meetings at the ministerial level and carries out core activity programs such as the Working Group on Dust Sandstorms. The North-East Asian Subregional Programme for Environmental Cooperation is a regional environmental cooperation mechanism with six members: the ROK, China, Japan, the Russian Federation, the DPRK, and Mongolia, the most active of which is the ROK, which is playing a leading role in the mechanism. The scope of the North-East Asian Subregional Programme for Environmental Cooperation's cooperative activities also varies from marine environment to air pollution, and activities are supported by a permanent secretariat located in the ROK. Furthermore, the Long-range Transboundary Air Pollutants in Northeast Asia project and the Acid Deposition Monitoring Network in East Asia have focused their efforts on air pollution matters such as acid rain. What is distinctive about these two institutions are that they are science-based environmental cooperation mechanisms that aim to gather scientific data and information on the status of the environment at the regional level.

Despite the fact that there currently is no legally binding multilateral treaty related to environment and sustainable development in Northeast Asia, there are several bilateral treaties regarding the marine environment in the region. For instance, the 1993 Agreement on Environmental Cooperation between the government of the ROK and the government of the People's Republic of China is the basis for bilateral cooperation between the two countries in terms of shared environmental issues, including the marine environment. The Joint Committee on Environmental Cooperation between Korea and China has its roots in this bilateral agreement (Ministry of Environment, Korea, 2015), and is responsible for handling issues regarding its implementation. The ROK's various ministries participate in this committee, but China's only participants are its Ministry of Foreign Affairs and Ministry of Environmental Protection. This limited involvement may be one of the reasons for the present limitations to effective cooperation between the two countries. Although environmental issues are multifaceted and thus require coordination among various ministries within a state, China's Ministry of Environmental Protection does not have sole discretion in managing the environmental and sustainable development agenda and thus lacks sufficient influence over the decision-making processes among its government agencies.

As can be seen from the previous discussion, Northeast Asia's regional environmental cooperation has evolved in a way that is different from that of other regions such as Europe. Even though there exist environmental problems of a similar nature at the regional level, Northeast Asian countries tend to prefer soft and non-legally binding institution building. Through this approach, Northeast Asia has put in place various environmental institutions encompassing marine- and air-related issues and other important regional environmental matters, engaging participation from government ministries and the scientific community.

Strengthening marine environment governance through building soft institutions: the case of the UNDP/GEF YSLME Project

The previous section showed how Northeast Asia has developed its own unique process of building environmental cooperation institutions. Of the various existing institutions, the most successful are those on marine environmental protection, such as the UNDP/GEF YSLME Project. This section will highlight this project in order to present a detailed analysis that explains the reasons for this success.

The UNDP/GEF YSLME Project has been recognized as one of the most successful regional cooperation projects of the UNDP's many existing Large Marine Ecosystem Projects (Kullenberg and Huber 2011). Even though there are many factors in Northeast Asia that impede the establishment of regional institutions, neighboring countries have been able to carry out environmental tasks in a concerted manner—for example, the cooperative joint cruise study conducted by China and the ROK to gather data on the Yellow Sea, and the creation of an independent regional institution (the YSLME Commission discussed in Part 2).[9] One of the key reasons behind the UNDP/GEF YSLME Project's success lies in the fact that relevant activities within it were created with an emphasis on cooperation and soft institution building, rather than on identifying, determining, and assigning legally binding state responsibilities and obligations in managing the common sea. In particular, the YSLME Project's notable achievements can be found in the endorsement of agreements on reducing fishing effort by the two countries, the active role of the Project Management Office, formulating regional-level policies based on scientific evidence, the ROK's proactive role in facilitating cooperation, and increasing the possibility of the DPRK's participation in regional environmental governance.

Agreements on reducing fishing efforts

Chinese fishing vessels often enter the ROK's exclusive economic zone in search for fish stocks and conduct prohibited fishing activities in this area, within which the ROK has full jurisdiction over the use and protection of marine resources. This has become a politically sensitive problem between the two states. Despite strong border surveillance and enforcement by the ROK government in the Yellow Sea, illegal fishing activities by Chinese vessels continue. This encroachment into the ROK's waters has led to the arrest of Chinese fishermen, and even to the loss of lives of both Chinese fishermen and Korean coastguards and can be explained by the rapid increase in demand for seafood in China (The Guardian 2014). The seriousness of marine pollution along China's coastal areas, in combination with overfishing and a shortage of fish stocks in Chinese waters, are what have motivated Chinese fishermen to cross into the ROK's jurisdiction.

Under these circumstances, the two countries have agreed on plans to reduce fishing efforts in the Yellow Sea region by 25%–30% by 2020 by carrying out the Strategic Action Plan for the YSLME Project (UNDP/GEF 2009). Considering that the ROK has already taken steps to decrease its number of fishing vessels based on its national scientific and policy considerations, China also needed to do likewise. Despite the potentially costly implication for China, its government accepted this UNDP/GEF YSLME recommendation. It seems that China perceived that this way of implementing regional policies to maintain sustainable fishing levels in the Yellow Sea would ultimately be to its benefit.

In fact, inside China, it appears that there were intense discussions between the State Oceanic Administration, which is responsible for the marine environment, and the Ministry of Agriculture, which is responsible for fisheries. The core of the debate was the YSLME Project's recommendation for a cooperation-based approach to reducing fishing efforts: although the Ministry of Agriculture was reluctant to actively reduce these, the State Oceanic Administration pushed strongly for it to agree to implement the policy recommendations presented by the YSLME Project's Strategic Action Programme. This was partially possible because there were significant financial gains and other advantages for the State Oceanic Administration if the UNDP/GEF YSLME Project was implemented.

The active role of the Project Management Office

The governance structure for the implementation of the UNDP/GEF YSLME Project, chiefly the role played by the Project Management Office, supported the soft, cooperation-based approach. Although both China and the ROK have pursued the formulation and implementation of up-to-date policy measures to protect the marine environment, expertise in the two countries is still lacking, and assistance is required in terms of innovative knowledge and skills on marine environment management. Furthermore, insufficient cooperation between China and the ROK on marine environment at the regional level also raised issues on how to improve the quality of cooperation between the two countries. In this case, the YSLME Project has played an important role in providing the necessary expertise through the global framework of the UNDP's Large Marine Ecosystem Projects, notably through the Project Management Office, which acted as the hub for knowledge sharing. The Project Management Office effectively provided essential information on developing regional activities on marine environmental protection for the governments and experts in the region. For example, it organized various training workshops, stakeholder meetings, and field seminars to create opportunities for interaction among regional and international experts and other stakeholders. This enhanced the facilitation of expertise and information sharing on the cutting-edge knowledge and skills needed at the regional level, avoiding competition that may have occurred otherwise.

The Project Management Office also carried out numerous scientific activities in implementing the YSLME Project. As there is generally a shared understanding in the region that science-based activities do not directly pose a threat to critical interests regarding state sovereignty, science-based activities were conducted relatively smoothly. To achieve this, the UNDP/GEF YSLME Project formed several Working Groups at the regional level. Each Working Group focused on specific issues such as pollution, ecosystem, and fisheries, in which leading scientists from each country participated (Kullenberg and Huber 2011). Collaboration on gathering and comparing regional scientific data was successful as a result of the Project Management Office's organization and facilitation, as well as support from participating governments. Once scientific inquiries were concluded, the Regional Science and Technical Panel further evaluated the gathered data to ensure the quality of the outcome of the activities of individual Working Groups before they were considered by the governments at the YSLME Project level.

The most important task on the YSLME Project also the most difficult: the Regional Cooperative Cruise Study. It aimed for scientists from both China and the ROK to study the features and characteristics of the Yellow Sea (Kullenberg and Huber 2011). As there were no precedents for conducting a joint study on the Yellow Sea, the study's location was cause for tension: the two governments' concern was the potential implication of this location on territorial jurisdictions. However, the Project Management Office's coordination between the two governments ultimately eased this tension by focusing the issue on only the scientific aspects and helped to produce an unprecedented report on the status of the Yellow Sea.

Science-based regional policy development

Third, the expert-based, bottom-up process of developing regional policies also facilitated marine environment cooperation between China and the ROK. Instead of a top-down policymaking process, the two governments relied on measures and data which were gathered and analyzed by experts from both inside and outside the region. Transboundary Diagnostic Analysis (TDA) was conducted by an international expert to identify the root causes of the marine environmental problems in the region (UNDP/GEF 2007). After a thorough chain of analysis, this TDA became the scientific basis for identifying the appropriate regional policy for improving the quality of the marine environment in the Yellow Sea. A detailed TDA encouraged participating governments to further consider the development of a regional master plan for Yellow Sea management and policymaking in the form of the Strategic Action Programme. With strong support from both governments, the Strategic Action Programme drafting group for the YSLME Project proposed regional policy measures for effective marine governance that are to be implemented by the governments by 2020. As these expert-based, scientific processes for carrying out and developing the TDA and Strategic Action Programme were supported by both China and the ROK, the final draft of the Strategic Action Programme was quickly endorsed by the governments, despite including politically sensitive issues such as fisheries and the creation of the YSLME Commission. These government endorsements thereby paved the way for the agreed regional-level policies on the Yellow Sea to be included in national policies.

The ROK's role in facilitating cooperation

Fourth, the ROK's proactive role facilitating cooperation in the Yellow Sea region enabled the YSLME Project to continue its operations and ultimately to arrive at a successful outcome. The first phase of the YSLME Project was completed in 2011, but during the period of project implementation (2004–2011), there was a significant change in terms of the eligibility of the ROK as a financial recipient from the GEF. When, in 2010, the ROK became a member of the OECD Development Assistance Committee, which consists of donor countries, it was no longer able to carry out the YSLME Project by relying on GEF funding. Faced with this situation, the ROK government committed to making substantial financial contributions so as to continue the project. In other words, it would have been difficult for the YSLME Project to have moved forward to its second phase had it not been for the ROK's pledge. Recognizing the importance of cooperative activities at the regional level to protect the marine environment, the ROK decided to make the necessary financial contributions, while China would continue to receive funding from GEF.

Increased possibility of the DPRK's participation

Finally, the cooperative nature of the UNDP/GEF YSLME Project increased the possibility of the DPRK's participation in this regional endeavor. Considering that the DPRK is one of the three coastal states in the Yellow Sea region, it is imperative that the DPRK participate in the mechanism. Given the importance of this involvement, the YSLME Project has continuously made efforts to invite the DPRK into this regional activity. As there are multiple incentives for the DPRK to join, it finally sent a formal letter of intention to participate in the second phase of the project, although it continues to be excluded as a result of UN Security Council sanctions. China and the ROK are willing to grant the DPRK observer status to enable it to participate to some degree until these sanctions are lifted.

In conclusion, the YSLME Project did not pursue a legally binding environmental treaty in the region. Instead, the cooperation-based soft institution-building process that has characterized the YSLME Project made significant contributions to the design and creation of regional measures on marine environment protection in the Yellow Sea. As a result, the proposed regional measures were subsequently adopted by China and the ROK and stand to become an integral part of each country's policies on marine ecosystem protection and management.

Conclusion

Building an effective institution to address common regional issues is always important. In the past, one of the prevalent methods for institution building was to transplant approaches that had been already created in developed countries to other locations. As was previously discussed, in the area of environment and sustainable development this would have implied relying on the convention protocol approach developed in Europe. Within this scheme, in order to address unprecedented regional environmental problems, European countries first agreed on a framework convention that provided a flexible forum to discuss detailed measures to protect the environment and realize sustainable development. Following this successful experience in Europe, some UN organizations developed their global programs based on this approach and applied it to other regions.

Although there are advantages to this legally binding treaty-based approach, such as providing transparency, treaty-making processes vary depending on the diverse challenges of different regions around the world. Environmental institution-building experiences in Northeast Asia demonstrate that the design of regional institutions should fully take into account the unique features of the region in order to ensure effective implementation. In Northeast Asia, where it is extremely difficult, if not impossible, for a multilateral treaty to be agreed on, countries have instead developed various (non-legally binding) soft institutions to address regional environmental problems.

One key example of developing an effective regional institution in Northeast Asia is the UNDP/GEF YSLME Project. As previously discussed, this project has suggested effective solutions in making regional policies and measures to protect one of the most severely polluted seas in the world without following the convention protocol approach. Since the project and its specific activities were designed in a cooperative manner, it was able to overcome political hurdles between China and the ROK, thereby producing significant achievements. It succeeded in adopting a regional target of reducing fishing by 25%–30% based on a cooperative scientific study conducted by experts from the two countries, despite the fact that illegal fishing remains a critical problem between China and the ROK. This agreement will ultimately contribute to solving the problem of illegal fishing by Chinese vessels in ROK waters and will also ensure sustainable fishing in the Yellow Sea region. Furthermore, the science-focused cooperative study undertaken by the two countries has produced the first scientific data on the Yellow Sea that can be used as a key source for devising marine policy at the regional level in the future.

These successful outcomes of the UNDP/GEF YSLME Project were possible because Project Management Office played an essential role in coordinating the relevant states and providing expertise. Another important determinant of success was the cooperative attitude between China and the ROK. Although the ROK became ineligible for GEF funding for the second phase of the project, it decided to continue participating in the second phase by covering its own financial obligations. On the other hand, China's government agencies made a grand compromise among themselves to reach an agreement on the regional target of reducing fishing efforts by 30%. A final factor that aided the effective implementation of the YSLME Project was its science-based approach: Working Groups of scientific experts were created, and the Regional Science and Technical Panel oversaw their output, guaranteeing their credibility. This therefore created a favorable environment for both governments to consider the suggested regional marine policy recommendations.

Drawing from the Northeast Asian experience, when countries in Latin America and other regions consider building regional mechanisms to protect the environment and realize sustainable development, there should be adequate consideration of an approach that would best fit the unique situation of the region. The examination of distinct regional challenges in order to design a cooperative mechanism that meets those needs would lead to building a more effective regional institution. Furthermore, even in times of regional tensions which can have a negative impact on regional stability, environmental cooperation can act as a conduit which can contribute to regional sustainability and prosperity.

Notes

1 U.S. Energy Information Administration (EIA). "International Energy Statistics, Total Carbon Dioxide Emissions from the Consumption of Energy." www.eia.gov/cfapps/ipdbproject/iedindex3.cfm?tid=90&pid=44&aid=8. CompareAllCountries.com. "Compare North Korea and Tunisia: Carbon dioxide emissions, thousands of tonnes." www.compareallcountries.com/North-Korea/Tunisia/Carbon_dioxide_emissions/
2 For a detailed discussion on regional environmental governance, see *Global Environmental Politics* 12, no. 3 (2012).
3 For a detailed discussion on the convention-protocol approach, see Susskind (1994).
4 UNEP. Mediterranean Action Plan for the Barcelona Convention. www.unepmap.org/index.php?module=content2&catid=001001004
5 UNECE. The Convention. www.unece.org/env/lrtap/lrtap_h1.html
6 UNECE. The Convention. www.unece.org/env/lrtap/lrtap_h1.html
7 In addition to the MERRAC in the ROK, there is the Special Monitoring and Coastal Environment Assessment Regional Activity Centre (CEARAC) in Japan, the Data and Information Network Regional Activity Centre (DINRAC) in China, and the Pollution Monitoring Regional Activity Centre (POMRAC) in Russia. NOWPAP, Regional Activity Centres. www.nowpap.org/
8 UNDP/GEF. Project Document. www.thegef.org/gef/sites/thegef.org/files/gef_prj_docs/GEFProjectDocuments/International%20Waters/Regional%20-%20(4343)%20-%20EAS-%20Implementation%20of%20the%20Yellow%20Sea%20LME%20Strategi/1-7-14_-_Project_Doc.pdf
9 For discussion on obstacles to creating regional environmental institutions in Northeast Asia, see, for example, Chung (1999).

References

Balsiger, Jörg, and Stacy D. VanDeveer. 2012. "Navigating Regional Environmental Governance." *Global Environmental Politics* 12, no. 3: 1–17.

Chung, Suh-Yong. 1999. "Is the Mediterranean Regional Cooperation Model Applicable to Northeast Asia?" *The Georgetown International Environmental Law Review* 11: 363–399.

CompareAllCountries.com. "Compare North Korea and Tunisia: Carbon dioxide emissions, thousands of tonnes." http://www.compareallcountries.com/North-Korea/Tunisia/Carbon_dioxide_emissions/

Drifte, Reinhart. 2005. "Transboundary Pollution as an Issue in Northeast Asian Politics." Asia Working Paper 12. London: Asia Research Centre (ARC), London School of Economics and Political Science.

Fukurai, Hiroshi. 2012. "Introduction: The Fukushima Dai-Ichi Nuclear Disaster and the Future of Nuclear Energy Programs in Japan and East Asia." *Pacific Rim Law & Policy Journal* 21, no. 3: 427–31.

The Guardian. 2014. "Chinese Fishing Boat Captain Dies in South Korea Sea Clash." October 10. www.theguardian.com/world/2014/oct/10/chinese-fishing-boat-captain-dies-in-south-korea-sea-clash

Kullenberg, Gunnar and Michael E. Huber. 2011. "Reducing Environmental Stress in the Yellow Sea Large Marine Ecosystem: Final Evaluation Report." UNDP.

Ministry of Environment, Korea. 2014. Particulate Matter. www.airkorea.or.kr/web/bbs/airpds/15830/?sch_key=0&sch_value=

Ministry of Environment, Korea. 2015. Bilateral and Multilateral Environmental Cooperation. http://eng.me.go.kr/eng/web/index.do?menuId=422

NOWPAP. Regional Activity Centres. http://www.nowpap.org/

Susskind, Lawrence E. 1994. *Environmental Diplomacy: Negotiating More Effective Global Agreements*. Oxford: Oxford University Press.

Timmermann, Martina. 2008. "Introduction: Institutionalizing Northeast Asia: Challenges and Opportunities." In *Institutionalizing Northeast Asia: Regional Steps Towards Global Governance*, edited by Martina Timmermann and Jitsuo Tsuchiyama. Tokyo and New York: United Nations University Press: 1–18.

UNDP/GEF. 2007. "Reducing Environmental Stress in the Yellow Sea Large Marine Ecosystem." Transboundary Diagnostic Analysis. UNDP/GEF Project.

UNDP/GEF. 2009. "Reducing Environmental Stress in the Yellow Sea Large Marine Ecosystem." Strategic Action Programme. UNDP/GEF Project.

U.S. Energy Information Administration (EIA). International Energy Statistics, Total Carbon Dioxide Emissions from the Consumption of Energy. www.eia.gov/cfapps/ipdbproject/iedindex3.cfm?tid=90&pid=44&aid=8

11 The multilateral trading system and regional public goods

Miguel Rodríguez Mendoza and
Craig VanGrasstek

Introduction

Where is the international trading system heading, and what might countries do to direct its course? These questions are greatly complicated by the division of that system into two distinct layers. One is the multilateral trading system, at the center of which is the World Trade Organization (WTO). The WTO is now entering its third decade of existence, after having replaced the General Agreement on Tariffs and Trade (GATT) of 1947–94. The other layer is a large and growing system of regional trade agreements (RTAs), consisting mostly of free trade agreements but also including customs unions and common markets. Whereas the WTO is founded upon the principle of unconditional most-favored-nation (MFN) treatment among all its members, RTAs take a more discriminatory approach. Whether they are bilateral, regional, or plurilateral, RTAs typically restrict their benefits to the members of the agreements.

The multilateral trading system faces two challenges, one of which also threatens to slow, halt, or even reverse the proliferation of RTAs. The first challenge is proliferation itself. The great irony of the WTO is that its establishment marked the culmination of a half-century of progress toward a multilateral trade regime, but came just when its members began negotiating discriminatory agreements in earnest. RTAs had been few and far between during the GATT years, but over the past two decades, countries have negotiated them with increasing frequency. RTAs have grown in number, in the depth of their commitments, and in the size of their combinations. Whereas giants such as the European Union, Japan, and the United States had long shown restraint in their negotiation of RTAs, reaching these agreements with smaller partners but dealing with one another solely within the framework of the multilateral system, in recent years they have sought to break through that glass ceiling in a series of transatlantic, transpacific, and other trade negotiations.

While these developments point toward the widening and deepening of RTAs, quite probably at the expense of the multilateral system, both layers of the trading system face an additional threat. Trade negotiations of all stripes have lately come under attack, be they regional or multilateral, with anti-globalization sentiment rising everywhere—above all in the most developed countries. This trend was evident a decade ago, when megaregional negotiations in the Asia-Pacific region and the Americas both petered out, but the anti-trade voices have grown increasingly shrill in recent years. They could well succeed in killing, or at the very least delaying, major initiatives such as the Trans-Pacific Partnership (TPP). It is unclear whether even some of the existing arrangements will survive intact, as evidenced by the British vote to exit from the European Union and the renewed demands for US withdrawal from the North American Free Trade Agreement (NAFTA). Nor is the multilateral system itself immune, as shown by the repeated failures to "get to yes" in the Doha Round of multilateral trade talks.

There is a possibility that the rising level of trade-skeptic sentiment in developed countries could render moot the debate over multilateralism versus regionalism. At a time when policy makers in the major industrialized countries still wonder if trade liberalization is best achieved through negotiations with one partner at a time, or with several, or with all, and when some of these policy makers prefer an "all of the above" strategy, the more disgruntled segments of their electorates increasingly insist instead upon a "none of the above" option. It is beyond the limited scope of this analysis to forecast whether these latest developments amount to bumps in the road, as transitory as the many other jolts that have periodically arisen in the decades since the end of the Second World War, or if instead they signal a sharp turn in the direction of that road. The authors both hope and believe that the former interpretation is more supportable than the latter. It is true that there are good reasons to doubt the future of the TPP, and the success of transatlantic negotiations has also been put in doubt, but these are only the largest among many regional initiatives. No matter what happens to these two initiatives, the principal issues examined here seem likely to remain relevant.

While thus acknowledging that antiglobalization sentiment is real and profound, and could well have lasting consequences, this analysis nonetheless starts from the assumption that it will remain manageable. We argue that the multilateral system still matters, but that the re-emergence of discrimination poses an underlying threat to its core of ideal nondiscrimination. That system may be undermined by deals that would actually divert as much trade as they create, and that diminish the role of the WTO in global governance. The WTO was intended not only to have a legislative function (i.e. to negotiate new trade liberalization deals among its members), but also to play important roles through its executive, judicial, and research capacities. The question here is whether RTAs are best seen as complements or as substitutes for the WTO, and thus whether they serve to supplement or undermine the capacity of the WTO to achieve its objectives.

The available evidence might be read in two very different ways, depending on which approach one takes to the analysis of public goods. Those who adhere to the theory of "hegemonic stability" take a decidedly more pessimistic view than do the advocates of "global public goods." The first view stresses the importance of power in the creation of global institutions and sees both the decline of the WTO and the rise of RTAs as symptomatic of a degenerating system in which the global redistribution of power has led to a lack of leadership. The second view instead sees this development as a more democratic distribution of power and responsibility, as demonstrated both by the near-universal membership of the WTO and the positive contributions that RTAs may make to the system. These include the use of RTAs as a policy laboratory for negotiations on new issues, allowing countries to calibrate the speed and depth of their liberalization commitments.

The present paper does not seek to resolve the differences between these two schools of thought, as they are rooted at least as much in differing philosophical foundations as they are in empirical realities. We instead take a more pragmatic approach, arguing that the WTO and RTAs can co-exist in a harmonious and mutually reinforcing manner. They can embrace each other and take advantage of the rich experience gained in the making and implementation of trade rules.

This paper has three objectives. First, we describe the current state of play in the trading system, especially with respect to the increasing emphasis placed on regionalism over multilateralism. Second, we discuss the implications of this shift from a global and public goods perspective, considering both those aspects of regionalism that some believe may contribute to discrimination, as well as those that may strengthen the system. Finally, we provide recommendations on how the positive aspects of regionalism might be strengthened and its less desirable consequences ameliorated, in order to ensure that the net result is positive for the multilateral trading system.

The expansion of RTAs

Four phases can be identified in the negotiation of RTAs. The first lasted from the start of the GATT system through the early 1980s, when RTAs remained rare exceptions that were largely confined to the negotiation of agreements among countries in the same region. These were common both among developing countries and, in the case of Western Europe, developed countries. In this period the most typical agreements consisted of customs unions—or FTAs that masqueraded as customs unions—between more or less similar countries in the same geographic area. This was as true for North–North agreements in Europe as it was for South–South agreements in Asia, Africa, and especially the Americas. The main difference in RTAs at that time was between the open regionalism of the European agreements and the closed regionalism of most pacts among developing countries: whereas the members of the European associations engaged simultaneously in regional and multilateral liberalization, many of the agreements among developing countries were designed to be regional complements to a policy of import substitution industrialization.

The second phase, which roughly coincided with the Uruguay Round of multilateral trade negotiations (1986–94), saw an increase in the pace and direction of RTA talks. Here the dominant pattern shifted to North–North agreements between countries of manifestly different sizes (e.g. the US–Canada FTA) and North–South agreements in which the asymmetries were even greater (e.g. the many agreements that developing countries negotiated with the European Union and the United States). The only real difference between this second phase and the one that followed it, which more or less coincided with the inauguration of the WTO, was in the sheer quantity of agreements: whereas there were still comparatively few RTAs being negotiated around the time of the Uruguay Round, the pace has since accelerated greatly. The rate at which RTAs entered into effect rose from 2.1 per year in the late GATT years (1980–94), most of them coming at the end of that period, to 9.0 per year in 1995–2003, and 13.9 per year in 2004–14 with another 17 registered between January 2015 and June 2016.[1]

We now appear to be in a fourth and especially consequential phase. Starting around 2013 the major economies began to explore the possibility of megaregional agreements that would directly link them to one another. Of the six possible combinations of pairings between China, Japan, the European Union, and the United States, four are currently under negotiation. Arguably the most significant of these negotiations, at least when considered in the context of the WTO, is the Transatlantic Trade and Investment Partnership (TTIP) between the European Union and the United States. Negotiations are also underway between the European Union and Japan, between Japan and China, and the negotiations between Japan and the United States were part of the TPP. The only two arrangements that policymakers in these countries have yet to broach are US–China or EU–China agreements.

The potential impact of the megaregional agreements on the WTO system is much greater than that of run-of-the-mill RTAs. This can be appreciated in the first instance by the sheer size of the agreements and also in the precedents that they might set. Both the TPP and the TTIP involve countries representing a very large share of the world's population, economic activity, and trade. The TPP countries account for approximately 60% of global GDP and 40% of the world's population. The TTIP encompasses the world's largest economic relationship, involving 29 developed countries whose reciprocal trade and investment flows amounted to more than US$1 trillion in 2012.

Viewed in isolation, the rising number and size of RTAs should not be troubling. Pragmatic statesmen will typically point out that there is more than one way to skin a cat, and that if progress is blocked in the WTO then these alternative fora may instead do the trick. Multilateralists find fault with that logic on several grounds, not the least being a concern that the proliferation of RTAs may actually contribute to countries' inability to conclude new agreements in the WTO. From this perspective, the rise of RTAs and decline of the WTO are not merely concurrent, but a matter of cause and effect.

Two views on public goods: hegemonic stability versus global public goods

What are we to make of the paralysis in the WTO and the concurrent proliferation of RTAs? Before examining the practical impact of these agreements on the trading system, both positive and negative, it is important to place this development in a proper analytical context. What is at issue here is whether the world will continue to provide for itself the public good that is an open and nondiscriminatory trading system. There are also very different views on whether a system in which RTAs predominate can be considered a global public good and on how countries might best go about ensuring that the rise of discrimination does not undermine the WTO.

The notion of public goods helps to explain why open markets are difficult to establish, how that difficulty can sometimes be overcome as a general rule, and what specific exceptions are then proposed to that general rule. An open trading system is often presented as a classic example of a public good at the international level, but it is an especially difficult one to establish and maintain. Much of the scholarship on this issue has focused principally or exclusively on just one aspect of the public goods problem, namely the need for countries to find a way of overcoming the free-rider problem. The two solutions to that problem require either that a uniquely powerful country step in to provide the public good (as posited in the theory of hegemonic stability) or that this task be accomplished through a more democratic approach to global governance (as advocated by the proponents of global public goods).

The core characteristics of public goods remain at issue, and one should not take for granted that an international trading system that provides for greater openness will necessarily do so in a way that is both nonrivalrous and non-excludable. Countries may instead see the benefits of the trading system in zero-sum terms, and use various means—including the deliberate fragmentation of that system into separate blocs—in an effort to capture greater shares of the benefits for themselves.

The ideological orientation of free traders does not always sit well with the more atavistic instincts of policy makers. No matter how persuasive Adam Smith, David Ricardo, and their intellectual successors may have been on the mutually beneficial nature of free trade, elected officials and other statesmen from countries at all levels of economic development have repeatedly shown their natural predilection for an essentially mercantilist outlook on trade. As long as they see the trading system in zero-sum rather than positive-sum terms, both with respect to the national balance of trade (i.e. surpluses are seen as good and deficits are bad) and to the access that they enjoy to foreign markets (i.e. preferential access in a relatively closed market may look more attractive than nondiscriminatory access in an open market), policymakers are not likely to place as high a priority as economists do on the achievement of a truly open and nondiscriminatory trading system.

When viewed through the lens of public goods theory, it is quite evident that the rise of RTAs challenges the assumption that an open trading system is nonexcludable. As an ideal, the multilateral trading system has long sought to achieve three objectives: the reduction or elimination of trade barriers; an end to discrimination between trading partners; and the universal application of these rules to all countries. The WTO may be nominally achieving the third of those objectives, now that nearly every country in the world is either a member or is actively negotiating for its accession, but the proliferation of RTAs implies that countries are willing to sacrifice the second objective (non-discrimination) in pursuit of the first (liberalization).

Almost all of the trade liberalization that has been achieved since the launch of the Doha Round has come about through RTAs rather than multilateral negotiations. Countries have thus shown a preference for inherently discriminatory instruments that allow their members to exclude third parties from the benefits of these agreements. What we are increasingly seeing is a tension between a multilateral system in which membership is universal but new MFN liberalization is elusive, and a system of RTAs that is growing both in size and scope, but in which the participating countries exclude nonparticipants from their deals.

The theory of hegemonic stability is a power-centric explanation for the global trading system, one that stresses the vital role of a hegemon—a politically powerful and economically efficient country that has both the means and the motivation to establish an open trading system. Britain played this role in the 19th century, and the United States in the 20th. Those who adhere to this view take a pessimistic view of the system as it now stands, as the United States no longer plays the leadership role that it did in past generations. From this perspective, the glacial pace of progress in the WTO and the proliferation of RTAs—including the US decision to negotiate such agreements in the mid-1980s—are both symptomatic of a system in which liberalization and multilateralism are being replaced by discrimination and balkanization.

This theory draws a direct connection between changes in the global distribution of power and the rise of discrimination. Here one finds a similarity in the trajectories that the trading system followed during the British and US hegemonies, with each going through a comparable evolution in the way they structured their bilateral agreements. The treaties that the British started to negotiate in 1860 and the tariff-reduction agreement that the United States began pursuing in 1934 each included MFN clauses that formed the foundation of the multilateral system at the time. In their heydays, each of these hegemons were essential to establishing and opening up global markets, but each of them later turned to discriminatory alternatives when their own competitiveness declined.

Beginning in the late 19th century and culminating in the set of restrictive Imperial Preferences negotiated at the Ottawa Conference in 1932, Britain went from negotiating bilateral agreements on a nondiscriminatory basis to discriminatory commonwealth agreements that threatened to undo that accomplishment. The United States, in turn, began to negotiate FTAs during a period when there were serious doubts over the country's competitive position vis-à-vis Japan, and some see the proliferation of RTAs as a sign of declining US interest in supporting the multilateral system. That development, coupled with the increasing difficulty that US presidents have had in gaining congressional support for any type of liberalization—multilateral or discriminatory—is one of the defining characteristics of the trading system today.

The picture looks much brighter for those who stress the need for global public goods, a system in which open markets and other *desiderata* can be provided and maintained through collective effort. The advocates of this position conceive of international relations more democratically, arguing that global institutions have a positive function to perform and do not owe their existence solely to the interests of the most powerful country. This is a more optimistic outlook, one that looks favorably on both the WTO, which is a far more inclusive institution than was the GATT, and the rising number of RTAs. As stated above, nearly all countries are now either members of or applicants to the WTO, and the fact that many of them wish to go further still through the negotiation of RTAs is a positive sign.

The advocates of global public goods stress the collective gains over the individual costs of cooperation and contend that institutions such as the WTO need to be established and strengthened as a means of dealing with the world's problems. This will, they hope, provide a more enduring, equitable, and cooperative basis for democratic global governance than reliance on hegemony. In this environment, nation states "will witness continuing erosion of their capacities to implement national policy objectives unless they take further steps to cooperate in addressing international spill overs and systemic risks" (Kaul, Grunberg, and Stern 1999, p.451).

It is difficult to resolve the differences between these two schools of thought in an objective fashion, primarily because these are rooted in the distinct philosophical assumptions of their proponents. We will not attempt here to suggest that either approach is universally superior, but will instead consider how each of them might conceive of the problem that the trading system faces. To simplify, this can be reduced to Lawrence's (1991) question of whether RTAs are best seen as "stumbling blocks" or "building blocks" for the multilateral system, a differentiation that is widely used today when considering the impact of RTAs on the multilateral trading system.

RTAs as "stumbling blocks"

There are two different levels at which RTAs may be seen as a threat to the multilateral trading system. The simplest and most traditional approach is to judge RTAs by the amount of trade that they either create or divert. That yardstick was especially apt at a time when trade negotiators dealt almost exclusively with tariffs and other border measures affecting trade in goods. A more complex question, and one that has become more pertinent with the expanding scope of issues in the system, is whether RTAs contribute to or undermine the other functions of the multilateral trading system.

The debate over the impact that discriminatory agreements and arrangements may have on the multilateral trading system is nearly as old as the system itself. Just a few years after the GATT came into being, Jacob Viner argued that trade creation occurs when "one of the members of the customs union will now newly import [an item] from the other but which it formerly did not import at all because the price of the protected domestic product was lower than the price at any foreign source plus the duty" (Viner 1950, p.43). Conversely, commodities are subject to trade diversion when "one of the members of the customs union will now newly import [the items] from the other whereas before the customs union it imported them from a third country, because that was the cheapest possible source of supply even after payment of duty" (Viner 1950, p.43).[2] The standard formula for determining the net benefits of any given RTA is thus a simple matter of arithmetic: does the total trade created exceed the value of the trade that is merely diverted?

Economists have never reached a consensus on whether discriminatory agreements offer a net benefit to the trading system. There is no shortage of analysts who have used Viner's logic to reach a very negative conclusion; they variously argue that the proliferation of RTAs may contribute to a balkanization of the trading system, the multiplication of competing rules of origin, and the creation of national constituencies that are more interested in preserving preferential arrangements with captive markets than they are in promoting new global deals.

From the perspective of a third (i.e. excluded) party, the issue of trade creation versus trade diversion is critically important. These parties will rarely experience any of the benefits from the new trade that is created but may very well bear the brunt of the trade-diversionary effects. These concerns may be especially high in the case of the current megaregional negotiations between the world's largest economies, especially the TPP and the TTIP. Should these agreements survive the current resurgence of antitrade sentiment, they may act to divert trade from other countries in various ways. Those countries that currently engage in nonpreferential trade with the TPP and TTIP countries will continue to pay MFN tariffs on products that the TPP/TTIP countries will now trade duty-free with one another; those countries that currently enjoy preferential access to the TPP/TTIP markets will experience erosion in their margins of preference; and the impact on countries with preferential access may deteriorate further if the TPP/TTIP countries negotiate more favorable rules of origin in these agreements than one finds in other trade agreements and programs.

Reliance on RTAs can also mean reducing the likelihood of reaching meaningful deals on certain topics. It is a common mistake to think of RTAs and multilateral agreements solely in terms of scale, on the assumption that the one is merely a smaller version of the other. There are instead important qualitative distinctions, as the contents of WTO and RTA agreements often differ greatly. There are some issues that cannot be effectively handled in anything short of a multilateral agreement. Agricultural production subsidies are the best example of such an issue: whereas it is quite simple to discriminate between partners in the application of tariffs on imports, there is no practical way to restrict the impact of production subsidies on some countries while exempting others.

The question of how RTAs affect the role of the WTO in global governance is more complicated. Although the WTO's legislative function may be important, serving as it does to negotiate agreements to reduce trade barriers and devise other rules, we should not forget that the institution also has other functions. Its judicial role is especially significant, as the WTO is widely recognized as having the most robust dispute settlement system of any international economic organization. While RTAs have dispute settlement provisions of their own, they will typically rely much more heavily on negotiated solutions to disputes—often between countries of greatly different sizes and levels of development. In the WTO disputes are adjudicated in the first instance by panelists from third countries,[3] and any appeals are handled by the highly regarded experts in the Appellate Body. It is doubtful that any bilateral or regional dispute settlement system could achieve a comparable level of objectivity and professionalism.

RTAs as "building blocks"

The positive case for RTAs touches on some of the same issues and evidence as the negative case, but sees the data through a different lens. Starting from the same Vinerian problem outlined above, the friends of RTAs will typically argue that the trade created by these agreements is indeed greater than the trade they divert. They will usually also appeal to other virtues of RTAs, noting that these agreements deal with new and complex issues and thus establish precedents for the inclusion of new subject matter within the scope of trade policy. Some argue that discrimination can serve to advance issues that might otherwise stagnate and to make agreements more enforceable.

Just as RTAs have grown in number, they have also expanded in scope and in depth. They may arguably have been "light" agreements during the first waves of bilateral and regional trade negotiations, when many of them were partial scope agreements, but this is no longer the case for most RTAs. They often contain disciplines that are wider in scope, deeper in their integration, and significantly more sophisticated than those of the multilateral trading system. They may cover areas not yet regulated by the WTO, such as investment, social and environmental issues, and regulatory coherence. Some RTAs also take innovative approaches to dealing with supply chains and the fragmentation of value addition in the global economy.

It would be a mistake to consider the third-country impact of the megaregional agreements solely in Vinerian terms. First, the current level of MFN tariffs is relatively low: many of the items imported by the European Union, Japan, and the United States are either duty-free on an MFN basis or face MFN duty rates that are so low as to constitute a nuisance rather than an obstacle. Many of the exceptional products that remain subject to relatively high tariffs, and hence may be most susceptible to real trade-diverting effects, are in fields that the major developed countries have almost entirely abandoned (e.g. apparel and leather products). These agreements are thus more significant for what they achieve on nontariff topics. Issues such as the regulation of trade in services, investment, competition policy, and intellectual property rights are likely to have an even greater impact on trade and investment in the 21st century than tariffs did in the 20th century, and the megaregional negotiations could fashion the template for new deals on these issues.

Toward a more pragmatic approach

Through the history of the multilateral trading system, there has always been a gap between how its members treat discrimination in principle and in practice. The elimination of discrimination is supposed to be one of the core objectives of the multilateral system. That is evident from the preambles of both the GATT and the WTO, each of which called for "the substantial reduction of tariffs and other barriers to trade and . . . the elimination of discriminatory treatment." The original GATT negotiators followed up by making universal and unconditional MFN treatment the core principle of the GATT, enshrining it in Article I.

From the very start, however, trade negotiators have also provided for the negotiation of discriminatory agreements that ran counter to the MFN principle. GATT Article XXIV allows for the negotiation of FTAs and customs unions, and since 1979 this loophole has been supplemented by the Decision on Differential and More Favorable Treatment Reciprocity and Fuller Participation of Developing Countries—better known as the Enabling Clause—intended to facilitate the negotiation of RTAs among developing countries. Later developments include Article V of the General Agreement on Trade in Services (GATS), which is essentially a repeat of GATT Article XXIV, and the inauguration in 2006 of the WTO's "transparency" mechanism for RTAs. All of these instruments facilitate the reconciliation of discrimination with the multilateral system, legally if not philosophically.

All WTO members look with suspicion on other countries' RTAs but are even more strongly committed than ever to protecting their own RTAs. The result has been the creation of a system that requires the notification and examination of these agreements and also imposes certain standards that these agreements are required to meet, but there has never been any serious effort made in the GATT or the WTO systems to ensure that these standards are enforced. An RTA is required to cover "substantially all of the trade" between the countries that conclude it, for example, but there is no consensus on what constitutes "substantially all." Thus, agreements are (usually) notified, and (slowly) examined, but never with any credible threat that they might be found not to meet the legal obligations established in GATT Article XXIV and/or GATS Article V.

We argue that the question is not so much whether the WTO can or should discipline RTAs, but rather how the WTO could embrace RTAs and build upon them. In other words, how can we mitigate the real challenges posed by RTAs while harnessing the many opportunities that RTAs create for sustainable development? The WTO has much to learn from RTAs and much to offer them as well, and the same can be said of RTAs vis-à-vis the WTO. Exploring these interactions goes beyond the simple requirements of GATT Article XXIV or GATS Article V.

We need to start from the premise that RTAs are here to stay and will continue to proliferate in the near future, no matter what happens to such high-profile initiatives as the TPP and TTIP. How then might we make RTAs and the WTO more responsive to each other? What should be developed is a more organic relationship between the WTO and RTAs. RTAs need not be dismissed as second-best options and should instead be recognized as valuable in their own right. Indeed, today's RTAs have the potential to be as complex and sophisticated as the WTO, and there is a body of rules and practices that have been developed at the regional level that the multilateral trading system could benefit from. In essence, a new approach to the relationship between the WTO and RTAs should be put in practice to allow the multilateral and regional frameworks to mutually reinforce one another.

One approach would be to help countries "multilateralize" their RTAs under the auspices of the WTO. That is much easier said than done. Multilateral trade talks now tackle multiple issues and involve an ever-growing number of countries. In this context, the multilateralization of RTA regulations would most likely require changes to the WTO's negotiating modalities, including a shift away from the unanimity rule and the "single undertaking" principle to enable deals to be struck more quickly among a critical mass of members. Such a coalition would need to encompass at least some of the largest trading nations to have a meaningful impact. The multilateralization process could start as a plurilateral agreement, whereby a subset of WTO members commit to a binding set of rules that applies only to them and that can be enforced in a WTO dispute settlement system. The members that choose not to join the deal would not be bound by its requirements, although they may benefit from it. This process would be fully voluntary, but discussions about multilateralization could be encouraged through various fora.

Among the fora that might foster such a process is a dialogue program launched by the International Centre on Trade and Sustainable Development (ICTSD) and called the E15 Initiative (E15), which has brought together a significant number of international experts in a series of policy dialogues that are geared toward strengthening the global trade and investment system.[4] One product of this initiative has been a proposal put forward by the Inter-American Development Bank to establish an RTA Exchange, a dedicated clearing-house of information on regional and bilateral deals and a place to discuss all matters related to regional trade pacts, their rules and practices (see Box 11.1).

Such an RTA Exchange could feature inter alia an annual forum in which countries share their best practices and discuss challenges they have faced in negotiating and implementing their RTAs. The RTA Exchange could also include an informative and interactive website that would be filled with RTA-related data, information, and fresh ideas for policymakers, companies, and analysts to employ.

Box 11.1 The RTA Exchange

- Discussions among E15 experts on RTAs led ICTSD and the IADB, joined subsequently by the Asian Development Bank (ADB), to propose and support the creation of the RTA Exchange, an initiative whose basic contours were agreed during the last WTO Ministerial Conference at Bali, in December 2013.
- The RTA Exchange is being conceived as an independent platform to systematically explore the possibilities for convergence and coherence between RTAs and the multilateral trading system, thus building synergies between them. It is intended to be developed into a leading forum where relevant actors in the RTA world and the WTO—negotiators, policy makers, analysts, regional development institutions, NGOs, and private sector representatives—could converge both physically and virtually to share experiences, ideas, insights, and proposals to make RTAs and the WTO more responsive to each other.
- The services of the RTA Exchange could be made available to all as a "public good" and this will certainly benefit the smaller developing countries that are often outsiders to RTAs and typically face more constraints in accessing the knowledge and information needed to engage fully in these debates. It is being structured based on the following main components:
  - (a) A web-based interface;
  - (b) A policy-oriented research and analysis program to be carried out by the participating institutions; and
  - (c) A regular dialogue and experience-sharing program for policy makers and practitioners.
- The RTA Exchange aims to become a "knowledge broker"; it will build as much as possible on existing information and analysis, but will also undertake specific research where gaps exist and fresh analysis is required to advance the "convergence" role of the RTA Exchange.
- Ultimately the aim of the RTA Exchange, as indicated before, is to provide a venue where interested stakeholders from the RTA and WTO would interact with each other, discuss relevant policy issues around RTA convergence, and identify options to multilateralize best practices or, as appropriate, regionalize best multilateral practices. It could provide this service through a combination of annual conferences, informal roundtables, briefing sessions, expert meetings, and regional dialogues.

(continued)

(continued)

- • Finally, it is important to underline that although the RTA Exchange could well develop in the future as a new, independent "institution," the initiative is currently being undertaken by a "consortium" of three institutions, namely the Inter-American Development Bank, the ADB, and the International Centre on Trade and Sustainable Development, ICTSD.

Source: Suominen (2014).

These proposals would not provide a complete solution to the problem, but would at least offer further opportunities for countries to incorporate the best of the RTAs into the multilateral system. Or to cast them in the language of public goods, they could offer means by which the countries that have come together to provide regional public goods can discuss better ways to make the benefits of those public goods more global.

To conclude, the principal questions that we have dealt with here are (1) whether RTAs are best seen as complements or as substitutes for the WTO, and thus (2) whether RTAs serve to supplement or undermine the contribution that the WTO makes to global governance. The perspective that one takes on these questions depends in part on how one chooses to view the public goods aspects of the problem. If one takes a power-centric view of the system, stressing the need for leadership and a central role for the WTO, the rise of the RTAs appears to be a challenge or even a threat. From this perspective, RTAs are problematic efforts to transform a true public good into an excludable club good, and one that undermines the WTO in numerous ways.

If one instead sees the issue through the lens of global public goods, those same developments seem more like an opportunity. From that perspective, RTAs allow like-minded countries to pair up in an effort to go farther than the negotiating environment of the WTO will allow, while also allowing them to demonstrate to the rest of the WTO membership what might be done on new issues.

We argue that the net value of RTAs depends on whether countries have the wisdom and the will to incorporate them more fully into the multilateral trading system. While it is important to acknowledge the challenges that RTAs pose, insofar as they not only compete with the WTO but may indeed act to undermine it, one must also recognize that they have the capacity to buttress the global trading system. If countries manage to make the most of this opportunity, they will endorse the hopes of those who call for the strengthening of global public goods, and help move both the WTO and RTAs toward reinforcing and "embracing" each other, and to enhance the positive contribution each can make to a more solid and stable multilateral trading system.

Notes

1 Note that all data on RTAs presented here is based on the WTO's Regional Trade Agreements Information System at http://rtais.wto.org/UI/PublicMaintainRTAHome.aspx, which is in turn based on the information that members provide to the secretariat. It does not include any RTAs that, for whatever reason, may not have been notified.
2 It should be noted that while Viner wrote only about customs unions, his argument was equally applicable to FTAs and other forms of RTA.
3 Note that some RTAs do provide for the use of third-country panelists to adjudicate trade disputes between the parties, but this would appear to be the exception rather than the rule. This approach may be more common in the specific case of investment disputes, where RTAs often provide for referral of a case to the International Centre for the Settlement of Investment Disputes (ICSID) or other established bodies.
4 The E15 Initiative (E15) was launched in 2011 by the Geneva-based International Centre on Trade and Sustainable Development (ICTSD).

References

Kaul, Inge, Isabelle Grunberg, and Marc Stern, eds. 1999. *Global Public Goods: International Cooperation in the 21st Century.* New York: United Nations Development Program.

Lawrence, Robert Z. 1991. "Emerging Regional Arrangements: Building Blocks or Stumbling Blocks." In *Finance and the International Economy,* edited by Richard O'Brien. New York: Oxford University Press.

Suominen, Kati. 2014. *RTA Exchange: Organizing the World's Information on Regional Trade Agreements.* Geneva: International Centre for Trade and Sustainable Development. http://e15initiative.org/wp-content/uploads/2014/12/E15_RTA_Suominen_FINAL.pdf (accessed June 24 2016).

Viner, Jacob. 1950. *The Customs Union Issue.* New York: Carnegie Endowment for International Peace.

Part IV

Old and new regions in a multiplex world

12 European regional public goods

Insiders and outsiders

Michelle Egan

Introduction

European integration has been struggling over the past decade due to a series of crises that has challenged the ability of the European Union (EU) to deal with the resulting political and economic volatility. Concerns about negative growth, rising inequality, and prolonged austerity, along with migration pressures from streams of refugees entering Europe, have created a climate where growing divisions have led to the southern periphery—Italy, Portugal, Spain, and Greece—shouldering the brunt of the economic and migration burden. As the EU member states hit hardest by the recent economic crisis respond to the extended influx of migrants reaching their shores, heated debates have been sparked about financial burdens, with widely differing views about the need for Europe-wide policy coordination. Unlike in the areas of trade and finance—where EU member states have been willing to expose their economies and societies to exogenous, competitive pressures, driven by treaty-based commitments to create a single continent-wide market—no such liberal regime has emerged for migration, where the model is one of closure and boundaries (Ferrara 2005). While European integration has promoted cross-border cooperation to improve social outcomes, public goods are increasingly excludable as the EU simultaneously dissolves internal borders while hardening external borders. What we see in Europe is a dualism between insiders and outsiders: national membership confers specific advantages in terms of access to regional public goods, while national citizenship confers market and social rights that are not afforded to those outside the bloc to the same degree. Regional public goods may also lead to stratification between insiders and outsiders not just as a consequence of membership but due to constraints and exclusions within the EU itself, raising questions about the dynamics of "free riding," as well as the unintended consequences of providing public goods in a heterogeneous polity with distinct economic and policy preferences and ideologies (Bonoli and Natali 2012). Does the provision of regional public goods in Europe reflect the preferences of some states over others? How can the provision of regional public goods generate democratic legitimacy, foster economic development, and ensure credible commitments in a climate of austerity and populism?

For Europe, with its deeply institutionalized structure, it is not the scope and provision of regional public goods, it is evaluating their effectiveness across different national contexts and dealing with the resulting backlash against efforts to provide collective action that encroaches on national autonomy.

This paper focuses on the provision of regional public goods (RPGs) within the EU, by examining the interrelated issues of trade, integration, and economic development in a climate of increased austerity and social dislocation. This chapter is organized as follows. Part 2 discusses the range of RPGs in Europe. Part 3 focuses on the evolution of trade integration and regional and social policy as two case studies. Part 4 emphasizes the impact of constraints on public finances in providing RPGs. Part 5 discusses the evaluation and impact of RPGs so as to highlight both the weakness and strengths of policy design and instruments, as well as the impact of sequencing on the provision of public goods. Part 6 then concludes.

The evolution of regional public goods in Europe

For more than six decades, the EU has been a major driver of regionalism, creating an array of formal institutions and collaborative mechanisms to promote RPGs. European integration has promoted a range of goods and services in environmental, transportation, social, and regional policy that are clearly identified as European public goods.[1] The EU has pushed forward with efforts to create a single market by addressing barriers to trade, coordinating common policies to prevent externalities, and seeking to address economic imbalances by promoting regional and social coherence. In contrast to many other regional efforts, the EU has also enhanced economic, political, and social rights, through legal provisions including the EU Charter of Fundamental Rights that provides guarantees for EU citizens, from freedom of association to data privacy. This has shifted the EU from primarily a market-centered project to one that is concerned about social citizenship, distributive justice, and democratic legitimacy. Although the EU was once considered one of the foremost proponents of RPGs, officials have struggled to build on this promise in the last decade, during which they established a new treaty, shored up banks, improved fiscal surveillance, and have tried to address declining competitiveness, rising labor costs, and flagging economic performance. Fiscal austerity has mobilized populist anti-austerity parties that have gained in the polls in countries facing large immigration flows, and huge sovereign debt. Frustration toward European integration—which is often used as a scapegoat for the failures of effective governance—and political dissatisfaction have hampered collective action to address Europe's challenges.

Yet the current narrative on Europe masks the degree to which the provision of public goods is both a central element of European economic recovery and a key building block for European integration. Recent initiatives focus on improving competitiveness, investment, and economic development so that European public goods provide an ever-expanding range of supply-side improvements.[2] With public investment below pre-crisis levels in Europe, such efforts to stimulate economic growth face budgetary challenges as well as concerns about crowding out private investment. Although public goods perform the classic functions of stabilization, redistribution, and allocation, the promotion and impact of public goods provision is a key issue for public administration and economic development scholars, bearing in mind the imposition of austerity measures in the aftermath of the global financial crisis.

Although the debate about public goods has been dominated by theories of federalism—particularly fiscal federalism, which concerns the assignment of competences to different jurisdictions within nation states—the roles and functions of the state have changed, which requires a reconsideration of the role and provision of public goods to include the regional dimension.[3] The EU has provided both tangible and nontangible public goods that include physical infrastructure such as trans-European networks aimed at modernizing services and markets;[4] economic development measures to reduce regional income disparities;[5] provision of guaranteed public services to ensure access, fairness, and transparency;[6] protection of consumer welfare; macroeconomic stabilization; fair market access; and external border control and burden-sharing mechanisms to deal with issues that go beyond territorial boundaries[7] (see Table 12.1).

Table 12.1 Range of European Public Goods

Sectors	Functions
Trade	Apply common external tariff, remove trade barriers, free movement provisions, reduce transactions costs, expand domestic market, facilitate trade, and apply common product standards
Competition policy	Ensure fair market access, prevent private distortions through monopolistic or predatory behavior, provide level playing field, protect consumer welfare, prevent public distortions through state aid and subsidies to protect market integration, assist interstate trade, and maintain effective competition
Transportation and communication	Ensure interoperability, reduce costs, apply common patent rules, safeguard consumer rights and provide security, intermodal transportation, cross-border services, digital access
Product safety, health, environment	Ensure market surveillance, product recall, quality, reliability, safety, transboundary cooperation, registration, testing, and certification, and avoid race to bottom and negative externalities
Regional economic development	Promote economic convergence, territorial cohesion, aid to specific distressed sectors, and investment, and reduce regional disparities in income and wealth
Economic and fiscal	Promote macroeconomic stabilization, recapitalization of banks and stress tests, banking union, exchange rate coordination, stability and growth pact (SGP), broad economic policy guidelines (BEPG), and fiscal compact
Internal security	Promote European Arrest Warrant, common asylum regime, partial common visa regime (Schengen), collective border control (Frontex), judicial cooperation, and police cooperation

Competences and public goods

Defining what should be included within the framework of public goods in the EU is complicated, as some would argue that it is constituted by the redistributive functions of the EU, such as cohesion policy and fiscal transfers, while others would include the provisions of competition policy, macroeconomic stabilization, and internal market liberalization. Finally, collective defense and security are also often considered key public goods (Thielemann and Armstrong 2013). The problem in this context is that competences to provide specific public goods within the EU are mixed. While formally the Lisbon Treaty outlines exclusive, shared, parallel, and mixed competence between the EU member states and the EU itself, in practice there are difficulties in drawing relevant borderlines that are not based on purely legal considerations (Rosas 2014). As the most densely integrated regional integration project, the EU has increasingly taken on new responsibilities, expanding its policy reach into areas traditionally associated with national authorities that results in allocation of new competences at the regional level, whether through political necessity (banking supervision, fiscal surveillance, and capital markets union), formal treaty changes (environmental and monetary policy), or integration through stealth (tax coordination, pensions) where inherent state prerogatives have become Europeanized (Majone 2005). Having designated trade initially as a public good, the EU then found that it needed to embrace new functions as increased cross-border trade and financial flows pushed for greater regulation of exchange rates and foreign direct investment, as well as environmental and consumer protection to deal with compound problems of anonymity, complexity, and concentrations of power to preserve market integration. Many processing, distribution, and consumption networks are distant from local production, generating a need for greater surveillance. The EU has increasingly provided assurances about quality, reliability, and safety through laws, regulations, and standards, as well as providing rules governing competition through the regulation of monopolies, the restructuring of industries, and the facilitation of new market entrants.

From an initial focus on a common market with a common external tariff, along with a treaty-based commitment to common commercial, competition, and agriculture policies, the transfer of policy competences from the national to the EU level has created a pattern of differentiated integration. Analysis of RPGs therefore needs to take account of the dynamics of differential versus unitary coverage. Since the EU has exclusive competence in fisheries, monetary policy, trade and competition, shared competence in the internal market, social and environmental policy, justice, safety, and transport, and supporting competence in health, education, and culture, the provision of RPGs will be impacted by the degree of enumerated powers. This is the case because domestic and political choices have restricted certain transfers of power to the regional level, leading to variations in terms of financial commitment, regulatory capacity, and political incentives to contribute to their provision. While

RPGs are created to address the unmet needs of society and aim to address complex political or societal issues through collective choice, much of the language of public goods tends to assume that policies can evolve on a *tabula rasa*, when in reality there is already an existing body of laws, policies, and practices. Past policies thus become an important part of the environment in which RPGs will emerge. While the transfer of institutional authority to the regional arena may be a means of fostering increased coordination, the inter-organizational politics of adjustment and accommodation are important factors in overcoming the joint-decision trap in which suboptimal outcomes may occur if specific states feel that the status quo is more advantageous than the newly proposed coordinated policies (Scharpf 1998). To overcome gridlock in negotiations, the production and consumption of RPGs may not be uniformly applicable across all jurisdictions. However, this insider/outsider model may not undermine the internal market, the economic, social, or territorial cohesion of the EU, nor result in bias or discrimination in trade and competition between member states.

Case studies: trade and market integration and regional and social policy

The economic goals of the original European Economic Community (EEC) were to eliminate protective barriers, curtail state monopolistic practices, and harmonize legislation to facilitate a common market. Though the economic freedoms of the EEC Treaty focused on a system of undistorted competition, driven by criteria based on the principle of nondiscrimination, the EU recognized the importance of collective economic development in the Treaty of Rome. In its preamble, it sought to "strengthen the unity of their economies and to ensure their harmonious development by reducing the differences existing between the various regions and the backwardness of the less favored regions" but provided limited institutional commitment toward this goal in that founding document. In fact, the goal of embedded liberalism was to ensure that trade liberalization was not in conflict with the broader provision of public welfare at the national level, so that market integration would benefit from increased social legitimacy (Ruggie 1982; Polanyi 1944).

Trade, welfare, and market integration

The EU has focused on constructing a "barrier free" market for the free flow of goods, capital, labor, and factors of production over the past seven decades, beginning with a common external tariff and customs union and then the removal of nontariff barriers. The EU has tried to address differences in cross-jurisdictional markets, ensuring that national standards and laws did not impede cross-border trade through enforcement of treaty commitments. Achieving the free movement of goods, persons, services, and capital (the "four freedoms") was difficult due to the requirements for unanimity that led to much political gridlock in the early period of regional integration (Egan 2001). Harmonization of policies proved both cumbersome and politically contentious. In response, the Court of Justice of the European Union (CJEU) provided the means to facilitate integration with the concept of mutual recognition.[8] This meant that states could retain their own domestic standards within their own jurisdiction but could not prevent the sale of goods and products that were deemed mutually equivalent in practice. Though mutual recognition provided for mutual reciprocity of rules, it is based on a high degree of trust, and a minimal convergence of regulatory objectives. Subsequently, the single market made progress in goods flows and capital flows, but liberalization of services and labor lagged behind due to political resistance. Efforts to promote labor mobility have included mutual recognition of professional qualifications, pension portability, and social security coordination, and labor rights have been extended to seasonal workers, students, pensioners, and the self-employed provided that they did not create a burden on the host state. All the same, such labor mobility is more limited than in the USA (Barslund, Busse, and Schwarzwälder 2015). Opposition has grown in many states to labor mobility, amidst concerns about access to welfare benefits and cheaper labor costs, causing a surge in anti-immigrant sentiment and the consequent EU-imposed mobility restrictions on Bulgarian and Romanian workers for seven years after their countries' accession. Services have been more controversial, as barriers to establishment rights and free movement of services have led to restrictions on market entry, increased resource costs, and discrimination between incumbents and foreign providers across a range of professional, business, and commercial services. The EU has managed to open up utilities to market competition: battered by weak demand and technological changes, the privatization of public monopolies and their infrastructure networks across Europe has brought to the fore the conflict between market freedoms and "public service" objectives.

Even if liberalizing public service markets strengthens general welfare, the prospect of mutual recognition of cross-border services and rights of establishment (to provide services beyond country of origin) has generated anxiety and protest over job losses and *délocalisation* (outsourcing). Protest against service liberalization has been compounded by increased regulatory heterogeneity among member states after enlargement. Redistributive issues often overshadow efficiency concerns in European debates, as service liberalization puts pressure on the national job market—simply by using the services freedom, labor from Central and Eastern Europe (CEE) could work on a temporary basis based on home-country wages, thus undercutting local employment practices and wages. While very differently regulated service providers might work simultaneously side-by-side with local providers, this may also generate significant redistributive consequences (Schmidt 2009, 2012). In this case, the economic decisions of a sole member state are likely to generate externalities in the single market. Not all legal entitlements generate broad RPGs, as mutual recognition as a market solution to regulatory diversity may help abolish labor market rigidities, exploit wage differentials, and provide competitive advantages for specific member states at the expense of those rules providing high levels of social protection. As this illustrates, the pursuit of one public good can conflict with the provision of another.

Regional imbalances, social cohesion, and economic development

Historically, efforts to promote economic development and address inequalities within the EEC were initially limited (Hooghe 1996). The expectation was that regional economic development would be the responsibility of the member states, although there was some recognition that divergent development would have critical social and political consequences for the nascent regional integration project. While the founding six members wanted to address low productivity, improve communications, and electrical power in order to increase living standards and industrial development, the only direct promotion of regional policy was through the mandate of the European Investment Bank (EIB) (Lewenhak 2012). The EIB initially made loans to poor regions, drafted as a protocol to the Treaty of Rome based on capital contributions from member states.[9] The EIB has been successful in obtaining funds for Community projects from international financial markets, providing both individual and cross-border assistance for projects, functioning as both a financial institution and development institution (Lewenhak 2012, p.6).

However, the persistent differences in per capita GDP and unemployment rates within regions have pushed the EU to increase its direct role in regional policy. With each subsequent enlargement, the EU has provided new instruments and funds to address the potential distributional effects of greater competition as a result of membership of the larger market. This focus on regional economic development was the result of the first accession, which incorporated Ireland, Denmark, and the United Kingdom into the union in 1973—the latter advocated for the European Regional Development Fund to address regional disparities through grants rather than loans, which became operational in 1975. There were concerns that these grants could become substitutes for national regional funding rather than a reflection of the policy's original intellectual and economic motivations. As a result, what began as a way of addressing market failures and disequilibrium shifted, as regional funds were associated with single market objectives and viewed as "side payments" assuring the active support of peripheral countries (Behrens and Smyrl 1999). As Pastor (2001) notes, "roughly 85% of ERDF-funded projects in the 1970s and 1980s were used for infrastructure, and 91% of its funds went to the poorest regions in five countries—France, Germany, Italy, Greece, and the United Kingdom," but this funding was significantly smaller than that allocated to agricultural policy. The funds were subsequently doubled in the wake of efforts to promote the single market program as the scope and mandate was transformed to address the potential costs of greater liberalization and competition for less developed economies. Under the Delors I Package, RPGs became an increased priority, in that the goals for cohesion were fundamental to the EEC project in terms of addressing convergence of basic incomes, rates of employment, and competitiveness, and promoting human capital to provide advantages for the EEC as a whole (European Commission 1996). The Delors II Package, created in the context of the Maastricht Treaty, created two more instruments, the European Investment Fund and the Cohesion Fund, for the benefit of the four poorest countries in the union at the time (Spain, Greece, Portugal, and Ireland). The use of cohesion funds has led to an expansion of objectives for cohesion policy to different target areas or issues so that most member states are eligible for some aid, raising concerns about the optimal allocation and targeting of funds. Thus, the expansion to include Austria, Sweden, and Finland led to the inclusion of adjustment funds for sparsely populated areas, something that allowed for funds to be directed to the Nordic states and hence broadened the base of recipients.

The subsequent inclusion of countries from CEE into the EU necessitated the reallocation of funds to facilitate this enlargement. Though funding was available pre-accession through the PHARE and SAPARD programs, cohesion policy has been declining in real terms as states have been reluctant to raise the overall amount of funds for structural programs.[10] However, in all of the new member states, a fully fledged regional policy has evolved, together with the creation of new regional administrative structures. Yet there remain reservations about the overall size and beneficiaries of cohesion policy in an enlarged EU. For some states, a sharp reduction in funding has impacted their programs: over the last decade, Spain has seen a 42% reduction in cohesion policy allocation and Britain one of 46%, which has led to governments seeking more public-private partnerships so as to make better use of more limited resources (Morata and Popartan 2008; Chapman 2008). For some states this has meant that the EU shapes the selection of projects due to their dependency on EU funding, whereas in other cases, EU funds have been more closely aligned with national economic development policies.

Similarly, social policy initiatives were also rudimentary in the early years of European integration. While the European Social Fund (ESF) was initially created to increase worker geographic and occupational mobility, and then vocational training, it was viewed as a marginal tool relative to market integration. Much of what the EU has promoted at the regional level is social regulation rather than social citizenship, as social entitlements have remained national (Majone 2003). Though there is recognition that regional policies can create dividends in terms of economies of scale, stabilizing financial systems, and security of supply, creating value through cooperation in areas beyond trade depends on a variety of factors including existing patterns of welfare systems and financing. The EU illustrates that providing RPGs requires a high degree of trust and equitable solutions, as well as substantial targeted resource commitment to overcome collective action problems. Yet surveys show that most citizens perceive industrial policy as a national issue and are unaware of the levels of European contributions; despite the largest amounts of European funding directed toward some of the poorest regions in Britain, the British population voted to leave the EU in large numbers in the 2016 referendum. Funds for science, agriculture, and education will initially be matched through domestic budgets, but questions have been raised about the ability to sustain adequate levels of domestic investment.[11]

Financing public goods in a climate of budgetary austerity

What types of RPGs are feasible given the increased budgetary constraints and imposition of austerity measures in EU member states? Most analysts focus on the limited size of the EU budget to illustrate that it is roughly 1% of GDP, and hence does not have the same macroeconomic impact as in federal states such as Germany and the United States. Only in monetary affairs does the EU have significant power, setting monetary policy through the European Central Bank. Thus the EU cannot provide the same type of public goods as states due to its limited public finances and administrative capacity. At roughly €142 billion in 2014, the EU budget is significantly larger than the national budget of 17 of its 28 member states, and accounts for an estimated 60% of total public capital expenditure in Portugal, 48% in Greece, and 24% in Spain (Robinson 2009). The European Structural and Investment Funds have become the main source of public investment in some states that have undergone extensive budget cuts as public debt levels have exceeded 100% of GDP. In the EU as a whole, investment declined by 20% in real terms between 2008–2013 as public investment rates dropped by 60% at the national and regional level in Spain, Ireland, and Greece (Dijkstra 2014). However, expenditures are larger than the actual EU budget due to the leverage that investment policies can provide through a mixture of long maturities, low interest rates, and sovereign guarantees to attract additional funding and investors. In the case of cohesion policy, the EU operates on principles of partnership and additionality, wherein EU funds are administered through partnerships in the region, thus leveraging local resources, and the funds must be additional to those of member states and cannot be substitutes for national funds (Hooghe 1998).

Budget debates have always been contentious within the EU as contributions are partly based on gross national income (GNI), with the question of budgetary imbalances leading to requests for rebates. This has been amplified in the current economic crisis, given that the budget is viewed as a tool of solidarity for net beneficiaries that are opposed to additional conditions being imposed on budgetary transfers, and a tool of growth by net contributors, which want more targeted spending cuts, given domestic austerity measures. However, redistribution of EU GNI across member states is not an explicit target of the EU budget as expenditures are based on specific strategic priorities and eligibility criteria, which have changed over time (see Table 12.1) (Allen 2008). Nor are all EU policies financed from the EU budget: some policies are financed by member states through their national budgets, making performance evaluation extremely complex. Yet an EU-wide budget financed almost entirely by member state contributions reduces the fiscal autonomy of the EU and creates a situation where the increasing emphasis on "just return" has increased budgetary conflict, making it difficult to review spending priorities as the budget is still heavily focused on agriculture and cohesion policies.[12]

However, the fiscal powers of the EU can be enhanced by the matched funding principle so that additional funding is provided by member states or private lenders, which increases the leverage generated by grants and loans from the EIB. The recent growth in EIB loans has coincided with a period in which the EU budget has widely been perceived to be under pressure, and is substantially greater than funds provided for EU regional policy (Robinson 2009). Since it offers long-term loans at low interest rates, the EIB is actually the dominant source of finance in many infrastructure projects, since it provides loans totaling some €40 billion per annum and facilitating around €200 billion per annum in expenditure.[13]

Given continued low levels of investment, the EU launched its Investment Plan in 2014 in response to the economic crisis. However, member states have been reluctant to fund such a large public goods project.[14] As states have undergone successive rounds of domestic public spending cuts, with austerity measures falling on the heavily indebted states in southern Europe, the plan is meant to kick-start growth. The goal is to use public guarantees to stimulate and attract private investment to provide RPGs, even though record low interest rates could provide specific opportunities to enhance investment in national public goods in less fiscally restrained countries.[15] The plan focuses on improving the single market by removing barriers to investment, providing access to capital for SMEs, and supporting long-term strategic infrastructure projects. There are concerns about whether RPGs are the optimal solution for promoting European recovery. In fact, the EU public funds that are being touted for this new initiative are not new funds, but rather have been shifted from other parts of the EU budget. The issue of geographic allocation of investment projects is also at issue, as investors will likely gravitate to more stable economies rather than crisis-ridden economies, despite their pressing need for additional economic stimulus.[16]

Evaluation and impact of regional public goods

There has been increased attention given to the role of performance evaluation and impact assessment within international organizations, driven in part by the public sector managerial reform movement, which has promoted indicators and measures to improve the efficiency and effectiveness of program objectives. Much of this literature for the EU has focused on implementation and compliance, in which the institutionalized system of cooperation in the EU is based on two different approaches: the growth of legalism, with attention to the effective transposition, implementation, and enforcement of laws, and the complementary development of nonlegally binding codes of conduct, recommendations, and peer review as relative "soft law" means to foster compliance with legal, administrative, and economic objectives within the EU (see Table 12.2). Some RPGs are subject to hard sanctions, whereby the entry criteria for monetary union

Table 12.2 Mechanisms and Instruments for European Public Goods Provision

Trade and Market Integration	*Regional and Social Policy Cohesion*
Instruments: treaty articles, Art. 4 TFEU, articles pertaining to free movement of labor, goods, services, capital, and competition Common External Tariff	Instruments: loans, quota system, financial instruments, co-financing, public-private partnerships
Objectives: Four Freedoms (goods, capital, services, labor, rights of establishment); market access, reduce protectionism and trade barriers	Objectives: regional economic development; Social cohesion in Treaty of Rome preamble; Lisbon Treaty and Europe 2020; territorial cohesion; social cohesion based on income disparities and need for social inclusion; and economic development through high GDP growth, employment, and competitiveness
Uniformity of coverage (except euro and Eurozone monetary policy)	Selective coverage based on eligibility criteria; specific objectives for funding; 75% of average GDP
Mechanisms: administrative and regulatory agencies, delegated acts, directives and regulations, mutual recognition, harmonization (regulatory approximation), delegation to private sector	Mechanisms: partnership, additionality, concentration and programming, subsidiarity
Compliance: litigation, alternative dispute resolution mechanisms, scoreboards, transposition rates (hard and soft law mechanisms)	Compliance: suspension of cohesion funds for excessive deficit under cohesion fund regulation, cooperation and verification mechanism (CVM) for Bulgaria and Romania
Prevent market distortions: use of trade remedies to protect single market: competition rules, notably state aids within single market and anti-dumping, bilateral safeguard measures, countervailing duties on third countries	Prevent market distortions: competition policy and regional aid review of scope of public authorities to invest in infrastructure without infringing the state aid rule
Evaluation and Performance: single market scoreboard, regulatory impact assessment, simplification of single market measures	Evaluation and Performance: economic convergence measured by per capita income, GDP, long-term growth and investment dynamics
Sequencing: capital expected to follow other freedoms; in reality, goods and capital more liberalized, services lagged, and labor mobility constrained by domestic political considerations	Sequencing: European social fund ESF and EAAGF in Treaty of Rome; post-enlargement funds ERDF, IMP; structural funds and cohesion; PHARE and SAPARD for CEE enlargement; consolidation of specific programs (e.g. RECHAR); each enlargement led to new measures, and objectives have both broadened and narrowed in response to economic, political, and technological pressures
Continual expansion of reach of single market over time to include new issue areas and policy domains, due to economic spillovers, and technological developments	Continual expansion of objectives and initiatives over time; resources support the result of political necessity to support integration and economic rationality

provides strengthened mechanisms against fiscal profligacy among member states that wish to adopt the euro, but limited sanctions within the Eurozone by creating the (now acknowledged and recognized) risk that national governments can accumulate excessive deficits and unsustainable levels of debt (Hodson and Maher 2004). Other public goods with more limited cooperation mechanisms include the open method of coordination and the Stability and Growth Pact, which provide qualitative indicators and benchmarks about employment practices, including social exclusion and recommendations about fiscal deficit, which results in a formal warning, noninterest bearing deposits, and subsequently nonrefundable fines subject to a somewhat flexible interpretation (Hodson and Maher 2004).

There is little assessment of the impact of such governance mechanisms, particularly from the perspective of RPGs. More specifically, the institutionalized forms of cooperation can vary in terms of obligation, delegation, and precision, which can provide flexibility in a more heterogeneous polity, but does raise concerns about credibility of commitments. Faced with a need to provide governance across multiple areas, the new styles of decision making are heavily dependent on nonhierarchical and mutually interdependent relationships, along with problem-solving styles aimed at building consensus through target setting. The most salient challenge is whether public goods can be sufficiently provided when different forms of soft law are employed, as the EU has shifted toward these new modes of governance with increasing frequency.

With regard to the two cases considered in this chapter, the EU has opted for different measures to assess the functioning of the single market (see Table 12.3). The four freedoms are subject to formal treaty rules, and transgressions due to continued protectionist trade barriers are subject to litigation before the Court of Justice of the EU (CJEU). This has led the CJEU to develop jurisprudence to address both quantitative restrictions and quotas, initially, and then nontariff barriers to the free movement of goods in order to promote intra-EU trade. While this has generated large volumes of case law addressing a variety of trade obstacles, national administrations often maintain specific domestic regulations—ostensibly for health, safety, and environmental reasons—intentionally or inadvertently favoring domestic

Table 12.3 Modes of Governance: How Does Europe Provide Public Goods?

Harmonization
Mutual recognition (regulatory equivalence)
Codes of conduct and voluntary accords
Benchmarking, best practice, and policy learning
Non-binding targets
Publication, naming, shaming, and scorecards
Self-regulation, co-regulation, and delegated governance
Litigation
Financial sanctions and penalties
Criminal investigations and proceedings

producers (Vogel 1997). Such policies that affect competition, access, and costs of market entry have led the EU to promote international regulatory coordination. This is backed by enforcement and compliance mechanisms to ensure the functioning of the single market. Through infringement proceedings, the European Commission (EC) has the right to bring legal action against member states for noncompliance if the issue is not resolved through voluntary member state compliance. The case is then referred to the CJEU, which is able to impose financial sanctions if a state continues to resist the judicial ruling.[17]

Despite legal enforcement mechanisms, the single market faces problems in terms of the transposition and implementation of EU laws at the domestic level, such that the "law on the ground turns out to be very different than the law on the books" (Monti 2010, p.96). The lack of legal coherence can undermine the credibility of the single market, as the correct application of European laws is critical for avoiding unnecessary delays or arbitrary discretion in accessing markets (Pelkmans and De Brito 2012). To address these problems, the EU has also introduced new tools to facilitate the informal resolution of problems encountered in the single market (Egan and Guimaries 2013). The EU has sought to address the collective action problem in public goods through diverse pragmatic solutions, including techniques such as target setting and publicizing performance through the creation of a Single Market Scoreboard.[18] Focusing on monitoring performance of the single market, the emphasis on naming and shaming comes with specific targets for improvement in terms of the implementation and transposition of EU laws across member states. Other evidence-based tools, such as the Single Market Review and Market Monitoring Tool, were applied to specific sectors to assess the performance of different markets and enhance market surveillance measures through efforts to eliminate performance gaps. The outcomes are published and ranked to provide for mutual learning about best practices, but also as a reputational tool to improve poor performance (Heritier 2001).

A second mechanism is through informal consultation, in which business complaints about trade barriers are addressed through exchanges of information, dialogue, and the discussion of potential resolutions without recourse to litigation through the soft law mechanism SOLVIT (Egan and Guimaries 2014). Companies can seek pragmatic solutions to market access problems, and the EC may also refer issues to this network-based approach if there is a good chance that the barriers can be removed without legal action (Egan and Guimaries 2014). The use of this mechanism has increased significantly over the past decade, suggesting that this facilitated coordination may provide an alternative resolution to trade barriers in the single market.[19] Such measures are part of a larger set of instruments and mechanisms that are in place to reinforce informal governance approaches, which also includes voluntary accords to reach agreement on collective goals through co-regulation and self-regulation (Heritier 2001; Egan 2001). This can involve self-regulation, whereby firms conduct their own testing and certification for product safety or accredit their production practices as meeting EU rules and standards. Delegated regulation has also emerged, in which the rules are defined by public authorities but the means to meet those standards are designed by the private sector through standardization (Büthe and Mattli 2011). The private bodies that undertake the work are viewed as collectively responsible for implementation, and should policy fail to produce collective outcomes, public authorities may take on the regulatory function. While voluntary coordination among the private sector delegates the costs of decision making and can provide the necessary technical expertise to create commonly agreed upon standards, compliance may be high due to the incentives created by participation in the process. Though firms may participate to reduce transaction costs, the inclusion of consumers and nongovernmental organizations also increases the value to stakeholders. This approach has been adopted in areas such as toy safety, energy efficiency programs, vehicle emissions, and cross border payment and transactions. If a specific member state is assertive in promoting its regulatory standards—for instance through regulatory dialogues and private rulemaking—and succeeds in persuading others to adopt them, it lends a competitive edge to domestic industry. This also means that if the EU is able to achieve common standards in various sectors, it can try to upload those standards to the international level. Many argue that firms exporting goods or services may need to change their own practices to secure market access, given the collective influence and scope of common EU regulations and standards (Young 2013).

The EU is thus influencing behavior beyond its borders—resulting in what is known as "trading up"—and this has been documented in a range of areas, from cosmetics to chemicals, where states have adjusted their own domestic regulations to meet EU regulations. Thus Australia, Canada, China, Japan, Russia, and South Korea have adjusted their domestic chemical regulations to meet the EU's regulation that restricts the use of certain substances and requires companies to find alternatives. Similarly, the EU's restriction on the release of hazardous substances into the environment has been adopted in different versions by China, Japan, and Korea (Bradford 2010; Young 2015). The effort to induce states to implement and enforce environmental and labor agreements as a condition of enhanced access to its market under its GSP+ scheme also illustrates the promotion of RPGs beyond its own regulatory borders (Menuier and Nicolaidis 2006). With external governance, there are also competitiveness concerns in areas of state aids, state-owned industries, and public subsidies since the strict promotion of competition rules internally can put EU firms at a competitive disadvantage vis-à-vis third countries such as India and China.[20] As the EU has divested its assets through privatization, seeking to cash in on buoyant markets for three decades, the changing relationship between state and market in the current economic environment has shifted the debate toward public administrative reforms to address budgetary deficits with crisis-hit economies of southern Europe selling state-owned public goods. In this environment, public goods may be used to mitigate the effects of market pressures, albeit without addressing the underlying structural problems in EU economies.

As an international institution, the EU also resorts to conditionality policies by using selective incentives and institutional capacity to shape domestic policies. These include the empowerment of domestic institutions as well as the imposition of certain regulatory rules and practices, ranging from competition policy to environmental standards, as the gravitational pull of EU membership induced compliance with the *acquis*. Despite the breadth of the EU agenda on institutional and policy change in CEE, there were few tools to measure effective implementing capacity. Though compliance with EU laws was initially viewed as successful, there were derogations and constraints placed on new members, including restrictions on labor mobility and a formal requirement to join the euro, leading to functional, spatial, and temporal variation rather than the uniform, harmonized, inclusive model of integration. This raises questions as to what is "regional" in terms of public goods, and whether the benefits that arise from scale in the provision of public goods are undermined when there are voluntary opt-outs, exclusions, and selective membership in specific policy domains. The resulting provisions of RPGs have come with more derogations and selective coverage, something that legal scholars, with their emphasis on the uniform application of laws, have viewed with concern (De Witte, Hanf, and Vos 2001). Yet in spite of this, the EU has found that states have reneged on their commitments upon accession, and so it has increasingly sought to lock in commitments and create post-accession monitoring and verification policies. The effect of this has been a marked slowing down of subsequent accession negotiations (Grabbe 2014). While post-accession financial instruments have continued to be an important resource in providing structural support, there is rising concern that this does not address the underlying problems of effective governance, bearing in mind the continued problems in terms of rule of law, corruption, and democratic practices in existing member states (Mungiu-Pippidi 2014).

Such leverage extends beyond European borders as the EU is often cited as uploading its social standards to international organizations such as the International Labour Organization, or inducing states to ratify and implement multilateral environmental agreements or labor standards as a condition for granting market access and trade preferences (Damro 2012). Being able to aggregate preferences and promote collective outcomes to generate RPGs has thus spilled over beyond EU markets, as the single market project has contributed to the development of the EU's regulatory capacity beyond borders. European regional integration efforts that cover an increasing range of goods and services provide governments with a chance to experiment with various rule-making and market-opening initiatives that allow us to learn from different comparative lessons and rule-making dynamics (Mattoo and Sauvé 2004).

This is also true in terms of social and cohesion policy, where the EU notion of convergence refers to the effort to close the wealth gap between the richest and poorest regions in the EU, measured in terms of per capita GDP relative to the EU average (European Commission, Directorate-General for Regional and Urban Policy 2007). In numerical terms, substantial convergence between individual new member state economies and the old member state averages have emerged over the previous ten years (Landesmann 2013; Epstein 2014). Since transition, CEE countries have been growing dynamically, with an average rate of growth for CEE-6[21] of around 3.8%, compared to the EU15[22] average growth rate of around 2.3%. The level of convergence is notable in Hungary and Poland, where GDP levels were close to 50% of EU15 in the 1990s; 20 years later, and following the accession of these countries to the EU, these levels have reached 75% of EU27[23] (Neissen 2013). Although cohesion has reduced regional disparities and reinforced regional convergence of GDP, there are concerns that this is due to fiscal transfers rather than increases in actual growth rates.[24]

While territorial cohesion is the most obvious example of distributive public goods, the figures mask the absorption capacity (to use EU jargon) of states in terms of their ability to meet the rules and criteria to utilize EU-mandated funds. In the cases of Bulgaria and Romania, they received about one-third of the allocation for the 2007–2013 budgetary period. Part of the problem has been the ability of new member states to provide co-financing for EU-funded projects (Baun and Marek 2008). While temporary derogations and concessions have been provided, there have been concerns about local and regional institutional capacity to manage the funds in question, despite the state receiving substantial funds in the pre-accession process to implement structural spending (Allen 2008; Keating and Hughes 2003). While such structural funds for economic cohesion have been amended to concentrate funds for specific issues and criteria, certain regions that have received aid in the past are no longer eligible. The shift from old to new member states has led to transitional periods and the continued coverage of the four "poor states" (Spain, Greece, Portugal, and Ireland), even though they had converged sufficiently to meet the criteria for monetary union. However, efforts to evaluate the impact of cohesion funds have not produced definitive results. While for symbolic reasons all member states continue to receive some financial aid, the absolute values remain small in terms of EU GDP. The effort to target lagging regions has generated mixed results, with some indications that the funds have diminishing returns in richer member states, while others indicate that they have performed well in Spain and Ireland in generating considerable investment and promoting growth (McMaster 2008). Overall, analysis of the impact of structural funds on regional GDP growth and convergence has been mixed (Becker, Egger, and von Ehrlich 2010; Beugelsdijk and Eijffinger 2005).

Yet evaluation must deal with both the intended and unintended impacts of the provision of RPGs. In terms of market integration, the removal of trade barriers has been uneven, and restrictions continue in both the services and labor markets. While the financial crisis has demonstrated that EU efforts with regard to financial market integration in terms of insolvency and risk management were weak, it has prompted more financial services regulation. The single market was built on a model of reduced transactions costs and economies of scale. It focused on creating an internal market without frontiers that subsequently enhanced competition and created more consumer choice in many areas. However, liberalization is now more contentious and the current economic crisis has led to a surge in economic nationalism that threatens the very cornerstone of the EU project (Monti 2010). It is widely acknowledged that remaining bottlenecks hamper innovation and growth in the single market, so efforts continue to coordinate rules in the digital economy, patents, and intellectual property rights (Monti 2010). The production of public goods is meant to address coordination failures where market fragmentation reduces barriers to innovation and investment and asymmetric information undermines consumer protection, while access and connectivity are meant to address digital inequalities.[25] Public investment in welfare-enhancing goods and services is meant to have a reinforcing effect on the single market. Equally important, this "modernization" of the single market stresses the need to balance social and economic rights to restore the legitimacy of market integration by focusing on social aspects of integration. This is important given the increased regulatory heterogeneity of member states and the perception that liberalization is a threat rather than an opportunity in a changing global economy.

The notion of the single market as a catalyst for growth in which differences are minimized has pitted social and market objectives against each other, with significant implications for RPGs. Scharpf (2002) highlighted this constitutional asymmetry by noting that the decoupling of social protection and economic integration was a product of national protection of their sovereign welfare states. He concludes, "at the national level, economic policy and social protection policy had and still have the same constitutional status . . . [but] once the European Court of Justice (CJEU) had established the doctrines of 'direct effect' and 'supremacy,' any rules of primary and secondary European law, as interpreted by the EC and the Court, would take precedence over all rules and practices based on national law, whether earlier or later, statutory or constitutional" (Scharpf 2002). While employment and social welfare policies at the national level had to be designed in the shadow of "constitutionalized" European law, the problem came with efforts to generate service liberalization in which labor costs are the principal determining factor in price differentials, as services are often temporary and usually labor intensive (Moses 2011). The subsequent legal judgments known as Viking[26] and Laval subjected the right to strike under national law to certain potential limitations deriving from EU law. This seemed a classic instance in labor law of "social dumping," in which an employer relocated certain operations to another country with lower wage rates (Estonia) in order to escape higher-cost labor rights in the country of origin (Finland). The CJEU found it could justify a restriction on the right to strike to ensure freedom of establishment, thus prioritizing market liberalization over social rights. The CJEU's Viking judgment brought to the fore the difficult issue of convergence—which is a crucial goal for the EU in admitting new member states from CEE, of which Estonia was a major beneficiary of EC cohesion funding. While regulatory convergence made Estonia's accession possible, the forces of convergence always operate under threat of backlash by social groups whose interests are threatened by market integration. In this case, Finnish workers found themselves at a competitive disadvantage as the Viking shipping line reflagged to use cheaper Estonian labor. Cohesion funds—the goal of which was to improve the legal and administrative infrastructure and attract FDI—enabled firms to take advantage of Estonia's lower labor costs. Distributional consequences of this type were unavoidable, of course, given the very different factor endowments—labor costs—between Finland and Estonia, and between old and new EU member states in general. The struggle over the creation of an integrated labor market in the EU brought to the fore the unintended consequences of providing different RPGs, as promoting economic development is expected to result in the increased convergence of prices and real wages, which can occur through the removal of legal barriers to free movement and the reduction of transportation and communication costs. In this case, the pressure for convergence took place between markets and polities with very different factor endowments, leading to a serious backlash over the distributional consequences of convergence (Lindseth 2016; O'Rourke and Williamson 1999).

Conclusions

Despite the growing chorus of disenchantment in Europe, as populist parties have surged in response to concerns related to inequality, productivity, and migration, there remains a role for regional organizations to act as catalysts for collective action by providing RPGs. In Europe, with extensive experience in collective governance, RPGs aim to create cross-border trade, macroeconomic stabilization, communications and transportation networks, as well as coordination on health, safety, and environmental issues through standards, testing, and certification practices to ensure quality, reliability, and safety, and social and economic cohesion to reduce cross-regional economic disparities. Many of these initiatives are original treaty aims and hence have been long-standing goals, whereas others have been added incrementally in response to the competitive pressures of integration, including environmental measures and digital access initiatives, or in response to perceived deficits in collective action as in the case of security and foreign policy coordination. Despite such ambitions, which have ranged from peaceful reconciliation to industrial development, competitiveness and economic growth, Europe has faced increased scrutiny about its ability to deliver public goods. European integration cannot be a technocratic exercise about solving problems; those solutions have to be politically accepted.

First, the provision of public goods is not uncontested. Left and right populist challenges to macroeconomic stabilization, market liberalization, or regulatory convergence have generated pushback from member states. This has included withdrawal from the European Union (Great Britain), resistance to services liberalization (France and Germany), maintenance of border restrictions (Hungary), and undermining of the rule of law and constitutional independence (Poland). While the impulse for collective action is economic rationality, the acceptance of such integration has broader political implications as RPG provisions are often contested by different states, regions, industries, and civil society interests.

Second, the promotion of RPGs may also have contradictory or unintended effects. The gap between the administrative effort to promote economic and social cohesion and constitutional perspectives on rights and market freedoms has led to difficulties in the EU integration process (Lindseth 2016). The constitutional asymmetry between national welfare and industrial rights and market rights at the EU level has led to the situation in which promoting cohesion to enhance the laws, regulations, and administrative capacity of new member states has led to a backlash in older member states whose interests are adversely impacted by different factor endowments—in this case labor costs—and the threat of social dumping. This also explains the free movement restrictions imposed by specific member states at the behest of labor organizations that are anxious about the downward pressures on real wages in their own domestic economies.[27] The irony, of course, was that cohesion funding—particularly pre-accession funding—has now paved the way for market freedoms to operate such that states with cheaper labor costs can exercise freedom of establishment under EU law. These new states have leveraged the cohesion funds to strengthen their administrative capacity, transportation networks, and investment culture to attract FDI to take advantage of the differences in labor unit costs that have not yet "converged" due to different factor endowments. This situation has led to tensions between functional pressures for integration and maintenance of specific social rights.

Third, strategic priorities are impacted by budgetary funds. The dependency on member state contributions to finance the European budget has resulted in exemptions, rebates, and specific ad hoc budgetary allocations that reduce the overall efficiency and transparency of resource allocation. As such, the budgetary issue is critical in assessing and evaluating institutional performance as the recent bailouts and stimulus programs have increased public debt, which affects the stability of the European budget, given the significant share of the GNI resource in the EU financing system. But even with a designated budget allocation, the performance of the public sector may impact states' ability to use the designated funds effectively as the backsliding of democracy, weak administrative capacity, and corruption concerns have resulted in threats of suspension of funding in several European states. There are also lingering problems of implementation and compliance so that designated rules, both formal and informal, are designed to ensure credible commitments to specified targets and goals.

Fourth, the provision of RPGs can have spillover effects, creating externalities that should be taken into consideration. Although the EU provides internal public goods to its members, it also provides external public goods through technical assistance, foreign aid, and preferential access to markets for nonmembers. Such public goods can impose costs in the form of conditionality requirements, asymmetrical leveraging, and restructuring of domestic rules and institutions that may not generate immediate benefits. Evaluations of RPGs should also look at their impact beyond territorial borders, since EU trade, aid, and governance practices cover many issue areas that generate regulatory cooperation, transnational feedback, and reactive sequencing in which applicant states, trade partners, and neighboring states change rules to conform to the *acquis* and upgrade their institutional architecture and regulatory capacity domestically to align with EU standards. The resulting regional architecture in Europe is one in which "insiders" are recipients of diverse public goods, but the impact of internal coordination may spill over to encompass or exclude "outsiders" as well. However, "outsiders" may just as easily find that the suspension of aid or accession negotiations can also restrict the opportunities for access, as providers of RPGs can rescind the supply of public goods (hence excludable in ways not traditionally envisaged in the public goods literature). While Europe has a well-developed infrastructure to coordinate the provision of public goods, the question is not simply the economic rationale for such coordination, but also the political consequences where constraints on sovereignty and autonomy arise from such institutionalized cooperation. The large contractions in the European economy that have emerged as a result of the Eurozone crisis have generated less appetite for deepening integration, negative growth in peripheral countries along with strong recovery in others, and have raised questions about the ability of Europe to provide a comprehensive solution to its problems. While European public goods can shape regulatory, allocative and redistributive outcomes in ways that differ from other regional efforts, it can also weaken national democratic institutions and can collapse trust in European institutions.

Appendix 1: Terms, acronyms, and abbreviations

Acquis: *Acquis communitaire*, the body of EU laws that have to be implemented by member states.

CVM: Cooperation and Verification Mechanism, regarding corruption, organized crime, and judicial reform as a safeguard measure against Bulgaria and Romania to ensure compliance with European norms.

EIB: European Investment Bank, established in 1957 and referenced in protocol in the Treaty of Rome.

ERDF: European Regional Development Fund, established in 1975 to focus on regional economic disparities and provide support for local and regional investment.

ESF: European Social Fund, established in the Treaty of Rome to deal with social dislocation and living standards and used for employee adaptability, employment access, and social inclusion.

ESM: European Stability Mechanism, to provide stability and bailout for Eurozone members under stress.

GSP+:   Generalized System of Preferences Plus, a preferential tariff system for developing countries.

IMP: Integrated Mediterranean Programmes, created to help the southern regions of the union through structural funds and EIB loans that were replaced by cohesion funds.

PHARE: One of the main pre-accession assistance instruments to assist applicant countries preparing to join the EU, originally for Hungary and Poland, then expanded to other countries, before being replaced by other instruments.

RECHAR: EU funding initiative to provide grants for the reconversion or development of depressed mining areas.

SAPARD: Special Accession Programme for Agriculture and Rural Development, to help implement the *acquis* in CEE prior to accession.

SGEI: Services of a general economic interest, economic activities that public authorities identify as being of particular importance to citizens and hence would be undersupplied if not provided by government (e.g. social services, postal services).

SOLVIT: An informal resolution mechanism created to deal with trade barriers through negotiation rather than litigation established in 2002.

TEN: Trans-European Networks, an infrastructure program to connect national transportation networks and promote transportation intermodality across Europe.

Notes

1 Much of the analysis of the EU in terms of global public goods focuses on its external promotion of goals and objectives, or fiscal assistance based on the notion of "normative power Europe" that focuses on the export of rules, values, and norms in terms of democracy, human rights, and good governance (Manners 2002). This chapter focuses on the provision of regional public goods internally within the EU to illustrate that RPGs can also be excludable to those that are not members of the "European club."

2 For example, the European Fund for Strategic Investment will have €21 billion of public funds: €8 billion from the EU budget, with a 50% guarantee, and another €5 billion from the European Investment Bank.

3 There is a large literature on global public goods in economics, but international lawyers have begun to focus on issues of governance and legitimacy in the production and distribution of public goods, conflicts between public goods, and how the pursuit of different public goods can be at cross-purposes.

4 The latest proposals involve Trans-European Networks (TEN). It should be noted that although a common transport policy was envisaged in Treaty of Rome, the European Parliament sued for inaction in this area, and there have been numerous initiatives to promote cross-border transportation links.

5 Economic and cohesion policies such as EU Structural and Investment Funds, the European Agricultural Fund for Rural Development, European Maritime Fisheries Fund, European Cohesion Fund, European Social Fund, and European Regional Development Fund.

6 The term "services of a general economic interest" (SGEI)—as distinct from a revenue-generating monopoly—has been used to differentiate areas that constitute non-excludable public goods from those sectors that can be subject to competition, and hence were initially viewed in terms of non-excludable public goods. However, the ECJ has found that such services can be opened up to competition (Case France Poste, C-559/12 P—*France* v Commission), hence the original article 90 which excluded utilities has now been viewed as incompatible with the competition policy provisions of treaty (Heritier 2001).

7 The creation of common asylum regime, immigration controls, and border management through the Schengen, Dublin, and Frontex initiatives are good illustrations of efforts to induce burden sharing in external border management which does lead to disproportionate and inequitable burdens in the provision of regional collective goods in Europe.

8 Rewe-Zentral AG v Bundesmonopolverwaltung für Branntwein (1979) Case 120/78, known as the Cassis De Dijon case, and other subsequent cases related to mutual recognition in services, such as Manfred Säger v Dennemeyer & Co. Ltd. (1991), which provided for mutual recognition without restriction in the absence of any legitimate justification.

9 www.cvce.eu/content/publication/1999/1/1/c638f726-0389-4fc8-ad0c-98b857251d48/publishable_en.pdf

10 In 2007–2014, EU funding for CEE amounted to €181.53 billion in aid, with Poland and Czech Republic receiving 50% of allocated funds. The majority of allocated grants are for regional development funds.

11 The UK currently receives around £4.5 billion (US$5.8 billion) a year in farming subsidies and structural funds for economic development, and another £1 billion to £1.5 billion in research funding.

12 Notre Europe www.institutdelors.eu/media/europe_for_growth__for_a_radical_change_in_financing_the_eu.pdf?pdf=ok

13 www.eib.org/infocentre/publications/all/financial-report-2014.htm. Priority areas are job growth and creation through innovation, skills, infrastructure, and small and medium enterprises.
14 http://ec.europa.eu/priorities/jobs-growth-investment/plan/index_en.htm
15 www.epc.eu/documents/uploads/pub_5420_growth_for_europe_-_is_the_juncker_plan_the_answer.pdf, 8
16 www.epc.eu/documents/uploads/pub_5420_growth_for_europe_-_is_the_juncker_plan_the_answer.pdf, 6
17 See Andrea Francovich and Danila Bonifaci and others v Italian Republic (1991, Cases C-6/90 and C-9/90).
18 http://ec.europa.eu/internal_market/scoreboard/
19 Our data indicates that between 2002 and 2013, an 84% resolution rate was achieved, although this varied among member states. It should also be noted that this coordination operates in the "shadow of hierarchy," in that the threat of litigation is still available if the issue is not resolved.
20 Comments of the Competition Law Association on the EU Commission's State Aid Action Plan, http://ec.europa.eu/competition/state_aid/reform/comments_saap/37551.pdf
21 Bulgaria, Czech Republic, Hungary, Poland, Romania, and Slovakia.
22 EU15 refers to the 15 EU member states prior to the accession of new countries in 2004. The EU15 comprised Austria, Belgium, Denmark, Finland, France, Germany, Greece, Ireland, Italy, Luxembourg, Netherlands, Portugal, Spain, Sweden, and the United Kingdom.
23 EU27 comprised Austria, Belgium, Bulgaria, Cyprus, Czech Republic, Denmark, Estonia, Finland, France, Germany, Greece, Hungary, Ireland, Italy, Latvia, Lithuania, Luxembourg, Malta, the Netherlands, Poland, Portugal, Romania, Slovak Republic, Slovenia, Spain, Sweden, and the United Kingdom.
24 http://ec.europa.eu/regional_policy/sources/docgener/studies/pdf/single_market/single_market_report.pdf, 9.
25 http://europa.eu/rapid/press-release_IP-15-4919_en.htm
26 International Transport Workers' Federation and Finnish Seamen's Union v Viking Line ABP and OÜ Viking Line Eesti (2007, Case C-438/05, ECR I-10779).
27 Cf. O'Rourke and Williamson 1999.

References

Allen, David. 2008. "Cohesion Policy Pre- and Post-Enlargement." In *EU Cohesion Policy After Enlargement*, edited by Michael J. Baun and Dan Marek. Basingstoke: Palgrave Macmillan.

Barslund, Mikkel, Matthias Busse, and Joscha Schwarzwälder. 2015. "Labour Mobility in Europe: An Untapped Resource?" *CEPS Policy Briefs* 237 (March).

Baun, Michael J., and Dan Marek. 2008. *EU Cohesion Policy After Enlargement*. Basingstoke: Palgrave Macmillan.

Becker, Sascha O., Peter H. Egger, and Maximilian von Ehrlich. 2010. "Too Much of a Good Thing? On the Growth Effects of the EU's Regional Policy." CEPR Discussion Paper No. DP8043.

Behrens, Petra, and Marc Smyrl. 1999. "A Conflict of Rationalities: EU Regional policy and the Single Market." *Journal of European Public Policy* 6, no. 3: 413–435.

Beugelsdijk, Maake, and Sylvester Eijffinger. 2005. "The Effectiveness of Structural Policy in the European Union: An Empirical Analysis for the EU-15 in 1995–2001." *Journal of Common Market Studies* 43, no. 1: 37–51.

Bonoli, Guiliano, and David Natali. 2012. *The Politics of the New Welfare State*. Oxford: Oxford University Press.

Bradford, A. 2010. "The Brussels Effect." *Northwestern University Law Review* 107, no. 1: 1–68.

Büthe, Tim, and Walter Mattli. 2011. *The New Global Rulers: The Privatization of Regulation in the World Economy*. Princeton, NJ: Princeton University Press.

Chapman, Rachel. 2008. "United Kingdom." In *EU Cohesion Policy After Enlargement*, edited by Michael J. Baun and Dan Marek. Basingstoke: Palgrave Macmillan.

Damro, Chad. "Market Power Europe." *Journal of European Public Policy* 19, no. 5: 682–99.

De Witte, Bruno, Dominik Hanf, and Ellen Vos. 2001. *Many Faces of Differentiation in EU Law*. Antwerp, Oxford, and New York: Intersentia.

Dijkstra, Lewis. 2014. *Investment for Jobs and Growth: Promoting Development and Good Governance in EU Regions and Cities: Sixth Report on Economic, Social, and Territorial Cohesion. Report on Economic, Social, and Territorial Cohesion*. Luxembourg: Publications Office.

Egan, Michelle. 2001. *Constructing a European Market*. Oxford: Oxford University Press.

Egan, Michelle, and Helena Guimaries. 2013. "Compliance in the Single Market." *Business and Politics* 14, no. 4: 1–28.

——. 2014. "Tackling Barriers to Trade in the Single Market." Paper presented at XII Euro-Latin Study Network on Integration and Trade (Elsnit), October 17–18, Florence, Italy. http://idbdocs.iadb.org/wsdocs/getdocument.aspx?docnum=39219456

Epstein, Rachel. 2014. "Overcoming 'Economic Backwardness' in the European Union." *Journal of Common Market Studies* 52, no. 1: 17–34.

European Commission. 1996. *First Report on Economic and Social Cohesion, 1996*. Luxembourg: Office for Official Publications of the European Communities.

European Commission, Directorate-General for Regional and Urban Policy. 2007. *Cohesion Policy 2007–13, Commentaries and Official Texts*. Luxemburg: Office for Official Publications of the European Communities.

Ferrara, Maurizio. 2005. *The Boundaries of Welfare. European Integration and the New Spatial Politics of Social Solidarity*. Oxford: Oxford University Press.

Grabbe, Heather. 2014. "Six Lessons of Enlargement Ten Years On: The EU's Transformative Power in Retrospect and Prospect." *Journal of Common Market Studies*, 52: 40–56.

Heritier, Adrienne. 2001. "New Modes of Governance in Europe: Policy-Making without Legislating?" MPI Collective Goods Preprint No. 2001/14.

Hodson, Dermott, and Imelda Maher. 2004. "Soft Law and Sanctions: Economic Policy Co-ordination and Reform of the Stability and Growth Pact." *Journal of European Public Policy* 11, no. 4.

Hooghe, Liesbet. 1996. *Cohesion Policy and European Integration*. Oxford: Oxford University Press.

——. 1998. "EU Cohesion Policy and Competing Models of European Capitalism." *Journal of Common Market Studies* 36: 457–477.

Keating, Michael, and James Hughes, eds. 2003. *The Regional Challenge in Central and Eastern Europe: Territorial Restructuring and European Integration Regionalism and Federalism*. Belgium: Peter Lang.

Landesmann, Michael. 2013. "The New North-South Divide in Europe: Can the European Convergence Model Be Resuscitated?" *wiiw Monthly Report* 1 (January): 3–13.

Lewenhak, Sheila. 2012. *The Role of the European Investment Bank*. Abingdon and New York: Routledge.

Lindseth, Peter. 2016. "Viking's 'Semantic Gaps': The Political Economy of EU Enlargement and the Challenge of Convergence." In *EU Law Stories*, edited by F. Nicola and B. Davies. Cambridge: Cambridge University Press.

McMaster, Irene. 2008. "Ireland." In *EU Cohesion Policy after Enlargement*, edited by Michael J. Baun and Dan Marek. Basingstoke: Palgrave Macmillan.

Majone, Giandomenico. 2003. "The European Community Between Social Policy and Social Regulation." *Journal of Common Market Studies* 31: 153–170.

———. 2005. *Dilemmas of European Integration: The Ambiguities and Pitfalls of Integration by Stealth*. Oxford: Oxford University Press.

Manners, Ian. 2002. "Normative Power Europe: A Contradiction in Terms?" *Journal of Common Market Studies* 40, no. 2: 235–258.

Mattoo, Aaditya, and Pierre Sauvé, eds. 2004. *Domestic Regulation and Service Trade Liberalization*. Washington, DC: The World Bank and Oxford University Press.

Menuier, Sophie, and Kalypso Nicolaidis. 2006. "The EU as a Conflicted Trade Power." *Journal of European Public Policy* 13, no. 6: 906–925.

Monti, Mario. 2010. *A New Strategy for the Single Market: At the Service of Europe's Economy and Society*. Brussels: European Commission.

Morata, Francesco, and Lucia Alexandra Popartan. 2008. "Spain." In *EU Cohesion Policy After Enlargement*, edited by Michael J. Baun and Dan Marek. Basingstoke: Palgrave Macmillan.

Moses, Jonathan. 2011. "Is Constitutional Symmetry Enough? Social Models and Market Integration in the US and Europe." *Journal of Common Market Studies* 49: 823–843.

Mungiu-Pippidi, Alina. 2014. "The Transformative Power of Europe Revisited." *Journal of Democracy* 25, no. 1: 20–32.

Neissen, Brigit. 2013. "Erste Group Research CEE Special Report: Fixed Income." February 20.

O'Rourke, Kevin, and Jeffrey G. Williamson. 1999. *Globalization and History*. Boston: MIT Press.

Pastor, Robert. 2001. *Toward a North American Community: Lessons from the Old World for the New*. Washington, DC: Institute for International Economics.

Pelkmans, Jacques, and Annabele De Brito. 2012. *Enforcement in the Single Market*. Brussels: CEPS.

Polanyi, Karl. 1944. *The Great Transformation*. Basic Books: New York.

Robinson, Nick. 2009. "The European Investment Bank: The EU's Neglected Institution." *Journal of Common Market Studies* 47: 651–673.

Rosas, Allan. 2014. "Exclusive, Shared, and National Competence in the Context of EU External Institutions: Do Such Distinctions Matter?" In *The European Union in the World: Essays in Honor of Marc Maresceau*, edited by Inge Govaere, Erwan Lannon, Peter Van Elsuwege, Stanislas Adam, and Marc Maresceau. Leiden: Ninjhoff, pp. 17–44.

Ruggie, John G. 1982. "International Regimes, Transactions, and Change: Embedded Liberalism in the Postwar Economic Order." *International Organization* 36, no. 2: 375–415.

Scharpf, Fritz. 1998. "The Joint Decision Trap: Lessons from German Federalism and European Integration." *Public Administration* 66: 239–78.

———. 2002. "The European Social Model." *Journal of Common Market Studies* 40: 645–670.

Schmidt, Susanne K. 2009. "When Efficiency Results in Redistribution: The Conflict over the Single Services Market." *Journal of European Public Policy* 32, no. 4.

——. 2012. "Who Cares about Nationality? The Path-Dependent Case Law of the ECJ from Goods to Citizens." *Journal of European Public Policy* 19, no. 1: 8–24.

Thielemann, Eiko. R, and Carolyn Armstrong. 2013. "Understanding European Asylum Cooperation under the Schengen/Dublin System: A Public Goods Framework." *European Security* 22, no. 2: 148–164.

Vogel, David. 1997. *Trading Up*. Cambridge, MA: Harvard University Press.

Young, Alasdair. 2013. "Regulators Beyond Borders: The External Impact of the EU's Rule." Paper presented at the 13th Biennial European Union Studies Association Conference, Baltimore, May 9–11, 2013.

——. 2015. "Liberalizing Trade, Not Exporting Rules: The Limits to Regulatory Coordination in the EU's 'New Generation' Preferential Trade." *Journal of European Public Policy* 22/9: 1253–1275.

13 Regional public goods in North America

Tom Long and Manuel Suárez-Mier

Introduction

The North American Leaders Summit, held on June 29 2016 in Ottawa, brought together three telegenic heads of state: recently elected Prime Minister Justin Trudeau of Canada, President Enrique Peña Nieto of Mexico, and President Barack Obama of the United States of America (USA). The "three amigos" offered a positive picture of integration and cooperation on issues ranging from energy and the environment to trade and the Trans-Pacific Partnership. The pleasant photo op belied a complicated reality for North America, however. Cooperation had stagnated for years as Trudeau's predecessor declined to schedule a summit in retaliation for Obama's hesitation and ultimate rejection of a major oil pipeline. The US Congress and both major presidential candidates threatened to reject the TPP, while the Republican nominee promised to "break" the region's fundamental trade accord and build a wall on the USA–Mexico border. Mexico struggled with the implementation of once-touted reforms, while concerns over security and governance continued. The moment highlighted the need for and possibilities of trilateral cooperation, but also underlined the existential risks for North America's future as a region.

Until the previous 25 years, "North America" has rarely been considered a region, and until then, it encompassed only the USA and Canada.[1] Only in the early 1990s, when Mexico sought a free trade agreement with the USA, did a tri-national region begin to emerge. For most of the three countries' histories, the shared continental geography was defined by the dominant presence of the USA and the potential or actual regional "bads" that emerged from it. During the 19th century, the USA threatened Canada's and Mexico's territorial integrity and independence—a threat made real when the USA annexed half of Mexico's territory in 1848 and followed with incursions into Mexico lasting into World War I. That threat dissipated in the following decades, but both Mexico and Canada adopted policies intended to keep their powerful neighbor at a distance by limiting investment, the presence of American companies, and the presence of US media.

Despite those policies, geography helped propel the flow of trade and people among the three countries. The ultimate goal of regional public goods (RPGs) is understood as promoting peace and prosperity. In North America, peace—at least at the interstate level—took shape even as policies aimed at regional prosperity received limited and sporadic attention. Cooperation grew more quickly between the USA and Canada, with 92 bilateral treaties signed between 1948 and 1965, compared to 38 between the USA and Mexico.[2] The year 1965 was an early watershed: the Canada–United States Automotive Products Agreement represented an early step in the production of RPGs aimed at enhancing regional prosperity. Regionalism took a quantum leap forward in 1988, with the negotiation of an FTA between the USA and Canada. Canada sought the agreement as a way to emerge from economic stagnation, and the agreement's model for RPGs relied heavily on an open US market. The agreement broke ground by including nontariff barriers, trade in services, and dispute resolution. RPG production centered on increased trade and investment; however, it indirectly deepened US–Canadian cooperation in a number of spheres. Clearer dispute resolution procedures helped produce greater rule of law at the bilateral level, which would become even more important in the ensuing trilateral accord.

The North American Free Trade Agreement (NAFTA) formally expanded the region to Mexico—catching up with economic and social trends—and enhanced the demand for and potential of RPGs. NAFTA was founded on the premise that important RPGs would be generated by the closer economic integration of the three countries. In particular, it was assumed that the virtual disappearance of trade barriers in North America would increase trade in a spectacular form—which it did—and that higher volumes of trade would result in faster rates of economic growth, particularly for Mexico, the smallest of the three economies. Unfortunately, this latter assumption did not hold true, since the average rate of growth of the Mexican economy has remained disappointingly low since NAFTA came into effect in 1994.

NAFTA represented a different approach to regionalism, though with similarities to the types that Amitav Acharya discusses in Chapter 3 of this volume. As a region defined by asymmetry and economically dependent on the huge US market, it has aspects of hegemonic regionalism. However, North America was brought into being by Canadian and Mexican initiatives, and the US government has rarely dedicated great attention to the region. In its economic aspects and its legalism, NAFTA represented an integrationist effort. However, it has not followed the European model of building regional bureaucracies, nor ASEAN's model of frequent consultation and engagement with external powers. There has been relatively limited spillover in the neofunctionalist sense of growing demands for cooperation and institutionalization across issue areas. Through NAFTA, the three countries took steps away from protectionism and nationalist policies, but at a governmental level have shown little initiative to go beyond that. Some of these relative gains have been reversed since 2001, after which stagnation has become the rule. North America has prized the national over the supranational, and in almost all cases, Canada, Mexico, and the USA engage with the rest of the world as individual states, not as a region. Despite these differences, we argue that North America should be treated as a region. Geography provides an obvious rationale; more important are the myriad connections among the three countries, which range from production chains to family networks. Using an RPG framework, we describe goods that have been created in the region and areas in which those goods are lacking.

With the important exceptions of trade and investment, many of the RPGs forecasted to be the major accomplishments of the new trading bloc did not materialize, particularly rapid and sustained economic growth in Mexico. Other RPGs that were not so obvious at the launching of NAFTA, like enhancing the rule of law in Mexico and at the regional level, with positive effects for foreign investment throughout the region, were more salient. While enhanced rule of law has benefited actors at the regional levels of the economies, NAFTA did not—and probably could not—create rule of law that would spill over to the economies as a whole. As such, important sectoral and geographic disparities in goods provision remain. As a recent McKinsey Global Institute study by Bolio et al. (2014) demonstrates, while productivity of the "modern" sector of the Mexican economy with close ties to NAFTA grew at a compounded annual rate of 5.8% per year between 1999 and 2009, the productivity of the "traditional" firms that cater to the domestic market, including those in the informal economy, has fallen at an annual compounded rate of 6.5%. RPGs only partially compensate for weak goods production at the national and local levels.

This paper will briefly examine the concept of RPGs as it applies to North America. Focusing on the role of these goods, it contextualizes today's situation with a succinct account of North American integration. The paper argues that rule of law has emerged as one of the most important RPGs in North America, directed largely at regional economic transactions. While these effects have been important, the provision of rule of law is fragmentary and has not produced the degree of spillover that was hoped for. Finally, we conclude by examining the future prospects of RPG provision in North America.

Overview of the region before regional integration agreements

Before 1988, US–Canadian economic cooperation was guided by the multilateral trade framework that the USA had promoted after World War II with the creation of the General Agreement on Trade and Tariffs (GATT). Both states were founding GATT members, unlike Mexico, which joined nearly four decades later. Until the negotiation of the US–Canadian FTA (CUSFTA), the USA showed a strong preference for global, multilateral economic RPGs. However, there were more limited earlier agreements, which can be seen as RPG inputs, produced in other areas. Between 1948 and 1992, when NAFTA negotiations began in earnest, Canada, the USA, and Mexico had signed 451 treaties between them, with more than 100 for each category of connectivity, peace and security, and natural resources and the environment (see Figure 13.1).[3] Besides eliminating barriers to trade and investment, the basic purpose of CUSFTA, especially in the eyes of the Canadians, was to establish a dispute settlement system that eliminated high-handed unilateral actions from the USA.

While remaining outside the GATT, Mexico pursued an inward-looking, protectionist policy of import substitution, based on the ideas promoted by Raúl Prebisch and the United Nations' Economic Commission for Latin America and the Caribbean (ECLAC) that nations needed to industrialize to escape their "secularly deteriorating terms of trade" as commodity exporters. Mexico pursued a number of integration agreements with Latin America, such as LAFTA (1960) and SELA (1975), but none led to substantial economic integration or produced important RPGs. These failures contrast with the success, albeit limited to trade and investment, of NAFTA. The former were politically propelled and maintained protectionism, while NAFTA involved an open trade agenda, with few exceptions, that traded economic nationalism for an integrated trade and investment area.

Starting in 1988, Mexico's newly elected president Carlos Salinas sought to anchor recent market-friendly reforms through trade deals. Before turning to the north, Salinas had sought closer economic ties with Europe and

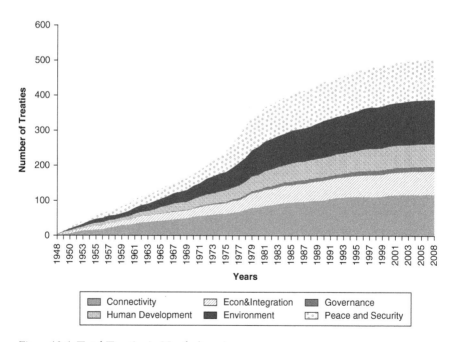

Figure 13.1 Total Treaties in North America.

Source: Liu and Kahn, Regional Public Goods Database (Chapter 2).

Japan, only to be rejected by both. President George Bush, however, quickly accepted Salinas' request for a bilateral pact. The presidents-elect established a good personal rapport, dubbed the "spirit of Houston," after a meeting in the Texan city a few weeks before their respective inaugurations. In August 1990, President Bush indicated to Congress that he intended to move forward with a bilateral agreement, at which point Canada reversed its earlier reticence and asked to join (Boskin 2014). Thus began the three-nation North American economic region.

The pursuit of NAFTA

Although the Mexican government faced internal skepticism about free trade with the USA, Mexicans did not expect any serious opposition to the trade talks. However, US labor unions, human rights NGOs, environmental groups, populist politicians like businessman Ross Perot, the Congressional Black Caucus, and the right wing of the Republican Party opposed granting Bush fast-track authority to negotiate with Mexico. It became clear that the Mexican government had to engage in Congressional politics to overcome objections from opponents of free trade with Mexico—though few had expressed reservations about the earlier Canadian accord or ongoing GATT round.[4]

Once the fast-track vote was won and formal talks began, the negotiation proceeded at a rapid pace, though not fast enough to get NAFTA through Congress before the presidential election of 1992. When Bill Clinton unseated Bush, with help from anti-NAFTA crusader Ross Perot, who won 18.9% of the vote, it opened a new phase in the formally completed negotiations. Responding to trade unions and environmental activists, Clinton insisted that NAFTA would include side agreements on these areas. These were finalized in September 1993, and the whole bill was sent to Congress. The House approved NAFTA by a slim margin of 34 votes on November 17; the Senate passed NAFTA three days later with 61 votes in favor and 38 against. NAFTA took effect on January 1 1994 (see Long 2015, chapter 4).

As stated in the agreement's objectives, the most important RPGs expected from NAFTA were in the following areas:

- The elimination of trade barriers and the facilitation of "the cross-border movement of goods and services" between the three nations.
- The promotion of "fair competition."
- Regional investment.
- Protection of intellectual property rights.
- Institutionalization of the agreement's implementation and administration, with mechanisms for dispute resolution (NAFTA Secretariat 1993).

Fulfilling these obligations in North America demanded a major transformation of the institutional and legal landscape, particularly for Mexico, whose standards had to catch up with those of the other two countries. Success was not evenly achieved, but trade and investment grew quickly in NAFTA's first decade (see Figure 13.2). The dispute resolution system created by the agreement has worked remarkably well.

The first RPG that surfaced unexpectedly in the region was the result of the currency crisis that hit Mexico in December 1994, when unprecedented political violence caused jitters in the financial markets. A combination of these fears, plus the ensuing issuing of large amounts of US-dollar–denominated short-term debt, an insufficiently flexible exchange rate system, and the inexpert management of the situation by a rookie administration, led to a devaluation in which the Mexican peso lost two-thirds of its value against the US dollar, causing panic in the financial and foreign exchange markets. The risk that this situation would get out of control less than a year after NAFTA came into force drove President Clinton to skirt Congress and prepare an unprecedented US$50 billion rescue package based on the Exchange Stabilization Fund and resources from the IMF, the World Bank, Canada, the European Union (EU), and Japan. The crisis rapidly dissipated and, after a deep recession, Mexico began to grow again within six quarters and repaid all its debt in 1997, well ahead of schedule. It is doubtful whether the USA would have undertaken this rescue operation had it not been for NAFTA.

Bolstered by RPGs in trade, rule of law, and macroeconomic stability, the creation of NAFTA achieved remarkable success in its first seven years. Between 1994 and 2001, its share of the global GDP went from 30% to 36%, as all other regions of the world lost ground. The EU fell by 1 percentage point, to 25%, despite having increased its membership; Asia[5] went from 25%

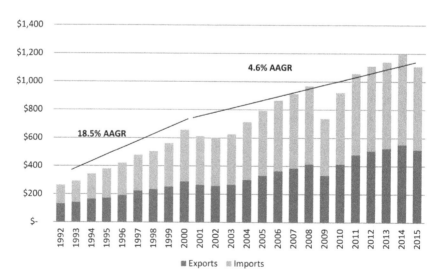

Figure 13.2 US Trade with North America (billions of US$).

Source: Pastor (2011, p.25).

to 22%; while the rest of the world lost 2 percentage points to reach just 17% of the total in 2001. In this period North America emerged as a formidable region that exceeded the EU in terms of economic size and productivity. The three economies and societies were progressively connected by trade, investment, pipelines, tourism, and immigration (see Figure 13.3). In early 2001, the presidents of Mexico and the USA proposed a North American economic community. In April they traveled to Canada to consult with its prime minister: "It seemed like the high point of North American integration, and as it turned out, it was" (Pastor 2011, p.23).

By the end of 2001, the North American landscape had dramatically changed. The continental economy slowed with the end of the dot-com boom in the USA. The downturn was amplified by the terrorist attacks of September 11 2001. Instead of responding regionally, the USA tightened its own borders, which slowed trade during a recession. The attacks led to a surge in nationalist, frequently nativist, sentiments that undermined efforts to find regional solutions regarding security—such as the Security and Prosperity Partnership—or migration. Perversely, as the need grew to better manage massive transnational flows, improve security, and enhance rule of law, the willingness of the three governments and their publics to produce them faded. The results of these failures are not encouraging. It is estimated that the region's share of the world's GDP in 2015 is between 25% and 27%, depending on the level of the exchange rates of their three currencies, a serious drop from the 36% reached in 2001. The three governments have largely failed to use NAFTA as a platform on which to build a more competitive region and address a new agenda beyond that of the trade agreement's mandate.

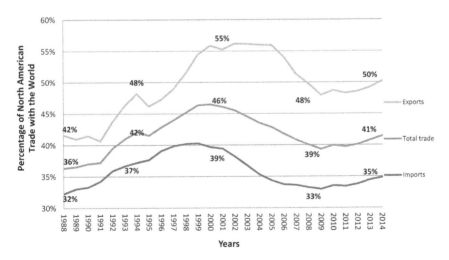

Figure 13.3 Integration: Intra-North American Trade as Percentage of North American Trade with the World.

Source: Pastor (2011, p.27).

RPGs in North America

Since NAFTA, transnational flows of nearly every variety have grown dramatically; however, the response has not always been regional in nature. North America's founding document is firmly situated in national principles— NAFTA's negotiators avoided hints of supranationalism. NAFTA's founding document makes it clear that none of the parties sought an expansive regionalism (Long 2014; Cameron and Tomlin 2000). Since the mid-2000s, trilateralism has frequently been replaced by dual-bilateralism. In a sense, this is a return to an historical pattern in North America. According to UN registries, there is only one trilateral treaty in North America—a 1976 environmental treaty. (NAFTA is not a treaty, so it is not included, signaling limitations with the data.) Mexico and Canada have only reported six bilateral treaties since 1948. However, the USA has 281 treaties with Canada and 216 with Mexico (see Figure 13.4).[6]

Despite NAFTA's national nature, it has led to the creation of important RPGs. We define RPGs in North America as a type of public good that "provides nonexclusive and nonrival benefits to individuals in a well-defined region" (this builds on Sandler 2004; Estevadeordal, Frantz, and Nguyen 2004; and Chapter 1 of this volume). Estevadeordal et al. (2004) note that RPGs are often an outcome of regional cooperation agreements, of which NAFTA was an early and widely copied example. The dramatic increases in trade and

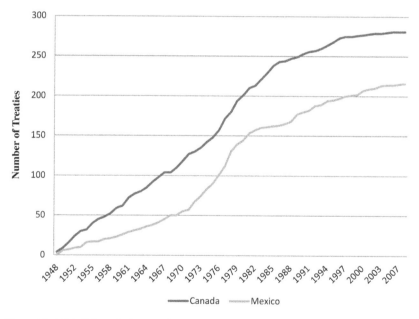

Figure 13.4 US Bilateral Treaties by Partner.

Source: Liu and Kahn, Regional Public Goods Database (Chapter 2).

investment that came with NAFTA were accompanied by much larger flows of migration and illicit traffic, all of which affected the demand for and provision of RPGs.

In the North American context, it is particularly important to highlight the interplay across different levels of government as this is relevant to the demand for and production of RPGs. Domestic, not regional, problems have been a greater factor in Mexico's disappointing economic growth over the past two decades. RPGs are unlikely to be a panacea for problems of peace and prosperity. A more adequate approach should start with the question of complementarity: where can RPGs make positive contributions? (See Chapter 6.) As RPGs cannot resolve many fundamentally domestic issues, weak provision of public goods at the national level can lower levels of regional goods.

Sandler (2006, p.10) offers a framework for examining the "aggregation technology" for RPGs—in essence, how the nature of RPG provision varies depending on the type of impure public good. Two of the types of aggregation Sandler discusses are particularly relevant. Sandler describes "weighted sum" aggregation of RPGs—"provision is no longer perfectly substitutable among countries" (Sandler 2004, p.18). The creation and benefits of the RPG are not equally shared. Second, Sandler discusses "weaker link" public goods, which are diminished by the unequal creation of that good across the region. With weaker link goods, the lowest level of provision has the greatest impact on the overall level of the RPG. Sandler's framework provides a way to conceptualize the provision of rule of law as an RPG that is not uniform across geographies or levels of analysis.

Sandler's analysis remains regional; however, RPGs have local and national effects. Similarly, deficient governance at the local and national level may reduce the availability of goods across the region. In this case, the weaker link in the production of rule of law in many sectors occurs in Mexico, largely due to lower state capacity. Insufficient provision by Mexico affects the total benefits of the RPG available to people and businesses across the region, but harms Mexico most of all. This is clear in terms of transnational security, particularly in the criminal justice system: Mexico suffers most—in social and economic terms—from the weakness of rule of law. The deficit affects the entirety of North America (and Central America, too) with decreasing intensity as it radiates outwards. While additional contributions from other states in the region to this weaker link RPG may produce benefits, the effects will be unequally distributed.

Rule of law as a regional public good

Though rule of law has often been treated as a public good at the local and national levels, this has rarely been the case regionally. In this section, we examine the concept of rule of law as a weaker link good with partial overlap and limited spillover across local, national, and regional levels. Like the related concept of governance, rule of law displays certain similarities across levels of analysis:[7] 1) public and transparent rules, 2) equivalent application of these rules, and 3) open and public decision-making procedures. At the national level, where rule of law has been most studied, Guillermo O'Donnell (2004) defined it as existing when "whatever law exists is written down and publicly promulgated by an appropriate authority before the events meant to be regulated by it, and is fairly applied by relevant state institutions including the judiciary . . . the administrative application or judicial adjudication of legal rules is consistent across equivalent cases; is made without taking into consideration the class, status, or relative amounts of power held by the parties in such cases; and applies procedures that are pre-established, knowable, and allow a fair chance for the views and interests at stake in each case to be properly voiced."

There are at least three reasons to consider regional rule of law in North America. Rule of law provides social order. There is a long tradition in International Relations of considering "international society" (Bull 1977, 1984, and Hurrell 2007), and the stronger web of connections makes the regional level even more "social." NAFTA also spurred more frequent and institutionalized interactions of officials among the three countries (Aspinwall 2009). NAFTA created clearer rules to structure transactions between and among member states, providing clarity at the regional level for trade and investment. Second, NAFTA created procedures that resolve some of the disputes that can arise from these transactions (completing equivalent application and openness as part of rule of law). Institutionalized dispute resolution replaces the threat of arbitrary US protectionism with regional rule of law, through which all three countries benefit. Finally, regional rule of law has enhanced, albeit imperfectly, the rule of law at the domestic level. In transnational cases, business disputes can be settled in the courts of the country of the claimant's choosing. Through this, Mexico "borrowed" the US judiciary and rule of law for some issues, thereby bringing a regional dimension even to domestic rule of law in the three countries.

NAFTA sought to promote a partial spillover from the regional level to the Mexican domestic context. While RPGs may partially overcome deficits at the national and local levels, this spillover exists unevenly across geographies and issue areas. Deficits at local and national levels also undermine regional rule of law. Like many goods, the demand, production, and consumption of rule of law are not evenly distributed across the North American region. Nor has this good been evenly distributed among social and economic sectors.

The rule of law as a regional public good: the case of Mexico

North America's prospects could be improved by enhancing the production of RPGs, such as rule of law. Among the countries of North America, it remains clear that Mexico has the least reliable legal system and weakest rule of law. While NAFTA contributed to an improvement in rule of law for some sections of the economy, for much of the population the situation has become worse. The share of employment in the "modern" sector, defined by size as firms employing 500 workers or more, has remained constant in the period mentioned at 20% of the labor force; the share of the "traditional" firms, with 10 employees or less, has grown from 39% to 42%; while the segment in between these, firms with 11 to 500 employees, which could be characterized as the bridge connecting the two, has seen its share fall. The falling productivity of the traditional part of the economy has resulted in wages for low-skilled workers that fell between 1999 and 2009 by 2.4% per year, while the salaries of the workers in the "modern" segment have remained stagnant despite the impressive gains in productivity (Bolio et al. 2014). Stagnant or falling wages are not what was expected from North America economic integration. The deepening split between modern and traditional also has a geographic dimension, since the former are located in the north and center of the country, closer to the US border and with much better physical and social infrastructure, while the latter are concentrated in the south. In this sense, NAFTA resulted in deepening the division of the country into two segments: one that prospers and grows, and another which remains impoverished.

Mexico's market-oriented reforms of the 1980s and 1990s, as profound as they appeared to be, did not alter longstanding institutional weaknesses. The reforms were full of contradictions. Despite their liberalizing logic, some sectors remained protected from international competition. Privatizations did not adequately consider the transformation and better integration of the economy's structure. Many regulations were eliminated, but others continued to stifle innovation, and subsidies did not disappear. In the face of entrenched interests and political opposition, Mexico's reform process largely stagnated. When the PRI returned to power in 2012, President Peña Nieto (whose term in office is due to expire in 2018) forged a political coalition behind a "Pact for Mexico," to advance energy, fiscal, telecommunications, education, and other reforms (Sada 2013). The energy reform welcomed private and foreign investment to the oil and gas business in Mexico for the first time in almost 80 years and increased competition in the electrical sector. This reduced the dominance of state-owned monopolies *Petróleos Mexicanos* and the Federal Electricity Commission in those key sectors. The reforms follow NAFTA's logic of bringing strategic areas under the cover of the US legal system to assure foreign and domestic investors. It is too early to assess the reforms' political sustainability and economic effects; some reforms, including energy and education, have drawn determined opposition as the president's approval ratings have deteriorated. However, the opening of key sectors excluded from NAFTA may provide momentum for closer regional integration, especially in energy.

Though much of its production has come via externalities or has been ad hoc, North America has some multilateral institutions that contribute to regional rule of law. First, NAFTA created panels for trade dispute resolution. Second, NAFTA created clearer rules for investment and institutionalized mechanisms for the settlement of disputes between investors and the states-party. These new mechanisms expanded the rule of law, primarily for international businesses and investors, though also to Mexican firms associated with foreign investors in complex supply chains. The agreements help to keep politics at arms' length in state–investor disagreements (Brower 2015). Third, NAFTA created some (weak) mechanisms, through which citizens and civil society groups can appeal at the international level in pursuit of compliance with national law and NAFTA obligations. These mechanisms enhanced the clarity of regional transactions, serving as a "club good" for economic actors within the three countries, promoting intra-North American investment. However, regionally produced rule of law primarily benefits only the sectors of those societies that are engaged in licit international transactions. It does not provide the same benefits to regions with low participation in international transactions, nor does it address the worrying trade in illicit goods among the three countries, mostly between Mexico and the United States. These are, mainly, illegal drugs and illegally trafficked people from the south flowing north and weapons and money from the north flowing south. The overall economic magnitude of illicit trade is unknown, for obvious reasons, but official estimates place the USA–Mexico drug trade at about 5% of the amount of legal bilateral trade in goods and services, which will approach US$600 billion in 2016.[8] Although law enforcement officials of both countries believe that the enormous growth in legal trade can help mask the illicit flows, particularly facilitating cash transfers and money laundering, trade experts have pointed to closer, more effective cooperation between the United States and Mexico, engendered by legal trade flows. More to the point, the expansion of this illicit trade, and the violence and corruption surrounding it, weakens the benefits of rule of law as a regional public good.

Dispute resolution mechanisms were important for all the actors involved, though in different ways. Mexico and Canada worried primarily about whether the USA—particularly a protectionist Congress—could undermine their gains in market access through unilateral measures, as we saw when President Obama adopted "buy American" provisions at the start of the Great Recession that are illegal under NAFTA. At the time, the USA and Canada sought investment protections and dispute resolution because of concerns about the political climate and weak judicial system in Mexico, and US investors worried about the risk of expropriation in Mexico and protection of intellectual property. These concerns were crystallized in two separate parts of the agreement, Chapters 11 and 19.

NAFTA's chapter 11 sought to regionalize and rationalize disputes between states and investors. For decades, when companies had grievances about their investments in other countries, they sought the protection of their home government, hoping to gain diplomatic pressure on their behalf. This took the dispute out of the legal and economic realms and placed it squarely in the political. Transparency and predictability suffered. Handling grievances under national courts—a principle long advanced in Latin America dating back to the Drago and Calvo doctrines—offered little assurance to investors if these courts were viewed as subject to political influence or as biased toward national actors. Put differently, chapter 11 was intended to bring the rule of law to these disputes, understood as the fair and consistent application of transparent, public, pre-existing rules. As Brower (2015) wrote: "a rule-based system must have an enforcement mechanism if its substantive rules are to have any meaning over the long term."

The evolving nature of investor–state disputes demonstrates that rule of law concerns were not limited strictly to Mexico. In recent cases, Canadian provincial and local regulations have been seen as injuring foreign investors, drawing criticism from Canadian activists (Sinclair 2015). Through the end of 2014, there had been 77 investor–state disputes under chapter 11. Canada has been the subject of the greatest number of claims (35), though Mexico has paid a larger share of judgments (US$204 million). While there are debates about whether these rulings have infringed on governments' legitimate regulatory powers, the existence of a clear framework seems to have favored investment. In Mexico, where there was the greatest initial concern about transparent dispute settlement, nearly 60% of total inward FDI has originated from NAFTA partner countries, according to data from UNCTAD. This happened even as total inward FDI in Mexico increased more than 17 times from 1990 to 2013. Canada's increase has been nearly as dramatic (see Figure 13.5).

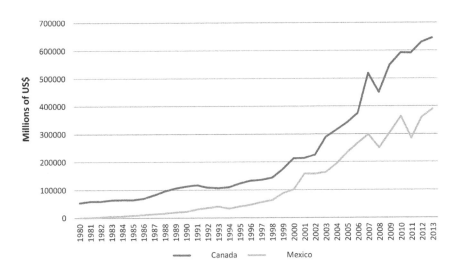

Figure 13.5 Inward FDI Stock, 1980–2013.

Source: Compiled by authors based on UNCTADstat, Foreign Direct Investment: Inward and Outward Flows and Stock Databse, http://unctadstat.unctad.org/

The limits of regional rule of law

The ability to resolve disputes pacifically at the regional level has not created spillover in terms of Mexico's ability to resolve disputes among its citizens with regularity and transparency. Mexico performs very poorly for various indicators related to rule of law and impunity. The country lacks the appropriate judicial infrastructure and rates of prosecution for crime are extremely low. A recent study on impunity noted that Mexico has just four judges for every 100,000 residents—less than a quarter of the average for the 59 countries involved in the study and half the rates for the USA (9.8) and Canada (8.4).[9] As the country has turned to the military to battle drug trafficking, extrajudicial punishment seems to be a growing problem and human rights abuses have become a source of serious concern. Similarly, a number of recent tragic incidents have revealed the depth of cartels' and gangs' penetration into local political systems, irrespective of which political party is in charge. The impact of these struggles goes beyond the local level.

According to the World Bank's estimates, rule of law in Mexico improved significantly around 2000, as the government transitioned for the first time to the opposition center-right National Action Party (PAN). This estimate declined as drug-related violence increased from 2006–2007 under the stewardship of a second PAN administration. Within this composite indicator, Mexico's scores on government effectiveness and regulatory quality have seen moderate increases, although they are offset by indicators related to violence (see Figure 13.6). These figures appear to blend two divergent trends in the Mexican economy.

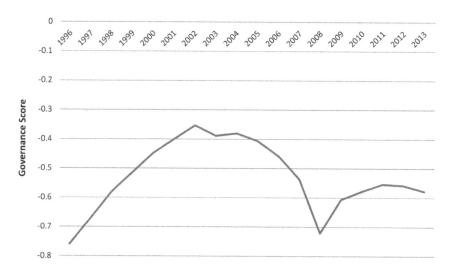

Figure 13.6 Rule of Law in Mexico.

Source: Worldwide Governance Indicators, World Bank DataBank.

Challenges with rule of law, whether national or regional, are not limited to Mexico. This is clearly visible in the dysfunctional US immigration system, where high levels of undocumented immigration create public "bads" with impacts across levels of governance, including for shaping more effective tax, social service, and labor market policies. As with many such issues, the need for RPGs in rule of law is directly linked to the expansion of transnational flows. While NAFTA created a regional market for goods, and to a lesser but important extent for services and capital, it did not legally unify labor markets.

As Estevadeordal et al. (2004, p.6) note, national commitments are crucial for adequate RPG creation. "If states are unwilling to envisage a role for regional cooperation to promote national development, it is unlikely that RPGs will be supplied at optimal levels." When one observes the current political scenario of North America, it is difficult to avoid skepticism about the likelihood of a more united North America. There is neither the interest nor the necessary attention on the part of the governments in question, with the possible exception of Mexico, which is immersed in a deep process of economic reforms and whose government is mired in a delicate political situation with very low approval from the population, which distract it from regional integration. While Trudeau favors multilateralism more than his predecessor, the emphasis on bilateral USA–Canada ties remains. For their part, US politicians have more often referred to NAFTA as a scapegoat, not as a framework for regional responses to shared problems.

Central RPGs: past production and future prospects

In Chapter 2, Liu and Kahn divide RPGs into six functional categories. While we have focused on the rule of law, in closing we will address other RPGs produced—or lacking—in each of these functional categories.

Economic cooperation and integration

NAFTA's focus was on the production of RPGs in trade and investment. At the regional level, these RPGs have produced greater prosperity, though with unequal distribution. However, trade and investment have not been the only economic RPGs in North America. At the macro level, there has been significant convergence among the three economies in terms of business cycles and interest rates, leading to a more predictable environment for companies that produce, invest, and trade in North America (Serra Puche 2015). NAFTA did not include formal agreements to coordinate fiscal and monetary policies, but informally communication among the treasuries and the central banks of the region is important. While for the most part convergence has been an externality of closer links among the three economies, it has at times been intentionally supported by government actions—most crucially in the significant US backing of Mexico during its 1994 peso crisis (De Long, De Long, and Robinson 1996; Edwards 1998).

Transnational production chains have been a significant, only partially anticipated aspect of NAFTA. About 40% of the value added in Mexican exports to the USA was produced in the USA (Wilson 2011). Mexican firms have benefited from their insertion into the regional economy, growing more competitive and productive through the adoption of modern business practices. However, the regional economy contributes to a bifurcation between the regionally and globally active and the purely domestic. Talent and capital are available to the former while being drawn away from the latter. In Mexico, this has been reflected in the growth of employment in the informal economy (60% of the workforce, by some measures, but just a quarter of the GDP) (Flores 2014) where productivity has declined. By definition, this huge informal sector is an area where the rule of law is largely absent and the provision of RPGs has very little effect. RPGs cannot entirely substitute the need to produce similar public goods at the national and sub-national levels.

Human and social development

Despite their proximity, educational exchanges in the region have been lacking. The number of students who study abroad in another North American country trails behind the numbers of those who head farther afield. Canada and Mexico combined to send about 72,000 students to the USA—fewer than Saudi Arabia, and far fewer than Asia, which sent a whopping 839,000.[10] As Robert Pastor frequently pointed out, there are hundreds of academic research centers in North America dedicated to other areas of the world, but few that focus on North America.[11] Support for greater educational exchanges among the three countries would create important RPGs. The leaders have recognized this need, pledging in 2016 to create the North American Center for Collaborative Development, based at the University of Arizona's Consortium for North American Higher Education Collaboration. Its promotion of research on shared challenges is sorely needed, though the commitment of funds and leadership is not yet clear. Summit pledges also included greater educational exchanges and programs to boost indigenous education and women's entrepreneurship (White House 2016).

RPG production has been more effective in certain professional areas, such as epidemiology. Governmental, academic, and private-sector actors in the health field undertake extensive planning and preparation to contain possible outbreaks of disease. There is close communication and collaboration among the three countries, thus mitigating one possible negative externality of increased regional flows. A 2007 plan created under the defunct Security and Prosperity Partnership helped guide the three countries' responses to a 2009 outbreak of H1N1 influenza. The plan has been augmented with lessons learned[12] and to address emerging diseases including Zika and chikungunya (White House 2016).

Natural resources, environment, and energy

North America has been defined by the extensive borders between the USA and its neighbors in terms of both the threats and opportunities that these entail. This is particularly clear regarding environmental challenges and opportunities for energy sector cooperation. Long before NAFTA, regional agreements sought to manage shared border resources and to limit transnational pollution.

Some of the stronger intergovernmental organizations to emerge from NAFTA concern environmental issues, where the challenges are very clearly transnational and sovereignty concerns have been less pronounced. Two merit mention: the North American Development Bank (Nadbank) and the Commission for Environmental Cooperation (CEC). The Nadbank has limited funding and a restricted mandate, but it has financed nearly 200 projects that address environmental and health issues on the USA–Mexico border. Though the CEC lacks sharp teeth—deliberately so according to the terms of NAFTA's environmental side agreement—it has provided a venue for appeals from civil society to the international level. NGOs can use the CEC to challenge national governments over the perceived failure to implement national environmental legislation. Though it lacks the power to sanction, the CEC's reports have served as a means to pressure governments into compliance.

In recent summits, North American leaders have forged a commitment to build upon Mexican energy reforms and the growth of energy production in the USA and Canada to create a more secure, integrated, and green North American energy market (White House 2015, 2016). Perhaps the biggest headlines from the 2016 Ottawa summit involved increasing clean energy production, boosting efficiency standards, and working to implement the Paris climate accords. While Mexico has sought to lead on the issue in its diplomacy and radical pledges to reduce CO_2 emissions, and Canada's new leadership has made bolder commitments on climate, the ability of the United States to deliver is complicated by sharp partisan divisions.

At a meeting of energy ministers in December 2014, the three countries sought to develop a regional comparative advantage in energy. This focused on "three strategic areas": joint statistics and mapping of energy resources and infrastructure; unconventional oil and gas; and modernization of energy infrastructure, institutions, and innovation (Natural Resources Canada 2014). Given the widespread impact of energy on both the economy and the environment, this should remain an important area for RPGs.

Peace and security

At the level of traditional interstate security, North America resembles Karl Deutsch's concept of a security community. There are no serious preparations for interstate conflict and there is an expectation that disagreements will be settled without resorting to threats of, or the use of, force (Deutsch 1957), with the possible exception of the Republican nominee for president being elected

in November 2016. However, the existence of a high-level security community has not lessened the impact of transnational and human security concerns,
which have become even more salient in recent years. Both the importance
and limitations of RPG rule of law can be seen in transnational security, a key
challenge for Mexico, in which the USA is particularly involved as the largest
market for drugs and a provider of illicit arms and official security support.

There has been significant regional cooperation is terms of transnational
security. However, these problems make clear that the limits of spillover vary
from one level of governance to another. US efforts to control drug trafficking
in Mexico in cooperation with the Mexican government have had no dis-
cernible effect on the level of traffic. Policy coordination has been effective in
some regards, such as intelligence cooperation aimed at capturing cartel leaders. However, it has been noticeably absent in others, such as in the control of
southbound arms shipments.

The strategy of aggressive policing has produced, at least in the short term,
greater human insecurity—and tremendous human and economic costs—without
notable improvements to the rule of law (Kenny, Serrano, and Sotomayor 2012).
According to official government statistics, impunity has actually worsened: nearly
94% of crimes are not reported or investigated. This figure was nearly as high for
crimes against businesses, of which 88% were not reported or investigated. While
Mexico has more police per capita than the international average,[13] just 22% of
Mexicans have some or much confidence in the police, according to a December
2014 poll by the newspaper *Reforma* (Grupo Reforma 2014). Nearly half of pris-
oners are being detained without having been sentenced.

Insecurity is the most blatant manifestation of inadequate rule of law. About
one-third of surveyed Mexican households reported having at least one person
who was a victim of a crime in 2014; only a fraction are officially reported.
Security concerns have a tremendous impact on Mexican businesses, too,
which face a national average cost of more than MXN55,700 (equivalent
to an average US$3,840 in 2015) annually as a result of crime and security
measures (INEGI 2014). However, there is a huge subnational variation, with
costs ranging as high as MXN90,000 per business unit in the aerospace hub
of Querétaro (INEGI). According to the same agency, one-third of economic
units (a category that includes both formal and informal goods and services
providers of all sizes, including many micro-enterprises) reported being victims
of crime in 2013. In this, too, there is a tremendous geographical variation,
ranging from 21% in the state of San Luis Potosí to 44% in Baja California.
Robbery, corruption, and extortion were the most common crimes against
business. Combined, INEGI estimates that crime costs households and businesses about 2% of GDP each year.

Connectivity

Insufficient investment in various aspects of connectivity has limited North
America's ability to take advantage of its shared geography. This has been

most notable in inadequate physical infrastructure, which has been strained by the massive expansion of trade flows. New and expanded crossings are needed, but have stalled. A long-planned new bridge for the world's most valuable border corridor, between Detroit and Windsor, is years behind schedule. Rail connections between the USA and Canada are outdated, even as they deal with tremendous quantities of freight. The planned Keystone XL pipeline has been shelved for the immediate future. Mexico's rail system, after decades of neglect, has received increased attention, although a new rail crossing on the USA–Mexico border opened only after years of delays. In many cases, connectivity worsened after 2001 due to the "thickening" of US borders (Pastor 2011), lessening the region's geographic advantages. This was exacerbated by policies that limited cross-border trucking between Mexico and the USA (in clear violation of the corresponding NAFTA provisions), and created expensive cabotage restrictions to American-flagged vessels in the USA resulting from the Jones Act, a remnant of Prohibition. The 2014 North American Leaders Summit called for a North American Transportation Plan as a "key deliverable," but this has not materialized. The 2016 summit omitted mention of costly physical infrastructure and instead focused on deploying technology to make crossing more efficient—a welcome, but probably insufficient step. The lack of infrastructure is replicated in other areas. Among OECD members, Mexico has the second-lowest number of fixed broadband internet subscriptions per 100 residents. The USA is number 16 of 34 countries; Canada is number 12. All lag even further behind in faster fiber-optic connections. There have been a number of recent positive steps, like the binational airport crossing in Tijuana–San Diego; the agreement to allow customs officials to do pre-clearing in the other country's territory; state-of-the-art customs-checking facilities going to Mexico; and trusted traveler programs and some improvements in screening procedures. However, for the most part these welcome developments barely compensate for post-9/11 border thickening instead of advancing the region beyond where it was 15 years ago. A lot more needs to be done if North America retains its role of the most productive region on earth.

Governance and institutions

In governance and institutions, North America diverges clearly from the European model. Some of the thin institutions of NAFTA, such as the labor secretariat, have been allowed to expire. Less formal gatherings, such as the North American Leaders Summit, have been infrequent and subject to political whims. And given the political discourse prevalent in the presidential campaigns of 2016, the chances of advancing a regional agenda appear dim.

From the perspective of RPGs, the crucial question for North America concerns multilevel governance. How can the regional level better promote the creation of RPGs that penetrate to national and subnational levels? Up to this point, the approach has been the opposite: how to lessen the impact of failures of governance and lack of rule of law at the subnational and national levels on regional transactions. The national and subnational weakness in rule of law presents a particular problem for North America, because regional institutions have few supranational capacities. Instead they rely heavily on national enforcement. However, NAFTA changed the landscape, creating new demands for cooperation. "[I]ncentives for cooperation in providing RPGs are greater when there are economic incentives and commercial interests in place" (Estevadeordal, Frantz, and Nguyen 2004). Certainly, these incentives and interests exist in the case of North America, but for the most part, efforts to produce RPGs have been ad hoc. Where they have been institutionalized, they have been thin and have reached across various levels of governance. Creating institutions that fulfill this role without overly impinging on the sovereignty of the three countries that have traditionally guarded it zealously is a difficult task.

Conclusions

In conclusion, North America's emergence as a region, and its production of RPGs, has been at once exemplary and incomplete. For the previous century, it has been a zone of interstate peace, but regional, transnational flows contribute to high levels of violence. It was a leader in regional trade integration, but that integration did not produce widely shared prosperity. Opponents of deeper regionalism have often stressed a desire to avoid Europe's bureaucratic model. However, they present a false choice: North America does not need larger bureaucracies to benefit from regionalism, but it does need greater political and fiscal investment in the creation of RPGs to manage shared problems and to enhance the foundations of shared prosperity. The opportunities for even incremental improvements in cooperation are substantial, even as the very basis of regional cooperation faces its greatest political challenges since the ratification of NAFTA.

Notes

1 For example, Deutsch (1957) discussed the USA and Canada as a security community. During the Cold War, air-defense institution NORAD did not include Mexico, which was instead included in Latin American defense pacts.
2 See the Regional Public Goods Database described by Liu and Kahn in Chapter 2 of this volume.
3 See footnote 2.
4 The Mexican government undertook an unprecedented campaign throughout the USA, targeting the population of all congressional districts that had representatives that were undecided on the NAFTA issue, and encouraging them to write their member of congress in support of free trade with Mexico. The country spent US$50 million on such lobbying between 1990 and 1993.
5 Defined as including Japan, China, Hong Kong, Taiwan, South Korea, and the ten ASEAN nations.
6 See footnote 2.
7 On governance across levels of analysis, see Krahmann (2003).

8 Melissa Dell (2015) recently noted the variety of estimates of Mexican drug trafficking organizations' earnings in the US market. The State Department's own estimate ranges from US$13.6 to US$48.4 billion per year, with similar estimates from other US and Mexican government agencies. This stands in stark contrast to the estimated US$560 million in domestic sales in Mexico.

9 See Le Clercq Ortega, Antonio, and Rodríguez Sánchez Lara (2015) and "Judicial Systems," *Citizen Security Statistics for the Americas,* database, Organization of American States. Online: www.oas.org/dsp/observatorio/database/indicatorsdetails. aspx?lang=en&indicator=48

10 Data from US Immigration and Customs Enforcement, "SEVIS by the numbers," October 2014. Online: www.ice.gov/sites/default/files/documents/Document/2014/ by-the-numbers.pdf

11 This was a frequent complaint in Pastor's many books and articles, such as *The North American Idea* (2011, p.191). See also Gueorguieva (2007).

12 See the "North American Plan for Animal and Pandemic Influenza," April 2012. www.phe.gov/Preparedness/international/Documents/napapi.pdf

13 "Indice global de impunidad," Centros de Estudios sobre Impunidad y Justicia. www.udlap.mx/cesij/resumenejecutivo.aspx

References

Aspinwall, Mark. 2009. "NAFTA-Ization: Regionalization and Domestic Political Adjustment in the North American Economic Area." *Journal of Common Market Studies* 47: 1–24.

Bolio, Eduardo, Jaana Remes, Tomás Lajous, James Manyika, Morten Rossé, and Eugenia Ramirez. 2014. "A Tale of Two Mexicos: Growth and Prosperity in a Two-Speed Economy." London: McKinsey Global Institute.

Boskin, Michael J., ed. 2014. *NAFTA at 20: The North American Free Trade Agreement's Achievements and Challenges.* Stanford, CA: Hoover Institution Press.

Brower, Charles N. 2015. "Who Then Should Judge? Developing the International Rule of Law under NAFTA Chapter 11." *Chicago Journal of International Law* 2, no. 1.

Bull, Hedley. 1977. *The Anarchical Society: A Study of Order in World Politics.* New York: Columbia University Press.

Bull, Hedley. 1984. *The Expansion of International Society.* London: Clarendon Press.

Cameron, Maxwell A., and Brian W. Tomlin. 2000. *The Making of NAFTA: How the Deal Was Done.* Ithaca, NY: Cornell University Press.

Dell, Melissa. 2015. "Trafficking Networks and the Mexican Drug War." *The American Economic Review* 105:1738–79.

De Long, Bradford, Christopher De Long and Sherman Robinson. 1996. "The Case for Mexico's Rescue: The Peso Package Looks Even Better Now." *Foreign Affairs* 75: 8.

Deutsch, Karl Wolfgang. 1957. *Political Community in the North Atlantic Area.* Princeton, NJ: Princeton University Press.

Edwards, Sebastian. 1998. "The Mexican Peso Crisis: How Much Did We Know? When Did We Know It?" *The World Economy* 21, no. 1: 1–30.

Estevadeordal, Antoni, Brian Frantz, and Tam Robert Nguyen. 2004. *Regional Public Goods: From Theory to Practice.* Washington, DC: Inter-American Development Bank.

Flores, Zenyazen. 2014. "Economía informal representó 26% del PIB de 2003 a 2012: Inegi." *El Financiero.* July 30. www.elfinanciero.com.mx/economia/informal-informalidad-pib-inegi-eduardo-sojo.html

Grupo Reforma. 2014. "Disminuye confianza en instituciones." *Reforma.* December 12. http://grupoforma-blogs.com/encuestas/?p=5233

Gueorguieva, Vassia. 2007. "North American Studies Centers: An Overview." *Norteamérica* 2, no. 2.

Hurrell, Andrew. 2007. *On Global Order: Power, Values, and the Constitution of International Society*. Oxford and New York: Oxford University Press.

Institución Nacional de Estadística y Geografía (INEGI). 2014. "Encuesta Nacional de Victimización de Empresas." Online database. www.inegi.org.mx/est/contenidos/ Proyectos/encuestas/establecimientos/otras/enve/2014/default.aspx (accessed May 9 2016).

Kenny, Paul, Mónica Serrano, and Arturo Sotomayor. 2012. *Mexico's Security Failure: Collapse Into Criminal Violence*. New York: Routledge.

Krahmann, Elke. 2003. "National, Regional, and Global Governance: One Phenomenon or Many?" *Global Governance* 9, no. 3: 323–346.

Le Clercq Ortega, Juan Antonio, and Gerardo Rodríguez Sánchez Lara. 2015. "Índice global de impunidad, 2015." Puebla, Mexico: Universidad de las América. www. udlap.mx/cesij/files/IGI_2015_digital.pdf

Long, Tom. 2014. "Echoes of 1992: The NAFTA Negotiation and North America Now." Washington, DC: Woodrow Wilson Center for International Scholars. www.wilsoncenter.org/sites/default/files/Long_NAFTA_and_Now_0.pdf

Long, Tom. 2015. *Latin America Confronts the United States: Asymmetry and Influence*. Cambridge and New York: Cambridge University Press.

NAFTA Secretariat. 1993. *North American Free Trade Agreement*, Article 102. www. nafta-sec-alena.org/Home/Legal-Texts/North-American-Free-Trade-Agreement

Natural Resources Canada. 2014. "News Release: Canada, United States and Mexico Enhance Leadership on North American Energy Cooperation." December 15. http://news.gc.ca/web/article-en.do?nid=914629

O'Donnell, Guillermo. 2004. "Why the Rule of Law Matters." *Journal of Democracy* 15, no. 4: 32–46.

Pastor, Robert A. 2011. *The North American Idea*. Oxford: Oxford University Press.

Sada, Andres. 2013. "What Is the Pacto por México?" Council of the Americas. March 11, 2013. www.as-coa.org/articles/explainer-what-pacto-por-méxico

Sandler, Todd. 2004. "Demand and institutions for regional public goods." In *Regional Public Goods: From Theory to Practice*, edited by A. Estevadeordal, B. Frantz, and T.R. Nguyen. Washington, DC: Inter-American Development Bank.

Sandler, Todd. 2006. "Regional Public Goods and International Organizations." *The Review of International Organizations* 1, no. 1: 5–25.

Serra Puche, J. 2015. *NAFTA and the Making of a Region*. Mexico City: Fondo de Cultura Económica.

Sinclair, Scott. 2015. "NAFTA Chapter 11 Investor–State Disputes to January 1, 2015." Canadian Centre for Policy Alternatives.

White House. 2015. "Joint Statement: United States-Mexico High Level Economic Dialogue." Office of the Press Secretary, January 6. www.whitehouse.gov/ the-press-office/2015/01/06/joint-statement-united-states-mexico-high-level-economic-dialogue

White House. 2016. United States Key Deliverables for the 2016 North American Leaders' Summit. Office of the Press Secretary, June 29. www.whitehouse.gov/ the-press-office/2016/06/29/fact-sheet-united-states-key-deliverables-2016-north-american-leaders (accessed August 1 2016).

Wilson, Christopher E. 2011. *Working Together: Economic Ties Between the United States and Mexico*. Washington, DC: Woodrow Wilson International Center for Scholars.

14 Public goods and regional organizations in Latin America and the Caribbean

Identity, goals, and implementation

Carlos Portales

Introduction

The provision of public goods in the international system has been linked to the existence of a hegemon, a power that is able to develop and enforce the rules of the system by providing desired public goods (Mandelbaum 2006). Since the end of World War II, the main country to perform this role in the international system has been the United States of America (USA). While it still provides substantial critical global public goods, it is no longer able to do so as it did in the late 20th century. Today, no country has replaced the USA in this regard, and the world is increasingly organized around groups of countries or regions. Beyond global public goods, the emerging multipolar/multiplex international system gives an important role to public goods produced regionally and subregionally. Regionalism and subregionalism become additional layers in the organization of the political and economic realms both by providing international security and by enabling participation in the international economy and in the creation of value chains (Fawcett 2013).[1]

The dynamics of development in a world of increasing interdependence with a less hegemonic international system requires a wider range of public goods. Thus the importance of regional public goods (RPGs) for guaranteeing peace and security and for providing rules and enhancing cooperation for development has increased. The public sector "producers" of these RPGs will increasingly be regional organizations, mechanisms of regional cooperation, and regional integration schemes, as well as intergovernmental institutions (Pacific Alliance) or ad hoc institutionalities (the Inter-American Development Bank initiative to support RPGs).

But regions are not a geographical given. The condition of being a region ("regionhood") has been linked to four elements: (1) a system of intentional actors (actors that are able to formulate decisions and act upon them); (2) a rational system with effective stated properties (ability to agree on values, to establish goals, and to use means to achieve them); (3) reciprocal recognition among actors; and (4) the ability to generate and communicate meaning and identity. A region has a common fate, certain similarities, proximity, and boundedness (Langenhove 2003). It is possible for a certain territory (i.e. a state) to belong to multiple regions. Different definitions of "region," even competing ones, may coexist in the same territories. Furthermore, in a world characterized by strong interdependence and closeness beyond overlapping regions, interregional and transregional arrangements are components of a world order. This suggests that in today´s interdependent world, global arrangements are still needed and cooperation among regions remains necessary (Fioramonti 2014).

What is the situation in the Americas in this regard? Is there only one definition of "region" or "identity"? What arrangements for cooperation are there? Do these work toward similar goals or do they seek different and even contradictory goals? How are regional organizations and other cooperation entities working to implement these? Do they cooperate or is there a lack of coordination among them?

Regionalism in the Americas

Since the USA and the Hispanic American republics[2] became independent (in the late 18th century and early 19th century, respectively), they have defined the Americas as being separate from the European (international) system and as having different goals. Non-entanglement and the Monroe Doctrine were central to the US posture until World War II: the Western Hemisphere should be free from European interference. Bolivarian and Hispanic-American 19th-century expressions—from the First Latin American Congress (Panama, 1826) to the Fourth Latin American Conference (Lima, 1864) showed a common concern for preserving the independence of Hispanic-American countries vis-à-vis European colonial powers. Although they were not able to form a regional organization, sovereignty and nonintervention were prominent shared values.

These perspectives led to a complex relationship in the incipient Inter-American System created by the USA and Latin American countries—including Brazil—at the first Pan-American Conference, held in Washington in 1889. Pan-Americanism was expressed as a desire for space for economic expansion plus a regional rule of law (the Roosevelt Corollary) among a group of countries that asserted their sovereignty, particularly over foreign private investment, and established nonintervention as a regional norm.

The region in the post-World War II order: security and conflict resolution as an RPG

Although the post-World War II international order was conceived as a universal system based on the United Nations (UN) and the Bretton Woods institutions, the UN Charter recognized that regional organizations contributed to the UN's goals and purposes. Latin American countries expressed their strong support of this at the 1945 San Francisco Conference. In 1948 they founded, with the USA, the Organization of American States (OAS), seeking RPGs based on common values. From the beginning, the OAS was an inter-American regional security and conflict resolution system that, recognizing the nonintervention principle, established bodies such as the Meeting of Consultation of Ministers of Foreign Affairs to collectively act when regional security was at stake. Latin America's desire to partake in the benefits of the Marshall Plan was not accepted by the USA, thus downplaying any economic RPGs. It would thus take more than ten years to create a regional development bank: the Inter-American Development Bank (IDB), which was founded in 1959, although the idea for it had first been raised at the 1889 Pan-American Conference.

Regional economic integration as an RPG: the beginnings

The creation of a common trade regime to expand domestic markets, allowing protection vis-à-vis the outside world, was the first economic RPG to be created in post-World War II Latin America. The Latin American Free Trade Association (LAFTA) was created in 1959 and envisioned a regional market. Subregional organizations followed: the Central American Common Market (CACM), created in 1960; and the Caribbean Free Trade Association (CARIFTA), created in 1965. But LAFTA was not able to achieve its objectives within the agreed period of negotiations. CACM was blocked after the 1969 war between Honduras and El Salvador due to contrasting perceptions of cost and benefits among its members, nor was it able to recover during the subsequent period of Central American civil wars. Only CARIFTA was able to evolve, and in 1975 became the Caribbean Common Market (CARICOM), thus advancing the integration aspirations of its small island members.

In 1969, five small and medium-sized LAFTA members launched a new integration scheme: the Andean Pact, adding preferential treatment for less developed members, industrial policies, and conditions on foreign investment. But these industrial and foreign investment policies were progressively abandoned, and even when a more comprehensive institutional arrangement was formally added, creating the Andean Community (CAN), the process lost steam.

In 1980, the Latin American Integration Association (ALADI) replaced LAFTA, softening trade liberalization objectives and keeping the scheme as an umbrella for existing arrangements while also allowing eventual further negotiations.

Democracy, liberalization, and regional integration: the 1990s

The fall of the Berlin Wall, the demise of the USSR, and the worldwide predominance of liberal values coincided with the end of almost all authoritarian regimes in Latin America, the reassertion of human rights, and growing cooperation in the protection of democratic governments. The OAS played a significant role establishing institutions fostering human rights and democracy as RPGs— its support of the expanded operation of the Inter-American Commission on Human Rights (IACHR), the functioning of the Inter-American Court on

Human Rights, and the process that led to the Inter-American Democratic Charter (IADC) in 2001 all highlighted the new consensus at the turn of the millennium.

After the Latin American debt crisis, the end of the "lost" decade of the 1980s, and in the context of globalization, economic integration objectives were adapted to a more open world trade system. CAN adopted liberalizing reforms in 1989, abandoning the inward-oriented model of development and opening up to external markets. In 1991, Brazil and Argentina spearheaded the creation of the Common Market of the South (MERCOSUR), which also included Paraguay and Uruguay.[3] This process was less favorable to open markets but in its first decade it cautiously attempted some liberalization. At that time, Mexico had begun negotiations for the North American Free Trade Area (NAFTA), while Chile, a country with a significantly open market, launched negotiations for multiple bilateral free trade agreements (FTAs). Central American countries also relaunched their integration process and created the Central American Integration System (SICA). Old 1960s product-by-product negotiations were replaced in FTA negotiations with across-the-board tariff reductions with exception lists, thus weakening tariffs as trade barriers within the region. At the same time, further commitments to liberalization in services and in investment rules and the establishment of conflict resolution mechanisms have not been realized or were only partially agreed on.

Furthermore, liberalization of markets, a more limited role of the state, and an increased role for the private sector led to the Summit of the Americas decision to negotiate a common hemispheric framework that included the USA and Canada. The process for a Free Trade Area of the Americas (FTAA), launched in 1994, was a very ambitious inter-American attempt to agree on common trade rules and disciplines. In practice, the prolonged negotiations allowed antagonist voices to develop, and the process finally stalled in 2005.

The 21st century: overlapping regional organizations

At the beginning of the 21st century, domestic policy changes in a number of countries blocked the development of open policies. Venezuela, then Ecuador and Bolivia softened or abandoned open trade policies, stalling CAN and particularly its negotiations with external partners. Venezuela withdrew from CAN in 2006, and Bolivia and Ecuador did not join Colombia and Peru in CAN negotiations for an association agreement with the European Union (EU) (although Ecuador later agreed to one on its own). Likewise, CAN members were unable to jointly negotiate an FTA with the USA, and only Peru (2009) and Colombia (2012) did so bilaterally. Given this history, CAN remains a framework in which preferences among members have already been agreed.

After economic crises in Brazil (1998–1999) and Argentina (1999–2002), MERCOSUR did not continue its process of liberalization. Indeed, the advent of new government coalitions in both countries barely maintained the framework that had previously been agreed upon, and MERCOSUR has not finished negotiations with significant world trade partners, concentrating instead on regional enlargement and accepting countries with a strong protectionist stance (Venezuela and Bolivia) as full members.

Over the last decade, Latin America and the Caribbean (LAC) have created new mechanisms of cooperation, but many do not emphasize common trade policies. Other RPGs have been promoted in the areas of conflict resolution, defense, connectivity, and even international political representation, as well as RPGs that respond to functional cooperation areas, such as health, education, the environment, and so on. As a result, there are regional organizations promoting different RPGs, sometimes multiple regional organizations focusing on similar RPG functions, although not always from the same angle.

The Union of South American Nations (UNASUR) was officially formed in 2008. Its origins lie in a Brazilian initiative[4] focusing on connectivity through the Regional Initiative for Infrastructure in South America (IIRSA), which was started in 2000. The process evolved and led to the creation of the South American Community of Nations in 2004, which sought to define a new region, South America, with a different identity to those of North and Central America. The process culminated in the creation of UNASUR, blending this new geographic definition with a wide range of new public goods, including de-emphasizing open markets (a mark of Venezuela's involvement). UNASUR covers conflict resolution (through its Council of Heads of State and Government); 22 areas of ministerial or sectoral cooperation, including institutions of mutual defense, the South American Defense Council (SADC); and represents a new regional identity (South America). UNASUR has thus been acting in parallel to the OAS or has replaced it in dealing with several conflicts—both international and domestic—within South America, such in the Bolivian regional crisis of 2008 and in the acceptance of US use of Colombian military bases in 2009. SADC is independent of existing inter-American security and defense institutions. UNASUR has created electoral observation missions, duplicating those of the OAS, and it represents South America as a region in summits with African countries and the Arab nations.[5]

Another entity, the Bolivarian Alliance for the Peoples of Our America—Peoples' Trade Treaty (ALBA-TCP) was created by Venezuela and Cuba in 2004 to promote an alternative to globalization (opposing free trade regimes) through intergovernmental cooperation. Supported by Petrocaribe—a low-cost oil transfer program—it involved 12 countries[6] in 2015. ALBA has also developed political coordination among its members in international organizations.

Other countries that were committed to taking better advantage of more open markets and increasing participation in foreign trade reached FTAs with the USA, agreements with the EU, and some Asia-Pacific countries. Central American countries thus achieved the CAFTA-DR agreement with the USA in 2004, and another with the EU signed in 2012 and provisionally applied since 2013. Peru (2009) and Colombia (2012) also reached FTAs with the

USA and association agreements with the EU (2012, provisionally applied since 2014). In 2011, countries that had been following their own path—Mexico, which signed NAFTA with the USA and Canada in 1994; and Chile, which had the largest number of bilateral FTAs[7]—joined Peru and Colombia to form the Pacific Alliance (PA), so as to further increase integration and coordination on the world economic scene. The PA countries already had mutual FTAs; all had FTAs with the USA and Canada and association agreements with the EU; and Mexico, Chile, and Peru belong to Asia-Pacific Economic Cooperation (APEC) and are parties to the Trans-Pacific Partnership (TPP), currently in the process of being approved and ratified (Nolte and Wehner 2013; Foxley and Meller 2014).

With regard to political identity, the Community of Latin American and Caribbean States (CELAC) was created in 2011, and is the first all-encompassing organization for LAC political cooperation. It has its roots in the experience of the Contadora Group, which expressed the voices of Mexico, Colombia, Venezuela, and Panama in the 1980s so as to solve Central American wars through negotiation and diplomacy. Contadora was followed in 1986 by the Rio Group (RG), a consultative political body created by the above members plus Argentina, Brazil, Peru, and Uruguay to support the new democracies and represent the Latin American point of view in world affairs. The progressive enlargement of the Rio Group to include all of the Caribbean countries led to the creation of CELAC, a new entity to represent LAC interests. While some ALBA countries see CELAC as a substitute for the OAS—minus the USA and Canada—others seek compatibilities between the two organizations. Up to now, CELAC has worked toward a broad consensus among a variety of actors with very different policy orientations and represents the LAC as a region—with a low common denominator—in dialogues with the European Union (EULAC)[8] and China (CELAC–China Forum and, particularly, the China–Latin America Foreign Ministers' Dialogue).

Regional public goods and regional organizations

The Cold War period

Regionalism was built based on two different perspectives—inter-American and Latin American—and these focused on different issue areas. The inter-American organizations, that is, the OAS and the Inter-American Treaty of Reciprocal Assistance (IATRA), promoted regional security and conflict resolution (although in the 1980s conflicting perspectives developed between the USA and a group of Latin American countries over the Central American conflicts, thus the OAS played no major role in the resolution of those conflicts).

Human rights and democracy were also founding principles of the postwar Inter-American System. Regional institutions for the promotion of human rights began to be developed at the end of the 1950s and matured in the 1980s (Goldman 2009). Inter-American institutions for the protection and promotion of democracy have been strengthened since the end of the 1980s (Pasqualucci 2003, pp.1–25 and pp.326–350).

Latin American organizations were designed to build regional and subregional economic integration starting with trade agreements. They were not able to achieve their objectives because of frequent policy shifts. During the Cold War, Latin American regions and subregional economic agreements did not include the USA.

From the end of the Cold War to the turn of the 21st century

From the late 1980s to the start of the 21st century, inter-American and Latin American organizations converged in attempts to provide several RPGs. Although the 1989 US invasion of Panama revealed a deep disagreement between the USA and Latin America, by 1991 both sides agreed to emphasize the defense of new democratic regimes and to refocus security perspectives, which led to the 2003 Mexico Declaration on Security in the Hemisphere. The Latin American reaction to 9/11 supported the concept of Hemispheric Security and expressed strong solidarity with the USA.

After Panama, cooperation for the protection and promotion of democracy developed, as a result of which OAS electoral observation machinery was strengthened, automatic responses to coup d'états were established in 1991, and, finally, the IADC was passed on September 11 2001. During this period, the Rio Group developed very active positions that converged with those of the OAS.

Convergence in the 1990s also developed in the fields of international trade and economics. Latin American countries adopted more open international economic policies, and regional agreements followed the same lines, which enabled the decision made at the Summit of the Americas to start negotiations for the FTAA, the first attempt to establish common trade rules as an RPG with an inter-American framework.

The 21st century

Regional tendencies shifted again and diverged in the first few years of the 21st century. The backlash of the shortcomings of the economic and trade reforms of the 1990s, known as the Washington Consensus; the emergence of antiglobalization efforts; and the rise to power of skeptics of trade liberalization in several LAC countries led to alternative models. The failure of the FTAA negotiations and the stalled multilateral trade negotiations led to the proliferation of trade agreements with more limited scope, in some cases including major trade powers and in others only among LAC countries. New regional organizations—Latin American, South American, and subregional—were created around different issues and had different and even conflicting identities.

How to define RPGs and how to attain them had become a subject of controversy. Difficulties in upholding a common definition of trade policies led to the stagnation of the MERCOSUR and CAN.[9]

An additional trend has been the participation of some LAC countries in transregional arrangements like the TPP. Others have become part of new global arrangements (Brazil in BRICS; and Argentina, Brazil and Mexico in the G-20), but acting independently of regional links.

The failure to build an inter-American identity through trade rules (FTAA) led to several competing Latin American projects. Subregional identities were reaffirmed (for example, in Central America and the Caribbean) while others (the Andean nations) were eroded. New overlapping and even contradictory identities begun to emerge:

- a radical antiglobalization stance (ALBA-TCP) that aimed to influence other new regional organizations;
- a South American identity (South American Community of Nations) that initially centered on Brazil, but that went on to include ALBA countries and became UNASUR;
- the transformation of the MERCOSUR project from a moderately protected market into one with strong mercantilist practices; and
- the organization of those countries with open trade views to better take advantage of globalization (the PA).[10]

Increasing complexity in the implementation of RPGs

Since the 1950s, the provision of RPGs in LAC has become increasingly complex, both because of the new issue areas covered and due to the multiple regional and subregional institutions involved. Starting with regional security and conflict resolution, the issue areas in question expanded to include regional and subregional trade, the opening up of economies to major external markets, connectivity, human rights, the protection and promotion of democracy, and external regional representation, as is shown in Table 14.1 which shows the increasing complexity in the provision of RPGs in LAC since the 1950s.

Regional security / conflict resolution

A framework for regional security and conflict resolution was provided by the OAS and was effective during the 1950s and 1960s, but it gradually became less effective and was unable to play a role during the Malvinas/Falklands War in 1982 and in the Central American wars of the 1980s (Shaw 2004, pp.59–149). Latin American countries developed independent views on the Central American situation (Arias Plan and Contadora Group) and ultimately organized themselves as the Rio Group.[11] The 1990s was a period of renewed cooperation between the USA and Latin America, with convergence between the OAS and the Rio Group around the protection of democracy. Regional security and conflict resolution became more diffuse during the 21st century (see Table 14.2).

In South America, UNASUR has joined the OAS—and in several cases practically replaced it—in dealing with conflicts, such as in Bolivia (2009) and

Table 14.1 Regional Public Goods in Latin America and the Caribbean

RPG	1950s	1960s	1970s	1980s	1990s	2000s	2010s
Regional Security/ Conflict Resolution	OAS	OAS	OAS	OAS (contested) RG	OAS + RG	OAS/UNASUR	OAS/UNASUR
Regional Trade	—	ALALC Bilateral — — CACM — CARIFTA	ALALC Bilateral CAN — CACM — CARIFTA	ALADI Bilateral CAN — CACM CARICOM	ALADI Bilateral CAN NAFTA (FTAA) SICA MERCOSUR — CARICOM	ALADI Bilateral CAN NAFTA (FTAA#) SICA MERCOSUR ALBA (contested) CARICOM	(ALADI) (Bilateral) (CAN) NAFTA – SICA (MERCOSUR) ALBA (contested) CARICOM Pacific Alliance
Economic Agreements with Major Markets	—	—	—	—	—	CAN–EU* MERCOSUR–EU*** Mexico–NAFTA Mexico–EU Chile–US Chile–EU Peru–US Peru–EU Central America–EU CAFTA–DR Mexico–Japan Chile–China China–Japan	CAN–EU** MERCOSUR–EU*** Colombia–US Chile, Peru, Mexico–TPP# Peru–China Costa Rica–China Peru–Japan

(continued)

Table 14.1 (continued)

RPG	1950s	1960s	1970s	1980s	1990s	2000s	2010s
Connectivity							
	–	–	–	–	–	IIRSA	UNASUR
						–	COSIPLAN
						PPP	Mesoamerica Project
Human Rights	[OAS]	OAS	OAS	OAS	OAS	OAS	OAS (contested)
Democracy	[OAS]	[OAS]	[OAS]	OAS	OAS+RG	OAS	OAS/UNASUR
External Regional	–	–	–	–	Rio Group	Rio Group	CELAC
Representation						UNASUR	UNASUR

Legend

Italics: minor results

* concluded only with Colombia and Peru
** concluded only with Ecuador
*** negotiations since 2005, not concluded
#negotiations not concluded
[....] formal statements
+working in the same direction
/working with different definitions

Table 14.2 Meetings of Consultation of Ministers of Foreign Affairs. OAS and the
Rio Treaty

Years	Meetings	Subject
1930s–40s	3	Hostilities in Europe/Japan attacks US
1950s	2	Communism/Caribbean–Dominican Republic
1960s	8	Cuba/Dominican Republic/strengthening alliance for progress
1970s	5	Ecuador–US tuna problem/Cuba/Costa Rica–Nicaragua
1980s	3	Ecuador–Peru/Malvinas-Falklands/Panama
1990s	1	Requested, no meeting
2000s	3	9/11 terrorist attack/Ecuador–Colombia
2010s	3	Nicaragua–Costa Rica/Ecuador–UK/Argentina debt

Source: Compiled by author from OAS website

Ecuador (2010), or has taken a conflicting position, as in Paraguay (2012).
Recently the Venezuela–Colombia conflict over border closure was referred to
UNASUR and has been blocked for consideration by the OAS. Nevertheless,
the OAS has started to deal with new regional security problems such as drugs
and citizen security. It is relevant to note the renewed importance of the
Bogotá Pact—an inter-American instrument—and the International Court of
Justice in the solution of 12 border delimitation disputes and other interna-
tional disputes in recent years.[12]

Finally, it is also important to remember that LAC is the only region in the
world that has avoided international armed conflict since 1995 with the conclusion of the brief Ecuador–Peru territorial dispute hostilities.

Regional trade

As was discussed above, regional trade agreements from the 1950s to the 1980s
were Latin American attempts to create regimes to provide RPGs. But the
first region-wide arrangement, ALALC, did not reach its goals and in 1980
become simply a framework to coordinate a web of mainly bilateral agreements (ALADI). The Andean Pact, formed in 1969, redesigned regional
integration and included industrial policies, limits on foreign investment, and
preferences for less developed countries. But it was unable to keep its policies
in place and abandoned its foreign investment policy and industrial projects
within a decade.

Other subregional organizations followed different paths: while CACM
had initial success, controversies over the distribution of the costs and benefits
of the process led to paralysis, followed by a decade of civil wars in Central
America. The English-speaking Caribbean expanded the membership of its
FTA (CARIFTA) and evolved into an expanded incomplete common market
(CARICOM).

Substantial reforms to international economic policies in the 1990s led
to openings to external markets, increased importance of the private sector
and a more limited role of the state, financial prudence, and macroeconomic

Table 14.3 Latin American and Caribbean Exports to the World (in billions of US$ and average annual growth rates, 1995–2015).

	1995	2000	2005	2010	2015	AAGR (%) 1995–2015
LATIN AMERICA AND THE CARIBBEAN	**223.4**	**354.8**	**565.2**	**867.7**	**899.5**	**7.2**
MESOAMERICA	**91.7**	**185.8**	**240.6**	**333.1**	**424.6**	**8.0**
Mexico	79.8	166.4	214.2	298.5	380.8	8.1
Central America	**11.9**	**19.3**	**26.4**	**34.6**	**43.9**	**6.7**
Costa Rica	2.8	5.5	6.7	9.0	9.4	6.3
El Salvador	1.7	2.9	3.4	4.5	5.5	6.2
Guatemala	1.9	2.7	5.4	8.5	10.8	9.0
Honduras	0.7	1.1	2.0	3.1	4.3	9.8
Nicaragua	0.5	0.6	1.7	3.4	4.8	11.9
Panama	0.6	0.8	1.0	0.7	0.7	0.9
Dominican Republic	3.8	5.7	6.3	5.4	8.4	4.1
SOUTH AMERICA	**126.3**	**161.5**	**310.6**	**517.6**	**458.1**	**6.7**
Argentina	21.0	26.4	40.4	68.2	56.8	5.1
Bolivia	1.1	1.5	2.9	6.9	8.7	10.8
Brazil	46.5	55.1	118.5	201.9	191.1	7.3
Chile	16.4	18.2	38.6	67.4	62.0	6.9
Colombia	9.8	13.1	21.2	39.8	35.6	6.7
Ecuador	4.3	4.8	10.1	17.5	18.4	7.5
Paraguay	2.0	2.2	3.2	6.5	8.4	7.4
Peru	5.4	6.8	17.8	35.8	33.4	9.5
Uruguay	2.1	2.3	3.4	6.7	7.3	6.4
Venezuela	17.6	31.2	54.5	66.9	36.4	3.7
CARIBBEAN	**5.5**	**7.5**	**14.0**	**17.0**	**16.8**	**5.7**

Source: IDB Integration and Trade Sector based on INTradeBID, United Nations Comtrade Database, World Trade Organization, and national sources.

Notes: AAGR represents average annual growth rate (%); Caribbean aggregate includes: Bahamas, Barbados, Belize, Guyana, Haiti, Jamaica, Suriname, and Trinidad and Tobago. Only the regional total is reported to minimize year-to-year variability at the national level.

stability, leading to changes in institutions of integration: CACM became SICA, the Andean Pact was transformed into CAN, and a new organization with a cautious approach to liberalization, MERCOSUR, was founded. At the same time, a new project, NAFTA, was agreed among Mexico, Canada, and the USA—the first trade agreement beyond Latin American borders—and several bilateral FTAs were reached under the umbrella of ALADI. A common economic vision led to the start of almost a decade of negotiations for the FTAA.

By the beginnings of the 2000s these integration schemes were changing. SICA, aiming to enter US and EU markets, was able to maintain and implement open policies. CAN was shaken by policy shifts in Venezuela, Bolivia and Ecuador, and MERCOSUR lost its appetite for open economic policies after economic crises in Argentina and Brazil.

How have these changes affected the actual trade performance of LAC? Table 14.3 shows the growth in exports to the world from LAC countries from 1995–2015. During this period, LAC's overall exports quadrupled, growing at an average rate of 7.2 percent per year. Mexico's exports grew more rapidly (8.1 percent average annual growth) than the rest of LAC (6.6 percent).

At the subregional level, Central American exports grew 6.7 percent per year between 1995 and 2015, with those of the five CACM members growing at an average rate of 7.9 percent. Exports of South America, comprised of CAN, MERCOSUR, and Chile, similarly grew at an annual average of 6.7 percent, and those of the Caribbean at 5.7 percent.

Together, exports of the Pacific Alliance countries (Chile, Colombia, Mexico, and Peru) increased by 7.9 percent annually, although this largely reflects Mexico's performance as the largest trading economy in the region.

Economic agreements with major markets

These were perceived as an RPG by some, while others rejected them or conditioned their negotiations to important concessions—mainly, but not only, in agriculture—of major trade powers that remain off the table. Thus, we have Central American countries reaching agreements with the USA and the EU; CAN is divided; Peru and Colombia have bilateral agreements with the USA and the EU; Ecuador only has an agreement with the EU; Mexico entered NAFTA with the USA and Canada and has an agreement with the EU; and Chile did the same bilaterally.

On the other hand, neither Bolivia nor Venezuela has pursued agreements with major external markets, and although MERCOSUR started negotiations with the EU, after more than a decade it has not been able to forge a trade pact. Although negotiations were resumed in 2016, an agreement still seems far from being reached. Indeed, MERCOSUR does not have trade agreements with any major commercial powers.

If we look at the driver for global trade today, the Asia-Pacific countries have 31 bilateral FTAs with LAC countries, two preferential trade agreements, and one multilateral transpacific trade agreement.[13]

In sum, today's scenario involves, on the one hand, Central America and the PA developing schemes of (sub)regional integration linked through FTAs and transregional agreements with major markets, the PA more deeply so than Central America. On the other hand, MERCOSUR trade rules are not being applied for Venezuela, and Bolivia has not fully implemented its accession. The current strong division over the Brazilian presidency during the second half of 2016 is raising questions about the institutional basis of MERCOSUR and risking the bloc's future (MercoPress 2016). Furthermore, while the four original members have accepted a dialogue to find convergences with the PA, Paraguay and Uruguay are already observers of the PA, the president of Argentina attended the recent PA Summit in Puerto Varas, and Uruguay is close to signing an FTA with Chile. Finally, ALBA has lost steam after the decline in oil prices and the crisis in Venezuela. Its government-to-government projects lack financial resources; its economies are following divergent paths; but political solidarity and common positions in many multilateral fora still remain.[14]

Connectivity

In the 21st century, connectivity is considered to be an RPG that is essential to integration. As previously mentioned, the South American Summit convened in 2000 by the president of Brazil led to the creation of IIRSA, which included the 12 countries of South America and would coordinate transportation, energy, and communication projects. In 2011, IIRSA became the technical body for the South American Council of Infrastructure and Planning (COSIPLAN) within UNASUR. COSIPLAN has agreed on the Strategic Action Plan 2012–2022, and in 2014 established priorities within its portfolio of 477 national, 95 binational, and five trinational projects, which represent a total investment of US$163.32 billion, organized into nine geographical Integration and Development Hubs. Some 12.4% of those projects had been completed by 2014 (US$ 20.35 billion) (UNASUR/COSIPLAN 2014).

In 2001, the president of Mexico launched the Plan Puebla-Panama, which included nine countries from Mexico to Colombia (subsequently joined by the Dominican Republic) with projects related to connectivity and the extraction of natural resources. In 2008 the Mesoamerican Project was launched centering on health, energy, transportation, trade facilitation, sustainable development, human development, tourism, disaster prevention and mitigation, and security (Mesoamerican Integration and Development Project 2015). A supplementary regional electric market has been created and the Central American Electrical Interconnection System (SIEPAC), which has a capacity for about 5% of Central America's total demand, has been operational since 2014 (Sáez 2014). Nonetheless, a stronger regulatory framework and the extension of lines to connect Mexico and Colombia (the tenth member country) would significantly enhance the regional electricity market (O'Connor and Viscidi 2015).

Human rights

The American Declaration of the Rights and Duties of Man was approved in 1948, at the same time as the OAS Charter, and preceded the Universal Declaration of Human Rights. Nevertheless, it took more than a decade to create the IACHR, which was established in 1959, and more than another decade to strengthen its powers. The IACHR promotes the observance and protection of human rights in the Americas, and its powers have been progressively increased by the decisions and actions of the OAS.

The IACHR began to play an active role through its visits *in loco*. The first visit was in 1965, following the US invasion of the Dominican Republic, and five more missions followed over the course of the 1960s. There were five more *in loco* visits in the 1970s, 23 visits in the 1980s, and 41 during the 1990s, before the number went down to 13 in the 2000s and 3 in the 2010s.

The IACHR also has issued 64 Country Reports since the 1960s, which analyze the situation in different countries and make recommendations to improve respect for human rights. In some cases, these reports have had significant impact and generated international pressure to protect human rights.

Since the 1970s, in its Annual Report to the General Assembly of the OAS, the IACHR has informed on human rights violations in some countries in addition to its country reports. From 1978 to 1994, the Annual Report included a chapter on the status of human rights in several states, highlighting the situation in 14 specific countries. A third step has been followed from 1996 onward: the Annual Report included a chapter reporting countries with human rights practices that require special attention, following criteria previously defined by the IACHR. Over 19 years, nine countries have been included in this method of reporting to the political body of the OAS.

Table 14.4 Inter-American Commission on Human Rights (1960–2014). Protection of Human Rights in Countries

Years	1960s	1970s	1980s	1990s	2000s	2010s
Missions *in loco*	5	5	23	41	13	3
Country Reports	6	13	15	15	12	2
Annual Report Chapter*	–	8	55	39	38	16

Source: compiled by author based on OAS website.

* The IAHRC Annual Report includes a chapter on the status of human rights in certain countries from 1978 to 1994. After spelling out its criteria, from 1996 on it included a chapter on countries with human rights practices that require special attention.

Besides reporting, the IACHR was authorized in 1965 to examine complaints or petitions regarding specific cases of human rights violations. The IACHR has received over 19,420 petitions, opening more than 12,000 cases. During the years 2010 and 2014 alone, 9,011 petitions were received by the IACHR and 1,082 were processed. In the same period, 16 Merit Reports[15] were published, 39 friendly settlements were reached between victims and states, and 81 cases were sent to the Inter-American Court of Justice. As part of these processes, 2,140 requests for precautionary measures were received by the IACHR, and in 219 cases precautionary measures were granted.

The Inter-American Court of Human Rights—an international tribunal with jurisdiction—was created in 1969 and has been in place since 1978. The court made its first decisions on contentious cases in 1987

Table 14.5 Decisions of the Inter-American Court of Human Rights (1987–2015), by Type of Decisions, Countries, and Period

	Decisions and Judgements	Provisional Measures	Monitors on Compliance
Country			
Argentina	20	19	15
Barbados	2	4	2
Bolivia	6	–	9
Brazil	7	32	8
Chile	8	–	13
Colombia	26	104	43
Costa Rica	2	7	5
Dominica	–	–	–
DominicanRepublic	5	15	4
Ecuador	22	8	29
ElSalvador	9	18	8
Grenada	–	–	–
Guatemala	31	90	52
Guyana	–	–	–
Haiti	2	6	–
Honduras	17	17	14
Jamaica	–	–	–
Mexico	10	38	14
Nicaragua	6	4	9
Panama	7	1	16
Paraguay	8	3	24
Peru	68	60	93
Suriname	9	–	6
TrinidadandTobago	5	18	2
Uruguay	3	–	1
Venezuela	21	91	17
Period			
1987–1999	63	93	2
2000–2015	231	443	382
1987–2015	294	536	384

Source: compiled by the author based on the Inter-American Court of Human Rights website, 2015

(on preliminary objections) and in 1988 (on merits).[16] A significant part of the region—25 countries—has enjoyed the protection of this supra-national system. Table 14.5 shows how the court has taken cases from different countries and how its work has been strengthened. The court's expanded role can be seen by comparing the number of decisions taken in 1987–1999 with those taken in the 2000s. Particular importance should be placed on the orders on provisionary measures and the monitoring of compliance with its judgments.

The IACHR system has been developed to provide human rights as an RPG: the commission has oversight over the whole hemisphere, while the court exercises jurisdiction over many countries. In the last decade, there have been attempts to limit their powers and even to question them. These ini-tiatives came mainly—although not exclusively—from ALBA countries, and two countries have withdrawn from its jurisdiction (Trinidad and Tobago in 1998 and Venezuela in 2012). But the system is the only regional legitimate instrument to promote and protect human rights while exercising jurisdiction. Extending the court's jurisdiction over all hemispheric countries would rein-force this RPG (Barretto Maia et al. 2015).

Democracy

As a common value, democracy is central to the preamble of the Charter of the OAS, but the creation of institutions to promote and protect did not come about until the 1990s. Following the end of authoritarian experiences in South America and the civil wars of Central America, the Rio Group and the OAS began to work toward protecting democratic regimes. OAS electoral observa-tion missions began in the 1960s and they were strengthened and expanded in the 1990s.[17]

The Santiago Commitment to Democracy and the Renewal of the Inter-American System was adopted in 1991 by OAS resolution 1080 (XXI). It created an automatic response to irregular interruption of democratic political institutional processes in any OAS member state. This opened a space for the collective protection of democratic processes. Resolution 1080 was applied during the 1990s and led to the approval of the IADC as described above.

Nevertheless, in the new millennium, the consensual values of the 1990s begun to be de-emphasized and even contested. Difficulties in the enforcement of the IADC followed the coup attempt against President Chávez in Venezuela in 2003, and the coup against President Zelaya in Honduras in 2009. The adop-tion of democratic clauses in other regional organizations (MERCOSUR, UNASUR) reaffirmed common purposes, but parallel mechanisms for imple-mentation allowed different reactions to circumstances in Paraguay in 2010 and in Ecuador in 2012. Furthermore, the effective electoral observation system at the OAS was duplicated in the 2010s by UNASUR's follow-up ("accompaniment") system, weakening international supervision of electoral procedures, which is key to fair and transparent elections (Heine and Weiffen 2015).

In sum, regional institutions to protect democracy as RPG have played a positive role in avoiding coup d'états, but they have been less able to support democratic practices when illiberal forms of government are exercised.

External regional representation

During the Cold War, there was no organized external representation of the region in the world system, showing the limits of regionalism during that period. Instead, inter-American organizations operated within the region. At the UN, a formal Latin American Group operated as a regional group for the formal work of the organization. Only during the 1990s did the Rio Group begin to establish formal dialogues with other regional groups and major powers at the UN, projecting an incipient regional Latin American identity. The formal dialogue of the Rio Group with the European Community in 1991 expanded into the EULAC Summit in 1999 (including Central American and Caribbean countries) and into the CELAC-EU mechanism after the creation of CELAC in 2011. It is important to remember that EULAC/EU–CELAC is mainly a biregional framework for political dialogue and that the EU has reached formal association agreements only with subregional entities or on a bilateral basis. CELAC has also established a forum with the People's Republic of China, and while there is a Chinese–Latin American policy, no common negotiating position has been reached with China by any Latin American country. In the 21st century, external regional representations were developed by UNASUR with the African Union (Africa–South America Summit, ASA) and with the Arab League (Summit of South American-Arab Countries, ASPA). Frameworks for dialogue were also established, but within South America only Brazil has an effective African policy, and the dialogue with the Arab League became paralyzed with the civil wars in Libya and Syria.[18]

Coordination (or the lack of coordination) in seeking RPGs

One further point worth highlighting is the increasing complexity arising from differing definitions of RPGs, overlapping memberships in international entities that seek to create those RPGs, and the low level of coordination among them.

Table 14.6 shows the multiple channels that work on RPGs: there are 120 ministerial and high-level meetings (M&HLM) in eight regional and subregional organizations with different and overlapping scopes. One can also see that regional (inter-American, Latin American, and South American) organizations are not working on common regional trade rules, nor on external trade negotiations—the traditional engine of integration. As has been noted, the FTAA failed in 2005; CELAC only acts as an umbrella for subregional and country negotiations with third parties (EU and China); and UNASUR is not seeking further trade integration because of the contrasting views of its

Table 14.6 Ministerial and High-Level Meetings by RPG and Regional and Subregional Organizations

	International Organization	OAS & SOA	CELAC	UNASUR	Mercosur	CAN	SICA	CARICOM	Pacific Alliance
RPGs									
Security/Conflict Resolution	Ministerial and high-level meeting								
	Foreign Policy	X	X	X	X	X	X	X	
	Defense	X	X WG	X SADC			X		
	Government/Public Security	*		X			X		
Trade & Integration	Trade	*	WG PALC	X	X	X	X	X	X
Human Rights	Human Rights	XIAHRS			X 1			X	X
Democracy	Democracy/Electoral Observation	X		X			MP		
Connectivity	Connectivity: Roads & Energy			IIRSA			MP	X	X 2
International Political Identity	External Political Representation		X	X	X		X	X	
Agreements with major markets	Economic agreements		X 3				X	X	X 4
Governance	Justice	X	X WG		X	X		X	
	Anti-Corruption	X	X	X WG					
Economic Cooperation (other than in Security/Conflict Resolution)	Treasury & Monetary Affairs	X 5	X	X 6	X	X	X	X	
	Industry/Development		X			X		X	X
	Infrastructure/Public Works/Transportation		X	X	X	X		X	X
	Agriculture	X IICA	X		X	X	X	X	
	Tourism	X	X		X	X	X	X	
	Energy	X	X	X	X	X	X	X	
	Sustainable Development/Environment	X	X WG	X	X	X	X	X	
	Science & Technology	X	X WG	X	X	X	X	X	

(continued)

Table 14.6 (continued)

International Organization		OAS & SOA	CELAC	UNASUR	Mercosur	CAN	SICA	CARICOM	Pacific Alliance
Social Affairs	**Labor**	X	X		X	X		X	
	Social Development	X	X	X	X	X	X	X	
	Women/Gender	X CIM	X WG		X	X	X	X	
	Health	X PAHO		X	X	X	X	X	
	Education	X	X	X	X	X	X	X	
	Culture	X	X	X	X	X	X		
	Drugs	X CICAD	X	X	X	X WG7			

Notes: X: Ministerial; X WG: High Level Working Group; MP: Mesoamerican Project. 1: HR promotion; 2: PA has 20 observer countries; 3: Acts as a political framework for agreements with EU and China; 4: Bilaterally and transregionally; 5: Finance Ministers meet around IDB meetings; 6: Banco del Sur is a unfinalized project around UNASUR; *: FTTA negotiations failed; X7: There are other CELAC Working Groups on migration, illicit trafficking of small arms, people of African descent, disaster risk management, planning and cooperation; SADC: South American Defense Council; PALC: Latin American and the Caribbean tariff preference; IAHRS: Inter American Human Rights System; IIRSA: Regional Initiative for Infrastructure in South America; IICA: Inter American Institute for Cooperation on Agriculture; CIM: Inter American Commission on Women; PAHO: Pan American Health Organization; CICAD: Inter American Drug Abuse Control Commission;

member countries. Entities such as CELAC and UNASUR have preferred to seek other forms of economic cooperation (nontrade related) and social cooperation, which has been labeled postliberal regionalism (Serbin, Martínez, and Ramanzini 2012).

UNASUR, CELAC, and MERCOSUR are three strongly overlapping organizations[19] working in the same areas: there are 17 M&HLMs in eight areas of economic cooperation (in areas other than trade) and another 17 M&HLMs in seven areas of social affairs. If we add the 32 M&HLMs of the subregional entities (CAN, SICA, and CARICOM), there are at total of 66 M&HLMs in LAC focusing on 15 areas of economic cooperation and social affairs. There are an additional 14 inter-American M&HLMs, for a total of 80 M&HLMs within the Americas to deal with these 15 areas. However, these eight international organizations and entities do not work in coordinated fashion (ECLAC 2014a).

RPGs: institutions, goals, and implementation

The evolution of the regional system over the last 70 years has led to the emergence of many regional organizations based on different identities (inter-American, Latin American and Caribbean, Central and South American) that seek RPGs. At the time of their creation, inter-American and Latin American organizations focused on different RPGs (mainly security and trade, respectively); however, during a short period in the 1990s, their goals expanded and intersected, and implementation in many cases was mutually reinforcing (human rights, democracy, and trade).

The current situation is complex: more regional organizations with overlapping goals coexist, but definitions of RPG do not necessarily coincide. OAS and UNASUR compete as *loci* for conflict prevention and resolution (Sanahuja and Verdes-Montenegro 2014).

The impressive development of the Inter-American System to protect human rights when national governments responsible for their enforcement are unable or unwilling to comply is still incomplete. Although the IACHR oversees the entire western hemisphere, its court is able to exercise jurisdiction only in countries that have consented to it. However, the universalization of the court's jurisdiction is a condition for strengthening the system. Greater resources and avoiding attacks from governments willing to weaken the system are very important in this regard.

The protection of democracy has also become a contested area between inter-American and South American organizations: the process that led to the IADC is now weakened, and there is no collective consideration of what constitutes a breakdown in democracy unless the government concerned accepts the intervention of a regional institution. Furthermore, there is now an alternative to the effective OAS electoral observation missions in the form of UNASUR's "accompaniment" missions.

Regarding common trade rules, after the failure of FTAA negotiations, the region has not one but several organizations. The PA continues to liberalize trade and strengthen participation in significant international markets through FTAs. In Central America, SICA/SIECA follows a similar strategy on a smaller scale. MERCOSUR has avoided further in-group trade liberalization and has not been able to agree on opening trade up with the main international markets. The incorporation of some ALBA countries into MERCOSUR raises questions as to whether its future direction will be one of reluctance to accept free trade or a decision to follow the new economic policies adopted by Argentina and (still pending) changes in Brazil. The MERCOSUR founders' acceptance of the PA proposal to find convergent forms of cooperation to overcome their differences and promote regional integration is today a potential route for further integration.

Connectivity (in infrastructure, energy, and telecommunications) as an RPG has been promoted by two major projects: IIRSA in South America and the Mesoamerican Project in Central America plus Mexico and Colombia. Although some results have been achieved, a great deal more needs to be done, particularly in terms of harmonizing rules to take full advantage of the physical infrastructure that has been developed.

To make RPGs possible, it will be indispensable to work toward a common definition of goals among existing regional organizations (ECLAC 2014b) and to develop specific projects in areas like connectivity (Perry 2013). Eliminating overlap and improving coordination in implementation, particularly common regulatory frameworks, are also musts for effective regional cooperation to provide RPGs.

Notes

1 Public goods have been promoted in Latin America both by regional organizations (Latin American Association of Free Trade, IDB) and subregional organizations (Central American Common Market, Andean Community, and CARICOM), as well as subregional banks (CABEI, CAF, and the FONPLATA integration fund), as previously explained.

2 The notion of Latin America was developed in the mid-19th century, but was institutionalized only in the creation of the United Nations' Economic Commission for Latin America (ECLA) in 1948. (Briceño Ruiz, Rivalora Puntigliano, and Casas Gragea 2012).

3 On March 26 1991, the four countries signed the Treaty of Asunción establishing the MERCOSUR.

4 Historically, Brazil only prioritized relations with Latin America for a short period. The Brazilian Empire perceived itself as having more affinities with Europe, and at the end of the 19th century the Republic of Brazil tried to enable the newly formed Inter-American System, an unwritten alliance with the USA and a South American subsystem. Brazil sided with the USA during both world wars, and only after World War II did Brazil adopt an overly Latin American identity, which extended to the military coup of 1964. With the return to democratic rule, Brazilian foreign policy once more began to focus on development-oriented and Latin American concerns. In 1990, following the creation of the MERCOSUR and in answer to NAFTA negotiations, Brazil begun to rapidly emphasize a new South American identity, one that was in line with its economic development model and global aspirations (Villafañe G. Santos 2014).

5 On UNASUR's self-image, see Ministerio de Relaciones Exteriores y Movilidad Humana de Ecuador (2014).
6 The ALBA member countries are Antigua and Barbuda, Bolivia, Cuba, Dominica, Ecuador, Grenada, Nicaragua, Saint Kitts and Nevis, Saint Lucia, Saint Vincent and the Grenadines, Suriname, and Venezuela. Seven ALBA countries also belong to CARICOM, four to UNASUR, one to SICA, two to CAN, and two to MERCOSUR (several countries belong to more than one subregional organization).
7 Chile has FTAs in force with 17 Latin American countries (1993–2010) plus an FTA with Canada (1997) and the USA (2004). Chile's average effective tariff with Latin America in 2014 was 0.98%.
8 The 2nd EU–CELAC/8th EU–LAC Summit held in Brussels in June 2015 has been described as a relationship running at multiple speeds: cruise speed with the PA, along old parameters with Central American and Caribbean countries, stalled with MERCOSUR, and marked by divisions and criticisms regarding the ALBA countries (Nuñez 2015). One could add a fifth speed: starting to move forward with Cuba.
9 The Andean Community, which includes Bolivia, Colombia, Ecuador, and Peru.
10 On the complex role of Brazil in these processes, see Malamud and Rodríguez (2014).
11 The Rio Group was mainly a political mechanism; it also played a role in conflict resolution as in the case of Colombian bombardment of the border with Ecuador in March 2008.
12 Mexico–US; Costa Rica–Nicaragua (4), Peru–Chile; Honduras–Brazil; Ecuador–Colombia; Bolivia–Chile (2), Nicaragua–Colombia (2).
13 Chile has 11 FTAs with Asia Pacific countries, Mexico has 6, Peru 5, Costa Rica 2, Panama 2, Colombia 1, El Salvador 1, Guatemala 1, Honduras 1, and Nicaragua 1; while Chile and MERCOSUR (Argentina, Brazil, Paraguay, and Uruguay) have PTAs with India. Chile and Peru belong to the P4 (with Brunei, New Zealand, and Singapore) while awaiting the ratification of the TTP.
14 ALBA countries show significant differences in their international economic relations: Nicaragua is a very special case, while the country uses the antiglobalization rhetoric of ALBA and follows their foreign policies it is also party to the market-oriented CAFTA-DR agreement with the United States, is an active member of SICA, and keeps a sound working relationship with the IMF. Ecuador's openness has been more limited but it has an association agreement with the EU. Cuba is trying to get foreign investment but remains a very centralized economy. Bolivia has had a strong process of development, mixing state and markets, structuring its foreign politics around global markets (mining) and Andean preferences. Its participation in MERCOSUR has mainly been political. The Caribbean's ALBA members have principally been recipients of Petrocaribe funds.
15 Merit Reports are decisions taken by the Inter-American Commission on Human Rights which contain conclusions about whether the facts of the case constitute human rights violations.
16 Today 23 countries are state parties to the Inter-American Convention of Human Rights. Eight Caribbean countries, the United States, Canada, Cuba, and Venezuela are not subject to the jurisdiction of the court. The Inter-American Commission on Human Rights, an organ of the OAS Charter, supervises human rights in all parties of the OAS.
17 Electoral observation missions have been sent to almost all OAS countries. Seven missions took place in the 1960s, eight in the 1970s, nine in the 1980s, 47 in the

1990s, 60 in the 2000s, and 37 in the 2010s. Only Barbados, Brazil, Canada, Chile, the United States, Trinidad and Tobago, and Uruguay have not received one.

18 There are important relations between Japan and LAC (in trade, finance, official development assistance, and particularly in investment), but they have followed a bilateral pattern. The 1990s Japan Rio Group dialogue never developed into a new forum.

19 MERCOSUR has five full members (Argentina, Brazil, Paraguay, Uruguay, and Venezuela), and Bolivia is in the process of becoming a full member. Chile, Colombia, Ecuador, and Peru are associate members, and Guyana and Suriname have framework agreements with it. These 12 countries together form UNASUR, and all are also among the 27 members of CELAC.

References

Barretto Maia, Camila, Edurne Cárdenas, Daniel Cerqueira, Raísa Cetra, Gastón Chillier, Mariana González Armijo, et al. 2015. *Desafíos del sistema interamericano de derechos humanos. Nuevos tiempos, viejos retos.* Bogotá: Centro de Estudios de Derecho, Justicia y Sociedad, Dejusticia. www.dplf.org/sites/default/files/desafc3ados20del20sistema20interamericano20de20derechos20humanos20versic 3b3n20final20pdf20para20web-2.pdf

Briceño Ruiz, José, Andrés Rivalora Puntigliano, and Angel M. Casas Gragea, eds. 2012. *Integración Latinoamericana y Caribeña.* Madrid: Fondo de Cultura Económica.

ECLAC (United Nations Economic Commission for Latin America and the Caribbean). 2014a. *Regional Integration: Towards an Inclusive Value Chain Strategy.* Santiago: ECLAC.

ECLAC (United Nations Economic Commission for Latin America and the Caribbean). 2014b. *La Alianza del Pacífico y el MERCOSUR. Hacia la convergencia en la diversidad.* Santiago: ECLAC.

Fawcett, Louise. 2013. "The History and Concept of Regionalism." UNU-CRIS Working Paper W-2013/5. Bruges: UNU Institute on Comparative Regional Integration Studies. http://cris.unu.edu/sites/cris.unu.edu/files/W-2013-5.pdf

Fioramonti, Lorenzo. 2014. "The Evolution of Supranational Regionalism: From Top-down Regulatory Governance to Sustainability Regions?" UNU-CRIS Working Papers W-2014/2. Bruges: UNU Institute on Comparative Regional Integration Studies. http://cris.unu.edu/sites/cris.unu.edu/files/W-2014-2.pdf

Foxley, Alejandro, and Patricio Meller, eds. 2014. *Alianza del Pacífico: en el proceso de integración Latinoamericana.* Santiago: Uqbar Editores.

Goldman, Robert K. 2009. "History and Action: The Inter-American Human Rights System and the Role of the Inter-American Commission on Human Rights." *Human Rights Quarterly* 31, no. 4 (November): 856–887.

Heine, Jorge, and Brigitte Weiffen. 2015. *21st Century Democracy Promotion in the Americas.* London and New York: Routledge Global Institutions.

Malamud, Andrés, and Julio C. Rodríguez. 2014. "A caballo entre la región y el mundo: el dualismo creciente de la política exterior brasileña." *Desarrollo Económico* 54, no. 212 (May–August).

Mandelbaum, Michael. 2006. *The Case for Goliath.* New York: Public Affairs.

MercoPress. 2016. "Mercosur in a State of Disarray; Venezuela's Presidency Disavowed by Argentina, Brazil and Paraguay." August 2. http://en.mercopress.com/2016/08/02/mercosur-in-a-state-of-disarray-venezuela-s-presidency-disavowed-by-argentina-brazil-and-paraguay

Mesoamerican Integration and Development Project. 2015. www.proyectomeso america.org

Ministerio de Relaciones Exteriores y Movilidad Humana de Ecuador. 2014. Report from the Seminario Internacional Integración y Convergencia en América del Sur, Quito, December 3–4. Quito: RisperGraf.

Nolte, Detlef, and Leslie Wehner. 2013. "The Pacific Alliance Casts Its Cloud over Latin America." *Giga Focus* 8.

O'Connor, Rebecca, and Lisa Viscidi. 2015. "Guatemalan Leadership and the Regional Electricity Market." *The Dialogue Blog*, August 20. www.thedialogue.org/ blogs/2015/08/guatemalan-leadership-t

Pasqualucci, Jo M. 2003. *The Practice and Procedure of the Inter-American Court of Human Rights*. London: Cambridge University Press.

Perry, Guillermo. 2013. "Regional Public Goods in Finance, Trade and Infrastructure." Documentos CEDE No 43. Bogotá: Centro de Estudios Socio Económico, Facultad de Economía, Universidad de Los Andes.

Sáez, Raúl E. 2014. "Notes on Regional Integration of Electricity Markets." Unpublished draft, October 2014.

Sanahuja, José Antonio, and Francisco J. Verdes-Montenegro Escánez. 2014. "Seguridad y defensa en Suramérica: regionalismo, cooperación y autonomía en el marco de UNASUR." In *¿Atlántico vs. Pacífico?: América Latina y el Caribe, los cambios regionales y los desafíos globales. Anuario de Integración Regional en América Latina y el Caribe*. Buenos Aires: CRIES.

Serbin, Andrés, Laneydi Martínez, and Haroldo Ramanzini Junior, eds. 2012. *El regionalismo "post-liberal" en América Latina y el Caribe. Nuevos actores, nuevos temas, nuevos desafíos, Anuario de Integración Regional en América Latina y el Caribe*. Buenos Aires: CRIES.

Shaw, Carolyn M. 2004. *Cooperation, Conflict and Consensus in the Organization of the American States*. New York: Palgrave Macmillan.

UNASUR/COSIPLAN (Union of South American Nations/South American Infrastructure and Planning Council). 2014. Project Portfolio 2014. www.iirsa. org/admin_iirsa_web/Uploads/Documents/cn25_montevideo14_Cartera_ COSIPLAN_2014_eng.pdf

Van Langenhove, Luk. 2003. "Theorising Regionhood." UNU/CRIS Working Paper W-2003/1. Bruges: UNU Institute on Comparative Regional Integration Studies. http://cris.unu.edu/sites/cris.unu.edu/files/W-2003-1.pdf

Villafañe G. Santos, Luis Claudio. 2014. *A América do Sul no Discurso Diplomático Brasileiro*. Brasilia: Fundação Alexandre de Gusmão do Ministério das Relações Exteriores.

15 Asia's financial stability as a regional and global public good

Masahiro Kawai[1]

Introduction: financial stability as a public good

Financial stability is an essential public good for any economy, as without it economic activity, growth, and employment are severely disrupted. Both the Asian financial crisis of 1997–98 and the global financial crisis of 2007–09 showed the large negative impact that crises can have on both crisis-originating economies and others affected by these.

As Asian economies have grown rapidly over the past 15 years and their collective GDP accounted for 31% of the world's GDP in 2015, up from 25% in 2000, maintaining financial stability in Asia is crucial to the stability of the global economy. This means that systemically important Asian economies, such as China, Japan, the Association of Southeast Asian Nations (ASEAN) countries as a group, and India need to pursue policies to keep their own financial systems sound and stable.

Financial stability in any region of the world would require an effective regional financial arrangement, which complements the global financial arrangement led by the International Monetary Fund (IMF). In 2000, following the Asian financial crisis of 1997–98, the ASEAN+3 countries (the ten member states of ASEAN plus China, Japan, and the Republic of Korea) launched the Chiang Mai Initiative (CMI), which was a network of bilateral currency swap arrangements, and the Economic Review and Policy Dialogue (ERPD), which was a regional surveillance process. The CMI and ERPD have been strengthened over time, particularly since the global financial crisis, including the multilateralization of the CMI (renamed the Chiang Mai Initiative Multilateralization, CMIM) and the establishment of the ASEAN+3 Macroeconomic Research Office (AMRO) as a surveillance unit for the CMIM and ERPD.

This paper explores the challenges faced by the CMIM, ERPD, and AMRO to promote regional financial stability. Several questions are posed:

- Does Asia have the capacity and expertise to manage possible future financial crises that might hit emerging and developing economies in the region?
- What needs to be done to make the CMIM, ERPD, and AMRO truly functional and effective?
- What type of relationship should the CMIM and AMRO establish with the IMF?

The paper is organized as follows. Section Two summarizes lessons learned from past financial crises, such as the Asian and global financial crises, and argues how regional financial arrangements can help promote financial stability at the national and regional levels. Section Three reviews the evolution of the CMI/CMIM, ERPD, and AMRO. Section Four discusses the experiences of regional financial arrangements developed in other parts of the world, particularly in Europe, to draw lessons for Asia. Section Five identifies challenges for the CMIM, ERPD, and AMRO and provides possible future directions, including their relationships with the IMF. Section Six concludes the paper.

Lessons from past financial crises

The most important lessons learned from past financial crises is that policy makers should prevent a financial crisis from taking place in the first place. The key principle should be: "Preventing a crisis is better than curing one." This entails the prevention or mitigation of the buildup of macroeconomic and financial vulnerabilities at the national level, which could lead to systemic risk and eventually a financial crisis. Once a financial crisis breaks out, appropriate crisis responses would be needed to keep a crisis from exerting significant negative influences on the economy and financial system. When a financial crisis evolves into a full-blown economic crisis and damages the whole economy and the financial sector, crisis resolution measures are needed. See Table 15.1 for a comprehensive summary of policy lessons learned from the Asian and global financial crises. Appropriate national measures would be the first priority, to be complemented by global and regional efforts.

Crisis prevention

The major preventive mechanisms would include: (i) implementing sound macroeconomic management (i.e. monetary, fiscal, exchange rate, and public debt) policies to avoid the buildup of systemic vulnerabilities such as excessive economic booms, credit expansion, and asset price bubbles; (ii) applying macroprudential regulation and supervision to monitor and act on economy-wide systemic risk; and (iii) managing large capital inflows and limiting "double-mismatch" problems. It is important to create a strong international financial architecture to send early warnings, induce effective international policy coordination, and thereby reduce systemic risk internationally.

In the prevention exercise, every country needs an effective framework of macrofinancial surveillance—i.e. surveillance that focuses on macroeconomic and financial sector developments and the interactions between the two—for effective macroprudential supervision. This surveillance is important because it can help spot problems and trigger policy action to reduce economy-wide risk. For emerging economies, managing capital inflows is also a significant challenge as capital flows tend to be procyclical, and large inflows can fuel domestic overheating and financial imbalances. Double mismatches in currency

Table 15.1 Summary of Policy Lessons from the Asian and Global Financial Crises

Objective	National Measures	Global Measures	Regional Measures
Preventing or reducing the risk of crises	*Implement sound macroeconomic management (monetary, fiscal, exchange rate, and public debt) policies*		
	• Pursue non-inflationary monetary policy • Maintain sound fiscal balances • Manage public debt prudently • Curtail excesses, booms and asset price bubbles • Avoid excessive currency overvaluation and persistent, large current account deficits	• Strengthen IMF surveillance and early warning systems, focusing on systemically important economies • Utilize private-sector monitoring agencies • Analyze global spillovers of policies and shocks	• Strengthen regional macroeconomic policy dialogue, and surveillance • Develop a regional early warning system • Analyze regional spillovers of policies and shocks
	Establish effective macroprudential regulation and supervision to monitor and act on systemic risk		
	• Establish a national systemic stability regulator or council to contain systemic risk • Improve information transparency and disclosure in financial and corporate sectors • Focus on consolidated supervision of systemically important institutions • Improve monitoring of household and corporate sectors • Reduce procyclicality of regulation	• Strengthen capacity, resources, and effectiveness of FSB to promote global systemic stability • Support implementation of international standards and codes, and best-practice corporate governance • Agree on internationally coordinated regulations to reduce systemic risk	• Establish a regional systemic stability council, such as the European Systemic Risk Board and the proposed Asian Financial Stability Dialogue • Strengthen regional monitoring of financial markets and systemically important (global and regional) financial firms
	Manage capital flows and limit double mismatches		
	• Pursue orderly capital account liberalization • Use capital flow management measures to contain excessive capital inflows • Avoid heavy reliance on foreign-currency denominated short-term capital inflows	• Collect and disseminate more data on short-term external debt • Provide country-specific policy advice on desired capital flow management measures	• Strengthen regional monitoring of capital flows • Coordinate capital flow management measures at the regional level
Responding to crises	*Provide timely liquidity of sufficient magnitude*		
	• Restore market confidence through consistent policy packages • Reduce moral hazard problems	• Strengthen IMF liquidity support • Encourage more countries to adopt the Flexible Credit Line and the Precautionary Liquidity Line	• Strengthen a regional liquidity support facility to contain crises and contagion

Resolving systemic crises

Support the financial sector within a consistent framework

- Extend guarantees of bank obligations
- Conduct stress tests to identify losses and capital needs of financial institutions
- Establish a consistent framework for NPL removal and recapitalization

- Harmonize national interventions in the financial system, such as bank deposit guarantees, at the regional level
- Establish a common international rule for public sector interventions in distressed financial systems
- Avoid financial protectionism

Adopt appropriate macroeconomic policies to mitigate the adverse feedback loop between financial and real sectors

- Adopt an appropriate monetary and fiscal policy mix contingent on the specific conditions of the economy
- Be prepared for extraordinary policies

- Strengthen regional ability to formulate conditionality
- Create a regional fiscal support system
- Streamline IMF conditionality
- Design international fiscal support programs for fiscally constrained economies

Establish frameworks for resolving financial firms' impaired assets and corporate and household debt

- Resolve financial firms' bad assets
- Strengthen legal and out-of-court procedures for corporate debt restructuring

- Finance regional programs to help accelerate bank and corporate restructuring
- Harmonize national frameworks for resolving financial firms' bad assets
- Provide international support

Introduce rules for exit of non-viable financial firms

- Establish clear procedures for exit of financial firms, and rehabilitation
- Establish legal and informal procedures for corporate insolvencies and workouts

- Harmonize insolvency procedures by adopting good practices
- Harmonize national resolution regimes for non-viable financial firms

Adopt international insolvency mechanisms for resolving internationally active financial firms and sovereign debt

- Strengthen national insolvency procedures of banks, non-bank financial institutions and corporations
- Negotiate with domestic & foreign creditors for orderly sovereign debt restructuring

- Develop regional insolvency procedures to support global efforts
- Develop regional mechanisms for sovereign debt restructuring
- Introduce international procedures for cross-border insolvencies
- Develop sovereign debt restructuring mechanisms

Source: Author, substantially revised version of Table 1 in Kawai, Newfarmer and Schmukler (2005).

and maturity—i.e. borrowing short in foreign currency and lending long in domestic currency—can be a source of financial crisis once capital flows reverse themselves and the exchange rate depreciates sharply.

From an international perspective, IMF surveillance plays a key role, particularly for emerging and developing economies. For a group of regional economies that are highly interdependent on each other, regional surveillance that focuses on cross-country spillovers is essential.

Crisis response

Once a crisis unfolds, the macroeconomic and financial authorities need to respond and manage the process so that the crisis does not grow to critical proportions. The crisis response tools that have been used in recent years include: (i) provision of timely and adequate liquidity; (ii) support of distressed but viable financial firms through guarantees, nonperforming loan removal, and recapitalization; and (iii) adoption of appropriate macroeconomic policies to mitigate the adverse feedback loop between the financial sector and the real economy, reflecting the specific conditions and reality of the economy.

However, if a financial crisis is associated with rapid deleveraging and sharp declines in asset prices, it is difficult to arrest this process and reverse it. In a sense, the unwinding of high leverage and the elimination of asset price bubbles are desirable, but they have serious consequences on the financial system and the real economy. The objective of crisis response is to mitigate the negative interactions between the financial and real sectors through a comprehensive set of monetary, fiscal, and financial sector policies.

For emerging and developing economies, the most urgent issue during a crisis is to secure international short-term liquidity. IMF is the usual provider of such liquidity with policy conditions. However, many emerging and developing countries prefer not to go to the IMF, particularly those in Asia due to the "IMF stigma." Regional liquidity support facilities such as the CMIM have an important role to play in those crisis or near-crisis countries which are not willing to accept IMF programs. But in the case of a large-scale crisis and/or a crisis involving multiple economies simultaneously, regional financial facilities alone may not be sufficient to contain the crisis and, as a result, the IMF may have to be invited in.

Crisis resolution

Crisis resolution measures include: (i) use of institutions and mechanisms for restructuring financial firms' impaired assets and, hence, corporate and/or household debt; (ii) use of national insolvency procedures for nonviable financial institutions; (iii) reliance on international cooperation for resolving nonviable internationally active financial firms, including clear burden-sharing mechanisms across countries; and (iv) use of international procedures for resolving sovereign debt that is not sustainable. The reality is that there is no clearly defined regime internationally for resolving financial firms that operate across borders, and therefore the crisis resolution process often creates international conflict leading to a stalemate.

In the case of emerging and developing economies, resolving unsustainable sovereign debt can be an important issue. During a financial crisis, public debt tends to rise, often to an unsustainable level, partly because of countercyclical fiscal policy to support aggregate demand and partly because of the socialization of private debt through the nationalization of insolvent banks. Once debt rises to an unsustainable level, orderly debt restructuring—such as debt reduction (or so-called haircut), interest reduction, and lengthening maturities—is needed to return the economy to healthy growth.

Development of Asia's financial arrangement as a regional public good

The Asian financial crisis of 1997–98 and its spread across the region revealed several important points: financial systems and economic conditions were closely linked across East Asia; the IMF alone should not have been relied upon for crisis management, and a regional self-help mechanism needed to be created to effectively prevent and respond to financial crises. Recognizing this, the finance ministers of the ASEAN+3 countries embarked on several new initiatives for regional financial cooperation in 2000:

- regional economic surveillance (ERPD);
- a regional liquidity support arrangement (CMI); and
- local currency bond market development initiatives.

The global financial crisis of 2007–09 demonstrated that the CMI was not ready to be used to respond to the impact of a crisis. While the crisis affected many Asian economies through the trade channel, it created shortages of international liquidity in a few countries—such as the Republic of Korea and Indonesia.

The Republic of Korea encountered sudden capital flow reversals in the aftermath of the collapse of Lehman Brothers in September 2008 and saw a rapid loss of foreign exchange reserves and sharp depreciation of the won, thereby sparking a mini currency crisis. Unwilling to go to the IMF or the CMI for liquidity support, the Korean authorities chose to secure a US$30 billion currency swap line from the United States Federal Reserve System.[2] This immediately had a positive, stabilizing impact on financial and foreign exchange markets in Seoul, suggesting that the financial turmoil was due to a temporary liquidity shortage.

Indonesia did not face even a mini currency crisis during the global financial crisis but it had some difficulty funding its fiscal needs internationally, and the rupiah depreciated sharply. The country requested that the US Federal Reserve extend a currency swap line but, unlike the case with the Republic of Korea, the request was denied. To cope with potential financial difficulties, the country instead obtained a US$5.5 billion "standby loan facility"—or "deferred draw-down option"—in 2009 with funds provided by Japan, Australia, the Asian Development Bank (ADB), and the World Bank. Thus, multilateral development banks and bilateral agencies played a critical role in helping Indonesia to secure financial resources during difficult times.

Progress on the CMI and ERPD

Figure 15.1 summarizes the developments of Asia's financial arrangement as potential regional public goods. The CMI and ERPD were introduced in 2000 and they were considered inseparable in 2005. The CMI was multilateralized to become the CMIM in 2010 and then underwent a major reform in 2012.

ERPD and AMRO

The ERPD is a regional economic surveillance process, designed to contribute to the prevention of financial crises through the early detection of irregularities, vulnerabilities, and systemic risks, and the swift implementation of remedial policy actions. It was intended to facilitate the following processes: analysis of the economic and financial conditions of the global, regional, and individual national economies; monitoring of regional capital flows and financial market developments; and the provision of policy recommendations for national authorities as well as joint actions on issues affecting

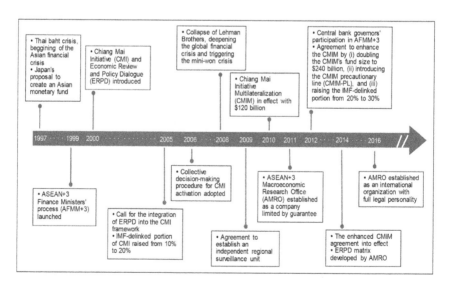

Figure 15.1 Developments of the CMI/CMIM, ERPD, and AMRO.

Source: Author's compilation from statements from ASEAN+3 Finance Ministers' and Central Bank Governors' Meetings, for various years.

the region. The expectation was that the authorities would implement better macroeconomic and financial sector policy at the national level as a result of peer pressure, and would pursue international policy coordination if needed.

Without strong support mechanisms for regional surveillance and in the absence of central bank governors in the process, however, the ERPD process was not as successful as initially expected, although gradual improvements were made over time. Recognizing these shortcomings, the ASEAN+3 finance ministers decided in Singapore in 2011 to create a surveillance unit, AMRO, in charge of regional economic surveillance and invited central bank governors to join the ASEAN+3 process in 2012.

CMI and multilateralization

The CMI is a regional liquidity support facility, which is intended to reduce the risk of currency crises and manage such crises or crisis contagion. It started as a combination of (i) a network of bilateral swap agreements among the Plus-3 countries—China, Japan, and the Republic of Korea—and between one of the Plus-3 countries and select ASEAN members; and (ii) the ASEAN Swap Arrangement. As early as May 2006, the ASEAN+3 finance ministers began to improve the functioning of the CMI and ERPD and to consider the multilateralization of the CMI. After step-by-step agreements were made, the CMIM was officially implemented in March 2010, expanding currency swaps to all ASEAN member states and Hong Kong. Its total size was set at US$120 billion, with the following member contributions: Japan and China contribute 32% each, Republic of Korea 16%, and ASEAN 20%. Maximum borrowing limits for members were also decided. The ERPD was considered an integral part of the CMIM. The AMRO was set up to "monitor and analyze regional economies" and to "contribute to the early detection of risks, swift implementation of remedial actions, and effective decision-making of the CMIM."[3] Essentially it was expected to lay the surveillance groundwork for the CMIM.

An important feature of the CMIM as of 2011 was that crisis-affected members requesting CMIM support could immediately obtain short-term liquidity assistance up to an amount equivalent to 20% of the maximum borrowing amount[4] and that the remaining 80% would be provided to the requesting member if accompanied by an IMF program. As such, the CMIM was closely linked to an IMF program and the lending conditions associated with this. The CMIM's link with the IMF was designed to address the concern that the currency crisis of a requesting member economy might be due to fundamental policy problems, rather than a temporary liquidity shortage, and that the potential moral hazard problem might be significant in the absence of rigorous policy conditionality. Essentially, the CMIM was intended for crisis lending and hence required conditionality. The lack of the region's capacity to formulate and enforce effective adjustment programs in times of crisis was a major reason for requiring the CMIM to be closely linked to IMF programs.[5]

Major reform of the CMIM in 2012

When the Republic of Korea faced a mini currency crisis in the fall of 2008, the country did not seek CMI assistance for three reasons. First, the Republic of Korea needed US$30 billion to calm the market, but the country's maximum borrowing limit under the CMI was only US$18.5 billion, which was too small in financial resources. Second, to obtain even this amount, the Republic of Korea would have been required to be under an IMF program due to the CMI's link to the IMF, as the drawing would have exceeded 20% of the borrowing limit. The authorities would have faced political objections in the country due to the IMF stigma—that is, negative perceptions of the IMF stemming from its actions in the 1997–98 financial crisis. Third, the Korean authorities considered the turbulence the country was going through to be a temporary liquidity shortage situation and not a currency crisis, and the CMI was not designed for near-crisis or precautionary situations. The country was fortunate in being able to secure a Federal Reserve currency swap line, while Indonesia was unable to do so. This illustrated the limitations of the CMI as it could not be used even by countries that were fundamentally sound, such as the Republic of Korea and Indonesia.

To address these problems, the ASEAN+3 authorities modified the CMIM substantially in 2012. The total size was doubled to US$240 billion and the IMF-delinked portion was raised from 20% to 30% of a country's maximum swap quota, with the possibility that it be raised to 40% in 2014 subject to review should conditions warrant (but no such rise has been made as of September 2016). This swap, called the CMIM Stability Facility (CMIM-SF), was intended for crisis response.[6]

At the same time, a new crisis prevention facility, called the Precautionary Line (CMIM-PL), was introduced.[7] The new facility is intended for precautionary purposes such as for temporary liquidity shortage and near-crisis situations. A member economy requesting this facility needs to be judged as pre-qualified in order to enjoy access to it. The qualification criteria were based on five areas: external position and market access; fiscal policy; monetary policy; financial sector soundness and supervision; and data adequacy. A member economy cannot draw on both CMIM-SF and CMIM-PL at the same time, and the maximum drawing, in either case, is the economy's swap quota.

ASEAN+3 Macroeconomic Research Office (AMRO)

AMRO was established initially as a private limited company in 2011, with its main mandate being to conduct macroeconomic and financial surveillance of global and regional economies and to contribute to early detection of risks, policy recommendations for remedial actions, and effective decision making of the CMIM. It became an international organization in 2016.

AMRO's scope of work and deliverables are somewhat different depending on whether a member economy is in a crisis situation or not. During a noncrisis period, AMRO conducts regional surveillance, analysis, and assessment to identify trends, issues, and risks, focusing on balance of payments and short-term capital flows. Based on this analysis and surveillance, it prepares monthly and quarterly reports on macroeconomic conditions and outlooks for member economies and biannual individual country surveillance reports, undertakes brief thematic studies on topical issues, and prepares assessments and reports for members requesting the CMIM-PL.

During a crisis period, AMRO is expected to provide an analysis of the economic and financial conditions of the CMIM program member economies, scrutinize the use and impact of the fund disbursed under a CMIM-SF agreement, and monitor compliance of the program economy with lending conditions.

Since 2012, the ASEAN+3 authorities have been developing the ERPD Matrix, consisting of various economic and financial indicators of all ASEAN+3 members. The matrix is intended to facilitate the assessment of the members' qualification for the CMIM crisis prevention facility. AMRO adopted the first set of measures to be included in the ERPD Matrix in 2014 with its focus on: (i) external position and market access (gross external debt as a percentage of GDP, gross short-term external debt as a percentage of foreign exchange reserves, the current account balance as a percentage of GDP, and foreign exchange reserves in months of imports); (ii) fiscal policy (revenue, expenditures, primary balance, overall fiscal balance, and central government debt, all as a percentage of GDP); (iii) monetary policy (policy framework and recent policy changes, headline inflation, core inflation, money growth, and credit growth as a year-on-year percentage); (iv) financial sector soundness and supervision (regulatory capital to risk-weighted assets, nonperforming loans to capital, nonperforming loans to total gross loans, return on assets, loan to deposit ratio, and residential real estate loans to total banking system loans as optional); and (v) data adequacy (primary evaluation based on ERPD matrices and supplementary evaluation based on AMRO economic reports). The authorities intend to continue to develop the matrix and elaborate the ways the matrix will be used for the smooth implementation of the CMIM-PL.

Experiences of regional financial arrangements in other parts of the world

This section examines regional financial arrangements developed in other parts of the world and attempts to draw lessons for Asia. Table 15.2 summarizes the features of the major regional financial arrangements and the IMF. Europe has the European Financial Stability Facility (EFSF) and the European Stability Mechanism (ESM). The Middle East and North Africa has the Arab Monetary Fund, Latin America has the Latin American Reserve Fund (FLAR, *Fondo Latinamericano de Reservas*), and North America has the North American Framework Agreement (NAFA). The BRICS countries (Brazil, Russia,

Table 15.2 Features of the IMF and Selected Regional Financial Arrangements

	International Monetary Fund (IMF)	European Financial Stability Facility (EFSF)	European Stability Mechanism (ESM)	Arab Monetary Fund (AMF)	Latin American Reserve Fund (FLAR)	North American Framework Agreement (NAFA)	BRICS Contingent Reserve Arrangement (CRA)	Chiang Mai Initiative Multilateralization (CMIM)
Year established	1944	2010	2012	1976	1978	1994	2015	2000
Headquarters	Washington, DC, US	Luxembourg		Abu Dhabi, United Arab Emirates	Bogotá, Colombia	None	Shanghai, China	None (AMRO in Singapore)
Fund size	US$660 billion	€440 billion	€704.8 billion	US$2.75 billion	US$3.9 billion	US$9 billion	US$100 billion	US$240 billion
Member economies	189	19 (All Eurozone member countries)		22 Arab countries in North Africa and the Middle East	8 Latin American countries (Bolivia, Colombia, Costa Rica, Ecuador, Paraguay, Peru, Uruguay, and Venezuela)	3 North American countries (Canada, Mexico, and the United States)	5 BRICS countries (Brazil, Russia, India, China and South Africa)	13 plus Hong Kong (10 ASEAN member states, China, Japan, the Republic of Korea, and Hong Kong)

Major objective	Macroeconomic stability, response to financial crisis	Preserving financial stability of the Eurozone through temporary financial assistance to Eurozone members (only) facing exceptional problems beyond their control	Correcting payment disequilibria and currency instability through short- to medium-term credit facilities	Supporting members' balance of payments with credits and guarantees	Provision of short-term liquidity support through 90-day central bank swaps, renewable up to 1 year	Provision of liquidity and precautionary support to protect against short-term balance of payments pressures	Provision of balance of payments and short-term liquidity support through currency swaps
Independent surveillance	National, regional, global surveillance	No independent surveillance (surveillance outsourced to the European Commission)	No independent surveillance (surveillance provided by IMF)	Independent surveillance	Independent surveillance	Surveillance relied on IMF Article IV consultation reports	Independent surveillance through ERPD (AMRO as a surveillance unit)
Relationship with the IMF	—	IMF participation sought "wherever possible." While not strictly required as a legal matter, linked to IMF programs as a matter of Council policy and members' domestic politics	Ordinary loans usually accompanied by an IMF program, but other types of assistance not necessarily linked	Not linked to the IMF	US treasury requires letter from IMF Managing Director	Beyond 30% of a member's borrowing limit, disbursements to be linked to an IMF program (never activated)	Beyond 30% of a member's borrowing limit, disbursements to be linked to an IMF program (never activated)

Source: Author's compilation and updates, adapted from Henning (2011, 2016) and Lamberte and Morgan (2014).

India, China, and South Africa) recently launched their Contingency Reserve Arrangement (CRA).

International Monetary Fund

The IMF has the prime responsibility for surveillance and short-term liquidity support. The scope of its surveillance is national (through Article IV consultation), regional (through Regional Economic Outlook reports), and global (through World Economic Outlook reports). It collaborates with the World Bank on the Financial Sector Assessment Program to promote sound financial systems in member countries. In recent years, the IMF has been increasingly focused on the interaction between macroeconomic and financial sector developments and the international spillovers of systemically important economies' policies and conditions.

The IMF pours large amounts of resources into its surveillance activity. In terms of human resources, the IMF is estimated to have devoted over 1,100 staff years to surveillance activities in fiscal year 2005, and hundreds of millions of US dollars per year in terms of financial resources (Takagi 2010; Lamberte and Morgan 2014).

The IMF has large financial resources for short-term liquidity support as its lending capacity was tripled to US$750 billion following the G20 agreement in 2009. Its major lending facilities include the Stand-By Arrangement (SBA) and the Rapid Financing Instrument (RFI), which typically involve policy conditions. In addition, it introduced new lending facilities—the Flexible Credit Line (FCL) and the Precautionary Liquidity Line (PLL)— for the purpose of crisis prevention.[8] Its quota resources have doubled to US$660 billion, following the 14th General Quota Review agreed in 2010 and implemented in 2016.

European arrangement

Two European institutions, the EFSF and ESM, have by far the largest financial resources among regional financial arrangements. The EFSF was established in 2010 as a temporary private firm based on the law of Luxembourg and was superseded by the ESM as a permanent international organization in 2012. The former will continue to exist for a long time as some loans it gave are long-term maturities. The two institutions have played important roles in the Troika programs of crisis-affected Eurozone countries, such as Greece, Ireland, Portugal, and Spain.[9] As the EFSF cannot enter into any new financial assistance programs, the ESM is now the sole and permanent mechanism for responding to new requests for financial assistance by Eurozone member states.

The ESM aims to safeguard financial stability within the Eurozone by providing financial assistance to Eurozone member states experiencing or threatened by financing difficulties. For this purpose, it has strong financing capacity. It finances its activity by issuing bonds and other debt instruments, backed by capital contributions provided by member states (with the subscribed capital of €704.8 billion). Instruments for financial assistance include loans, primary and secondary market purchases of sovereign bonds, precautionary programs, bank recapitalization through loans to governments, and direct bank recapitalization.

However, the ESM does not have sufficient surveillance capacity and thus has outsourced surveillance services to the European Commission (EC), which has more expertise. When the ESM provides financial assistance, called ESM Stability Support, to a requesting country, the EC and the European Central Bank (ECB) must conduct country assessment, and the country must agree to a macroeconomic adjustment program. The Troika system also utilizes the surveillance capacity of the IMF, which is considered to have much greater expertise and experience in this regard. The reason for involving the IMF is that it was initially feared that surveillance by European institutions alone might be too lenient on their European peers. The ESM indeed seeks active participation of the IMF both at technical and financial level, and a member country requesting ESM financial assistance is expected to address, wherever possible, a similar request to the IMF, although the latter is not strictly required as a legal matter. The ECB was initially reluctant to provide liquidity through purchases of Eurozone member states' sovereign debt, but it has begun doing so as well as providing liquidity support to the banking system.

The importance of the European experience lies in the large size of financial resources to be mobilized, utilizing the high-quality surveillance service provided by other institutions (the EC and the IMF) when its own surveillance capacity is limited, working with the IMF in crisis management, and collectively crafting a set of policy conditions. However, challenges remain as to who should discipline large economies such as Germany and France when they start facing problems.

Other regional arrangements

The Arab Monetary Fund and FLAR are relatively small in terms of financial resources and include only developing countries as their members. However, their relationships with the IMF and approaches to policy conditions are different. The Arab Monetary Fund has limited capacity for surveillance and, as a result, it relies on the IMF for this and its ordinary loans are usually accompanied by IMF programs. FLAR does not seem to have much surveillance capacity either, but it conducts its own surveillance and provides loans without involving IMF programs.

The Arab Monetary Fund's main objectives are to correct balance of payments disequilibria among its member states, remove payment restrictions between members, establish policies and modes of Arab monetary cooperation, promote financial investment abroad by member states, promote the development of Arab financial markets, pave the way towards the creation of a unified Arab currency, and promote trade among member states. For these purposes, the fund provides short-term and medium-term credit facilities to member states to help finance their overall balance of payments deficits; provides credits for settling current payments among member states; and manages funds placed under its charge by member states. Due to the limited surveillance and policy formulation capacity, the fund's financial assistance is almost always associated with IMF programs and policy conditions.

FLAR was set up in response to the Latin American region's need to have its own institution to solve external liquidity problems as a supplement to the global action taken by the IMF. Its activity has evolved from being a pure reserve pool that supports balance of payments problems to an institution contributing to the harmonization of monetary, foreign exchange, and financial policies and to the improvement of the investment conditions of the members' international reserves.[10] Economic surveillance is carried out by FLAR's economists. There is no policy conditionality and no link with the IMF. Nonetheless, throughout its history, no member country has ever defaulted on a loan provided by FLAR and none has required refinancing.

The NAFA is a regional financial arrangement established as a parallel financial agreement to the North American Free Trade Agreement (NAFTA) between Canada, Mexico, and the United States in 1994. It put together and enlarged three prior bilateral swap agreements between the three countries. The trilateral swaps were introduced in connection with a new consultative mechanism, the North American Financial Group, which brought US Treasury and Central Bank officials together for annual meetings on macroeconomic and financial matters. Provision of liquidity support under the NAFA would require the US treasury to request a letter from the IMF Managing Director assuring that the IMF would cooperate with the United States.

BRICS contingent reserve arrangement

Leaders of BRICS (Brazil, Russia, India, China, and South Africa) countries agreed to establish the BRICS CRA with a US$100 billion fund in July 2014 and the facility came into force in July 2015. China contributes US$41 billion, Brazil, Russia and India contribute US$18 billion each, and South Africa contributes US$5 billion, and members' voting shares are equal to their contribution shares. Maximum access limits are: US$20.5 billion for China, US$18 billion each for Brazil, Russia, and India, and US$10 billion for South Africa. The facility's objective is to protect against short-term balance of payments pressures by providing support through liquidity and precautionary instruments in the form of currency swaps with central banks.

As in the case of the CMIM, participating countries retain possession of committed resources until a request for assistance by one party is granted and a currency swap takes place. In addition, use of the first 30% of each member's maximum access is delinked from an IMF program but use beyond this ratio is linked to an IMF program and is subject to program arrangements with the IMF. But, unlike the CMIM, members are explicitly required to comply with

Article IV surveillance and disclosure obligations of the IMF. The reason for this requirement is that given the presence of financially fragile members—such as Brazil, Russia, and South Africa—the potential creditor members need to rely on the IMF's Article IV reports as the most credible source of economic and financial information on potential borrower countries. The CRA has not been activated yet.

Challenges to Asia's financial stability

Important advances have been made on the CMIM, ERPD, and AMRO, but the question remains whether this progress has been significant enough to make these institutional arrangements effective for preventing and countering currency crises. One of the most significant challenges is that as the CMIM has never been activated, it is not entirely clear how it might work once a crisis unfolds. There are four issues at play: the adequacy of CMIM resources; the effectiveness of ERPD and the role of AMRO; the CMIM's IMF link; and procedural clarity and certainty in activating the CMIM.

Adequacy of CMIM resources

Even with the increase in the total size of CMIM to US$240 billion, the maximum swap quota available to each member economy remains small for either crisis prevention or response (see Table 15.3). For example, the maximum swap quotas currently available for Indonesia, the Republic of Korea, and Thailand are US$23 billion, US$38 billion, and US$23 billion, respectively. These quotas are small compared to the IMF packages arranged during the crisis of 1997–98, particularly for the Republic of Korea (US$58.2 billion) and Indonesia (US$42.3 billion). Furthermore, the IMF-delinked portion available to a member is insufficient—even if the portion were to be further raised to 40%—in comparison to the IMF packages for these countries, or compared to the bilateral currency swap arrangement that the Korean authorities secured from the US Federal Reserve (US$30 billion) during the global financial crisis. To counter a currency crisis or liquidity shortage using the CMIM, therefore, its total size—particularly the amount available without an IMF link—should be expanded. Given the "IMF stigma," some redesigning of the CMIM would be desirable so that any member economy in a crisis or near-crisis situation can use the CMIM without an IMF program.

Several options are available for securing adequate financing for members in crisis or near-crisis situations. First, the total size of CMIM resources may be expanded at least twofold. This would significantly raise both the maximum swap quota and the IMF-delinked portion that each member can obtain at times of crisis or near-crisis. Second, purchasing multiples may be raised for ASEAN countries and the Republic of Korea, while those for China and Japan may be reduced as the latter two countries are unlikely to require

Table 15.3 Available Financial Resources under the CMIM

Members	Financial Contributions (US$ billion)	Maximum Swap Amount (US$ billion)	IMF-Delinked Amount (US$ billion)	
			IMF link of 30%	IMF link of 40%
Plus Three	**192.00**	**117.30**	**39.600**	**50.700**
China total	76.80	40.50	16.560	19.980
People's Republic of China	68.40	34.20	10.260	13.680
Hong Kong, China	8.40	6.30	6.300	6.300
Japan	76.80	38.40	11.520	15.360
Republic of Korea	38.40	38.40	11.520	15.360
ASEAN	**48.00**	**126.20**	**37.860**	**50.480**
Brunei Darussalam	0.06	0.30	0.090	0.120
Cambodia	0.24	1.20	0.360	0.480
Indonesia	9.104	22.76	6.828	9.104
Lao PDR	0.06	0.30	0.090	0.120
Malaysia	9.104	22.76	6.828	9.104
Myanmar	0.12	0.60	0.180	0.240
Philippines	9.104	22.76	6.828	9.104
Singapore	9.104	22.76	6.828	9.104
Thailand	9.104	22.76	6.828	9.104
Vietnam	2.00	10.00	3.000	4.000
ASEAN+3	**240.00**	**243.50**	**77.460**	**101.180**

Source: Ministry of Finance, Government of Japan.

Note: ASEAN=Association of South East Asian Nations; ASEAN+3=Association of South East Asian Nations Plus Three; CMIM=Chiang Mai Initiative Multilateralization; Lao PDR=Lao People's Democratic Republic. The last column was added by the author

CMIM assistance. For example, the purchasing multiples for China and Japan may become zero and those for ASEAN countries and the Republic of Korea may be raised by 45% without changing the total size of CMIM resources. Third, the IMF-delinked portion may be further increased, ultimately to 100%. This would make it easier for members in crises or near-crises to gain access to CMIM resources without IMF programs. Finally, a combination of these options may be implemented to substantially increase both the maximum swap quota and the IMF-delinked portion available for each member economy that would potentially need CMIM assistance.

   A more radical approach to securing sufficient financial resources for each member would be to transform the CMIM, which is a reserve pooling arrangement, into a fund where members contribute their capital (or quotas).

Once contribution multiples are set for member economies—for example, at 500%—those in crisis or near-crisis situations can draw adequate financial resources without relying on IMF financing and programs.

Effectiveness of the ERPD and the role of AMRO

Even though progress has been made on the ERPD and AMRO, experts consider their effectiveness questionable at best, especially for CMIM purposes (Azis 2012). The current ERPD process is still largely one of information sharing with weak peer review or policy coordination (Menon and Hill 2014) and has not moved to the more advanced due diligence stage, which would require a rigorous analysis of potential borrower economies from the perspective of potential creditors (Kawai and Houser 2008). AMRO remains a relatively modest organization in terms of budget and personnel. Ideally, the ASEAN+3 authorities should be able to rely on AMRO's assessments when making decisions about whether to lend, how much to lend, and what conditionality to apply. This means that the effectiveness of ERPD needs to improve and the role of AMRO needs to be strengthened as a CMIM support organization for economic surveillance and conditionality formulation.

Views are divided on the desired functional role of AMRO. As the IMF produces high-quality analyses of global and national economic developments, AMRO may play a primary role processing information provided by global and national agencies, in order to economize on its limited resources (Takagi, 2010). AMRO's surveillance may have an increasingly regional, rather than national, focus, with a clear mandate for addressing policy spillovers and finding scope for collective action. One of the advantages of AMRO is its close contact with regional policymakers (Siregar and Chabchitrchaidol 2014). Thus, the nonpublic nature of the current peer review process facilitates the provision of confidential advice and constructive criticism of policies at the highest official levels throughout the year. Henning (2011) suggests that AMRO could provide contrasting assessments of vulnerabilities within the region when it disagrees with the findings of the IMF. Another advantage of AMRO is its more frequent (quarterly and biannual) updating of assessments of member economies than the annual cycle for IMF Article IV consultation reports. It is important for AMRO to continue this practice.

Relying completely on the IMF for surveillance and conditionality formulation would not make much sense as there is a possibility that CMIM can be activated without IMF programs. Although AMRO may initially rely on the IMF for surveillance and conditionality setting, it needs to develop its own capacity to conduct surveillance, craft policy conditions, and monitor economic and policy performance.

Thus, while working with the IMF, AMRO may find its own comparative advantage. First, AMRO could continue to focus on national surveillance, while absorbing information provided by the IMF and other national and international organizations. It could accompany the IMF in its national surveillance—such as its Article IV consultation and the Financial Sector Assessment Program (currently carried out in conjunction with the World Bank)—and at the same time articulate its own assessment. Second, AMRO could focus more on regional surveillance and spillover issues and provide its own views on regional vulnerabilities. For example, even within the ASEAN+3 region, some common external shocks could affect different member economies differently. AMRO could analyze such differential impacts and provide advice on desired policy responses for different economies. Third, AMRO could gradually build its analytical capacity to assess a member economy's qualification for CMIM-PL assistance and to formulate its own independent conditionality in the event of CMIM activation without an IMF program. Once AMRO acquires adequate capacity in these areas, the CMIM's link with the IMF can be substantially reduced and ultimately eliminated.

Link with the IMF

Reducing the CMIM's link with the IMF would be one of the most important challenges for the ASEAN+3 countries. The reason is that use of the CMIM crisis response or precautionary facility requires an IMF link, which discourages any potential borrower member to rely on this facility. There are several ways to make the CMIM readily available for member economies seeking support.

When a member economy faces a temporary liquidity shortage, CMIM-PL could be made available to the pre-qualified member without requiring any IMF link or conditionality, up to the full amount of the swap quota. Quick access to a sufficient amount of swap line can restore market confidence and stabilize the situation, as happened in the Republic of Korea in the fall of 2008. If the problem persisted after using the CMIM-PL facility for a pre-specified time (for example, six months), then the situation would probably be one of crisis rather than a temporary liquidity shortage, and thus the support may be switched to CMIM-SF, which would require macroeconomic policy adjustments (Sussangkarn 2011).[11] At this stage the IMF may or may not be invited in, depending on the nature and magnitude of the crisis. Removing the IMF link at the initial phase would make it much more attractive for member economies to rely on the CMIM-PL swap.

When a member economy faces a currency crisis, rather than a temporary liquidity shortage, and the amount of liquidity support needed is small and within the swap limit, CMIM-SF support could be provided to an eligible economy without an IMF program but with independent policy conditions. Only when the crisis requires both very large amounts of financial support, exceeding the swap limit, and significant macroeconomic policy adjustment, the CMIM-SF would be advised to work with the IMF.

In this way, the CMIM would be the first line of defense for a temporary liquidity shortage problem (which would mobilize CMIM-PL) and for a small-scale currency crisis requiring macroeconomic policy adjustment (which would mobilize CMIM-SF), with the IMF joining to deal with large-scale crisis situations.[12]

At this point, the ASEAN+3 authorities seem to believe that AMRO's capacity remains limited in terms of assessing a member economy's qualification for CMIM-PL, conducting economic surveillance, and crafting independent policy conditions in the event of a crisis. Thus, the IMF may initially work with AMRO in supporting these tasks, with the expectation that they will be gradually shifted to AMRO as it builds its own analytical capacity.

Procedural clarity

Some experts argue that there is a lack of clarity over procedural matters relating to the activation of the CMIM, such as the precise economic information that is required for member authorities to make decisions, the steps to be taken before contacting the CMIM chair country, and procedures to be followed if the facility is needed very soon, say within a week, due to sudden liquidity shortages (Azis 2012). When financial turbulence or a liquidity shortage hits a member economy, a rapid response is essential to contain the turbulence or prevent it from developing into a currency crisis. For this purpose, a smooth and well-prepared mechanism of liquidity support is essential. The ASEAN+3 authorities have conducted CMIM test runs under several scenarios to identify potential gaps in implementing financial assistance in a timely manner. Test runs for the CMIM-SF facility involving the IMF (and other potential stakeholders such as the ADB) would also be useful.[13] Nonetheless, a crisis can come at any moment without clear indication, and there could still be a delay in action, particularly when chair countries are relatively inexperienced.

Part of the problem is that the CMIM lacks a permanent secretariat in charge of activating it. AMRO is a research and surveillance unit facilitating the ERPD and supporting the CMIM but is not a permanent secretariat for all aspects of it, including activation. To quickly respond to member economies' emergency needs, a permanent secretariat supporting CMIM activation is urgently needed. One option would be to locate such a secretariat in AMRO so as to ensure a quick response to crisis or near-crisis situations.

Conclusions

Asia's regional financial arrangement, introduced in 2000 as a response to the Asian financial crisis, has been strengthened since the outbreak of the global financial crisis. The CMIM—a multilateralized version of currency swap arrangements—has US$240 billion for both a crisis prevention and a crisis response facility, with the IMF-delinked portion at 30%. The AMRO—a surveillance unit for the ERPD and CMIM—has been gradually building its capacity.

The problem is that the CMIM (or its previous version, CMI) has never been activated, so some uncertainty exists as to whether and how the CMIM and AMRO would actually work in the event of its activation. The European experience suggests that surveillance is not an easy task, setting policy conditions would be a demanding, complex exercise, and enforcing the borrowing economy's compliance with lending conditions would be a challenge.

Asia can contribute to global financial stability by improving its regional financial (CMIM) and surveillance arrangements (ERPD) and eventually moving to create an Asian monetary fund (AMF). This fund would be supported by member economies' capital (or quota) contributions, conduct independent surveillance, assess the financing needs of members requesting support, activate support programs, formulate policy conditionality, and monitor policies and performance of program economies. To transform the current arrangements into an AMF, significant progress needs to be made in the quality of the ERPD process, AMRO's analytical capacity, and institution building. The ERPD process, which is in transition from the simple information-sharing stage to a peer review stage, will have to establish more advanced procedures to carry out due diligence—that is, rigorous scrutiny of a potential borrower economy. AMRO needs to strengthen its analytical capacity in surveillance and policy conditionality formulation and at the same time assume a greater functional role as a permanent secretariat for all aspects of the CMIM.

The enhanced CMIM and AMRO—and a future AMF—could serve as a complementary organization and a building block for the global financial architecture anchored by the IMF. For this purpose, AMRO needs to work closely with the IMF, exchanging information on a routine basis, conducting joint analyses— as for the Financial Sector Assessment Program and Article IV consultation—and intervening in crisis economies together if needed. However, this means that the IMF should also clarify its focus. As the coordinating global institution, the IMF has a clear role to ensure global consistency, but this should not imply that the IMF sets all the key agendas and that regional institutions—such as the CMIM and AMRO—should simply follow. Regional institutions have their own comparative advantage and can provide inputs to the IMF so as to improve the global financial architecture.

In addition, the IMF should reestablish itself as a credible, trustworthy institution. It would not otherwise be accepted in Asia as a true partner for the region. The IMF needs significant reforms of its operations and governance. On the operational side, the IMF must focus on the surveillance of systemically important economies (such as the USA, the Eurozone, and China) in an even-handed way. It must also scrutinize international spillovers of major economies' policies and provide policy recommendations to promote global macroeconomic and financial stability. In terms of governance reform, the long-delayed 2010 IMF reform was finally approved by the US Congress in December 2015 to facilitate its implementation, i.e. doubling IMF quota resources and increasing the voice of rising, emerging economies in the organization. The IMF should start discussing the next quota changes and is advised to consider disallowing any single member country to have the power of veto.

With continued reforms, emerging Asian members would likely provide the IMF with an opportunity to regain their trust as a partner for macroeconomic and financial stability in Asia.

Notes

1 This is a revised version of the paper presented at the workshop, "Regional Cooperation, Regional Public Goods and Sustainable Development," organized by American University and the Inter-American Development Bank and held in Washington, DC, on June 22–23, 2015.
2 Brazil, Mexico and Singapore also obtained similar currency swaps from the US Federal Reserve.
3 The Joint Ministerial Statement of the 13th ASEAN+3 Finance Ministers' Meeting, May 2 2010, Tashkent, Uzbekistan.
4 Initially the IMF-delinked portion of the CMI was 10% and it was raised to 20% in May 2005. It was further raised to 30% in May 2012.
5 Potential borrowers of the CMIM believed that the facility should not be linked to IMF programs.
6 The maturity of the CMIM-SF swap for the IMF-linked portion was lengthened from 90 days to one year and its supporting period lengthened from two years to three years, with a maximum of two renewals. The maturity for the IMF-delinked portion was lengthened from 90 days to six months and its supporting period lengthened from one year to two years, with a maximum of three renewals.
7 The maturity of the CMIM-PL was set at one year for the IMF-linked portion and six months for the IMF-delinked portion, with a maximum duration of two years for both cases.
8 The SBA is designed to help countries address short-term balance of payments problems, and disbursements are made conditional on achieving policy targets (conditionality). SBAs may be provided on a precautionary basis, that is, countries can choose not to draw upon approved amounts but retain the option to do so until conditions deteriorate. The RFI provides rapid financial assistance with limited conditionality to all members facing an urgent balance of payments need. Access under the RFI is subject to an annual limit of 37.5% of quota and a cumulative limit of 75% of quota. The FCL is designed for countries with very strong fundamentals, policies, and track records of policy implementation. It is arranged, at the member country's request, for countries meeting preset qualification criteria. Disbursements under the FCL are not conditional on implementation of specific policies, unlike the case of the SBA. There is flexibility to either draw on the credit line at the time it is approved or treat it as precautionary. The PLL is intended for countries with sound fundamentals and policies, and a track record of implementing such policies. PLL-qualifying countries may face moderate vulnerabilities and may not meet the FCL qualification standards, but they are not required to take substantial policy adjustments normally associated with SBAs. The PLL combines qualification (similar to the FCL but with a lower bar) with focused conditions that aim at addressing the identified remaining vulnerabilities. See IMF website: www.imf.org/external/np/exr/facts/howlend.htm
9 The European Troika includes the European Commission, the European Central Bank and the IMF.
10 As such FLAR acts as a financial intermediary and receives deposits from central banks, official institutions and multilateral agencies from the region, both from member and non-member states.

11 The length of the period before policy adjustments are required could be decided appropriately.

12 This is consistent with the principles for cooperation between the IMF and the regional financial arrangements, including the CMIM, developed by the Group of Twenty: "(i) cooperation between RFAs and the IMF should foster rigorous and even-handed surveillance and promote the common goals of regional and global financial and monetary stability; (ii) cooperation should respect the roles, independence, and decision-making processes of each institution, taking into account regional specificities in a flexible manner; (iii) while cooperation between RFAs and the IMF may be triggered by a crisis, ongoing collaboration should be promoted as way to build regional capacity for crisis prevention; (iv) cooperation should... include open sharing of information and joint missions where necessary.... (E)ach institution has comparative advantages.... RFAs have better understanding of regional circumstances and the IMF has a greater global surveillance capacity; (v) consistency of lending conditions should be sought to the extent possible ..., in particular as concerns policy conditions and facility pricing. However, some flexibility would be needed as regards adjustments to conditionality, if necessary, and on the timing of the reviews.... (D)efinitive decisions about financial assistance within a joint programme should be taken by the respective institutions participating in the programme; and (vi) RFAs must respect the preferred creditor status of the IMF." (Group of Twenty 2011). Henning (2016) further suggests that the G20, IMF, and RFAs adopt three broad guidelines: transparency; specialization along comparative advantage; and prohibition against competition in critical areas.

13 Just as Europe developed a Troika model for coordination with the IMF in managing the EU and Eurozone financial crises, Asia may also develop its own Troika model for such coordination, including the IMF and the ADB.

References

Azis, Iwan J. 2012. "Asian Regional Financial Safety Nets? Don't Hold Your Breath." *Public Policy Review* 8, no. 3: 321–340.

Group of Twenty (G20). 2011. "G20 Principles for Cooperation between the IMF and Regional Financing Arrangements." Endorsed by G20 Finance Ministers and Central Bank Governors, October 15.

Henning, Randall C. 2011. "Coordinating Regional and Multilateral Financial Institutions." Working Paper No. WP11-9. Washington, DC: Peterson Institute for International Economics.

Henning, Randall C. 2016. "Global and Regional Financial Governance: Designing Cooperation." Forthcoming as a Discussion Paper (August/September) of the Council on Foreign Relations, New York and Washington, DC.

Kawai, Masahiro, and Cindy Houser. 2008. "Evolving ASEAN+3 ERPD: Towards Peer Reviews or Due Diligence?" In OECD, *Shaping Policy Reform and Peer Review in Southeast Asia: Integrating Economies amid Diversity*, 65–98. Paris: Organisation for Economic Co-operation and Development.

Kawai, Masahiro, Richard Newfarmer, and Sergio L. Schmukler. 2005. "Financial Crises: Nine Lessons from East Asia." *Eastern Economic Journal* 31, no. 2 (Spring): 185–207.

Lamberte, Mario, and Peter Morgan. 2014. "Regional and Global Monetary Cooperation." In *Reform of the International Monetary System: An Asian Perspective*, edited by Masahiro Kawai, Mario Lamberte, and Peter Morgan, 225–253. Tokyo: Springer.

Menon, Jayant, and Hal Hill. 2014. "Does East Asia Have a Working Financial Safety Net?" *Asian Economic Journal*, 28: 1–17.

Siregar, Reza, and Akkharaphol Chabchitrchaidol. 2014. "Enhancing the Effectiveness of CMIM and AMRO: Challenges and Tasks." In *New Global Economic Architecture: The Asian Perspective*, edited by Masahiro Kawai, Peter Morgan, and Pradumna Rana, 55–82. Cheltenham, UK, and Northampton, MA, USA: Edward Elgar.

Sussangkarn, C. 2011. "The Chiang Mai Initiative Multilateralization: Origin, Development, and Outlook." *Asian Economic Policy Review* 6, no. 2: 203–220.

Takagi, Shinji. 2010. "Regional Surveillance for East Asia: How Can It Be Designed to Complement Global Surveillance?" ADB Working Paper Series on Regional Economic Integration 50. Manila: ADB.

16 From small markets to collective action

Regional public goods in Africa

Richard Newfarmer[1]

Introduction

As commodity prices languish and the global economy limps along in anemic recovery, the countries of Africa have increasingly looked to neighboring markets to expand trade and drive growth. Ironically, even while the European Union grapples with the powerful centrifugal forces of dissolution following the Brexit vote in 2016, Africa is pressing ahead with regional economic integration. Many older arrangements, such as the East African Community (EAC) and the Economic Community of West Africa States (ECOWAS), are undertaking progressively more steps toward deep integration, and the region has spawned new, even bolder initiatives in 2015—the Tripartite Free Trade Area and the even more ambitious Continental Free Trade Agreement—designed to lower trade and other barriers across the whole continent. Why is it that African countries seem to persist at integration while Europe, arguably the most successful historical experience of integration, would seem to have established its limits? This paper examines the drivers of integration, and looks at their successes and limitation in providing regional public goods that anchor greater integration, political stability, and economic opportunity.[2]

Since the wave of independence movements swept the African continent in the 1960s, nations within Africa have sought to create regional cooperation mechanisms. These have ranged from informal nonbinding cooperation agreements, through forums to discuss common problems, to binding plurilateral contracts with specific obligations, enforcement provisions, and multinational bureaucracies to implement and, in some cases, adjudicate rules. These collections of contractual rules and platforms of discussions, together with collective actions based on agreed principles, provide what might loosely be called "regional public goods" (RPGs) (Estevadordal and Goodman 2014).

Among regions of the developing world, Africa suffered one of the most brutal experiences of European colonialism. One legacy of this colonial history was the creation of nation-states, typically with arbitrary boundaries that ignored tribal cultures and histories, and unusually small markets. About one-third of these post-independence countries were landlocked and isolated from the global market. Colonialization often exacerbated tribal divisions through the creation of privileged ethnically defined elites that governed autocratically, resulting in seething tensions that have contributed to an usually high frequency of violent conflicts in many parts of Africa, even after independence.

This history suggests there are several reasons to expect that the regional provision of public goods—security, wider markets, infrastructure, and shared regulations—have the potential to improve the lives of people in Africa. Regional efforts could augment the efforts of other actors, both domestic and international, to help dampen conflicts, enhance security, and create a stable political order. Moreover, firms in small markets could begin to realize economies of scale through trade expansion and access to lower-cost shared infrastructure, such as energy, ports, and air transportation. Regional initiatives could lower trading costs across both sides of common borders, which is particularly important for landlocked countries seeking access to the global market. Governments could benefit from specialized expertise through sharing common regulations and even regulatory agencies. Finally, as Africa is the region with the lowest average per capita incomes, human capital is unusually scarce, so searching for ways to share knowledge and access technology are other forms in which regional cooperation efforts might be expected to pay dividends.

This political and economic logic of substantial mutual benefits gave rise to high expectations, but many observers were later disappointed. Porges, for example, gives this downbeat assessment of her reading of the literature in comparison with other regions: "although most Africa PTAs [preferential trade agreements] have a high level of ambition for integration, they have not been effective in eliminating intraregional trade and investment barriers and have struggled with (or succumbed to) economic conflict" (Porges 2011, p.470).

Regional cooperation in Africa: a long march with a quickening pace

The wave of African independence movements in the early 1960s gave rise to the first efforts toward African-led regional cooperation. A key date was the founding of the Organisation of African Unity (OAU) in 1963. It brought together 32 mostly newly independent countries around the objective of political collaboration to oppose the vestiges of white rule (notably in South Africa and Angola) and to maintain a neutral posture in the Cold War. Throughout the next decades, African governments went on to design a series of Pan-African development approaches which they felt were relevant to the needs of their people.[3]

Regional cooperation on economic issues began in earnest with the Abuja Treaty in 1991 that created the African Economic Community (AEC)[4] and regional economic communities (RECs) designed to foster economic integration over the following three decades. Other arrangements promoting regional cooperation generally concern security, environmental, and other issues, including the African Union (AU), founded in 2002 as the successor to the OAU; the New Partnership for Africa's Development (NEPAD), an African-led peer mechanism; the 12-state International Conference on the Great Lakes (ICGL), founded in 2000, which focuses on peace, democracy, and humanitarian issues; and the Manu River Union, reactivated in 2004 and comprising Liberia, Sierra Leone, Guinea, and (later) Côte d'Ivoire to promote trade integration as well as in health after the Ebola crisis of 2015, among others. Today, the AU recognizes eight principal RECs.

An integral part of regional cooperation agreements are specific trade arrangements offering preferential market access to neighbors. These now cover most of intra-African trade (see Figure 16.1).

Progress toward achieving the objectives of the Abuja Treaty and subsequent commitments has been slow. In its assessment, UNECA (2012) wrote "despite current initiatives, results remain mixed. Whereas certain RECs have achieved tangible outcomes . . . others have had relatively disappointing results" (UNECA 2012, p.13). The report underscores difficulties in harmonizing, monitoring, and assessing projects and programs designed to boost integration. While some regions have made considerable progress in setting up free trade areas and enlarged their membership—such as the EAC—others have

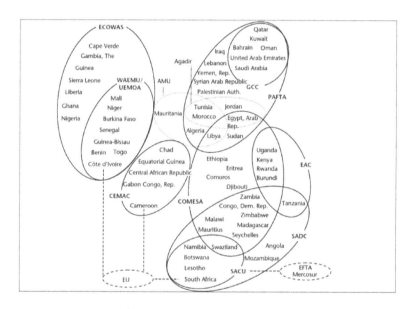

Figure 16.1 Africa's Regional Trade Agreements.

Source: Acharya et al. (2011, Figure 2.18), WTO Secretariat.

Note: AMU = Arab Maghreb Union, CEMAC = Economic and Monetary Community of Central Africa (Communauté Économique et Monétaire de l'Afrique Centrale), COMESA = Common Market for Eastern and Southern Africa, EAC = East African Community, ECOWAS = Economic Community of West African States, EFTA = European Free Trade Association, EU = European Union, GCC = Gulf Cooperation Council, MERCOSUR = Southern Cone Common Market, PAFTA = Pan-Arab Free Trade Area, SACU = Southern African Customs Union, SADC = Southern African Development Community, WAEMU/UEOMA = West African Economic and Monetary Union/Union Économique et Monétaire Ouest-Africaine.

undertaken commitments that have exceeded actual implementation, often by a large margin, such as ECOWAS, the Southern African Development Community (SADC), and the Intergovernmental Authority on Development (IGAD).

This has not dampened the apparent longing for an economically united Africa, which dates back to the Abuja Treaty. In December 2014, three RECs launched the Tripartite Free Trade Area (TFTA), covering the EAC, SADC, and Common Market for Eastern and Southern Africa (COMESA). This marked the culmination of the discussions that had begun in 2005 focusing on the harmonization of trade and infrastructure policies in these three RECs. This effort was aimed at combining 26 countries ranging from Egypt to South Africa into a free trade group accounting for 625 million people with an aggregate GDP of US$1 trillion. The area would subsume some 58% of the entire economic activity of Sub-Saharan Africa. Its immediate objective would be to expand trade and create a huge market to attract investment. This was seen as a stepping-stone toward a Continental Free Trade Area, which would materialize in 2019. The agenda focused on improving regional trading arrangements, including the removal of nontariff barriers; facilitating trade by lowering transit times in major corridors, including the pilot North–South corridor begun in 2007; joint planning of infrastructure, including roads, ICT, and air transportation; and free movement of business people within the TFTA region (see De Melo 2014; Laski 2015). This underscores the point that however fitful and uneven efforts had been across the continent, the underlying direction has been toward ever-greater regional cooperation designed to foster integration.

The political economy of integration in Africa

Political leaders pursue regional integration for a variety of reasons (see Schiff and Winters 2003). As in the case of Europe in the 1950s and 1960s, African countries have pursued integration to bolster political alliances. The OAU was largely born as a way of uniting in order to defend the interests of post-independence African nations against white colonial rule and its backlash. Similarly, the SADC originated in the 1980s as an alliance against apartheid in South Africa and has only more recently turned into a free trade area. In fact, Martin, Mayer, and Thoenig (2010) examined conflicts and RTAs between 1950 and 2000 (mainly outside of Africa), and concluded that geopolitical motivations played a statistically significant role in their formation. The agreements in North Africa and East Africa were born with an explicit long-term commitment to establish some (usually vague) eventual political federation.

Underlying these political motivations, however, was a critical economic issue: the constraints of the small average size of national markets. The median GDP size of African countries in 2013 was US$12.3 billion (that is, about one one-third the GDP of the city of Quebec, Canada, or Des Moines, Iowa, USA). All of Africa's economies measured at PPP would not be equal to Germany (Figure 16.2). This means that it is difficult for private producers to achieve reasonable scale economies without exporting and importing. Beyond

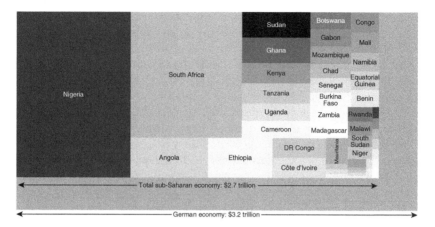

Figure 16.2 Africa's Unusually Small National Markets (GDP, PPP in US$).
Source: IEA 2014.

this, small domestic markets provide little allure for foreign investors, many of which are accustomed to building plants that serve large markets. Similarly, governments have found it economically advantageous to share infrastructure. This also means that countries can reap gains from sharing regulatory authorities (e.g. standards, customs procedures, etc.). Regional trading agreements offer an opportunity to establish cooperative arrangements across multiple government activities and markets.

The limitations of a small market are severe. Braun, Hausmann, and Pritchett (2004) calculate that a one-standard deviation change in market size would explain a 0.6% difference in growth: "Integration agreements can be interpreted as attempts between sovereign states reciprocally to renounce some of these rights [to restrict trade and migration and set macro policies] in order to facilitate economic activity" (Braun et al. 2004, p.139). They go on to argue, based on worldwide experience, that two factors explain post-independence growth: changes in market access (including access to foreign markets) and the change in the quality of policies (Braun et al. 2004, p.139).

In Africa (as no doubt elsewhere), the quality of policies was endogenous to governance generally, and particularly to the frequency of civil conflicts. After independence, Africa was plagued by despotic governance and civil wars with a frequency not experienced in other regions. Between 1960 and 1999, 20 African countries experienced a civil war, with the incidence of war peaking at 8 per year in the 1980s before declining to 7.5 in the 1990s, and roughly 3–4 after 2000 (Aryeetey et al. 2012). The roots of most conflicts eventually descended into tribal rivalries—Biafra's attempted succession from Nigeria in 1967–70; the Rwandan rebellion and eventual genocide of 1991–94; the simmering civil wars that began in the Democratic Republic of Congo in 1997,

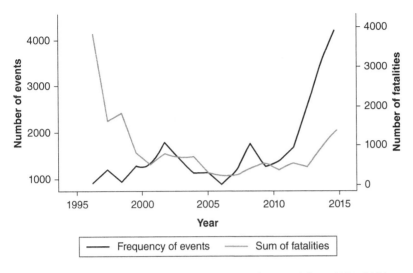

Figure 16.3 Frequency of Violent Events and Fatalities in Africa, 1997–2014.

Source: Armed Conflict Location and Events Dataset (ACLED) Conflict Patterns Across Africa, Real Time Analysis of African Political Violence, version 5 (http://www.acleddata.com).

Côte d'Ivoire in 2010–11, Somalia after 1991, and South Sudan in 2013, to name a few. Rebel movements were often born and harbored in neighboring countries in ways that ultimately influenced outcomes. In the long fight against apartheid in South Africa, the African National Congress survived in part through the support of the front-line states; Uganda's Yoweri Museveni gained important support from Tanzania in the 1980s; the Rwandan Patriotic Front was born in Uganda; and both sides of today's civil war in South Sudan have received sporadic external support—the rebels from Sudan and the government from Uganda.

More comprehensive analysis has exposed deeper causes behind these conflicts: natural resources (especially minerals) that were easy to loot (Angola and Sierra Leone), low per capita incomes and education that made recruiting labor and soldiers cheap (Mozambique and the CAR), and weakness in democratic institutions (Aryeetey et al. 2012).

Even though the Ibrahim Index of African Governance (IIAG) reveals a steady improvement in conflict levels through to 2010 (Mo Ibrahim Foundation 2014), the decrease in violence since the 1990s seems to have been reversed since 2012–2013 (Figure 16.3). The character of the new upsurge is different than in the early 1990s when civil wars predominated based on struggles for power with political purpose. With the exception of the civil war in South Sudan, today's drivers of civil conflict are mainly election-related violence, extremism, terrorist attacks, drug trafficking, maritime piracy, and criminality. Armed insurgents with nihilistic ideologies—such as Boko Haram in Nigeria, the Tuareg and Arab uprising in Mali, and the cross-border raids into Kenya of the Al-Shabaab from Somalia—have caused heavy, senseless casualties.

Whatever the motives, violence and insecurity devastate victims and destroy growth prospects. In an article diagnosing the causes of slow growth in African countries since independence, Collier and O'Connell (2008) describe four governance syndromes affecting resource-rich, coastal states, and resource-poor countries over the post-independence period. Their statistical analysis showed that political conflict rooted in tribal politics was the most powerful of the four impediments to economic growth in Africa. They calculated that conflict generates a 2% decline in the rate of economic growth. Shanta Devarajan et al. (2013) use cross-country regressions to show that countries which experience more than 100 casualties from violence against civilians in a given year would experience a decline in economic growth of 2.3%. As such, by far the greatest public good that regional cooperation arrangements can confer would be to help reduce conflict.

Can regional cooperation contribute to reducing conflict?

While the regional cooperation arrangements that flourished in Africa after 1990 were arguably more a result of peace than a cause, it seems likely that they contributed to improvements in social peace in the continent. One effect of such arrangements is that they create larger political units that recast both ethnically driven politics and external security threats. Collier and Venables (2008) used counterfactual analysis based upon several econometric studies of growth in Africa to discuss the effects of country size on three public goods essential to prosperity: security, economic policy, and infrastructure. If Africa had formed a political union, they contend that, even taking greater ethnic diversity into account, the size of this union would have reduced the risk of civil war by some 14%; similarly, a united Africa would have muted neighborhood arms competition and reduced defense spending, under certain assumptions, from 3.2% of GDP to 2.4%. Similarly, larger states would lead to better economic policies through several channels: a better civil service, a better media and thus more informed citizenry, and a faster pace of policy adjustment for economic reform. Finally, infrastructure benefits from economies of scale—particularly in transportation (e.g. rail), power, and connectivity. The links between infrastructure and trade are particularly important for resource-rich landlocked countries that need electricity for mining and have to export to global markets through neighboring countries.

The trade agreements embedded in the regional agreements have arguably played a direct role in this process by augmenting cross-border commercial relations.[5] Trade increases interdependence by raising the cost of conflict to the potentially warring states; moreover, trade is often accompanied by greater knowledge of neighbors and trading partners that evolve into cross-border friendships and business partnerships; and finally, RTAs typically entail new institutions for resolving commercial disputes before they escalate to conflict. Cross-country econometric studies seem to bear this out. Martin, Mayer, and Thoenig (2005) found that bilateral trade expansion does tend to reduce intrastate conflict among members because, they conjecture, regional integration increases the opportunity cost of war. Mansfield and Pevehouse (2000) found that membership of an RTA significantly decreases the likelihood of armed conflict, a conclusion supported by more recent evidence in the work of Lee and Pyun (2009). Martin et al. (2010) add an important qualification, namely that gains from RTAs and integration have to be sufficiently large before the conflict-dampening effects of RTAs gain traction. Chaffour and Maur (2011) highlight the institutional underpinnings to peace that arise from regional cooperation agreements, particularly trade agreements. RTAs, they contend, provide "an infrastructure for institutional dialogue and cooperation," with flexible instruments that comprise both binding and nonbinding legal agreements.[6]

Security is becoming a regional public good

Africans, often building on previous agreements, are playing a more proactive role in resolving festering conflicts. One of the objectives of the AU is the promotion of peace and security on the continent. It established a Peace and Security Council (PSC) in 2004, with the right to intervene in countries in situations of war crimes, genocide, and crimes against humanity. Any decision to intervene in a member state under Article 4 of the Constitutive Act will be made by the Assembly on the recommendation of the PSC. The AU worked on crises in Darfur, Comoros, Somalia, Democratic Republic of Congo, Burundi, and Côte d'Ivoire, among others; participated in peacekeeping operations in Somalia and Darfur; and imposed sanctions against persons undermining peace and security. The PSC is in the process of overseeing the establishment of a "standby force" available to be deployed at short notice upon the resolution of the AU General Assembly.

Beyond the AU, regional organizations are also actively involved in such initiatives. The Intergovernmental Authority on Development (IGAD) has been playing a weighty role in the Horn of Africa. Formed in 1986 as a successor organization to one dealing with a drought in the region, IGAD is comprised of Djibouti, Ethiopia, Eritrea, Kenya, Sudan, South Sudan, and Uganda. It was key in mobilizing troops for support of the government in Somalia beginning in 2006, and under the UN flag in 2007. Since the civil war began in South Sudan in December 2013, IGAD has led the mediation efforts of regional partners trying to end the conflict there. As the peace agreement signed in early 2016 broke down in July and civil war resumed, IGAD, the AU, and the UN were actively discussing sending in an armed force to protect civilians and try to reimpose peace—without the active support of the recalcitrant government.

Another example is the ICGL's effort to broker a peace deal in the Democratic Republic of Congo after the M23 rebellion that began in 2012. This organization brings together Angola, Burundi, the Central African Republic, the Republic of Congo, the Democratic Republic of Congo, Kenya, Uganda,

Rwanda, the Republic of South Sudan, Sudan, Tanzania, and Zambia, with a focus on peace, democracy, and humanitarian issues. International pressure from external actors, plus the efforts of a UN-authorized South Africa-led force that included troops from Tanzania and elsewhere, eventually quelled the M23 rebellion. This was part of a larger understanding that the new military force would go after the FDLR, a Hutu-led militia dedicated to overthrowing the Rwandan government, as well as the other three dozen militias at large in the Kivu provinces of the Democratic Republic of Congo. Progress to date has been elusive, and the militias, while suppressed, still emerge periodically.

A third example is the active condemnation of the violence in Burundi associated with President Pierre Nkurunziza's decision to seek a third term in office. In May 2015, several demonstrators were killed precipitating a short-lived military effort to wrest control of the government from civilian authorities. Leaders of the ICGL meeting in Luanda issued a declaration condemning both the violence and the unconstitutional change in government. The coup collapsed, though low-intensity strife continued into 2016 and serious issues of governance remain.

Finally, a continent-wide example of measures to reduce conflict and violence is NEPAD's Peer Review Mechanism, which seeks to have governments voluntarily provide a review of all governance, peace, and security issues. The process is similar in some aspects to the OECD peer review, and consists of five stages including a participatory self-assessment, a peer review conducted by heads of state, and preparation of a national action plan to improve deficient areas. To date, 17 peer reviews have been undertaken. While not wholly successful yet, the process has created an African-led platform to discuss security issues and improve governance (Maru and El Fassi 2015).

Economic integration agreements: design issues

Preferential trade agreements: beyond tariffs to regulation

The early African agreements only partially offset the problems of scale that followed independence. The early African agreements of the late 1990s were built around an import substitution model. These used high average external tariffs (and other barriers) to wall off member states from international competition in an effort to create a larger internal markets that were highly protected. Weaknesses soon became apparent: as was also the case in Latin America, the costs of new import substitution industries were high and quality was lower than internationally available comparable products. Member states typically had similar technological levels and factor endowments, so potential gains from integrating complementary economies were limited, and trade growth naturally stunted. Trade diversion rather than trade creation was the rule rather than the exception.[7] Over time, policy has moved away from import substitution, and external barriers across the region have fallen, though not yet to the levels found in the more integrated regions of East Asia and Eastern Europe.

A second characteristic is that these regional trade agreements are not confined solely to tariffs and regulation of merchandise trade, but for the most part seek deeper integration that extends to common approaches to regulation, the liberalization of selected services, and in some case even monetary and political federation. The Southern African Customs Union (SACU) was born as a currency union from its founding in the first decade of the 20th century; and the West African Economic and Monetary Union (UEMOA) and the Central African Economic and Monetary Community (CEMAC) were formed as currency unions, arising from the *Communauté financière africaine* (CFA) experience. Beyond this, the EAC aspires to become a currency union before the end of this decade—though it seems improbable that this deadline can be met—and to eventually move toward political federation. Nearly all agreements include provisions that would permit the integration of selected services markets (including finance), customs regulations, and some investment provisions (Table 16.1). Less common are general provisions permitting labor movement and government procurement.

Table 16.1 Different Coverage and Regulatory Content of RTAs

	CEMAC	COMESA	EAC	ECOWAS	SACU	SADC	UEMOA
Type of agreement	CU & M	CU	CU	CU	CU & M	FTA	CU & M
Aspired coverage:							
Currency	Yes	No	Yes	Yes	Yes	No	Yes
Goods	Yes	Yes	Yes	Yes	Yes	Yes	Yes
Services		Some	Some	Some	Some	Some	Some
Customs*	Yes	Yes	Yes	Yes	Yes	Yes	Yes
Intellectual Property		No	Yes	Yes	Yes	Yes	Yes
Investment	Yes	Yes	Yes	Yes		Yes	Yes
Labor	Yes		Yes				Yes
Competition		Yes			Yes		Yes
Dispute Resolution	no	Yes	Yes		Yes	Yes	Yes
Govt. Procurement	Yes						
Political Federation			Yes	Yes			

Source: WBG RTA database; WTO RTA database; World Bank (2005); Chauffour and Maur (2011).

Notes: CU = Currency union, M = Monetary union, FTA = Free trade agreement. *includes non-tariff measures.

Most RECs have set up procedures to reduce nontariff barriers. COMESA, SADC, and the EAC, for example, have set up an online registry that enables private operators and government officials to register complaints, which can then be resolved bilaterally. By 2013, according to UNECA, 329 complaints were lodged using these systems, and 227 were resolved (UNECA 2013, p.7). Nontariff barriers still persist, however: the EAC has set up a website with a list of nontariff barriers that are scheduled for removal or otherwise under discussion (see Kirk 2012) and SADC is doing likewise (see Gilson 2012).

Many of the agreements purport to allow freer movement of labor, especially for professional services. For example, COMESA, SADC, and CEMAC all now grant variations of a 90-day visa on arrival to citizens of states which are members of the FTA protocol; ECOWAS is taking this further by creating an ECOWAS passport that will replace national passports; within the EAC, Kenya, Rwanda, and Uganda have a bilateral agreement to allow citizens to freely establish themselves for work purposes in these EAC countries; Rwanda now issues visas on arrival to all African citizens (UNECA 2013, p.4).

Collaboration on border crossings

Governments in Africa have developed regional arrangements to promote several collaborative efforts to deepen trade ties—importantly, trade facilitation, physical infrastructure, and services.

Trade facilitation

Intraregional trade shares remain low relative to East Asia, Europe, and North America. One reason is high transportation costs. Reducing delays at the border and in transit can have a dramatic effect on reducing costs—and therefore on increasing exports. Even though time to market has been decreasing in Africa, exporter and importers there still require 50% more time than those in East Asia. These delays are compounded by the fact that 16 of Africa's 47 continental countries are landlocked: as these are already far from markets, crossing multiple borders with heavy delays drives up costs. Freund and Rocha (2011) estimate that trade volumes are 16% lower than what would be expected from normal gravity model relationships, and the difference is almost wholly accounted for by the time-to-export variable intended to proxy trade facilitation. A one-day reduction in inland travel times is equivalent to a 2% decrease in trading partners' import tariffs.

The overlap in PTAs and differences in tariff rates, nontariff measures, and rules of origin mean that the tariff code is extremely complex to administer. The same good may be subject to a different tariff depending on its origins and the paperwork submitted by the trader. Additionally, the level of training of customs agents is frequently not commensurate with the complexity of the tasks.[8] Delays at borders are common: Hummels (2001) calculates that, on average, a one-day delay drives up costs by about 0.8% around the world, and Djankov, Freund, and Pham (2010) found that each day in transit had the effect of reducing trade volumes by slightly more than 1%, on average.

For these reasons, trade facilitation is a major component of regional cooperation. Governments throughout Africa are paying much more attention to streamlining border crossings. In East Africa, for example, governments are working closely with the DFID-financed Trademark East Africa to computerize forms on both sides of the EAC border, create one-stop registration procedures, and harmonize the various agencies at the borders to reduce crossing times. RTAs provide a forum in which to discuss time savings in harmonization or mutual recognition of standards, cabotage rules governing trucking, insurance issues, and other regulations (see Rippel 2012).

Collaboration on physical infrastructure

Virtually all of the RECs have begun some form of joint planning for road and rail development as a way of promoting further integration. One example is the effort to complete the missing links in the Trans-African Highway. In 2012, African ministers of transportation adopted a region-wide plan that included network routes, design standards, and harmonization of safety, social, and environmental norms. Collaborative planning of international roads is now well established in virtually all the regional agreements. Similar efforts are underway in rail and air transportation (see UNECA 2013). Collective action, especially on transportation issues, is not confined to established groups. For example, the countries of the EAC's Northern Corridor (mainly Rwanda, Uganda, and Kenya) have been coordinating several projects, including a standard gauge railway project (US$13.5 billion) and a single airspace arrangement, signed last year during the 8th Northern Corridor Integration Projects Summit held in Nairobi, Kenya (All Africa News 2015).

Energy development is another area of regional cooperation in Africa. All of Africa has installed capacity for generation of about 90 GW, about half of which is located in South Africa. The entire population of Africa uses less electricity per year than Spain, and two-thirds of Africans—620 million people—do not have access to electricity (Africa Progress Panel 2015). The implication of this for trade and growth is profound. Firms across the region report that a measurable portion of sales annually are lost because plants suffering blackouts have to be shut down (Figure 16.4).

Regional collective actions, often with the support of donors, are helping to ameliorate these deficits. For example, the East African Power Master Plan was completed in 2011. It outlines the least-cost generation and transmission program for meeting regional electricity demand for 2013–38, and contains provisions for interconnection codes that will regulate transmission system design and technical operational requirements with common standards. Similarly, the West African Power Pool continued efforts to update the ECOWAS Master Plan for Production and Distribution adopted in 2011. ECOWAS intends to establish a regional electricity market (see UNECA 2013).

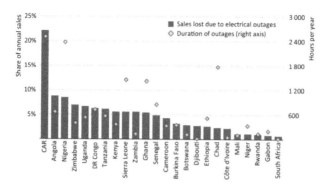

Figure 16.4 Duration of Electrical Outages and Impact on Business Sales in Selected African Countries.

Source: World Bank (2014); IEA analysis.

Notes: CAR = Central African Republic. Data is from the last available business survey for a given country.

No less important for connectivity than power and transportation is broadband access. Ten countries began working together in 2003 to bring broadband access to Africa through undersea fiber optic cables. The Eastern Africa Submarine Cable System (EASSy) was inaugurated in 2010 and runs from Mtunzini in South Africa to Port Sudan in Sudan, with landing points in nine countries and connections in at least ten landlocked countries (Figure 16.5). The US$200 million project delivers direct connectivity between East Africa and Europe/North America, with interconnections to the Americas, the Middle East, and Asia.

Collaboration on services

African services markets are not the most closed in the world: using the World Bank's Services Trade Restrictiveness Index (STRI), Africa compares favorably with East Asia and the Pacific, though it is far more closed than Latin America and Eastern and Central Europe, as well as the OECD in general. Indeed, only seven of the 22 African countries have restrictions that exceed the world average. Among services, the most restricted are to be found in professional services, telecommunications, and transportation. These sectors are among the most important in terms of inputs into the growth process, both for the domestic production and exports. Restrictions in transportation include cabotage rules that limit the cargos that trucks registered in one country can deliver to another; monopoly air transportation rights given to particular airlines that reduce service and drive up costs; state monopolies in rail traffic that often deteriorate into poor, high-cost services; and differing standards (e.g. axle and load requirements), which can restrict transit and cause trucking companies to waste valuable time loading and unloading.

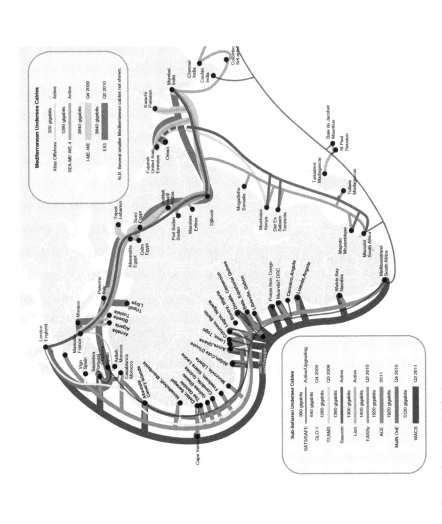

Figure 16.5 Eastern Africa Submarine Cable System.

Source: http://en.wikipedia.org/wiki/EASSy

Even though many sectors are relatively open, such as retail trade, others remain comparatively closed, such as finance, telecommunications, and professional services—at least as measured by the regulatory approvals necessary to enter the market. RTAs in Africa have not gone far regarding including services liberation. The EAC, like other agreements, does provide for some foreign entry (mode 3) in retail and cross-border supply, such as with digital services. Dihel, Fernandes, and Mattoo (2012) show how restrictions in professional services hamper growth by making it difficult for firms to access the knowledge and talent of lawyers, accountants, and engineers from foreign countries. The EAC's review of trade in services found 63 instances of laws that conflicted with EAC protocol provisions, mostly in professional services (73%) and road transportation (24%) (East African Community 2014).

Some initiatives are encouraging. The Northern Corridor countries of the EAC—Rwanda, Uganda, and Kenya—have begun issuing a single joint East African visas to foreign tourists. These same countries have also promoted telecommunication competition by banning roaming charges within the EAC; officials report that, as a consequence, usage has risen, prices to consumers have come down, and profits of companies have gone up. On balance, however, using services negotiations in RTAs in order to anchor more open markets in services, increase competition in their supply, and lower input costs is an opportunity that has been largely missed.

Effects of RTAs on trade and growth

Whether regional cooperation contributes to sustained peace and prosperity in the long run depends heavily on whether arrangements also contribute to increased trade, productivity, and rising incomes. Regional cooperation arrangements can affect trade and investment, and, through trade, economic growth. There is an abundant literature that shows that, in general, trade tends to raise growth rates over time, especially when combined with complementary policies affecting investment climate.[9] But do RTAs contribute to expanding trade? De Melo and Tsikata (2014) point to three ways regional agreements can increase trade: reductions in tariffs between members; reductions in nontariff measures; and improvements in trade facilitation, regional infrastructure, and policies and regulations that reduce trade costs. They found that in four of the six regions studied, intraregional trade (as measured by imports) has grown at about the same pace as external trade; the exceptions are the Pan-Arab Free Trade Area and SADC, where intraregional trade grew faster (Figure 16.6). Even so, the share of intraregional trade remains uniformly low—below 15% of the total trade in all agreements.

An issue of importance is whether increases in intraregional trade are truly new trade creation or are simply trade diversion with associated income losses. De Melo and Tsikata (2014) looked at this question in detail through the lens of different methodologies and conclude that "no clear pattern emerges across the RECs." ECOWAS, SADC, and UEMOA seem to benefit from

Figure 16.6 Intra-regional Imports as Percentage of Total, Before and After
RTA Effectiveness.

Source: DOTS, IMF (2013).

Note: The red dot on the plot line in each panel indicates the agreement's implementation date (and when the organization becomes active, in the case of ECOWAS). UEMOA
countries are excluded from ECOWAS. The spike in the ECOWAS import share in 1980
was due to zero import activity in Nigeria that year.

trade creation, while EAC evidence suggests trade diversion. Trade openness
for all RTA groups seems to increase but not directly attributable to RTAs.
Calculating an "average distance ratio" between regional trade and extraregional trade based on gravity models suggests that extraregional trade costs have
fallen more rapidly than within regions, and it is only the EAC where internal
costs have fallen faster, "displaying a regionalization of trade" (De Melo and
Tsikata 2014). They also implicitly compare the findings within Africa to those
in Head and Mayer (2013)'s detailed review of the gravity model literature;
the latter finds that FTAs worldwide increase trade by an average of 32%
after controlling for other factors (e.g. distance, relative size, etc.), albeit with
considerable variance around the mean. Trade effects of common currencies
are even larger. By comparison, increases in African trade appear to be much
smaller. Acharya et al. (2011), using different time period and gravity models,
also found evidence of trade creation within RTA regions.

In one of the most recent and innovative studies, Mayer and Thoenig (2016) assessed the consequences of existing and prospective trade integration in the EAC using a procedure that combined gravity model estimations with CGE prospective analysis. They found that the EAC customs union has been very successful in increasing bilateral trade among members by 213% on average. This is much more than COMESA, which led to an increase of 80%, or the SADC, which led to an increase of 110%. Moreover, the trade gains propelled improvements in income. Real GDP was estimated to have risen by 0.45% in the EAC relative to the counterfactual. Finally, the formation of the EAC has contributed to peace in the Great Lakes region. The statistical risk of bilateral conflicts between members was estimated to have decreased by 12%.

Moreover, using a prospective approach, they calculate that efficient implementation of the EAC common market area would lead to a further doubling of the gains in welfare achieved so far. They also find, however, that an EAC common currency is estimated to have only small trade and welfare effects that may not justify the risks and costs associated with it. The estimated benefits from integration with COMESA and SADC are relatively small, largely because the EAC already overlaps with both regional trade agreements, so the main value in the TFTA would lie in paving the way to a continent-wide free trade area.

A balanced reading of this literature would lead to the conclusion that the regional trade agreements have had an overall positive effect on overall trade and trade within the region, but have played a role secondary to trade expansion with global partners in contributing to the trade-led growth experienced in the last two decades. Still, it seems clear they have not fulfilled their full promise. Several factors account for this. First, the economies within regions produce many of the same products, so when comparing developments before and after a relatively short period, the gains from merchandise trade integration are likely to be low. Second, implementation of agreements has often lagged behind stated aspirations, so joining in one period may not confer benefits in the years immediately following the agreement. Third, reductions in intraregional tariffs have been offset by persistent nontariff barriers in the form of standards, trade delays at the border, and other factors—see Brenton and Isik (2012) and Cadot and Malouche (2012) for a full discussion. Beyond this, implementation of provisions anticipating reductions in barriers to trade in services, capital markets, common standards, government procurement, competition policy, and labor law have not been implemented in a timely fashion in virtually any agreement (East African Community 2014).

De Melo and Tsikata point to another, arguably more fundamental flaw in the sequencing of liberalization: "Until recently at least, regional integration in Africa was founded on a 20th century exchange of market access at the expense of outsiders and on the "linear model of integration" that neglected the importance of tackling behind-the-border impediments to trade. With the reduction in trade costs and subsequent fragmentation of production, 21st century regionalism is about a new bargain: an exchange of domestic market reforms for FDI which brings home the services activities necessary to participate in the global value chain" (East African Community 2014, p.19).

The slow progress on trade facilitation and slow integration of services markets and their resulting high costs has undermined the otherwise positive trade benefits of RTAs.

Conclusions

Have regional cooperation efforts in Africa contributed to a more peaceful and prosperous Africa by providing RPGs? While there is a lack of convincing econometrics to justify hard conclusions, the evidence seen through the lens of a 40-year history points to an affirmative answer. Small market economies, riven by ethnic divisions and insecurity, cannot grow. Landlocked countries, even with good governance, are too small to grow without access to neighboring markets, transportation to coasts, and access to global markets. Since independence, governments throughout the region have concluded an increasing number of agreements spanning politics, policy, and commerce; the intensity of economic linkages within regions has deepened, and regional cooperation has moved progressively into new areas of commerce, policy, and politics. Along the way, countries have exchanged market access and relinquished aspects of sovereignty to regional rules. This process has unleashed a dialectic of collective action that has resulted in access to wider markets, new investment, and new forms of collaboration. And this has contributed to raising incomes and reinforcing peace.

Moreover, the last three decades have seen ever more serious attempts by African leadership to provide security arrangements that lay the foundation for peace, a prerequisite for growth. Regional organizations have provided platforms for discussing boundary disputes, ending civil wars, and curbing excessive government repression and social conflicts. These efforts have not always been successful, and conflicts persist in several parts of Africa, driving down growth. In fact, violence may increase as growth weakens with the end of the commodity boom and a youth bulge of jobseekers enters a tighter labor market. Still, recent upsurges in violence seem more a function of these phenomena interacting with radical ideologies, drugs, and criminality than they do with more overt political, tribally based violence of past decades—presenting a new challenge to collective regional action.

Despite some obvious progress, regional cooperation agreements, when measured through the narrow lens of merchandise trade growth, have arguably fallen short of realizing their full potential to spur growth through deep integration. While growth in Africa, especially in nonconflict Africa, has recently been high by historical standards, intraregional trade has been only a weak driver of this growth, at best keeping pace with the growth of the economy. Moreover, diversification of export portfolios has proceeded slowly, and African regional groupings have had only incipient success in tapping into global value chains (see Kowalski et al. 2015).

There are several reasons for this lackluster trade performance. The most significant reason is probably the fact that similarities in economic structure permit far fewer gains from trade and specialization than trade with the rest of the world does. With manufactures accounting for a relatively low share of national output and relatively similar factor endowments and relative prices, the opportunities for intra-industry trade based on different factor prices are far more limited. Second, implementation has suffered the particularistic exclusions driven by private interests that are typical of all trade deals. These include product exclusions from free trade agreements, nontariff barriers, onerous rules of origin, incompatible standards, and regulatory barriers, which have undermined the otherwise beneficial attempts to liberalize trade and investment.[10]

Inappropriate sequencing, particularly of services liberalization, may be the most important policy-amenable obstacle. De Melo and Tsikata (2014) insightfully argue that politicians have focused excessively on goods liberalization to the exclusion of implementing other provisions that might be more important in expanding trade-led growth. They argue that the sequencing of RTAs in Africa has too often followed an "old model" in which goods are liberalized first, followed by trade facilitation, and then later—often much later—by services, which they claim is inappropriate in a world where value chains give primacy to trade logistics with their heavy reliance on service inputs. Efficient services—lower-cost transportation, telecoms, ports, accounting, and legal services—are central to growing merchandise and services exports (Mattoo and Sauvé 2011). Hoekman and Shepherd (2015) have shown that they are even more important for productivity growth in manufacturing—and that restrictive regulations are a major cause of underperforming services.

Collier and Venables (2008) argue that the shortcomings in regional integration in Africa stem not from a failure to fully implement trade agreements, but from an excessive focus on trade to the exclusion of political and therefore policy integration. Regional trade agreements tend to exacerbate inequalities between rich and poor countries, and rich cities and poor countryside, creating interest groups that undermine the implementation of agreements. They write that "The forces unleashed by scale economies . . . imply further forces for divergence . . . Hence, the politics of regional integration schemes among low-income countries are almost inevitably going to be fraught. A more promising alternative would be to base political union not on trade but on economic policy making and infrastructure where the scope for mutual gains is likely to be much greater" (Collier and Venables 2008, p.31).

While one might quibble with several aspects of this formulation,[11] the thrust of this admonition has apparently been heard. Countries are collaborating ever more on regional infrastructure and common economic policies. Among the aspects of economic integration, an impressionistic assessment would point to the important role of collective action on infrastructure. Increasing the supply of electric power, reducing transportation costs, and enhancing connectivity have huge and immediate benefits that increase economic opportunity. Similarly, coordination of macroeconomic and regulatory policies—for example, trucking regulations or product standards—lead to an enormous pay-off for low-cost investments. These elements of regional cooperation may well imply larger returns for the time policy makers invest in them than if they were to focus on tariff policy. It may also be the case that economists analyzing regional cooperation have focused excessively on only one element of success—trade creation—rather than recognizing the synergies that RTAs have for promoting collective action in other arenas, including peace and security.

The next phase of regional integration presents a challenging agenda. Conflicts still abound, and African leaders have their hands full. They are likely to enjoy ever less support from the big powers, whose attention is drawn to events elsewhere, such as clashes in the Ukraine and mounting tensions in the South China Sea, as the politics of austerity that have followed the Great Recession exact their toll on domestic political comity and erode past consensus on development assistance. The emergence of global value chains as a central feature of the world economy presents an opportunity for a new form of industrialization, but Africa, with its high trade and infrastructure costs and thick borders, will have to create more efficient services if it is to capitalize on its enormous natural resources and use globalization to create a dynamic productive base. In this new world of trade in tasks and services, Africa's comparatively high external tariffs will have to give way to a more open regionalism, where its producers can have access to inputs and the latest technology at world prices (a lesson to be learned from East Asia). Finally, the pace of implementing accords for regional integration will have to accelerate if the region wishes to maintain its recent high growth rates and accelerate its development. The role for regionally provided public goods in this process will only expand.

Notes

1 The author would like to thank Jaime de Melo of the University of Geneva, and the editors, Antoni Estevadeordal and Louis Goodman, for their thoughtful comments. Any errors remain the responsibility of the author.

2 The paper looks only at regional agreements in Africa and does not deal with North-South agreements. The most prominent North-South agreements include the Economic Partnership Agreements between the EU and the major sub-regions in Africa, which began to be signed from 2008 onward. The EU also has a separate trade agreement with South Africa. The EFTA countries—Iceland, Liechtenstein, Norway, and Switzerland—have also signed FTAs with Morocco and SACU. The USA has only one FTA with an African country, Morocco, signed in 2006, though others are under consideration.

3 These initiatives included: the Lagos Plan of Action (1980), the Final Act of Lagos (1980), Africa's Priority Programme for Economic Recovery (1986–1990), the African Alternative Framework to Structural Adjustment Programme (1989), the African (Arusha) Charter for Popular Participation and Development (1990), and the Abuja Treaty (1991), among others. Later, in 2002, the OAU gave way to the more ambitious African Union, with its executive functions, parliament, and peacekeeping mandates.

4 Regional cooperation arrangements in Africa date back to the turn of the twentieth century when, under the aegis of British rule, the South African Customs Union was established in 1910, comprising the Union of South Africa and the High Commission Territories of Bechuanaland, Basutoland and Swaziland. In 1969, when these territories became independent, the agreement went on to comprise the Republic of South Africa, Botswana, Lesotho, and Swaziland, and Namibia joined after its independence in 1990. The Abuja Treaty was significant because it attempted to lay out a roadmap for African unification.

5 As early as 1889, Wilfred Pareto noted that "customs unions and other systems of closer commercial relations [could serve] as a means of the improvement of political relations and maintenance of peace" (quoted in World Bank 2005, p.38).

6 Miroudot writes: "BITs influence the policy determinants of FDI, but PTAs also improve the economic determinants and have been found to have a stronger impact on investment" (Miroudot 2011, p.320).

7 The World Bank (2005) calculated intra-regional trade and external imports and exports for many agreements worldwide using data for 1948–2000. African agreements, save for SACU and possibly ECOWAS, showed signs of trade diversion in these calculations; namely, trade with the world decreased while intraregional trade increased, controlling for other factors.

8 Several reviews highlight the fact that rules can be overly restrictive—though according to some analyses rules of origin in African RTAs are less restrictive than say in NAFTA (see Estevadordal and Suominen 2003, and Brenton 2006). In fact, for many products in these several agreements, the preference margins are so low that traders find it cheaper to pay the MFN tariff than fill out the paperwork.

9 Newfarmer and Sztajerowska (2012) reviewed 14 econometric studies since 2000 (roughly the year of Dani Rodrik's trenchant critique of the early studies), and noted that 13 found that trade had a positive and significant impact on growth. This relationship holds true for Africa. An important qualification is that realizing the potential benefits of trade opening requires complementary policies affecting the investment climate (particularly regulation), social safety nets, and trade facilitation (see Hoekman and Olarrega 2007; Bolaky and Freund 2004; and Winters 2004). Brückner and Lederman (2012) adopted econometric techniques that correct for the endogeneity bias associated with reverse causality and omitted country variables. Their control variables included rainfall, OECD growth, and political institutions, among others. They found that trade openness causes economic growth: a 1% increase in the ratio of trade over gross domestic product is associated with a short-run increase in growth of approximately 0.5% per year, and with an even larger effect in the long term, reaching about 0.8% after ten years. Ethnic conflict can obviously undermine this relationship.

10 Comprehensive reviews of these can be found in EAC (2014); K'Ombudo et al. (2014); Argent (2014).

11 It is not clear that those living in landlocked countries or in small cities are likely to lose in absolute terms from enhanced integration, any more than Arizona loses from integrating with California or Norway does with Europe. Moreover, it is hard to argue that the small landlocked countries are the source of political drag on implementation. For example, Rwanda joined the EAC despite the fact that early modeling indicated the country might suffer welfare losses (Carrère and De Melo 2008); and Rwanda has been a strong proponent of liberalizing accords within the EAC since joining—with continued high growth.

References

Acharya, Rohini, Jo-Anne Crawford, Maryla Maliszewska, and Christelle Renard. 2011. "Landscape." In *Preferential Trade Agreements: Policies for Development*, edited by Jean-Pierre Chaffour and Jean-Christophe Mauer. Washington, DC: World Bank.

Africa Progress Panel. 2015. *Power, People Planet: Seizing Africa's Energy and Climate Opportunities*. Geneva: Africa Progress Panel.

All Africa News. 2015. East Africa: Kagame in Uganda for Northern Corridor Summit. *All Africa News*. June 5.

Argent, Jonathan. 2014. "Review of EAC Common External Tariff." Mimeo. Nairobi: Trademark East Africa.

Aryeetey, Ernest, Shanta Devarajan, Ravi Kanbur, and Louis Kasekende. 2012. "Overview." In *Oxford Companion to the Economics of Africa*, edited by E. Aryeetey, Shanta Devarajan, Ravi Kanbur, and Louis Kasekende. Oxford: Oxford University Press.

Bolaky, Bineswaree, and Caroline Freund. 2004. "Trade, Regulations, and Growth." World Bank Policy Working Paper. Washington, DC: World Bank.

Braun, Matias, Ricardo Hausmann, and Lant Pritchett. 2004. "The Proliferation of Sovereigns: Are There Lessons for Integration?" In *Integrating the Americas: FTAA and Beyond*, edited by Antoni Estevadeordal, Dani Rodrik, Alan Taylor, and Andres Velasco. Cambridge, MA: Harvard University Press.

Brückner, Markus, and Daniel Lederman. 2012. "Trade Causes Growth in Sub-Saharan Africa." Policy Research Working Paper Series No. 6007. Washington, DC: World Bank.

Cadot, Olivier, and Mariem Malouche, eds. 2012. *Non-Tariff Measures—A Fresh Look at Trade Policy's New Frontier*. Washington, DC: World Bank.

Carrère, Céline, and Jaime De Melo. 2008. "Trade Policy Harmonization in EAC: Revenue and Welfare Implications for Burundi and Rwanda, Coordinating Integration with COMESA." Mimeo. Washington, DC: World Bank.

Chauffour, Jean-Pierre, and Jean-Christophe Maur, eds. 2011. *Preferential Trade Agreements: Policies for Development*. Washington, DC: World Bank.

Collier, Paul, and Stephen O'Connell. 2008. "Opportunities and Choices." Mimeo. Oxford: CSAE.

Collier, Paul, and Tony Venables, 2008. "Trace and Economic Performance: Does Africa's Fragmentation Matter?" Mimeo. Oxford: CSAE.

De Melo, Jaime. 2014. "The Tripartite Free Trade Africa: Is It the Way to Deepen Integration in Africa?" *Africa in Focus Blog*. November 4. www.brookings.edu/blogs/africa-in-focus/posts/2014/11/04-tripartite-free-trade-area-integration-africa-de-melo

De Melo, Jaime, and Yvonne Tsikata, 2014. "Regional Integration in Africa: Challenges and Prospects." World Institute for Development Economics Research Working Paper 2014/037.

Devarajan, Shanta, Delfin Go, Maryla Maliszewska, Israel Osorio-Rodart, and Hans Timmer. 2013. "Stress-Testing Africa's Recent Growth and Poverty Performance." World Bank Policy Research Paper No. 6517. Washington, DC: World Bank.

Dihel, Nora, Ana Fernandes, and Aaditya Mattoo. 2012. "Developing Professional Services in Africa." In *De-Fragmenting Africa: Deepening Regional Trade Integration in Goods and Services*, edited by Paul Brenton and Gozde Isik. Washington, DC: World Bank.

Djankov, Simeon, Caroline Freund, and Cong Pham. 2010. "Trading on Time." *Review of Economics and Statistics* 92, no. 1 (February): 166–173.

East African Community (EAC). 2014. *East African Common Market Scorecard, 2014: Tracking Compliance in the Movement of Capital, Services, and Goods.* Arusha: EAC.

Estevadeordal, Antoni, and Louis Goodman. 2014. "Regional Cooperation, Regional Public Goods and Sustainable Development." Unpublished paper.

Freund, Caroline, and Nadia Rocha. 2011. "What Constrains Africa's Exports?" *World Bank Economic Review* 25, no. 3.

Gilson, Ian. 2012. "Deepening Regional Integration to Eliminate the Fragmented Goods Market in Southern Africa." In *De-Fragmenting Africa: Deepening Regional Trade Integration in Goods and Services,* edited by Paul Brenton and Gozde Isik. Washington, DC: World Bank.

Head, K., and T. Mayer. 2013. "What Separates Us? Sources of Resistance to Globalization." *Canadian Journal of Economics* 46, no. 4: 1196–1231.

Hoekman, Bernard, and Marcelo Olarreaga, eds. 2007. *Global Trade and Poor Nations: The Poverty Impacts and Policy Implications of Liberalization.* Paris: Brookings Institution Press and Yale Center for the Study of Globalization and Sciences-Po.

Hoekman, Bernard, and Ben Shepherd. 2015. "Services, Firm Performance, and Exports: The Case of the East African Community." Mimeo. London: International Growth Centre.

Hummels, Davis. 2001. *Time as a Trade Barrier.* Purdue University, mimeo.

International Energy Agency (IEA). 2014. *Africa Energy Outlook.* Paris: OECD/IEA.

Kirk, Robert. 2012. "Addressing Trade Restrictive Non-Tariff Measures on Goods Trade in the East African Community." In *De-Fragmenting Africa: Deepening Regional Trade Integration in Goods and Services,* edited by Paul Brenton and Gozde Isik. Washington, DC: World Bank.

K'Ombudo, Alfred Ombudo, Peter Kusek, Roberto Echandi, and Rodrigo Polanco. 2014. *East African Common Market Scorecard 2014. Tracking EAC Compliance in the Movement of Capital, Services and Goods: Main report.* Washington, DC: World Bank.

Kowalski, Przemyslaw, Javier Lopez Gonzalez, Alexandros Ragoussis, and Cristian Ugarte. 2015. "Participation of Developing Countries in Global Value Chains: Implications for Trade and Trade-Related Policies." OECD Trade Policy Papers No. 179. Paris: OECD.

Laski, Anne. 2015. "Anticipating Regional Integration in Africa." *International Growth Centre Blog.* January 26. www.theigc.org/blog/anticipating-regional-integration-in-africa/

Lee, J.-W. and J.H. Pyun. 2009. "Does Trade Integration Contribute to Peace?" Asian Development Bank Working Paper on Regional Integration No. 24. Manila: Asian Development Bank.

Mansfield, Edward, and John Pevehouse. 2000. "Trade Blocs, Trade Flows, and International Conflict." *International Organization* 54, no. 4: 775–808.

Mayer, Thierry, and Mathias Thoenig. 2016. "Regional Trade Agreements and the Pacification of East Africa." IGC Working Paper, April. London: International Growth Centre.

Martin, Philippe, Thierry Mayer, and Mathias Thoenig. 2005. "Make Trade, Not War." CEPR Discussion Paper No. 5218. London: CEPR.

Martin, Philippe, Thierry Mayer, and Mathias Thoenig. 2010. "The Geography of Conflicts and Free Trade Agreements." CEPR Discussion Paper No. 7740. London: CEPR.

Maru, Mehari Taddele, and Sahra El Fassi. 2015. "Can the Regional Economic Communities Support Implementation of the African Governance Architecture (AGA)?" Paper 181, October. Maastricht: ECDPM.

Mattoo, Aaditya and Pierre Sauvé. 2011. "Services." In *Preferential Trade Agreements: Policies for Development*, edited by Jean-Pierre Chauffour and Jean-Christophe Maur. Washington, DC: World Bank.

Miroudot, Sébastien. 2011. "Investment." In *Preferential Trade Agreements: Policies for Development*, edited by Jean-Pierre Chauffour and Jean-Christophe Maur. Washington, DC: World Bank.

Mo Ibrahim Foundation. 2014. *Ibrahim Indicators of African Governance: Summary Report 2014*. London and Dakar: Mo Ibrahim Foundation.

Newfarmer, Richard, and Monika Sztajerowska. 2012. "Trade and Employment in a Fast-Changing World." In *Policy Priorities for International Trade and Jobs*, edited by Douglas Lippoldt. Paris: OECD.

Porges, Amelia. 2011. "Dispute Settlement." In *Preferential Trade Agreements: Policies for Development*, edited by Jean-Pierre Chauffour and Jean-Christophe Maur. Washington, DC: World Bank.

Rippel, Barbara. 2012. "Why Trade Facilitation is Important to Africa." In *De-Fragmenting Africa: Deepening Regional Trade Integration in Goods and Services,* edited by Paul Brenton and Gozde Isik. Washington, DC: World Bank.

Schiff, Maurice, and Alan Winters. 2003. *Regional Integration and Development*. Washington, DC: World Bank.

UNECA. 2012. *Assessing Regional Integration in Africa V: Towards an African Continental Free Trade Area*. Addis Ababa: UNECA.

UNECA. 2013. *Harmonizing Policies to Transform the Trading Environment*. Addis Ababa: UNECA.

Winters, Alan L. 2004. "Trade Liberalisation and Economic Performance: An Overview." *The Economic Journal* 114: F4–F21.

World Bank. 2005. *Global Economic Prospects: Trade, Regionalism, and Development*. Washington, DC: World Bank.

World Bank. 2014. *Africa's Pulse, April 2014*. Washington, DC: World Bank.

Index

xenophobia 133
Xi Jinping 145

Yellow Dust/ Asian Dust 209, 213
Yemen 187

Young, Alasdair. 252
Young, Oran R. 48, 49

zero-sum views of trade 226
Zwillenberg, Paul. 186f